Caraleigh

Caraleigh

*A History of South Raleigh's
Mill Village Neighborhood,
1891 to Today*

Steven A. Hill

McFarland & Company, Inc., Publishers
Jefferson, North Carolina

ISBN (print) 978-1-4766-8738-4
ISBN (ebook) 978-1-4766-4678-7

LIBRARY OF CONGRESS AND BRITISH LIBRARY
CATALOGUING DATA ARE AVAILABLE

Library of Congress Control Number 2022016321

© 2022 Steven A. Hill. All rights reserved

No part of this book may be reproduced or transmitted in any form or by any means, electronic or mechanical, including photocopying or recording, or by any information storage and retrieval system, without permission in writing from the publisher.

On the cover *clockwise from top left:* balloting at Caraleigh for Raleigh's annexation of the mill village, 1957–58 (Raleigh, *News & Observer* newspaper/ State Archives of North Carolina); Caraleigh Cotton Mills, Raleigh, c. 1910 (State Archives of North Carolina Audio-Visual Collections, PhC.68 Carolina Power and Light Photograph Collection); overhead view of Caraleigh Mills taken from the southside, looking north, with downtown Raleigh's tall buildings visible at the top right. On the left edge, a few newly constructed CitySpace Homes sit, close to Caraleigh's swimming pool (courtesy Christopher E. Sauls)

Printed in the United States of America

McFarland & Company, Inc., Publishers
Box 611, Jefferson, North Carolina 28640
www.mcfarlandpub.com

For Marnie and Katie

Table of Contents

Preface   1
Timeline: Caraleigh, North Carolina   4
Introduction   6

1. The Genesis of Caraleigh   15
2. Raleigh's Most Reliable and Substantial Men   32
3. African Americans at Caraleigh   65
4. Raleigh's Pure Water Question   72
5. Mill Patriarchy and Child Labor   99
6. World War I to the 1920s   115
7. The Great Depression Era to World War II   121
8. Old Mill, New Owners   137
9. In Raleigh's Orbit   141
10. 1980s–2020s: From Sow's Ear to Silk Purse   161

Chapter Notes   185
Bibliography   221
Index   227

Preface

The subject of this book is Caraleigh, a neighborhood of Raleigh located just over a mile south of the city's center, inside the I-40 Beltline and a short walk from the State Farmers' Market. My research started when my wife and I purchased a condominium unit at the Historic Caraleigh Mills in February 2019. The former textile factory, built in 1891–1892, is comprised of several closely situated buildings on Maywood Avenue.

When we first stood in the shadow of Caraleigh Mills, my wife and I were confronted by the two-story main building's ancient bricks made from the mud of the very land upon which we stood. Our senses were filled with a palpable sense of history. The majesty and massiveness of Caraleigh made our decision to buy an easy one. And after entering the condominium complex, my historical curiosity heightened. Tastefully displayed throughout the interior hallways of the 84-unit condominium complex are enlarged black and white photos of early 20th-century mill workers and a few century-old images of Caraleigh itself. I recognized some of the pictures as the work of the famous photographer Lewis Hine (1874–1940), sparking a slew of questions that cascaded in my mind: Was there child labor here? Did Lewis Hine actually visit Caraleigh? And most importantly for me, what historical studies have been written about Caraleigh?

This was the start of the research for this book, well-timed for release in 2022, especially with the predicted creation of the "massive Downtown South project" on lands adjacent to, or were part of, the original Caraleigh community that spanned 200 acres.[1] The Downtown South development proposes the creation of a $2.2 billion mixed-use development at the southern entry of downtown Raleigh, with added housing, retail stores, restaurants, hotels, all of which is planned to centralize around a 20,000-seat sports and entertainment stadium.[2] Raleigh's 21st-century tycoons have targeted south Raleigh for the city's profitable expansion, just as they had in the 1890s. To be sure, the goals and names of modern business leaders have changed, but some of the concerns over the last century remain comparable.

Caraleigh was described in the 1890s as an integral part of Raleigh's future growth, reinforced with newspaper headlines that announced there was a "Boom in Real Estate" in the state capital.[3] Development of the area in the late 19th century proceeded despite numerous warnings of potential environmental dangers. Similarly in 2020, the proposed development of in south Raleigh have met both praise and skepticism about the plan's ability to enhance and enrich the lives of its residents.[4] Fears in the 21st century are that increased property values could displace

The front entrance to Historic Caraleigh Mills residential condominium complex in 2020 (photograph by the author).

current residents and could also bring flooding from nearby waterways, namely Walnut Creek.[5]

Caraleigh's story reveals that Raleigh has a long history of friction between the promises of economic expansion and fears of potential hazards from proposed growth in the Walnut Creek area. Compromise and conflict among developers, builders, residents, and city officials over the last 130 years has resulted in Raleigh's imbalanced trajectory of growth that began during the city's recovery from the Civil War and continued through to the present. Raleigh's trajectory of expansion benefited north Raleigh, with an established reputation for expensive real estate and urbane sophistication, and disabled south Raleigh, notoriously known for inexpensive land, poverty, and crime. When discussing the Downtown South development project in December 2020, Henry Hinton, a popular North Carolina radio personality out of Greenville, North Carolina, referred to the Downtown South plan as an effort to improve a "blighted" part of the city.[6] Hinton's perception of this part of Raleigh begs answer to questions of why, how, and when did south Raleigh earn such disdain. By shining a light upon some of the people, events, and stories of Caraleigh that helped frame south Raleigh's development, I attempt to fill in some of the blanks in Raleigh's history.

Some visitors to Caraleigh in 2021 would proclaim the old mill village a gentrifying neighborhood, where new houses are under construction alongside the rehabilitated mill, in the presence of a locally popular microbrewery, the Trophy Brewery. But the glimmers of transformative social, demographic, and economic change tepidly started decades before, in the 1970s. Long known for its mostly poor and working-class population, Caraleigh appears to have succumbed to an invasion of middle-class residents, many of whom could be characterized as part of the subculture of 21st-century hipsters.[7]

The analysis of Caraleigh is a case study in the local historians' laboratory of historical change. And for Caraleigh, changes it endured from 1892 to 2020 were mostly of the unkind sort. The phenomenon of change, central to unraveling and recounting Caraleigh's past, are deeply rooted in macroscopic forces of state, national and international scale. In the course of preserving, commemorating, and investigating Caraleigh's past, Raleigh's history will be coerced into review. Readers should be unafraid, because, as historian Joseph Amato has aptly stated, "people of every place and time deserve a history"[8] and "what is history without revision?"[9]

Chronology is an important aspect of history. But this book is not simply a chronicle of events. To enhance readers' contextual understanding of Caraleigh, I have included the findings of other researchers about topics germane to Caraleigh's historical development.

My research methods include extensive investigation of newspaper resources, as well as physical and digital visits to numerous North Carolina Archives: University of North Carolina at Chapel Hill's Wilson Library, Duke University's David M. Rubenstein Library, and the Olivia Raney Local History Library.

Many are my personal and scholarly debts for this book, but gratitude must start with my wife, Marnie, who has unfailingly encouraged my work. North Carolina historians who have provided a model for me to follow include Sarah Caroline Thuesen and Jerry E. Gershenhorn, and Rodney Pierce. To East Carolina University and its Department of History, I am forever indebted to Philip Adler, Bodo Nischan, Mona Russell, John Tilley, Michael A. Palmer, Gerald J. Prokopowicz and Christopher A. Oakley. Professor Emeritus Charles W. Calhoun is especially treasured for his rigorous and unyielding expectations of me. In assistance with obtaining high resolution images and use permissions, Ian Dunn of the North Carolina Archives and Scott Sharpe of the *News and Observer* were crucial. For review, guidance, and development of the manuscript, I am grateful to Rita Staton, Professor Leon Shargel, as well as Walker G. Roberts and Mariah Hachmeister, and Michelle M. Petteway. For previous scholarly investigation of Caraleigh, I stand on the shoulders of Daniel L. Watkins that proved significantly helpful. Deserving plaudits for sharing their experiences in Caraleigh, I thank Betty and James Gerardi, William Dumont, the Rev. Rex Watkins, Connie Crumpler, and Frances Collins.

Timeline: Caraleigh, North Carolina

1890—W.G. Upchurch purchases 200 acres of land, one mile south of Raleigh City limits

1891—Caraleigh Cotton Mills and Land Company and the Caraleigh Fertilizer Plant established on January 24, 1891

1892—Fire nearly destroys the Caraleigh Phosphate and Fertilizer Plant

1894—Typhoid and malarial fevers strike Caraleigh workers

1895—Caraleigh founder and first president W.G. Upchurch dies

1895—J.J. Thomas assumes presidency of Caraleigh Cotton Mills

1897—Night School started for Caraleigh's working children

1898—A.A. Thompson cited as the third president of Caraleigh Mills

1898—Wake Forest College purchases $50,000 in Caraleigh Mills bonds

1903—The Caraleigh School created, later rededicated as the Eliza Pool School in 1924

1903—The Walnut Creek Council No. 55 branch of the Junior Order of United American Mechanics established at Caraleigh

1904—The Caraleigh Baptist Church established

1907—African American workers at the Caraleigh Phosphate and Fertilizer plant strike

1911—The second president of Caraleigh Mills, J.J. Thomas dies

1914—Fifty weavers at the Caraleigh Mills strike

1915—Caraleigh's welfare work programs commence

1920—A.A. Thompson, the third president of Caraleigh Mills dies

1920—Striking Caraleigh mill employees and their families evicted from mill-owned houses

1924—Caraleigh Cemetery on Bunker Hill created

1930—Caraleigh Mills closes

1930—*News and Observer* reports starvation and destitution at Caraleigh

1933–1941—Caraleigh property becomes a regular stop for traveling circuses

1934—Caraleigh Mills Phosphate Plant destroyed in fire

1937—*News and Observer* claimed 40 percent of Caraleigh's children were under-nourished

1938—The Caraleigh textile buildings expectant of new owners, Raleigh Mills Company

1939—Work starts on the new Raleigh Water Works plant, later named for Ernest Battle Bain

1942—A U.S. Post Office substation of Raleigh opened at Horton's store on Maywood Avenue

1943—Premier Worsted Mill buys the Caraleigh Mills building

1951—The American Woolen Company purchase the Caraleigh textile complex

1952—Raleigh's City Council creates of a one-mile zoning area outside the city's limits

1953—One mile of streets paved in Caraleigh by the State Highway Department

1956—Residents deliver petitions to the Raleigh City Council opposing creation of a subdivision for African American housing on South Saunders Street, near Caraleigh

1956—The Fred Whitaker Company purchases, the Caraleigh Mills textile buildings

1957—Raleigh annexes Caraleigh, December 31, 1957

1961—The Fred Whitaker Company plant at Caraleigh develops the Spacedye process

1973—Miriam P. Block elected to Raleigh's City Council

1974—James and Betty Gerardi move to Caraleigh and initiate gentrification

1986—South Saunders Road widened to six lanes

1994—William J. Dumont purchases and rehabilitates his first Caraleigh home

1999—The Fred Whitaker Company ends operations at Caraleigh

2000—Caraleigh's first prefabricated, manufactured home in Raleigh's City limits constructed

2001—Barney Joyner and Vaughn King join forces in the renovation of Caraleigh Mills

2001—Caraleigh entered in the National Register of Historic Places as a Historic Landmark

2002—Caraleigh Mills textile building declared a Raleigh Historic Landmark

2003—Renovation of the Caraleigh Mills complex completed; first condominium unit sold

2011—A tornado rips through Caraleigh

2017—Publication of the Southern Gateway Corridor Study Final Report

2019—*Downtown South Raleigh, North Carolina: A ULI Advisory Services Panel Report* published

Introduction

Caraleigh originally had three parts: the textile mills, the phosphate and fertilizer plant, and its village, a company-created hamlet for its white cotton mill laborers, commonly referred to as operatives. Caraleigh was welcomed in Raleigh as a harbinger of prosperity for a city still struggling to regain its economic composure after defeat in the Civil War. From the start of operations in 1892 through the 1920s, Caraleigh yielded handsome profits for its investors; but for its workers, Caraleigh provided low pay and public health disasters. Disentangling south Raleigh's textile mill history reveals woeful instances of tragedy, as well as forgotten episodes of the state's social, business, political, racial, and public health history from the 1890s to the early 2000s.

Throughout the last 130 years, real estate developers and businessmen have dangled alluring charms of economic progress before the city of Raleigh's hungry eyes. Results of these promises have been disparate and are most visible in the capital city's northern and southern sections. History has shown that north Raleigh's romance with business investment has been functional and fruitful, while south Raleigh's courtship with the same admirers have been mere trysts, destructive dalliances, short-lived and ephemeral assignations, strained, violent, and at times even deadly.

Assurances of wealth creation in south Raleigh in 2020 have been accompanied with skepticism. If the goals of 21st-century business visionaries are achieved, as they were in 1892, will economic development benefit everyone in Raleigh, or will it once again endanger the health and lives of the many for the benefit of the few? In order to avoid repetition of past mistakes, a full-throated telling of south Raleigh's previous experiments in economic renewal at Caraleigh should be undertaken.

Some of the state's early experiences with public health involving the waters of Walnut Creek make up Caraleigh's story. Walnut Creek was the source of Raleigh and Caraleigh's drinking water, which once poisoned at Caraleigh, sickened or killed mill workers and Raleighites. The Environmental Protection Agency in 2006 related that the Caraleigh Phosphate and Fertilizer Works was the site of one of Raleigh's largest fires in 1892 that released tons of sulfuric acid that continued to leach into Raleigh's water supply "in great volumes each time it rained."[1] Caraleigh's past waterborne disasters surely deserve representation in the discussion about south Raleigh's future development in south Raleigh.

Caraleigh's history—parsed in three component parts—clarifies south Raleigh's genesis. The birth of Caraleigh in 1891 marked south Raleigh's start; the death of

Caraleigh's textile mill in 1930 initiated south Raleigh's unsavory reputation; and finally, the glimmer of Caraleigh's rebirth that started in the mid–1970s and was robustly revealed in 2003 with the conversion of the old Caraleigh Mills textile building into high end condominiums.

And though not within city limits of Raleigh until 1957, Caraleigh was always embraced as a factor in the "very growth and history of the city of Raleigh."[2] Yet, Raleigh's 20th-century material progress has been better reflected in north Raleigh than in south Raleigh. Real estate developer John Kane acknowledged this phenomenon in 2019 when he stated that the Downtown South project would a "game-changer" for the capital city and for that part of Raleigh that "has not had the love that it needs, and we are trying to give it that love and that investment" needed to grow.[3] History has long been recognized as the fruit of power, and Caraleigh testifies to this hierarchical theory of the past's telling. The historical record of Caraleigh's powerful leaders and its laborers—both white and African American—have been incompletely told in varying degrees. Historical records respectfully revered the cotton capitalists, while documented remembrance of Caraleigh's African American laborers have been subdued, stuck in the biased, pro-white supremacist primary sources constituting the few crumbs of their memory.[4]

This book is arranged chronologically in chapters. Starting with the contextualization of Caraleigh's origins in the post–Civil War era, the book concludes in 2020 with anticipation of the Downtown South project, predicted to envelop Caraleigh. Chapters 1 to 6 investigate Caraleigh's birth, connecting its origins to the baneful memories and consequences of the Confederate defeat in the Civil War and ignominy of Union occupation during Reconstruction. Subsequent chapters consider Caraleigh's founders and their supporters who determined the development of Caraleigh and the education of its residents, Caraleigh's African American workers at the fertilizer plant, and the twin waterborne disasters that befell Caraleigh in 1892 and 1894, as well as child labor practices. An in depth examination of Caraleigh's early history unavoidably offers oblique insights into some dark corners of Raleigh's history needing exposure, with refreshed consideration of Raleigh's many lesser-and-better-known events and personalities. In so doing, readers will see how the state's lionized politico-businessmen ruled Caraleigh, concomitantly influencing the capital city's pattern of growth for more than a century.

Chapters 7 to 10 explain how, despite the mills' 1930 closing, Caraleigh's community remained alive, abandoned by its alma mater to struggle through the Great Depression.

Caraleigh's mill buildings were reopened under a succession of other textile companies from 1938 to 1999. Nevertheless, the mill village suffered through long term, downward textile industry trends. Multiple problems added to the mill village's geographical isolation from Raleigh, combining to exact a punishing toll on Caraleigh's residents. Economic, psychological, social, and political perils illustrate the origins of Raleigh's 20th-century dichotomy whereby north Raleigh prospered and south Raleigh atrophied. Starting in the 1970s, Caraleigh started to slowly inch towards rebirth with the actions of local homeowners and investors who led to the 2003 conversion of the Caraleigh textile building into an 84-unit condominium complex. Caraleigh's life as a residential community was a watershed moment for south

Raleigh's rebirth, but more improvement appeared to be on the horizon. And while Caraleigh's future in 2020 appears prosperous, close scrutiny of its past lends insight to the city's uneven economic and social stratification that resulted in an affluent north Raleigh and a pauperized "south Raleigh ghetto."[5]

Visitors to North Carolina's capital in 1891 interested to see Raleigh's progress were instructed to "by all means be taken to Caraleigh."[6] Caraleigh proved that the state's capital was "enjoying a healthy boom,"[7] drawing large crowds who walked from the city to watch Caraleigh's construction, inspiring expressions of wonderment at the "magical transformation" taking place; Raleigh's residents ventured "to see and ponder over the many changes" that the building of the "largest textile mill in Raleigh" would bring.[8]

Raleighites had always claimed it, but Caraleigh was outside city limits until annexed on December 31, 1957.[9] Newspapermen augured and augmented Caraleigh's success from inception, making it a desired addition of the state's capital city. The start of Caraleigh's construction in 1891 and its "two large manufactories" caused the *State Chronicle* to proclaim that "this year of 1891 will be the most prosperous in the history of Raleigh," asking, "cannot our citizens feel proud of Raleigh?"[10] Boasts about Raleigh's "fine progress" in the *News and Observer* in January 1892 urged collective pride and continued unity in the city's advancements:

> Recently, we have built a cotton and a wagon factory and have begun the Caraleigh mills; have put up electric lights and electric cars; have constructed water works and sewers, and have laid broader and deeper foundations for the progress and prosperity of the city. Let us all stand together and keep up the good work.[11]

Image of Caraleigh's chimney taken from the mills' courtyard (photograph by the author).

Excessive cheerleading for Caraleigh Mills in the 1890s overshadowed misgivings about situating Caraleigh's operation and housing for workers on land that was described as swampy and malarial. And despite the precautionary step of sending "a committee to visit Southern cities with mills of like character" to see the "best methods" of "conducting the fertilizer business," disaster awaited.[12] Fearful predictions proved warranted, with Caraleigh Mills' workers being sickened, nearly to death. The fertilizer plant was located down the Maywood Avenue, where African American workers were frequently maimed and killed. But the dangers of Caraleigh extended to Raleigh's population who suffered, too. The city's drinking water came from Walnut Creek, which was behind the cotton mill and the fertilizer works: A "great terra cotta piping for the extension of the intake service of the Raleigh's water works" ... ran "immediately under the acid chamber" at Caraleigh's "phosphate and fertilizer plant"[13] creating a sickening experience for the city that went unresolved for decades.[14]

The creation of Caraleigh Mills—and the town it spawned—aroused a flurry of providential predictions of halcyon days to come, while news of Caraleigh's demise as a functioning textile mill 39 years later was muted. During Caraleigh's zenith of prosperity, from 1892 to the 1920s, stories of Caraleigh were celebratory, with few criticisms publicly aired. If Caraleigh's flaws were openly discussed, subsequent and voluminous newspaper features about Caraleigh eclipsed the naysayers. Lengthy newspaper articles across the state chronicled Caraleigh's development,

The Caraleigh Phosphate and Fertilizer Plant was located on Maywood Avenue, just down the street from the Caraleigh the textile mill. The Phosphate and Fertilizer plant was destroyed by fire in 1934 (State Archives of North Carolina).

often sidestepping, or forgetting, its occasionally recorded foibles. Decades of hortatory, jubilant rhetoric concerning Caraleigh largely submerged doubts, bequeathing mostly one-sided primary sources for later historians to draw upon. A clear example of the single source bias phenomenon can be viewed in an indispensable source for the county's history published in 2008: *Wake: Capital County of North Carolina, Vol. II, Reconstruction to 1920.* In discussing tragic events at "Caraleigh Hill" in 1894, the authors drew upon one 1938 *News and Observer* article about "Caraleigh Hill around the turn of the century."[15] In so doing, significant historical details about tragic events went unmentioned, such as courtroom proceedings involving Caraleigh, the significance of contradictory medical experts' testimony, and any discussion of potential culpability for Caraleigh's owners.

The historiography of North Carolina's textile mills yields only passing acknowledgment of Caraleigh. Most treatments of Caraleigh, both academic and non-academic, have ignored or mollified its tragic past. Thus, Caraleigh's historiography echoed the fawning praise showered upon the enterprise and its leadership. Interestingly, the few dedicated studies of Caraleigh have been fragmentary, sometimes misstating facts and leaving gaps in Caraleigh's—and the state's—story. One 1974 manuscript about Caraleigh poignantly asked, "why has this part of Raleigh's history been forgotten so soon?"[16] When it comes to Caraleigh, and Raleigh for that matter, there has been a history problem.

History often operates in this fashion, when the popularly approved and accepted narrative fails to reflect the complete story. And, having been told and retold, recitation of the incomplete narrative becomes unchallenged truth. Historian Michel-Rolph Trouillot, author of *Silencing the Past*, made important points about the mechanics of history. For Trouillot, "what history is" was less significant than "how history works."[17] In his view, the production of historical narrative was a dialectical process among competing groups. The alternative historical accounts of less powerful groups were most often accompanied with an inability to access the means of the production of their narratives.[18] The veracity of any particular story about the past has been "at best, the story about power, a story of those who won."[19] In the case of Caraleigh, the investors and officers of Caraleigh were the winners whose self-aggrandizing stories were repeated in newspapers and history books written between the late 1800s and most of the 1900s. Trouillot argued that the exclusion of alternate narratives can render readers of single-source historicity "complaisant hostages of the pasts they create."[20]

This book bears witness to the achievements and transgressions of Caraleigh's leaders, many of whom fought to preserve slavery, or were the sons of Confederate soldiers. Caraleigh's officers, most of whom comprised the state's oligarchy, were members of a Raleigh-centered plutocracy of financial, business, and political elites whose values shaped Caraleigh; these were highly respected men, many of whom were buried in Raleigh's Oakwood Cemetery, alongside the state's most "great and gifted."[21]

Investors and supporters of Caraleigh were, to one degree or another, "Redeemers"—southern Democrats who sought the end of Reconstruction, promoted the resurrection of white supremacy, and the political, economic, and social subordination of African Americans. Summoning memories of the Civil War and Reconstruction to incite fear that "Federal bayonets" could one day return to the South,

North Carolina's Democratic Party called for unity to regain political power in the late 1890s to the early 1900s.[22] Hence, the politics of the Democratic Party magnified racial antipathies and Southern traditions to maintain power.[23] Redeemers guided the postbellum growth of the region and the achievement of a "Solid South," the goal demanded the Democratic Party's exclusive rule in the region.[24]

The Democrat Party leadership thought that they would best guide regional progress and prevent any future federal interference into the South's system of race relations. In his 1949 book, *Southern Politics in State and Nation*, political scientist V.O. Key, Jr., described North Carolina and its state government as a "progressive plutocracy" ruled by a coterie of bankers, lawyers, and businessmen from 1890s to the 1950s.[25] Historian Karl E. Campbell neatly summed up the defining ideas of the progressive plutocrats:

> The progressive plutocracy ran the state on the basis of racism, religion, and reform. White supremacy was the absolute foundation of the new progressive plutocracy. Conservative Evangelical Protestantism provided its moral energy, especially in the crusade for prohibition.[26]

Caraleigh's directors and supporters fit squarely into the fold of the progressive plutocracy who advanced a form of progressivism that they believed would result in state government efficiency and an expansion of public services to citizens. The tenets of the progressive plutocrats agreed with New South industrialization that needed their oversight of state government to avert any interference to its "system of racialized capitalism."[27]

This book confirms and extends the scholarship of Dwight B. Billings, Jr., author of *Planters and the Making of a New South*.[28] Billings found that the South's antebellum tradition of plantation authority was "translated into mill villages," with textile leaders' power extending over African Americans as well as "the white workers in mill towns."[29] While clearly stating that the power of a "repressive state" aided mill directors' authoritarian control of mill workers, Billings less forcefully suggested that North Carolina's state power was used to buttress textile mill villages' caste system, the undermining of potential labor unrest, as well as the building of schools and roads.[30] Caraleigh's history confirms the use of state power, updating Billings' mere suggestion of state support and affirming its brazen implementation. Examples of Caraleigh's connection and use of state power exhibited itself frequently. For one, stockholders received their dividends at meetings held in the mayor's office,[31] and in another example, the state allowed prison laborers to build a railway link to Caraleigh's mill and fertilizer plant.[32]

The men who organized, directed, or supported Caraleigh from 1892 to 1930 were reputedly "Raleigh's most reliable and substantial" businessmen.[33] Of the 24 examined in this book, two were gubernatorial candidates Ashley Horne and Augustus Summerfield Merrimon; others were prominent bankers and businessmen such as John T. Pullen, James J. Thomas and Raleigh Mayor A.A Thompson, and one was a newspaper editor, Josephus Daniels.[34] Caraleigh's politically potent progenitors commanded great respect and swayed the development of Caraleigh, and how it was portrayed. In a state ruled by "a white supremacist Democratic Party," state subsidized historians extended their version of Caraleigh's history, praising those who set in motion the state's racialized march to progress for most of the 20th century.[35]

In telling Caraleigh's story, this book demonstrates that its founders set in motion the economic, ideological, and social realities at Caraleigh that were celebrated by historians who composed narrative accounts focusing on the "great white men" of the state.[36] Historians such as Samuel A. Ashe, Robert D.W. Connor, J.G. de Roulhac Hamilton, wrote favorably about many of Caraleigh's founders, and in so doing echoed their endorsement of slavery, white supremacy, and disdain for Republicans and Reconstruction, among other things.[37]

Caraleigh's documented memory constructed for later generations remained within the accepted boundaries of socioeconomic and political structures of the postbellum South, one starkly divided between the powerful and the powerless. By managing the Victorian era facade of social responsibility via protective patriarchal benevolence, Caraleigh's founders and supporters—such as John T. Pullen, Needham B. Broughton and Josephus Daniels—preserved the antebellum principles of agrarian power and race-based privilege. Thus, through Caraleigh's sponsorship of its church and school, the morality of the Raleigh's elites molded the minds of Caraleigh's mill workers who mistakenly believed that their paternalistic guardians had their best interests in mind.

Caraleigh preserved the pre–Civil War labor structure with the use of available, inexpensive labor. With slavery abolished, Gilded Age North Carolina planter-industrialists maximized the use of low-cost workers in cotton mills and fertilizer plants, with some alterations. The Swedish economist and sociologist Gunnar Myrdal observed these changes in his 1944 magnum opus, *An American Dilemma: The Negro Problem and Modern Democracy*, where he recognized that the South's antebellum textile industry, though insignificant, had been largely driven by "Negro labor, partly slave labor."[38] However, the South's postbellum textile industry largely excluded African Americans.[39] The elimination of blacks from the mills arose from realities particular to the South between the 1880s and 1920s: first was development of a Southern "civil welfare movement" to provide employment opportunities for poor white farm families that left black workers unneeded; second was the employment of white women in mills. White Southerners disallowed black men from work alongside white women during the Jim Crow era.[40]

And in this context, the mill captains directed the play of power at Caraleigh, imbuing residents with their philosophy of race for decades thereafter. The powerful leaders of Caraleigh, along with their boosters, subsequently formed Caraleigh's historical narrative, whereby favorable local news reports of the mill and their founders smothered those that were critical. Nevertheless, as both dominant and subordinate narratives start with the creation of documentation of some kind, the retrieval of Caraleigh's suppressed sources allows the voices of marginalized groups to be heard. Effective historical silencing does not require a conspiracy, or a political consensus, although Caraleigh appears to have had both; the roots of Caraleigh's silencing were "structural."[41] The overall atmospherics of the era reinforced the composition of the region's "deeply held beliefs" of resurrection and rebirth that made the prospect of Caraleigh's possible failure publicly unimaginable.[42]

Scholarly opinions about North Carolina's textile mill founders remain a topic of conversation in the 21st century, but much of the information available about Caraleigh and its founders has been only lightly explored. The scant sources about Caraleigh that exist demonstrate obvious bias, shining a favorable light upon the overly feted Southern captains of the textile industry. In 2017, Peter A. Coclanis, the Albert R. Newsome Distinguished Professor of History and director of the Global Research Institute at UNC–Chapel Hill, emphasized the positive role of the late-19th-century textile mill businessmen in reviving the state's pitiful economic situation after the Civil War and Reconstruction. Hence, Coclanis buttressed a positive memory of mill directors, leaving out the exploitation of its cotton mill workers and their use of child laborers; however, Coclanis alluded to the sins of the textile titans, confessing that "some of these builders were worthy targets." In a large sense, then, this book can be viewed as a study of some of those "worthy targets" and how their actions resonate in Raleigh today.[43]

1

The Genesis of Caraleigh

Craze for Cotton Mills

From 1880s to the early 1900s, textile mills were hoped to extract the South out of the economic quicksand it had been slogging through since the surrender at Appomattox in 1865. The success of Southern textile mills was deemed a sacred "new duty" to achieve prosperity through home grown effort, thus creating a psychological nexus between the mills and the sacrifices of the Civil War and humiliations of Reconstruction.[1] Cotton mills were the vehicles by which the "triumphs of Southern capitalism," were to be realized.[2] Of course, those who pooled their wealth together to create the mills in the postbellum South were admired and lavished with praise. After all, mill captains personified the main artery that diffused "dynamic power" into the South's "future hopes and unborn aspirations."[3]

The first historian of North Carolina's cotton mills, Holland Thompson, noted in 1906 that cotton mill industrialism was "doing what bayonets could not do," thus highlighting the enmity that much of the South held towards the victors of the Civil War.[4] During the era known as the New South—from the 1880s to early 1900s—cotton was believed to be as essential to the region's prosperity as it had been prior to the Civil War. Instead of simply growing cotton and sending it off to northern mills to be made into finished fabric, as had been done in the antebellum years, the South developed its own capacities to fully reap the rewards of textile manufacturing.

Cotton mills became Southern symbols of salvation. As institutions bearing economic, social, and emotional importance enshrined in the psyche of the former Confederacy, textile mills represented "the New South and its promise of salvation."[5] Similarly, the vision behind Caraleigh's cotton mills and its phosphate and fertilizer plant was perceived a defiant proclamation of Southern independence from the Northern conquerors, as reflected in the *News and Observer* in 1895: "For a long while farmers of the South" had "been sending their money and products North to pay for Northern manufacturers for fertilizers."[6] The South, having realized the "folly of enriching other sections" of the nation at the South's expense, was now building its own fertilizer factories "with home capital, patronized by home people."[7]

A "craze" for textile mill building struck North Carolina between the 1880s and the 1910s.[8] There were 60 textile mills in North Carolina in 1885; by 1915, there were 318. The number of spindles and looms a factory possessed was used to measure its production capacity; the total number of spindles in North Carolina was estimated to be 200,000; this rose to 3.88 million by 1915. The number of looms in the state were

Caraleigh Mills depicted in the 1923 *Southern Textile Bulletin*.

counted at 2,500 in 1885 and by 1915, that number jumped to 67,288.[9] In the South as a whole, from 1880 to 1890, the number of textile establishments rose 48.4 percent and between 1890 to 1900, that number climbed to 67.6 percent.[10] In 1906, Holland Thompson stated that mills were present from the coast to the mountains in North Carolina, with the average mill having 8,000 spindles, the largest 75,000 spindles, and the smallest, 680.[11]

Historians point to 1880 as the watershed year of renewed economic consciousness in the South, the start era of the New South.[12] North Carolina experienced a

Caraleigh Mills, Raleigh, North Carolina; c. 1890s. View of the mill complex from Maywood Avenue. Caraleigh Mills opened in 1892 (photograph by Brimley, H.H. [Herbert Hutchinson], 1861–1946. State Archives of North Carolina).

1. The Genesis of Caraleigh

slow drift into the contest for Southern industrial achievement that quickened dramatically after 1890.[13] By 1900, the Tar Heel state reportedly led the South in number of mills. Raleigh was not immune to the region's "cotton mill fever," as local journalists were calling it.[14]

The planned birth of Caraleigh Mills followed already established practices from England, where the Industrial Revolution started, and in the New England section of the United States.[15] The design of the textile buildings in the 1890s followed "New England factory" insurance company design specifications. Caraleigh, too, used fire-mitigating "slow burning construction" materials and design, most notably the extensive use of brick, a flat rooftop, and heavy interior timber, fire resistant beams as shown in the image below.[16]

The tradition of company-built homes for textile workers followed English 1700s precedent and was replicated in the New England states in the early 1800s and later in the Southern states.[17] Scholars have identified at least two models for textile mills and their communities: the Slater System, named for its British namesake, Samuel Slater, and the Waltham System, named after the Massachusetts mill town where it originated.

The Slater System was formed around smaller, family oriented, village-style communities that were subordinate to the primary importance of company profits. The system made room for an improved quality of life for operatives who could earn a living in favorable working conditions. This textile mill labor system proclaimed to have created a workplace with the health and welfare of the worker in mind, aiming at a holistic lifestyle that included leisure time outside of work. Owners of a mill

The use of heavy timber construction in cotton mills was developed for its fire-resistant qualities. This system of construction was later identified as "slow-burning," or "mill construction" (State Archives of North Carolina).

who followed this system would be directly "involved with the day-to-day life of the community, often living in the town themselves."[18] Concomitantly, the Slater System also relied on outside agents not employed at the mill who would further process raw materials that could not yet be automated with available technology.

The Waltham System was designed solely for commercial profit. Its creator, Bostonian capitalist Francis Cabot Lowell, along with fellow businessmen, created the Boston Manufacturing Company. Lowell's plans mirrored the best practices of English mills, replicating their structurally efficient management methods and applying them to their operations in the mill city of Waltham, Massachusetts. As the first modern corporation that was run by shareholders, who "put up the investment required to build a robust mill city," Lowell's endeavor was unique.[19] For their investment, shareholders expected a profitable monetary return. This differed from the Slater System in that the owners of this corporation would have little to do with the day-to-day running of the mill. Shareholders provided capital and employed others to oversee and manage the mill and its town by proxy. The reach of Waltham System investors often extended beyond the mill to adjoining profit-yielding operations, enabling investors to make money on other facets connected to the operation of the mill and the life of its village.[20]

Caraleigh was formed through the investment of a number of stockholders from Raleigh and other parts of the state.[21] As a "joint stock company," Caraleigh displayed elements of both the Slater and Waltham Systems. For instance, operations at both Caraleigh's cotton mill and phosphate and fertilizer plant were conducted through hired managers rather than investors; however, evidence shows that this was not always the case. Caraleigh's directors, investors, and supporters were often directly involved in workers' lives via church functions, political events, school activities, picnics, and more.[22] The company built Caraleigh's houses, its church, its school, and its graveyard. In August 1899, a picnic held at Caraleigh provided a petite example of the far-reaching company support that also included notables from Raleigh's aristocracy. Raleigh's *Morning Post* reported that "barbecue and Brunswick stew" was served up to officers and employees of the mill, along with invited guests including William G. Upchurch, A.A. Thompson, Frank O. Moring, Capt. J.J. Thomas and Carey J. Hunter and John T. Pullen.[23]

Raleigh had three cotton mills in 1895—Pilot Mills, Raleigh Mills, and Caraleigh Mills—with Raleigh Mills being the city's first and Caraleigh the largest of the three.[24] Conceived on January 24, 1891, the "great enterprise" of the Caraleigh Cotton Mills and Land Improvement Company, as well as its phosphate and fertilizer plant, embodied the state's ambitions during a "genuine building boom" in Raleigh.[25] Situated on sparsely populated farmland just south of the city, on land belonging to W.G. Upchurch, Caraleigh Mills, and the small community it created, attracted much public attention. Caraleigh Mills, "one of the largest in the state," was recognized as a significant contribution to the state's "Cotton Mill Campaign,"[26] one of the "biggest and most solid enterprises" ever inaugurated in Raleigh.[27] As construction progressed throughout the fall of 1891, the *State Chronicle* reported that the "new manufacturing suburb" was becoming the "haunt of sight-seer," because there was "much to see" including the "rise and progress of the biggest manufacturing industry hereabouts."[28] Soon Caraleigh grew into a "busy suburb," especially after it commenced production operations in August 1892.[29]

1. The Genesis of Caraleigh

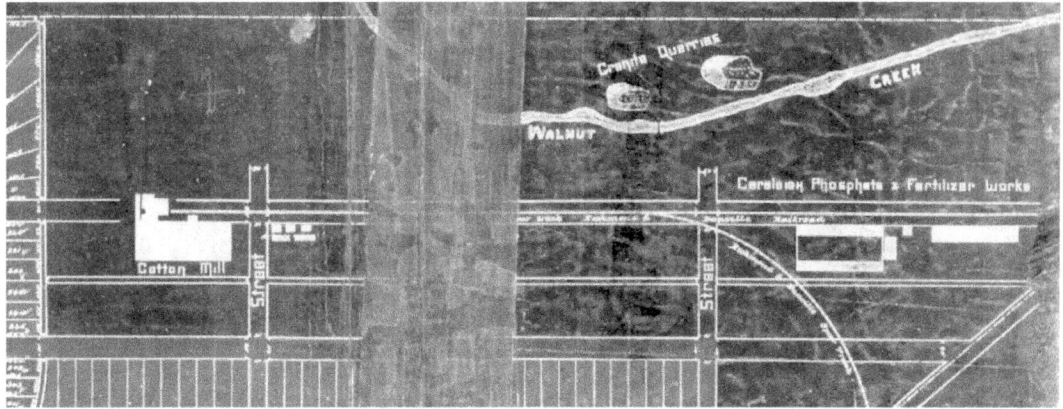

Map showing location of Caraleigh Cotton Mills and the Phosphate and Fertilizer plant (Wake County, North Carolina, Register of Deeds, Consolidated Property Index. BM1885–00152 Caraleigh Mills Co.).

The creation of cotton mills in the South most often attracted small-town investors; this differed from other major industries that required larger investments, such as in iron and railroad businesses. Although Caraleigh also depended on local sources of financial backing, Caraleigh's supporters were some of the most powerful men in the state, well-known bankers, lawyers, merchants, and politicians such as Ashley Horne, Augustus Summerfield Merrimon, R.H. Battle, Julian Shakespeare Carr, and others.[30] The support these men offered resulted in Caraleigh's favorable treatment in the press, as well as financial resources to construct one of the larger textile plants in the state. The numbers measuring Caraleigh's undertaking spoke to the seriousness of the effort. Its capital stock was $125,000,[31] and, as the *Evening Visitor* reported, a "force of about a hundred hands" of construction workers were needed to create the foundation of the main building.[32] The stone foundation was "eight feet high and massive," measuring 268 by 100 feet.[33] The building's "lofty chimney" was "visible from several miles from the Southward," and could be clearly seen "from the top of the capitol."[34] Fantastic reports of 10,000 textile-producing spindles in the "large and handsome" two-story building inspired much needed hope for brighter economic forecasts for the future, representing the city's quest for industrialization through cotton mill manufacturing.[35]

Caraleigh's phosphate and fertilizer plant was lauded throughout the state for being a remarkable accomplishment, boasting a two story acid chamber, housed in a 400 foot long impressively tall wooden structure that covered about 100,000 square feet of total space.[36] The same building's interior consisted of a "series of vast tanks," 30 feet high that required "ninety tons of lead" and sulphuric acid for the creation of "acid phosphate."[37] The triumph of Caraleigh's fertilizer plant was proclaimed in 1898 with an annual production of 20,000 tons of fertilizer and by 1916, the plant was named Wake County's "largest single enterprise," with a capital stock of $300,000.[38] The *News and Observer* reported in 1926 that the Caraleigh Phosphate and Fertilizer Works was "one of the most complete fertilizer plants of its kind in the country."[39] However, unlike Caraleigh's Cotton Mills buildings, the fertilizer structures would last only until 1934, being destroyed in a reportedly spectacular blaze.[40]

Sept. 7, 1906.

Letterhead from the Caraleigh Phosphate and Fertilizer Works (State Archives of North Carolina, Utilities Commission, Chief of Clerk's Office, Corporation Commission Cases 2332–2382, 1906, folder 2337).

The Civil War and the subsequent ignominy of the Union Army's occupation of North Carolina during Reconstruction deeply influenced Caraleigh's founders. The news of Caraleigh's predicted success was welcome in a state still reeling from Civil War–era psychological and economic devastation, with its most pressing internal concern being its need for money. Caraleigh aided in mental recovery from still resonant psychological scars of April 1865, when "wave after wave of blue-uniformed troops poured" into Wake County and the city of Raleigh.[41] The number of Union troops were estimated to be around 100,000, a number that was 16 times the city's population and three times that of Wake County.

The conflict between the states of the Confederacy and the Union, fought from 1861 to 1865, had devastated the Southern economy: a tenth of all white males had perished, the credit system was powerless, and two thirds of its infrastructure was wiped out, including railroads, bridges, buildings, and homes.[42] Compared to prewar estimates, the average value of real property had diminished by 50 percent and farmland had been devalued by 70 percent. By 1870, the average wealth in states outside of the South was $1,086 per capita; in the South, it was $376.[43] The emancipation of slaves transformed the social and agrarian system. Supply merchants, who provided farmers with loans and supplies in return for a lien on the farmers' land, demanded that indebted farmers turn more to cash crops, namely cotton and tobacco, to earn cash quickly.[44]

To salve its wounds, Southerners turned to cotton and its manufacture with deep energy and "passion," according to journalist Wilbur J. Cash, with output of Southern cotton crops doubling between 1875 and 1890 and tripling a decade after.[45] During the Civil War, cotton growers in India, Egypt, and Brazil had filled the cotton needs of European markets and Northern states' textile factories. But by 1875 this changed with the start of the South's cotton comeback. Evidence was seen in unprecedented commercial growth, attracting young men to Raleigh to pursue wealth through any business connected to the production and sale of cotton.[46]

While cotton mills existed in the South before the Civil War, it was from 1880 to

1. The Genesis of Caraleigh

Exterior photograph of Caraleigh Mills with addition under construction, around 1920 (State Archives of North Carolina).

1905 that textile production hit fever pitch, as reflected in the total number of spindles of thread in Southern mills that rose from 11,898 in 1860 to 110,00 by 1905.[47] In conjunction with this increase, consumer consumption of raw cotton increased sevenfold between 1880 and 1900. The value of the South's cotton mills multiplied nearly nine times, capital investment rose from 11.1 million to 124.6 million, and the number of "operatives," as mill workers were called, increased from 16,714 to 97,494.[48] The furious pace of growth in the textile industry left such an indelible impression on the South that it influenced how they perceived themselves and how outsiders viewed the South, too. Thus, study of the South between 1865 and the early 1900s requires an understanding of the dramatic growth of its textile mill industry; and by extension, analysis of North Carolina and its capital city demand commensurate attention.[49]

Raleigh by the mid–1890s was thought of as one of the South's "premier interior markets" for cotton, calling the state's capital "essentially a cotton town."[50] With hopes for economic resurrection in their corner of the former Confederacy, Caraleigh's founders moved with a fervor unseen in the Raleigh "since the surrender" in 1865.[51] The *News and Observer* anticipated that Caraleigh would soon bring a "hum of spindles and looms" that would "make music within ear-shot of our city."[52]

All three of Raleigh's textile mills in 1895 were located "just outside" the border of the city: the Raleigh Cotton Mills was "North of the city," the Pilot Cotton Mills was located "beyond the city limits" on the northern side and Caraleigh, in

A cotton picker machine attached to a 5 horse-power motor located inside Caraleigh Cotton Mills in Raleigh, North Carolina, 1910 (Brimley Photograph Collection, State Archives of North Carolina).

the south.[53] Being situated on the periphery of the city, Raleigh's cotton mills abided by the prescriptions of Daniel A. Tompkins, a leading proponent of the New South movement who recognized that Southerners were by nature agrarian, and that laborers and executives alike possessed long-held suspicions of cities. But beyond rural biases, there were practical reasons for situating themselves a few miles outside of municipal limits; these benefits, maintained Tompkins, included the construction, ownership, and control of mill workers' homes, the evasion of local property taxes, as well as circumvention of any city government jurisdiction. According to historian Brent D. Glass, the textile industry's rejection of cities was a major reason for the "state's unique standing as one of the most industrial but least urbanized states in the nation."[54] Thus, the stereotypical view of the Caraleigh village was formed, because it was populated with white mill laborers in a city that self-identified as a white collar town. The distinction between Caraleigh and its nearby metropolis would persist, developing into sources of tension—racially, socially, politically, and economically—for nearly a century.[55]

Late-19th-century industrial factories required investment capital and raw power to run its machinery. Caraleigh represented an attractive investment opportunity in the 1890s for several reasons. First, its location was near enough to Raleigh

1. The Genesis of Caraleigh

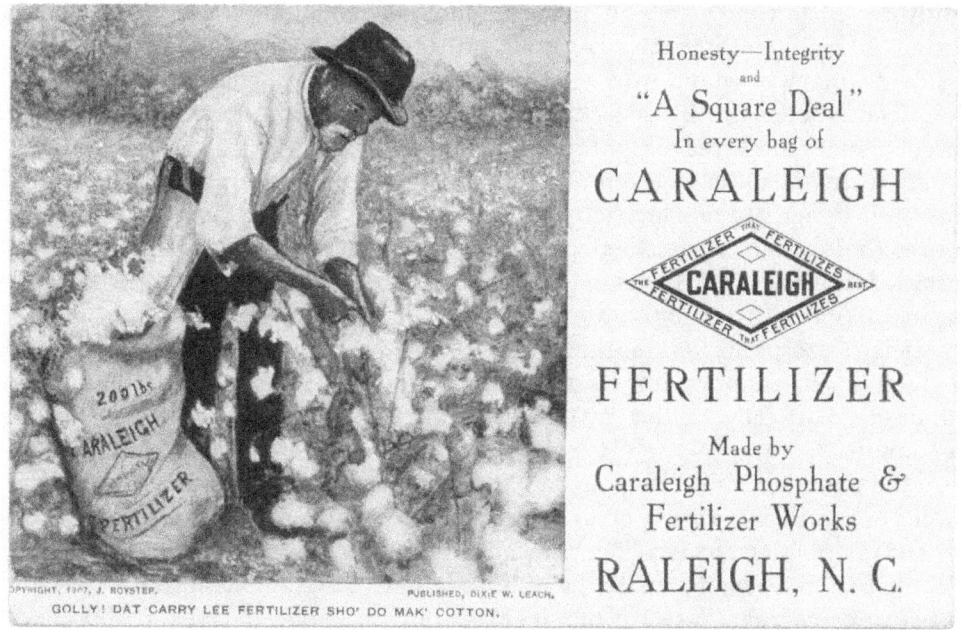

An African American picking cotton on a Caraleigh Phosphate and Fertilizer Works advertisement card; note the wording upper right: "Honesty—Integrity and 'A Square Deal' in every bag of Caraleigh Fertilizer" (Durwood Barbour Collection of North Carolina Postcards [P077], North Carolina Collection Photographic Archives, Wilson Library).

to enjoy Raleigh's urban privileges, yet distant enough from city limits to avoid taxation.[56] Secondly, Caraleigh's connection to the state's railroad lines made it efficient to import and export cotton and its products.[57] In the open rural space just south of Raleigh, Caraleigh's founders were given broad powers to "build and improve, lease and rent real estate, lay off and open streets and establish and maintain police regulations as may be necessary to protect its property."[58] The founders' great freedom to do as they pleased included the right to create and maintain necessary utilities: water works, water mains, gasworks and gas mains, all things electrical, street railways, and tramways.[59]

Caraleigh's two factories—the textile mills along with the phosphate and fertilizer plant—were located on a street that Caraleigh's founders named Maywood, likely after the nearby Maywood Dairy Farm. Situated close to the Norfolk-Southern Railway, Caraleigh's builders, with the help of forced prison labor, added a railroad spur line that led directly to the mill building and another to the Caraleigh phosphate plant.[60] The main line of the North Carolina Railroad, built between 1851 and 1856, was connected to southwest Raleigh and the north bank of Walnut Creek, through property of Dix Hill, the state's hospital for the mentally ill. The proximity to Raleigh, combined with "its own tracks of the Southern railroad," provided Caraleigh "excellent shipping and receiving" capabilities, as well as making Caraleigh a regular stop for travelers, permitting individual embarkation and debarkation.[61]

By 1899, Caraleigh's textile operation was consuming about 2,000 bales of cotton annually, much of which came from its own 200 acres of land, where its owners cultivated cotton and also built and sold "adorable" suburban housing on lots measuring "50 by 100 feet."[62] The village of Caraleigh housed anywhere from 160 to 250 residents, many of whom worked at the mill, making Caraleigh a company town described as "a pretty mill settlement" with operatives who lived in "one hundred and seventy homes" of "three to eight rooms each."[63]

Early textile mills required running water for power generation, but Caraleigh was built to operate on electricity.[64] Electricity allowed for a more mobile power source for locations such as Raleigh that were further inland. The City of Raleigh installed its first electric lights in 1885, and six years later, Caraleigh Mills was making use of 300 electric lamps powered with an Edison dynamo generator.[65] By 1898, Caraleigh's prosperity was marked with an increase in the company's capital stock, as the company announced to its stockholders, to "three hundred fifty shares, of one hundred dollars each," with a "guaranteed cumulative dividend of eight per centum per annum."[66]

The Caraleigh Mills Company was a study in vertical integration. The textile mill owned or controlled a variety of necessary resources as well as railroad links to its supply and distribution chain, which reduced costs and improved efficiencies. For example, the bricks needed to create the mill buildings' "large and handsome" two story structure came from "W.G. Upchurch's brick yard on Caraleigh lands" that produced and sold one to two million bricks annually.[67] Though appearing monolithic, Caraleigh's textile mill operation was made up of several buildings. The original two story mill building of 1892 makes up the majority of the textile operation. But numerous nearby smaller additions were added, buildings of two and one stories. The collective structure developed during five waves of construction: the original in 1892, another around 1900, a 1910 addition, a 1919 wing and warehouse, and in the late 1950s, several one-story concrete block additions with flat roofs. The cotton needed to weave into finished fabric was grown in Caraleigh's cotton fields or bought locally.[68] The adjacent Caraleigh Phosphate and Fertilizer Works, among the "best equipped fertilizer manufactories in the country," was established to support the growth of that cotton.[69]

Caraleigh's enterprises benefited from cotton farmers' misfortunes in the late 1800s when prices dramatically fell, causing an exodus of farm families from the countryside who sought work at the textile mills and increasing the demand for commercial fertilizers.[70] Cotton prices dropped on average 24 percent between 1876 and 1896, resulting in overproduction and subsequent widespread use of commercial fertilizers to nutrify weakened soil, as most of the state's cotton and tobacco farmers made widespread use of commercial fertilizers.[71] Many of the founders of the mill were also directly involved with the Phosphate and Fertilizer Works; for example, the first president of Caraleigh Mills, W.G. Upchurch, was a director in both the mill and the phosphate concern.[72] The company's directors were its seven to ten principal stockholders, who were likewise "largely the same stockholders" as those of the phosphate works.[73]

Caraleigh's Redeemers

Caraleigh's founders, investors, and boosters were shaped in the context of four distinct periods of Southern history: the antebellum period from 1820 to 1860, the Civil War from 1861 to 1865, Reconstruction, ending in 1877,[74] and lastly, the "New South" era, a period economic uplift for Southerners that started around 1880 through the early 1900s.[75] Besides economic recovery from the Civil War, values of the Old South informed Caraleigh's architects' decisions about how the mill and its village were to be molded, thus verifying the research of historian Holland Thompson's in *From the Cotton Field to the Cotton Mill*.[76] Thompson in 1906 maintained that the "essential attributes" of Southern political and social culture were intensified during the Civil War and fixed "more firmly" during Reconstruction and these "convictions" persisted through the early 1900s.[77] That textile mills represented economic change for North Carolina was clear to Holland Thompson, but he also believed that "the influence of the old civilization is felt through the expression of the new," but were modified in "almost every detail."[78]

Most of Caraleigh's executives were "Redeemers," Southern Democrats who led the region through the end of Reconstruction and sought the restoration of white supremacy and black subordination. The idea of the "New South" centered on the notions of industrialization, urbanization, and racial harmony, a vision originally credited to Henry W. Grady's whose suppositions and proposals were pronounced in the 1874 *Atlanta Daily Herald* editorial, "The New South."[79] Two other men—Walter Hines Page and Daniel A. Tompkins—both North Carolinians, assisted in developing what became known as the "New South Creed," an informal set of ideas to guide the post–Confederate South to regain national dominance, stressing economic development, sectional reconciliation, and improved education.[80]

Walter Hines Page was a recognized proponent of the "New South" viewpoint and a Wake County native, newspaper editor, author, and owner of Raleigh's *State Chronicle* newspaper until he sold it to Caraleigh Mills's ally, Josephus Daniels, in 1885.[81] The third of the New South architects was Charlotte industrialist, author, and publisher Daniel A. Tompkins, who had an ownership stake in numerous publishing concerns: *Charlotte Daily Observer*, *Charlotte Evening News*, and the *Greenville [South Carolina] News* and the *Observer Printing House*. Tompkins' publications were de facto propaganda outlets for cotton mills in the industrial New South. Feature stories about Caraleigh depicted the village as a seeming paradise with "attractive lawns, flowers, and pretty gardens," and where the company provided education and health care for villagers.[82] Tompkins' papers hailed Caraleigh's workers as "good citizens" who had no equal, because "there was not a more enterprising community in the state."[83]

Caraleigh Mills was part of the South's postbellum quest for a "glorious material and industrial triumph,"[84] where the region's ascendency was envisioned to culminate in victory through native "Southern will power," according to C. Vann Woodward.[85] The New South Creed was a simple set of beliefs that became an essential feature of the Southern philosophy. The creed was a "powerful shaping force" that was expressed in question and answer form, "a sort of catechism, a statement of religious beliefs" to be internalized through memorization and recitation[86]:

Why Did the North Defeat the South?

Question: Why Did the North Defeat the South?
  Answer: The South could not compete with the North because the South relied too much on cotton and slave-based agriculture. The South failed to develop industries

and cities and towns. Southern leaders were too interested in politics and too uninterested in work and making money.

Question: What should the South do?
Answer: The South must build factories and cities. Farmers must grow a wider range of crops and use the best methods and tools for farming.

Question: What kind of relationship should the South have with the rest of the nation?
Answer: Harmonious. Disharmony wastes energy and, more important, discourages people who might invest in the New South.

Question: What about relations between blacks and whites?
Answer: Those must also be harmonious.

Question: Does that mean racial equality?
Answer: No! Southern whites must dominate the South. Whites are naturally superior and more civilized and know what is best for blacks. Blacks may have certain civil and political rights, but they cannot have power in proportion to their numbers. Social equality is unacceptable. Miscegenation and interracial marriage are abhorrent.[87]

Raleigh was fertile ground for Caraleigh to enact the New South philosophy that called for healing sectional differences, racial peace, and a new economic and social order centered on industry and a scientific, diversified form of agriculture. Following this formula, it was hoped that the South would achieve victory and be a dominate power within a reunited nation.[88] In this context, Caraleigh Mills represented Raleigh's boldest effort to embrace the South's "consciousness of a new economic era."[89] In the 1890s, newspaper reports of Caraleigh were penned in the optimistic tones of foreordained Southern triumphalism, as a collective hero's tale of miraculous recovery, an indicative omen of prosperity denied for decades.[90] Lyrical newspaper commentary wrapped Caraleigh in the righteousness of Southern energy and regional pride:

> …as the Southland grows and as the commonwealth grows Raleigh will likewise grow, and the managers and shareholders in the Caraleigh Mills know that as Raleigh grows, Caraleigh must necessarily grow. Every bale of Caraleigh suitings that are sent is a good advertisement for Caraleigh, Raleigh, and the State.[91]

The "Caraleigh Anthem" that was sung at the mill's opening echoed the buoyant attitude of a revitalized South:

> The Caraleigh Mills are large and strong
> And they are running every day,
> At morn and eve both loud and long,
> Their whistle blows this way,
> (Three Toots)
> Their colors red white and strong,
> They're a mixture of blue and gray,
> Their brown and pink will last you long
> And their whistle blows this way,
> (Three Toots)
> O, yes, I am a Southern girl,
> I glory in their name,
> And boast it with far great pride
> Than glittering wealth or fame.
> My home-spun dress is plain I know,
> But think of the good I do,

1. The Genesis of Caraleigh

> When wearing this dress I advertise
> The Caraleigh colors true.
> The Southern land is glorious land,
> With cotton mills aglow,
> And Southern girls for Southern mills
> Will wear their goods you know
> We've waited for the Caraleigh Mills,
> Oh! We've waited very long
> But now we hear on each work day,
> Their whistle clear and strong
> (Three Toots)
> Chorus
> Hurrah! Hurrah!
> For Caraleigh Mills
> Hurrah!
> The mills with colors good and true,
> Bring custom from afar[92]

Late 19th-century and 20th-century North Carolina newspapers and historians showed spaniel reverence for the mill captains of Caraleigh. Glowing reportage about Caraleigh persevered for decades. In 1895, the *News and Observer* characterized Caraleigh's start as propitiously and destined for success, a phenomenal undertaking in the production of cloth unsurpassed anywhere in the nation[93] The *News and Observer* reported in 1897 that cotton grown in Wake County could be brought to Caraleigh where it would be "spun and bleached and dyed and woven and finished into the finest" of fabrics.[94] In 1898, the *Morning Post* described Caraleigh as "a very superb enterprise, supplied with the best machinery and equipment made, utilizing several hundred intelligent, happy looking employees."[95] Caraleigh in 1899 was reported to be the "first complete cotton manufacturing plant in the South," where raw cotton entered the factory and exited the factory finished product.[96] In 1917, Caraleigh's workers still appeared to the *Charlotte News* "to be perfectly contented ... from general appearances they are well blessed with this world's comforts and pleasures."[97] Remembered for being able to "compete on even terms with the great textile mills of New England," Caraleigh was "capable of equalling [sic] textile products not only from New England, but of Old England, as well."[98]

Raleigh's "most progressive citizens" reinforced the idea that Caraleigh's triumph was an irreversible truth. The *News and Observer* in 1899 underscored the prominence of Caraleigh's leaders, who possessed standing in the state that was "of the highest" caliber, men who "needed no introduction to the public."[99] Caraleigh's architects were not simply a collection of small-town investors who mobilized their resources within their own communities. They were counted among the foremost business and political leaders in Raleigh and the state. Caraleigh's founders embodied the spirit of the era, with their indubitable leadership providing an assured sense of a brighter economic future and psychological salvation at a time when some believed that North Carolina was "poor and backward."[100] Even before Caraleigh had started operations, Raleigh's *Evening Visitor* rallied readers to support W.G. Upchurch and Caraleigh.

> Our friend, Mr. W.G. Upchurch, is the moving spirit in the matter, and he is a "moving man," sure enough. He has put his shoulders to the wheel in this business and he will

shove it along with all his well known energy. The mills will be one of the most valuable adjuncts to the industries of Raleigh yet made, and shows that our city is fast entering the arena as a manufacturing centre. While our little provincial towns are howling with promises, Raleigh is substantially at work with her most progressive citizens in the front. The beauty of it is we take no step backward. We make sure of being right, and "then go ahead."[101]

Caraleigh's name itself was significant, connecting to what some historians of language refer to "name magic," the belief that psychological "power exists in a name."[102] Knowledge of a name was believed to "imbue the qualities" of that person or place in those who spoke it.[103] The *News and Observer* declared as much when it opined that Caraleigh was a "union of the words Carolina and Raleigh" and that this semantic birth was "infused with all the meaning that progress and success can give [and be] forever dedicated to industrial growth and prosperity."[104] Caraleigh, the *News and Observer* wrote, delighted "the heart of every sincere Raleighite,"[105] Thus imbued with a broad sense of purpose by virtue of its very name, Caraleigh appeared to possess the spirit and life energy of the region, state, and city. Caraleigh's stature was further buttressed through the names of the founders themselves, a number of whom were revered for their heroics during the Civil War, resistance to the despised Union Army's occupation, as well as their postbellum business accomplishments. The names of Caraleigh's founders inspired confidence in Caraleigh and its raison d'être, corroborating C. Vann Woodward's assertation that "important institutions of that day sought to identify themselves with the romantic cult of the Confederacy" to gain prestige.[106]

The evolution of Caraleigh's historical record heavily favored its affluential founders, avoided their shortcomings, and muted or excised disparaging experiences at Caraleigh from public record. Caraleigh was part of the "white men triumphant" storyline popularized during the Democratic Party's crusade against Republicans and Populists in the late 1800s and early 1900s.[107] The latter two political parties combined their energies to create what was known as the Fusion Movement that gained political power in the state at the expense of the Democratic Party in the elections of 1894 and 1896. James L. Hunt's scholarship in the *North Carolina Historical Review* in 2020 investigated the lives of historians who created the state's historical narrative about North Carolina Populism. Hunt's analysis of North Carolina's first cadre of state paid, professionally trained historians found that their careers and values influenced their writing about the Democratic Party's war against Populism in the state's history. In so doing, Hunt provides increased clarity about Caraleigh's place in "the process of twentieth-century historical writing."[108]

Before 1900, non–Ph.D. holding authors wrote North Carolina history. Afterwards, the position of the "wage-earning historian" materialized, a state subsidized and salaried storyteller whose services were beholden to a Democratic Party that resolutely embraced "Jim Crow capitalism."[109] Politicians of the Democratic Party and their appointees controlled state government in 1903 and created the North Carolina Historical Commission. Later in the 1920s, the same men formed the *North Carolina Historical Review* and the University of North Carolina Press, ensuring that a "usable history" explained the past to impart moral, economic, and political foundation for contemporary politics, as well as direction for a desired future.[110] The coterie of state employed historians were reliant upon the favor of the Democratic Party and approval of conservative business leaders who bankrolled the state's colleges and universities.[111]

North Carolina's first professionally trained academic historians supported the Democratic Party's core goals to support public education, urban industrial capitalism, as well as economic and political suppression of African Americans.

Among the vanguard of the state's dedicated Democratic white supremacist historians were Joseph Gregoire de Roulhac Hamilton and R.D.W. Connor. In Hamilton's telling of the Populist era, the sinister agents were Republicans, especially black Republicans. According to Hamilton, when Populists formed a political alliance with Republicans to rob the Democrats of power, it enabled the appointment of black officeholders and black voting; therefore, Populists became the architects of their own demise. The "white men triumphant" theme of Hamilton's historical storyline was popularized during the Democratic Party's crusade against Populism from 1898 to 1900 in *The History of North Carolina*, of which series Hamilton wrote volume three. Of the six volumes, three contained ingratiating biographies of the state's white elite, among whom were many Caraleigh leaders. These men were, according to Hamilton, the state's "best men," industrialists, bankers, railroad managers, lawyers, physicians.[112]

An acolyte of Hamilton's was R.D.W. Connor (1878–1950) who wrote volume one of the *History of North Carolina*. Connor did his utmost to ensure that the Democratic Party's policy of white supremacy extended to the state's official historical record and to curriculum taught to school children. While Connor influenced curriculum for children throughout the state, Connor's contact with Caraleigh was not limited to the written word.[113]

R.D.W. Connor commemorated Robert E. Lee's birthday with Caraleigh's school children in 1912 (photograph by the author).

The commemoration and celebration of the Confederacy and its leaders, as well as reconciliation with the Union were important learning objectives for North Carolina's school-aged children in the first decades of 20th century. Heroic reverence for Confederate leaders was taught, believing they epitomized the best Christian and Southern values. From 1900 to the 1920s, local chapters of the United Daughters of the Confederacy filled Southern schools with portraits of Robert E. Lee and Jefferson Davis. Robert E. Lee's birthday saw ceremonies in his honor frequently occurring in schools.[114]

On January 19, 1912, Robert E. Lee's birthday was observed at all of Raleigh's public schools with speeches that emphasized Lee's "devotion to duty," a "commendable custom," according to the *Raleigh Times*. The ministers preaching the gospel of General Lee to Raleigh's pupils in 1912 were men of significant standing in the state. Visiting speakers honored Lee, the "Great Southern Chieftain," and provided children with details about his "noble life," hoping to shape the character of the city's youth[115]: Mr. J.W. Bailey was sent to the Raleigh High School; F.M. Harper to the Thompson School; Colonel F.A. Olds to the Wiley School; Dr. Charles Lee Smith to the Centennial School; and Robert Digges Wimberly Connor spoke at the Caraleigh School.[116]

Significantly, R.D.W. Connor was not only North Carolina's first official archivist, but also rose to become the first Archivist of the United States.[117] Historian James L. Hunt described R.D.W. Connor as someone whose intention was to ensure that white supremacy in the state "extended to written history."[118] Caraleigh's children listened with "with deep interest" to the Secretary of the State Historical Association who taught them a lesson about the legendary Confederate general.[119] The *News and Observer* provided a summary of Connor's words at Caraleigh that day:

> The patriotism of General Lee was told of and his love of the Union was presented as a part of the principles which actuated his life and the splendid esteem in which he was held by the world was told, it being emphasized that his life today is one that is influencing the world, that it was a life of the best type, worthy of emulation.[120]

A copy of Connor's lesson to Caraleigh's the children about the "inspiring subject" of Robert E. Lee's life has not been preserved; however, a broader survey of Connor's works details what he believed should be taught to the state's children and adults. Connor wrote *The Story of the Old North State* in 1906, a textbook for school children, with several revealing entries.[121] R.D.W. Connor on slavery:

> At the close of the war the old slaves still loved their old masters, and the old masters still treated their old slaves kindly. There was no unkind feeling between them until the carpet-baggers came. These men tried to set the negroes against the southern white people.[122]

R.D.W. Connor on the Ku Klux Klan (KKK):

> People said they were the ghosts of soldiers who had come back from the battle-fields to punish wicked negroes and carpet-baggers. The negroes believed these stories, and in many places would not follow the carpet-baggers, as they had done. The letters "K.K.K." stood for Ku Klux Klan, a society formed by the white people in certain counties to oppose the Union League and punish negroes who were guilty of crimes. Everything about it was secret, and nobody except members knew who belonged to it. It did many things that were wrong and against the law, but it made bad men behave themselves.[123]

R.D.W. Connor on the end of Reconstruction:

> The Union soldiers were gone; both the Union League and the Klu Klux Klan had been broken up; and the white people were again the rulers of North Carolina.[124]

As editor of *A Manual of North Carolina Issued by the North Carolina Historical Commission for the Use of Members of the General Assembly Session 1913*, Connor was arbiter of what information was included or excluded in the state's historical record. One entry in the manual provided a brief history of the State Capitol building, in which Connor quoted the 1909 work of fellow historian Samuel A. Ashe:

> And these walls have witnessed the reversal of that State policy forced on an unwilling people by the mailed hand of the conquering power, and the full restoration of Anglo-Saxon control. Never in history has a people been so clearly and effectually vindicated as those gallant souls of North Carolina, who, emulating the constancy of Hamilcar, swore their children to undying opposition to those who would destroy their civilization.[125]

Governor Charles B. Aycock appointed Connor to the nascent North Carolina Historical Commission in 1903, after which Connor became known as "the founding father of the North Carolina Office of Archives and History."[126] In 1934, President Franklin D. Roosevelt appointed R.D.W. Connor to be the first Archivist of the United States.[127]

Broadly speaking, Caraleigh's powerful originators could best be described as businessmen, bankers, civic and religious leaders, politicians, and Confederate veterans of the Civil War. Some fit all of these characterizations, others only a few. The public placed great faith in the state's patriarchs who provided what the South wanted, cotton manufacturing and gainful employment for "underemployed agrarians who desperately sought employment in textile mills as an alternative employment."[128] While directing the South's social and economic order, the mill directors earned enormous amounts of public esteem that Harriet Herring recognized in *Passing of the Mill Village: Revolution in a Southern Institution*: "Small wonder that the region accepted as wise the social as well as the economic activities of the leaders who provided the profits and the employment."[129]

The state's newspapers acted as propaganda outlets for Caraleigh (*Morning Post* [Raleigh], January 10, 1894).

2

Raleigh's Most Reliable and Substantial Men

The Founders and Their Terroir

The standard plan for new mills in the South after the Civil War was to attract substantial men in the community who possessed widespread confidence in the highest degree, regardless of qualifications or previous training.[1] Historians claim that the examination of mill founders is essential, because each mill's progenitors set the culture of mill communities according to their own values. In Caraleigh's case, its founders included bankers, businessmen, politicians, journalists, doctors, lawyers, teachers, planters, Civil War veterans, and even clergymen. Oftentimes, the descriptions of Caraleigh's captains approached those of demigods, resembling hagiography more than chronicle. Combined, Caraleigh's headmen represented a solid force of Southern willpower, one that would drive the highly propagandized story of Caraleigh's triumph to reality, at least in the minds of contemporaries.

In 1906, Holland Thompson in *From the Cotton Field to the Cotton Mill* found that the power of the mill managers was manifest in "all" social organizations of the mill village.[2] And because the behavior of the mill worker was a reflection on that particular mill and its leadership, factory managers attempted to control "the conduct of their operatives" where there was "little separation of private and industrial life."[3]

In 1929, Harriet L. Herring's *Welfare Work in Mill Villages* asserted that the "character of the individual mill is often set by the character of the man or men who fathered it."[4] In 1967, George B. Tindall posited in *The Emergence of the New South, 1913–1945* that the perceived function of the mill captains was to care for their people as community benefactors whose influence on their workers was "difficult to exaggerate."[5] Tindall cited one mill owner who believed their job was "making American citizens."[6] In 1974, the enduring power of the mill upon Caraleigh's community was observed in the *News and Observer*, admitting that Caraleigh had "spun not only cotton but also the lives of its workers," supervising life and death: living "in company houses and ... buried in a company cemetery."[7] In 1992, the scholarship of Brent D. Glass in *The Textile Industry in North Carolina: A History* reaffirmed the impact of the textile men who embraced the core beliefs of the state's aristocracy, projecting an image of social responsibility and enacting "paternalistic control" over their workers to preserve this benevolent image.[8] Under the aegis of textile mill authority, mill villages perpetuated the Victorian values of "order and stability" that adhered to a hierarchical ideology of society.[9]

Directors, Investors and Supporters

The Caraleigh Mills Company, as well as the Phosphate and Fertilizer Plant, had similar organizational structures consisting of a president, vice president, secretary, and a treasurer, with the latter two offices able to be held by one person. There were up to ten directors, one of whom was elected as the president by the Board of Directors.[10] The biographies that follow promise not to be comprehensive; rather, they aim to understand each person's connection to Caraleigh and explore how their values and ideals affected Caraleigh's development, as expressed in their own words, actions, and associations.

Augustus Summerfield Merrimon (1830–92) was North Carolina's seventh Supreme Court Chief Justice and one of the most prominent of North Carolina's citizens when he died in 1892.[11] A few months before Merrimon's death, he acted as chairman of the board at Caraleigh's first board meeting for the organization of the Caraleigh Cotton Mills and Land Improvement Company and was elected its first named director.[12] A.S. Merrimon was born on a plantation in Transylvania County, was a veteran of the Confederate Army, a gubernatorial candidate in 1872, and served as a United States Senator from 1873 to 1879; from 1889 to 1892, Merrimon was a member of North Carolina's Supreme Court, rising to the position of Chief Justice.[13]

A.S. Merrimon's youth was spent in Haywood County, working on farms and in sawmills while he "studied law between the plow handles" alongside fellow student Zebulon B. Vance.[14] In 1852–3, Merrimon was licensed to practice law, and in 1860, he was elected to the North Carolina House of Commons as a Union Whig, in opposition to the secession of states from the Union.[15] After President Abraham Lincoln called for troops from the state, Merrimon enlisted in the Confederate Army

Augustus S. Merrimon was a Confederate veteran of the Civil War, gubernatorial candidate, United States Senator, North Carolina's seventh Supreme Court Chief Justice, and the first director of the Caraleigh Cotton Mills and Land Improvement Company (photograph by the North Carolina Museum of History).

and served until the end of the war. Merrimon aided Zebulon Vance's election to the governorship in 1862 and during the conflict was appointed solicitor for the Eighth Confederate Congressional district, a position he used to try to end violence between pro–Confederate and Unionist factions in the western part of North Carolina.[16]

After the Civil War, Merrimon committed himself to resisting acts of Congress and Republican Party politicians who sought to dismantle North Carolina's antebellum traditions, as recorded in the *Asheville-Citizen Times*:

> Returning to the bar, Mr. Merrimon removed to Raleigh and at once entered upon a lucrative practice. At that time steps to subvert the existing State government were being rapidly taken. The negroes were being enrolled as voters and a convention was called to frame a new constitution. Mr. Merrimon threw himself into the struggle and sought to arrest the destruction of the State institutions.[17]

In 1866, Merrimon accepted the legislature's appointment as a Superior Court Judge, a position he resigned from in 1867 after refusing to carry out orders from military commander to enforce martial law in disregard to state law.[18] During the Kirk-Holden War in 1870, Merrimon intervened to assist prisoners detained upon orders from Governor Holden and was one of the lawyers who prosecuted Governor Holden for "high crimes and misdemeanors against North Carolina."[19]

In 1872, Merrimon was a Democratic Party candidate for governor. During the political contest, Merrimon was noted to be an ally of the Ku Klux Klan, an opponent of racial integration, as well as an opponent of the 1868 North Carolina State Constitution,[20] arguing that, if passed, it would force "white children and colored children" to attend the same schools and require biracial state militia companies.[21] The *Wilmington Messenger* recounted an incident during the election campaign of 1872 that they thought shed light upon Judge Merrimon's character.[22] The Democratic Party's State Committee of New York sent a representative to North Carolina in order to pitch an underhanded plan designed to increase the "negro vote," because, as the New York Democrats believed, African Americans were too afraid to be seen to vote a Democratic ticket.[23] The scheme involved "tissue paper ballots" whereby "the negroes could pretend to vote the Republican ticket, while really voting the Democratic ticket."[24] When presented with the proposed strategy, witnessed by the reporter, the judge flatly refused, stating that he would have no part of any plan or arrangement that was dishonest. According to the newspaper, this showed Judge Merrimon to be "the bearing of a man of white soul, perfect honor, genuine manhood—an ornament to his race and to his native North Carolina."[25]

While his bid for the governorship failed, Merrimon served in the United States Senate from 1873 to 1879. Governor Thomas J. Jarvis appointed Merrimon to fill a vacancy on the State Supreme Court in 1883, to which Merrimon was subsequently elected and reelected in 1886, rising to become Chief Justice in 1889, a position he served until death on November 14, 1892, at age 62.[26]

The details surrounding the Chief Justice's death provide a window on not only Merrimon's stature, but also the social, political, and racial climate of Raleigh the year that Caraleigh was founded. Merrimon's death on November 14, 1892, was lamented throughout the city and first proclaimed publicly at 4:30 in the morning with ringing of the bell at city hall. At 1 o'clock the governor announced the Judge's death to the council of State and ordered all public buildings closed for two days to mourn the loss of the "eminent citizen, statesman and jurist."[27] State officers were ordered to assemble at Judge Merrimon's home the next day to escort Merrimon's remains to the state Supreme Court to lie in state until 3 p.m. and to take the body for funeral rites to Edenton Street United Methodist Church, among the largest churches in the city. As planned, a casket covered in black cloth bearing Chief Justice Merrimon's remains were placed in a hearse with the assistance of active pall bearers, "eight well known colored men of Raleigh."[28] Honorary pall bearers were members of the state bar, officers of the National Bank of Raleigh, "with which Mr. Merrimon had been long connected," and two officers of Caraleigh Mills: Ed Chambers Smith, W.G. Upchurch.[29] Merrimon was then buried alongside other prominent North Carolinians at the Oakwood Cemetery in Raleigh.[30] In 1894, two years after Merrimon's death, his son William B. Merrimon, himself a businessman "well-known throughout the state," became a member of the Caraleigh Phosphate and Fertilizer Company's board of directors.[31]

William George Washington Upchurch (1837–95) was the first president of Caraleigh Mills, as well as a director of Caraleigh Phosphate and Fertilizer Works.[32] Upchurch was commended for being the "moving spirit" in the establishment of Caraleigh and without peer in the 19th-century Raleigh business community, because of his work being deeply "interwoven into the industrial fabric of the city."[33] A major landholder in the area that would become Caraleigh, Upchurch stood to benefit financially with Caraleigh's location.[34]

In 1858, Upchurch worked as a salesman for his uncle, William C. Upchurch in Raleigh. And during the Civil War, W.G. Upchurch worked as a clerk in the office of the *Raleigh Standard*. After the war, Upchurch formed numerous business partnerships and, by 1878 was a leader in the "wholesale grocery and cotton commission business."[35] Upchurch was saluted for being "the substantial wheat grower in Wake" County[36]; he sat on the State Board of Agriculture and the Raleigh City Council and served as "director and vice president of the National Bank of Raleigh."[37]

James J. Thomas (1831–1911) was a leader in both "great enterprises" at Caraleigh, being both the first president of the Caraleigh Phosphate and Fertilizer plant and the first vice-president of the cotton mill at Caraleigh and its second president after W.G. Upchurch's death.[38] Hailed as a "Captain of Industry" and leading figure

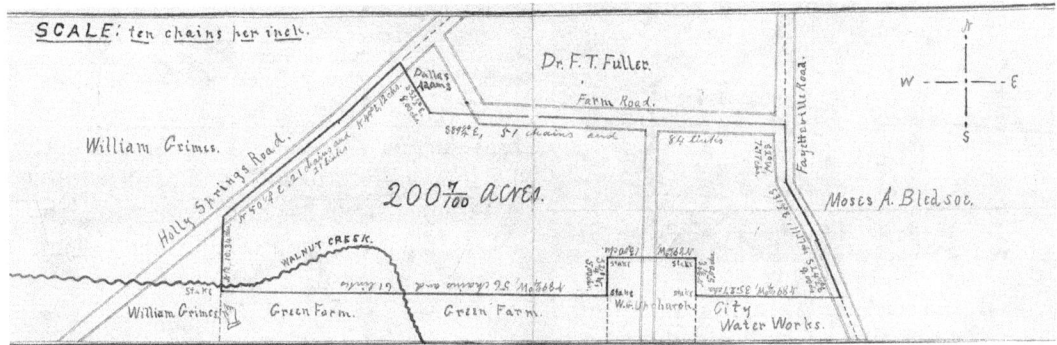

Hand drawn map showing W.G. Upchurch's purchase of a little over 200 acres of land in 1890 that would become Caraleigh (Raleigh Banking and Trust Company Papers 1831–1928 Correspondence 1876–1928, Deeds, Land Papers 1831–1923, n.d. P.C. 136.1, North Carolina State Archives, Raleigh, North Carolina).

in the financial life of North Carolina's capital city after the Civil War,[39] J.J. Thomas was known as a "most prudent and successful" businessman and banker, whose "sterling honesty" and "good judgement" led him to amass a fortune and inspire faith in him.[40] When the Commercial and Farmers bank was created, "Capt. J.J. Thomas" was elected its leader. Thomas's reputation allowed depositors to "sleep soundly," because, according to the *News and Observer*, his name was a "synonym of safety and fidelity."[41] Although not immersed in politics, Thomas was estimated to be a "thorough democrat of the Jefferson school."[42]

Before the Civil War, Thomas worked as a salesman and clerk and later as a merchant in the dry goods business, where he remained until the outbreak of hostilities between the states in 1861. Thomas volunteered for the Confederate Army and was commissioned a first lieutenant and promoted later to the rank of Major. Upon recommendation of General R.E. Lee, Thomas was appointed assistant division quartermaster in the Army of Northern Virginia.

During the conflict, Thomas participated in the Battle of Drury's Bluff and in combat around Richmond, Virginia; notably, he participated in the Battle of Gettysburg, and after three days' fight there, Thomas was, along with many other Confederate soldiers, captured at Greencastle, Pennsylvania, but was subsequently liberated on the same day of capture.[43] Owing to the frequent absence of superior officers, Major Thomas assumed the duties of division quartermaster, which was the position he held until the surrender at Appomattox Court House in April 1865.

In the postwar period, Thomas maintained his Confederate affiliations as the "beloved president of the Wake County Confederate Veterans Association," where he was known as a "friend of all who wore the gray."[44] Following the conflict, Thomas worked in a "commission business" in Baltimore until his return to Raleigh in 1872 when he partnered with B.P. Williamson, and future Caraleigh Mills president W.G. Upchurch, to form the Williamson, Upchurch, and Thomas wholesale grocery commission firm.

At Thomas's funeral, some of the most noteworthy citizens of North Carolina were among the honorary pall bearers—former Confederate General Robert F. Hoke; philanthropist and banker John T. Pullen; newspaper editor Josephus Daniels; Alfred A. Thompson, former Raleigh mayor and third president of Caraleigh Mills; Ashley Horne, banker, businessman, director of the Caraleigh Phosphate and Fertilizer Company, gubernatorial candidate and Confederate veteran.[45]

Oil portrait of Ashley Horne. Painted in 1914 by Mary L.H. Williams and presented to the State of North Carolina by the NC Div. of the United Daughters of the Confederacy in honor of his contributions to the state (photograph by the North Carolina Museum of History).

Ashley Horne (1841–1913) was a farmer, Confederate veteran, businessman, and aspirant to the governorship of North Carolina in 1908. He was from Clayton, North Carolina, and was considered one of richest and best-known men in the state, and a most loyal Democrat.[46] Remembered as one of "one of the corner-stones of the Caraleigh company," Ashley Horne was vice president of the Caraleigh Phosphate Mills and a "director of the Caraleigh Cotton Mills."[47]

Horne became a prosperous farmer and businessman after the Civil War and was recognized as one of the "Great Merchant-Planters,"[48] and one of the "largest and wealthiest farmers, merchants and manufacturers in the State."[49] The subject of a hero's tale, Horne's wartime story attained legendary status of epic proportions about how he "walked home from Appomattox barefooted" following "four years of bloody war," a tale that was repeated for years in newspapers throughout the state.[50] His service as a Confederate soldier and rise to affluence in business, fueled his entry into Jim Crow era North Carolina politics. Characterized as a "lifelong Jeffersonian Democrat" who was "loyal and faithful to his party," Horne served as a state senator from 1884 to 1885 and nearly won nomination to be state treasurer in 1896. Despite having support from Julian S. Carr, one of the wealthiest men in the state who was the president of the Ashely Horne Democratic Club, Horne lost a bid to become governor in 1908.[51]

Ashley Horne was proud of his military service and served as a major in General Julian S. Carr's staff of the State Association of Confederate Veterans. "Colonel Horne" received North Carolina lawmakers' praise in 1913 when he financed the creation of the "Horne Memorial to Women of the Confederacy" statue located on Raleigh's Capitol Square until its removal in 2020.[52]

Horne's political views aligned with the racially charged Democratic Party in North Carolina around the turn of the century, and was also "in full sympathy with the case of temperance, the work of religion and the influence of the church in human life."[53] When asked in 1899 if he supported "the Amendment" of 1900, which was designed to disenfranchise African American voters, Horne's reply was "most emphatically and uncompromisingly in the affirmative,"

The *Monument to North Carolina Women of the Confederacy* was dedicated on June 10, 1914 (Library of Congress).

Raleigh protesters vandalized memorials dedicated to the Confederacy on the evening of June 19, 2020. The next morning, Governor Roy Cooper ordered the removal of the *Women of the Confederacy* monument (used by permission of the *News and Observer*).

since he was "a strong believer in liberating the great old State of North Carolina from the constant fear of black rule...."[54] He believed that North Carolina's future included being "politically the vindicator of white suffrage and the domination of the Anglo-Saxon race."[55] In discussion about his suitability for public office, Horne cited his military service and support for the Ku Klux Klan.

> I have fought for my country and have been with the Clansman when we had to fight for our women and children and the one inheritance, I have to leave to my only son is my Democracy and to that I shall ever be true.[56]

Ashley Horne's death in 1913 was greatly lamented throughout the state. Laid to rest at his family's cemetery in Clayton, North Carolina, large crowds of mourners attended the funeral services.

> It was a tribute from men and women of standing high in the State, from men and women of all ranks of life, and a touching feature was that great crowds of negroes who had been in Col. Horne's employ or who were workers in Johnston county were among those who mourned.[57]

Richard Henry Battle (1835–1912). Reputedly among "the ablest and most prominent lawyers in the state," R.H. Battle hailed from one of the most distinguished families in North Carolina with roots dating back to the 1600s.[58] So, when Caraleigh publicly proclaimed that its stockholders included "the leading men of Raleigh and other points," R.H. Battle's name served as proof.[59]

Battle graduated from the University of North Carolina–Chapel Hill in 1854 and spent four years at the university as a tutor of Greek and mathematics prior to practicing law in 1858.[60] Afterwards, Battle practiced law in Wadesboro and developed numerous business and banking interests in Raleigh, serving as a director of the Citizens National Bank of Raleigh, president of the North Carolina Home Insurance Agency, and directorship of three cotton mills: Raleigh Cotton Mills, Neuse River Cotton Mills, and Caraleigh Cotton Mills.[61]

In the Civil War, Battle achieved the rank of captain in the Confederate Army and was Governor Vance's private secretary from the day of his inauguration on September 8, 1862, until 1864, thereafter being appointed State Auditor. In this capacity, Battle continued to provide daily legal counsel to Vance until April 12, 1865, the day before the Union Army occupied Raleigh.[62] After the Confederate surrender, Battle was a member of the Constitutional Convention of 1875 and in 1880, was an alderman of the city of Raleigh, as well as a member of the State House of Representatives; he was a leading member of the state Democratic Party's executive committee, and Battle was the party's chairman from 1884 to 1888.[63]

Richard Henry Battle was a Civil War veteran, private secretary to Governor Zebulon Vance, prominent lawyer, and director of the Raleigh Cotton Mills, Neuse River Cotton Mills, and Caraleigh Cotton Mills (*Morning Post* [Raleigh], August 23, 1900).

Along with Caraleigh investors and directors V.C. Royster and J.J. Thomas, R.H. Battle was a member of the North Carolina Monumental Association, whose "noble purpose," in 1892, was to "erect a worthy monument in the capitol square to the memory of the Confederate Soldiers from North Carolina."[64] In 1900, when the bronze statue of "North Carolina's best loved son, Zebulon Baird Vance" was dedicated in Raleigh's Capitol Square, Battle delivered the keynote address celebrating Governor Vance's memory.[65] Battle recalled that Vance was initially hesitant to support North Carolina's secession from the union of states in 1861, but that changed:

> "The prevailing sentiment in Raleigh was then intensely Union, and the indignation of many was aroused to a high pitch. Threats of violence were being muttered from citizen to citizen, and there was danger of riot and of insult, or worse, to the indiscreet visitors." But when secession was deemed necessary for North Carolina, Vance "drew the sword and threw away the scabbard when he entered the army" ever ready to sacrifice his life to the cause; "he foresaw the desolation and degradation of his beloved State, if it failed, and he imagined unexampled horrors as the result of the sudden emancipation of 4,000,000 slaves. And then the ardent wish of his heart that the honor of North Carolina should be maintained, and the faith she had pledged to the sister states of the South redeemed, to the utmost!"[66]

Battle maintained numerous civic responsibilities: as a trustee of the University of North Carolina from 1879 to 1912 and in 1891 was its secretary-treasurer of the board; as Rex Hospital's president of its board of trustees, as president of the Board of Trustees of the Olivia Raney Library in Raleigh; as president of the trustees of the

When the bronze statue of Zebulon Baird Vance was dedicated in Raleigh's Capitol Square in 1900, R.H. Battle delivered the keynote address (photograph by the author).

Raleigh Cemetery Association, which created and maintained Oakwood Cemetery; as president of the trustees of Raleigh Associated Charities; as a trustee of both St. Mary's and St. Augustine's schools in Raleigh; as president and vice-president of the advisory board of the North Carolina Agricultural Society.[67]

Upon death, Richard H. Battle was remembered for leading a life of "distinguished public services and noble virtues" and was buried at Oakwood Cemetery.[68]

Julian Shakespeare Carr (1845–1924) was a native of Chapel Hill, North Carolina, and was an industrialist, philanthropist, and Civil War veteran. Julian S. Carr held stock in Caraleigh Cotton Mills and was one of the original founders of Caraleigh listed in North Carolina's Act of Incorporation.[69] Carr was born in Chapel Hill, where he attended the University of North Carolina from 1862 to 1864. His enlistment in the Third North Carolina Cavalry of the Confederate Army interrupted his studies, which he resumed from 1865 to 1866.

From 1868 to 1870, he relocated to Little Rock, Arkansas, for reasons of business. Carr joined a tobacco manufacturing firm where he pioneered an advertising campaign using the Bull Durham trademark to publicize his firm's tobacco manufacturing. Soon, Carr's advertising attained worldwide fame for his company, which his own wealth allowed him to purchase in toto. Carr sold his tobacco manufacturing business in 1898 to the American Tobacco Company for almost three million dollars. Afterwards, Carr engaged in banking, hosiery and cotton mills, railroads, electric and telephone companies, and bought a small weekly newspaper in Durham, converting it to a daily newspaper.

Carr was a generous philanthropist who used his wealth to benefit the Methodist church, the University of North Carolina, and Confederate veterans; he also supported numerous educational institutions, including several colleges such as Davidson, Wake Forest, St. Mary's, Elon, Trinity, and Greensboro, and others. As a

Julian S. Carr stands second from the left, November 22, 1923 (Library of Congress).

Trinity College trustee, Carr led the effort to move the school from Randolph County to Durham, where it later became Duke University. Carr was one of the donors that started the Durham Public Library, North Carolina's first publicly supported library, in 1897. As commander of the United Confederate Veterans in North Carolina, he was known as General Carr. An active member of the Democratic Party, he donated money and was a delegate to party conventions. In 1900, North Carolina and Idaho cast their votes for Carr as vice-president in 1900.[70]

John Turner Pullen (1852–1913) had a relationship with Caraleigh that was both educational and religious. In 1897, Pullen spearheaded the creation of a "night school" for Caraleigh's "young employed" and was credited for building the first church at Caraleigh Mills.[71] J.T. Pullen, born and reared in Wake County, was a banker, philanthropist, author, church founder, and lay preacher.[72] Remembered as a "Man universally Beloved and Doer of Kind Deeds" and as the "most loved man in Raleigh," Pullen devoted much of his time to religious matters.[73]

Pullen conducted church services at Caraleigh and when workers were gravely ill in the summer of 1894, he visited and consoled the suffering and preached abstinence from alcohol to Caraleigh's mill community.[74] A central figure in Caraleigh's Baptist church founding story, Pullen earned favorable mention during the church's centennial celebration.

Deacon John T. Pullen of the Fayetteville Street Baptist Church had for years prior to the 1904 founding of the Caraleigh Baptist Church organized a series of cottage prayer services and a Sunday School that met from time to time in different homes in the new mill village. A need for a building was soon recognized and he had said: "Get me the land, and I'll get you the building." Alf. Thompson, President of the mill company heard of the proposal. His company furnished the lot, and Mr. Pullen was as good as his word; he furnished the building. He called it the Caraleigh Hill Mission.[75]

John T. Pullen, born and reared in Wake County, was a banker, philanthropist, author, church founder, and lay preacher (Annual of the North Carolina Baptist State Convention, 1913).

Josephus Daniels described Pullen as an almsgiver to the poor.[76] And when Charles B. Aycock was elected governor, Josephus Daniels, in his capacity as president of the Chamber of Commerce, appointed Pullen to be part of the inauguration committee in 1900.[77] Pullen was a widely respected figure in Raleigh and appeared to be the measure by which other men were evaluated. During the funeral oration for Ashley Horne, it was stated that Ashley Horne was a "true man, a sincere man," similar to "Charles B. Aycock, John T. Pullen, ..."[78]

Oakwood Cemetery was John Turner Pullen's final resting place.[79]

Needham Bryant Broughton (1848–1914) was a businessman in the printing trade, prominent Baptist church leader, and Democratic Party politician known for devotion to service in the public education. As early as 1874, Broughton led bipartisan and interracial efforts to reform city government in Raleigh.[80] According to the *News and Observer* in 1914, N.B. Broughton demonstrated leadership in "all contests for good government, for law and order."[81] Known as a "constructive, religious statesman," Broughton's association with Caraleigh was with the creation of Caraleigh's Baptist church and his temperance activities there in conjunction with his leadership role in the Anti-Saloon League.[82]

Born and reared in Wake County, Broughton was just six years of age when his father died. At age eight, Broughton came to Raleigh to attend public schools. At age 12, he apprenticed as a printer.[83] Eventually Broughton found work at *The Raleigh Register* until 1864, then proceeded to *The Congressional Globe* in Washington, D.C., then on to New York City as a typesetter at *The Herald*. By 1871, Broughton returned to Raleigh and partnered with Cornelius Bryant Edwards to buy the printing firm of Major W.A. Smith, reconstituting it as Edwards and Broughton.[84] The firm eventually became the largest printing company in North Carolina and from 1887 to 1894, printed most state publications.[85]

Broughton was part of the "Big Three," a trifecta of influential men that included Alfred A. Thompson and R.H. Lewis, who called for increased taxation in the late 1880s to support Raleigh's public schools. In recognition of Broughton's education work,[86] Needham Broughton High School was dedicated to his memory in 1929.[87] Broughton was also a trustee for Meredith College, the North Carolina Agricultural and Mechanic College (now North Carolina State University), Wake Forest College, the Oxford Orphan Asylum, and the State School for the Deaf, Dumb and Blind.[88]

Broughton's name was most synonymous with religion, specifically Raleigh's Tabernacle Baptist, as well as Caraleigh's Baptist Church. Building upon the initial efforts of John T. Pullen who started the "Caraleigh Hill Mission" in 1899,[89] Deacon Broughton led the initial meeting that conceived and officially named the Caraleigh Baptist Church.[90] Motivated by what he thought were increased conditions of immorality in and around Raleigh, Broughton saw Caraleigh's church as an outpost of moral virtue against growing "conditions of immorality" in the city that "threatened Raleigh's manhood."[91] Along with Caraleigh church co-founder the Rev. Sylvester Betts, Broughton lamented the number of "disreputable houses" in east Raleigh, the "incubator of shame," where city officials were accused of permitting prostitution to flourish unchecked.[92] Following an extended absence from Raleigh, the Reverend Betts was "amazed" at the shameful increase in prostitution and suggested that "praying hands should visit these houses and try to persuade the women to leave and lead better lives."[93]

Broughton suggested more forceful methods, favoring the use of police to enforce Baptist codes of morality, calling for "strong, bold, aggressive city government" action,[94] asserting that responsibility for the "appalling conditions" rested with the "mayor and police" who lacked the "stamina to enforce the law and rid the city of evil."[95] Broughton believed that as long as Raleigh was content "with a weak city government," its citizens "may expect to be overrun with lewd women, gamblers, 'blind tigers' [illegal bars] and the like."[96] In his proposal to "redeem the city," Broughton called for action at the polls to vote for politicians with the "moral courage to put an end to these evils."[97]

Mill village churches were an extension of the authority of the mill's management upon its employees outside of the workplace. This was dynamic existed to control and influence mill operatives' behaviors. Caraleigh Mills sponsorship of its village church indoctrinated workers with the values of mill directors and Raleigh's church leaders.[98] The influence of N.B. Broughton and the Reverend Betts was evident at Caraleigh's Baptist church, which believed in vigorous

Needham B. Broughton, one of the Founders of Edwards & Broughton Printing Company, Tabernacle Baptist Church in Raleigh, and the Caraleigh Baptist Church (photograph by the North Carolina Museum of History).

enforcement of Baptist morality rules involving lewd behavior and alcohol consumption. At Caraleigh, the Reverend Betts, A.A. Thompson, J.T. Pullen, N.B. Broughton and others vigorously supported the Democratic Party's push to excise the "saloon curse" from Caraleigh and the state.[99] In 1902, Broughton became the president of the North Carolina Anti-Saloon League and was still in a leadership role when North Carolina's temperance forces attained approval for state-wide prohibition in 1908.[100]

Caraleigh's own church history posited that the pursuit of financial stability and "protecting the reputation" of the new church were goals of paramount importance.[101] Accordingly, Caraleigh's church took quick action withdrawing members who had been judged immoral. In July 1904, one morally lax congregant was "restored to fellowship" in October after a public admission of guilt and "asking the church to forgive him."[102] The nature of his sin was unspecified, but others were documented. In November of that same year, the church's "eavesdropping committee" warned a "brother" to end his consumption of alcohol and repent or else face exclusion.[103] Church records indicated that another church member was disciplined for use of profanity, and in another instance, "a sister in the church" was discharged from the church for dancing.[104] In 1905, it was ruled that any male church member absent from two consecutive church conferences would result in an "investigation" by the deacons of the church.[105]

As with most Caraleigh leaders, Broughton was among the "true blue Democrats" during a period of racially driven politics.[106] Assisting in the statewide terror campaign of the 1890s and early 1900s, Broughton was played a significant role in reclaiming political power from African Americans and their white allies, Republicans.[107] Between 1898 and 1900, the Democrats' racially driven campaign was marked by two climactic events. First was the Wilmington Race Riot in November 1898, when the Republican rule of the city ended with the violent attack of African Americans and their white allies.[108] Second, one in which Broughton played a noteworthy role, was the Democratic Party's amendment to the state constitution in 1900 to politically disenfranchise African Americans, which became law via popular vote.[109] Democrats hailed the exclusion of the black vote as a legislative necessity to "end the crime of Reconstruction" and erase the "dread of Republican supremacy."[110]

The combined voter strength of the Republican and Populist parties resulted in what Democrats called the Fusion Movement in North Carolina in the 1890s, resulting in political setbacks for the Democratic Party in the statewide elections of 1894 and 1896.[111] Broughton ran for state office in 1896 and lost to James Hunter Young, the state's leading African American Fusionist.[112] J.H. Young's 1896 victory over Broughton for a seat in the state House of Representatives was by a thin margin: 4,719 votes for Broughton and 4,721 for Young.[113] Fusionists and Populists voted to give Young "Broughton's seat"[114] and according to Josephus Daniels, Broughton was robbed, asserting that Broughton won by ten votes (4731 to 4721), and Young "who was not elected," held "his seat by fraud."[115]

J.H. Young, born in 1858, was the recognized county and statewide advocate for African American civil rights, becoming the archenemy of Josephus Daniels and N.B. Broughton, both of whom were Young's most committed critics.[116] Young's 1893 acquisition of the *Raleigh Gazette* provided him platform from which to combat his ideological adversaries in the Democratic Party, especially Josephus Daniels.[117]

Statewide newspaper reports cast Broughton's defeat in racial dimensions, attributing it as a casualty of the Fusion movement. The *Smithfield Herald* wrote that Broughton's loss in 1896 to "Jim Young, a negro," was a "clear case of stealing a seat in the Legislature for a negro man to represent a county in which the negro is in the minority."[118] On January 9, 1897, *Gazette* scoffed at the *News and Observer's* accusations of ballot tampering and assured readers of the veracity of Young's victory.[119] In September 1898, Broughton's loss continued to be discussed in the *Smithfield Herald*, which gave a flattering sketch of Broughton as a hesitant politician who was "a good citizen, a kind man, an honor to his race and people" with friends "all over the state."[120]

Broughton's 1896 defeat continued to cast its shadow in 1900 when he sought the office of state senator; more than a few Democrats saw Broughton's 1900 nomination as racial revenge, an opportunity for a "wrong to be righted."[121] The memory of Broughton's political martyrdom energized the Democratic Party's platform of racial hatred into the new century. Historian Helen G. Edmonds wrote in *The Negro and Fusion Politics in North Carolina: 1894–1901* that "two men who fought this Negro with all their influence as men, Democrats, and printers were Josephus Daniels and Needham Broughton."[122]

Broughton's leadership in the Democratic Party started prior to 1900, when as early as 1888, many in the party wanted Broughton to be their candidate for Congress; he was the "chairman of the Executive Committee of the Fourth Congressional district."[123] And in May 1892, Broughton was nominated to be permanent chairman of the state's party at the Wake County Democratic Party Convention, because he was "a true democrat."[124] As election day approached in 1892, Broughton, alongside Josephus Daniels, urged "the democrats of Raleigh township to do their full duty" in voting for Democratic Party candidates at the "Cleveland-Carr Club."[125] Broughton's acceptance speech for the party's nomination to run for office in 1900 revealed unmistakable dedication to other party principles besides temperance[126]:

> I want to tell you that I shall represent every interest and every man in Wake County. [Applause]. I come to this position, if I am elected, and I shall be, through the people and not through myself. You are going to select here today a ticket worthy of you and of Wake County and we are speedily coming to the day when white men and white men only will rule North Carolina. [Applause].[127]

In 1900, when the Democratic Party sought to eliminate the African American vote via the implementation of literacy tests, they recruited Needham Broughton to convince fearful illiterate white voters who thought they, too, would be disenfranchised.[128] The *News and Observer* wrote in support of Broughton's candidacy, saying "They know he [Broughton] is honest and truthful," and "when he tells them that the amendment does not disenfranchise them, they will believe him implicitly."[129] Josephus Daniels extolled Broughton's virtues as "a strong and an ideal candidate," someone who was "well known in every section of Wake County."[130]

Throughout the 20th and the 21st centuries, biographies of Needham Broughton downplayed his role in the heated racial politics of the day, mollifying his political activities as primarily being motivated to promote education or to the banning of alcohol, a cause he linked to Christian zeal.[131] A 1971 biography of Needham Broughton in *100 Years, 100 Men: 1871–1971* dedicated one paragraph out of eighteen to Broughton's political activities:

For purely political affairs, Mr. Broughton does not seem to have had much taste, but he served for a period as chairman of the executive committee of the Democratic Party of his district; he refused, however, to allow his name to be considered when his friends thought he might have been nominated for Representative in Congress. In 1900, he was elected to the State Senate, and had a part in important educational legislation of that year. "In public duties that were not political he was, when called upon, always ready and always conspicuously strong and efficient."[132]

Broughton's entry in North Carolina's digital encyclopedia, www.NCpedia, reprinted from a 1979 biography in the *Dictionary of North Carolina Biography*, similarly minimized Broughton's political activism. Of the 490 words of Broughton's biography, 15 summed up his political leadership:

> In 1900, Broughton accepted the Democratic nomination to the North Carolina Senate from Wake County in order to prevent its going to a "wet" candidate. He was elected but did not seek a second term.[133]

In the county's standard history, *Wake: Capital County of North Carolina*, Broughton and his partner in the printing business, Cornelius Bryant Edwards, were described as Democrats, as well as "devout" Baptists, and humanitarians, Prohibitionists.[134] Broughton's loss to Young in the 1896 election was covered in a brief footnote. But John M. Haley's 1987 biography of African American reformer, teacher, and political activist Charles N. Hunter was more descriptive about Broughton's political actions and motivations. Haley's work described how Broughton sought Hunter's support with temperance, while concomitantly giving voice to Broughton's loss to Young in the political context of the day.[135] In explaining Broughton's friendship with Hunter, Broughton's long held opinion concerning African Americans was provided: Broughton "believed that the best solution to the 'Negro Problem' was to scatter blacks all over the country because their congestion in the South impeded their political, social, commercial, and religious advancement."[136]

In 1930, a representative of the Junior Order of the American Mechanics, a whites only fraternal organization central to social life in Caraleigh, wrote to support the naming of a Raleigh high school in Broughton's honor:

> Mr. Broughton was a man of great native ability, an executive and a successful business man, who for nearly a half a century was one of Raleigh's most public-spirited citizens, both in religious and civic life. There are many living who can recall his generous nature and his constant efforts for the benefit of the masses and his many benefactions to those in distress.[137]

When he died in 1914, Broughton was remembered as "a friend" of the "colored people," and a man who was sought "in every great movement of his times," especially in matters related to state of North Carolina.[138] Needham B. Broughton was buried at the Oakwood Cemetery on May 27, 1914.[139]

Joseph Redington Chamberlain (1861–1926) was at the forefront of North Carolina's fertilizer manufacturing industry that developed in the late 19th century.[140] Described as being "instrumental in building both" the cotton mill, and the phosphate and fertilizer plant at Caraleigh, Chamberlain was on Caraleigh Mills' board of directors in 1892 and was the first vice president of Caraleigh's phosphate and fertilizer plant, eventually assuming its presidency by 1896, a position in which he remained for three decades.[141]

A native of New York, Chamberlain was a member of the first faculty appointed to teach at the North Carolina College of Agriculture and Mechanic Arts in 1889, where he was head of the department of agriculture, livestock, and dairying, serving as a college professor until 1892.[142] Chamberlain also served as an agriculturist for the North Carolina Agricultural Experiment Station in Raleigh, a director on the State Board of Agriculture, and an officer and principal stockholder in Caraleigh Cotton Mills and other companies, including the Farmers' Cotton Oil Company of Wilson, North Carolina, the Farmers' Guano Company of Norfolk, Virginia, and the Raleigh Telephone Company. He was also an officer in the Raleigh Cotton Mills, one of the founders of the Capudine Chemical Company, founder of the Wake Seed Company and the Copperville Mining Company, and a director of the Raleigh Banking and Trust Company.[143]

Joseph Reddington Chamberlain was instrumental in building both the Caraleigh cotton mills, and its phosphate and fertilizer plant (*Who's Who in Raleigh; A Collection of Personal Cartoons and Biographical Sketches of the Staunch "Trees" That Make the "Oak City,"* **Adolph Oettinger Goodwin, Raleigh, printed by Commercial Printing Co., 1916).**

A top tier businessman in Raleigh, J.R. Chamberlain was known throughout the state for his agricultural expertise, and was noted for being a "Republican," a potentially damning fact in a state where being associated with "Republican evils" was considered an unpardonable sin.[144] Chamberlain's political affiliation helped in 1921 when the Republican Party controlled national government and his Republican identification positioned him to speak on behalf of farmers in the state against a proposed tariff on potash, a potassium-rich salt, sine qua non for fertilizer production. Though not breaking ranks with his party, Chamberlain thought the potash tariff harmful for "farmers of North Carolina and other agricultural states."[145]

In the "Populist-Republican times" from around 1895–1897, Chamberlain aligned with the "Fusionists," a political group comprised of members of both the Republican Party and the Populist Party whose combined efforts diminished

Democratic Party power throughout the state, notably with the election of Daniel L. Russell to the governorship; Chamberlain, who was "elected by the fusionists as one of the board of agriculture" and described as "Russell's tool," was often at the center of political intrigue at the college.[146] Chamberlain resigned from the North Carolina College of Agriculture and Mechanic Arts, allegedly after students in 1892 protested his "teaching methods."[147]

In some publications, it appeared that Chamberlain was given tacit pardon for his dual shortcomings of being both a Northerner and Republican and also was considered "first among North Carolina's progressive citizens to engage in manufacture of fertilizers."[148] In 1916, Chamberlain's biographical entry in *Who's Who in Raleigh* attempted to conciliate Chamberlain's faults, dissociating him with the Union troops of the Civil War and Reconstruction era, saying that he was a Northerner but one "who a quarter of a century later was to invade the southland on an entirely different mission."[149] Chamberlain's biography recruited the idea of sectional harmony from the New South Creed in warmly embracing their adopted son, asserting that the "conflict of '61 to '65 had all but been forgotten" and that Chamberlain's "arrival here was as welcome as the resistance to the northern troops was bitter."[150]

An obituary in the *News and Observer* on April 29, 1926, noted that Chamberlain as "one of Raleigh's most prominent citizens" and was buried in Oakwood Cemetery.[151]

Thomas Henry Briggs (1847–1928) was a merchant, banker, and religious leader, who was born in Raleigh and was one of Caraleigh's original founding members.[152] He hailed from an "Old Raleigh Family" whose ancestors took part in the city's founding in 1792.[153] Briggs' early education was at the school of Mrs. James P. Taylor and then attendance at Lovejoy's Academy, both prepared Briggs for successful graduation from Wake Forest College in 1870. Upon graduation, Briggs and his brother immediately joined forces in the creation of a wholesale and retail hardware business that their father had started in 1865.[154]

T.H. Briggs was active in Raleigh's community development throughout his life. He was an organizer of Raleigh's YMCA, and alongside Caraleigh Mills' first president W.G. Upchurch, and others, was a founder of the Wake County Cattle Club.[155] As a leading banker, Briggs had executive roles in the Commercial National Bank and the Wake County Savings Bank. He helped to develop the state's educational system as treasurer and trustee of Wake Forest College, trustee of the Agricultural and Mechanical College in Greensboro, and member of the Raleigh School Committee. As treasurer of Wake Forest College in 1898, Briggs directed the school's profits from bonds sold and its proceeds reinvested into Caraleigh Mills; the college's purchase of "$50,000 in bonds from the Caraleigh Mills" gave the school a first mortgage on the entire property of Caraleigh Mills and would pay "6 percent interest."[156]

An active supporter of the Baptist church, Briggs organized Sunday schools and aided in religious outreach and extension work. About one year prior to his death, Briggs was lauded in the *News and Observer* for having been a member of the First Baptist Church for "65 years" and a member of the "Sunday School of the church for 72 years," in addition to having served "a long number of years on the board of deacons."[157] Interestingly, in 1906, President Theodore Roosevelt in 1906 appointed T.H. Briggs' son, W.G. Briggs, North Carolina's postmaster. With the prestigious appointment, the *Raleigh Times* offered an apologia of sorts, reporting that "although from a democratic family, Mr. [W.G] Briggs aligned himself with the Republican party before he became of age."[158]

On the day of T.H. Briggs' funeral and burial at the Oakwood Cemetery, despite a steady rainstorm, over 1000 people showed up to pay respects.[159]

Carey Johnson Hunter (1857–1923) was a well-known leader in industrial, educational, and religious endeavors in Raleigh and throughout the state.[160] Listed as a principal stockholder in Caraleigh in 1898, Hunter graduated from Wake Forest College in 1881, afterward starting his business career in the mercantile business in Greenville, North Carolina.[161] In 1888, he accepted a position at Union Central Life Insurance Company for the states of North Carolina and, later, Virginia. Hunter's business acumen earned him directorship positions in numerous organizations: Commercial National Bank[162]; Capudine Chemical Company; the Melrose Knitting Company; Caraleigh Cotton Mills. Additionally, he acted as president of the Parker-Hunter Realty Company, and the Mutual Publishing Company.

The Briggs Hardware Building located in downtown survives as Raleigh's last commercial building from the 1800s and was the city's first skyscraper. The first building at this site was completed in 1865 and the second in 1874 (photograph by the author).

As an educational leader, Hunter was a trustee at Wake Forest College and Meredith College. Hunter was chairman of the Executive Committee of the Mission Board of the Baptist State Convention and president of the Biblical Recorder Publishing Company.[163]

Service to the state for Hunter included membership in the Executive Committee of the North Carolina Agricultural Society and leadership in organizing the Annual State Fair. Governor Charles B. Aycock appointed Hunter to the State Board of Public Charities, a position that was subsequently renewed under later governors.[164]

Carey won wide acclaim for his role as the first president of Raleigh's Young

Men's Christian Association (YMCA) and his continued work on the state board after his tenure as president.[165] At a 1911 fundraising event for the creation of a modern building for Raleigh's YMCA, where "Mr. Alf. Thompson, ex-mayor of the city of Raleigh, and one of its leading citizens, presided at the head table, acting as toastmaster," speakers portrayed the creation of the YMCA as a regional effort to build up their cities, in fulfillment of the New South Creed. Hunter's speech alluded to what he saw as the South's need for sectional successes, in agonistic terms, stating that "We American people believe in success," citing "the West," which did "things with a rush that had made a wilderness to bloom in a few years," and Japan, "because of its wonderful development," and finally, "the South" which he asserted was "attracting the eyes of the nation now, because it is bringing things to pass. We have demonstrated that we can do things." After his speech, Hunter introduced the "Dinner Resolution" to launch the fundraising action to the assembled dignitaries, stating in part their shared belief "that every interest in our growing cities calls for an up-to-date Young Men's Christian Association building."[166] Another friend to Caraleigh, Josephus Daniels continued the notion that the YMCA would further buttress their Southern city: "We established a slogan for Raleigh: Bigger, Busier, Better Raleigh. We have grown bigger and busier and now we are taking the step to better Raleigh."[167]

C.J. Hunter's funeral included honorary pallbearers J.R. Chamberlain, and Josephus Daniels, and burial at Oakwood Cemetery.[168]

Allison Francis Page (1824–99) was an elected director of Caraleigh Mills and founder of the Commercial and Farmers Bank of Raleigh, along with Caraleigh dignitaries J.J. Thomas, A.A. Thompson, Ashley Horne, and Carey J. Hunter.[169] "Frank" Page was born in Wake County, about a dozen miles north of Raleigh,[170] but the center of his profitable enterprises was in Moore County, where over 75 years of life, he accrued a fortune in the railroad and lumber businesses, earning him the moniker "Lumber King."[171]

Page was lauded for establishing the town of Aberdeen, in Moore County, and for practically building "the town of Cary" and for "building up Raleigh" with "some of the handsomest structures in the city."[172] When local citizens wished to name the town now known as Cary, North Carolina, for Page, he declined. Instead of naming the town Page Depot, Page chose to name it for Ohio prohibitionist Samuel Fenton Cary in 1871.[173] Page served as the first mayor and postmaster of Cary. He built the Mansion Park Hotel, in Raleigh, a top-tier hotel without a saloon and also contributed to the construction of churches for both white and African American Christians. Frank Page's eight children became prominent in state, national and international circles, most notably Walter Hines Page, a leader in the New South movement, scholar, editor, and United States minister to Great Britain during Woodrow Wilson's presidency.[174] And in memorial to the Raleigh's "Sesqui-Centennial celebration" in 1942, A.F. Page, along with W.G. Upchurch, were remembered as being among "Raleigh's Builders."[175]

"Colonel" Page was a "loyal son of Methodism and a pillar of faith," a man of "large brain, and large heart," whose philanthropic donations of thousands of dollars helped make the Methodist "Orphanage and Preachers' Home" a reality.[176] Politically, Page aligned with the Whig Party that was against slavery and the South's secession from the Union in the 1850s. A.F. Page was married twice and had eight children.[177]

In his final will and testament, Page requested and directed that his body be interred in Oakwood Cemetery and that all of debts be paid through the sale of his holdings of Caraleigh Mills stock.[178]

Richard Beverly Raney (1860–1909) was one of the directors of Caraleigh phosphate plant and its cotton mills in 1894.[179] Because he was the "popular host of the Yarborough" House in Raleigh, Raney's position at the hotel made him an influential person in the capital city in the late 1800s to the early 1900s.[180] For decades, the Yarborough was the de facto social and political center of the city, a place where politicians met to discuss legislation prior to casting their votes. An axiom of Raleigh in the late 1800s was that "more laws have been passed in the Yarborough than in the Capitol building."[181]

Raney's personal interests focused on travel and books and business interests that were broad in scope. Investments included the North Carolina Wagon Factory, the Raleigh Cotton Mills, the Caraleigh Cotton Mills, and the Caraleigh Phosphate concern. He also had directorships of the South Piedmont Land and Manufacturing Company of Greensboro, the West End Hotel in Winston, and the Commercial and Farmers Bank of Raleigh. Raney was an original administrator of the Commercial National Bank for which he was a director and the Standard Gas and Electric Company, where he was vice-president and director.[182] Serving as general agent for North Carolina at the Penn Mutual Life Insurance Company, Raney concomitantly managed farms in Wake and Warren counties.[183]

Not unlike many of his generation who were too young to participate in the Civil War, the conflict impacted Raney. He was the youngest of ten children, and two of Raney's brothers served in the Confederate Army; one died of "fever" while bearing arms.[184] Raney's first wife, Olivia Blount Cowper, born in 1861,[185] with Raney's mother-in-law sister to Confederate General Bryan Grimes.[186] In addition to Olivia Raney's Confederate pedigree, her family's background was of the most respectable sort, with her father Pulaski Cowper, president of North Carolina Home Insurance Company, and her maternal grandfather, John Gray Blount, who had been the largest landowner in the state.[187] Raney's second marriage was to Kate Whiting Denson whose father was a Confederate officer.[188]

In the inauguration ceremonies for Charles B. Aycock to the state's governorship, Raney was appointed to various committees for the event.[189] When the Raleigh Chamber of Commerce met in 1907 and needed a new president, the chamber followed Josephus Daniels's motion to elect Raney.[190]

Less than two years after their marriage, Olivia Raney died in 1896 during childbirth. In Olivia Raney's honor, Raney financed a three-story free circulating library opened to the public in 1901; the Olivia Raney Library, for "use of the white people" of Raleigh, provided the city with not only a library but also an auditorium for musical and dramatic productions.[191] The three story library building overlooked the grounds of the capital to the east, with an entrance of "Corinthian Doric order, executed in brownstone" and was said to have a variety of books on all subjects.[192] Plaudits were heaped upon R.B. Raney for his "great deed" in giving "away his comfortable fortune" to construct the memorial library. The *Farmer and Mechanic* reported that there was "not a library in the South so well arranged."[193]

When R.B. Raney died, the mayor of Raleigh extolled his life as worthy of the "highest place in the memory of our people."[194] Having been a director of the Raleigh

Cemetery Association, alongside R.H. Battle, Richard Beverly Raney was assured a final resting place at the Oakwood Cemetery.[195]

Vermont Connecticut Royster (1848–1922) was one of Caraleigh's investors. Royster, "for two generations," was regarded as an outstanding citizen and important businessman, known throughout the South as the state's candy magnate.[196] Although too young to fight in the Civil War, "Mr. Royster did his bit for the Confederacy" by running errands for the Adjutant General's office in Raleigh. Making the best out of defeat and Union occupation, Royster then sold candy to the soldiers of the "invading armies of Sherman," eventually establishing a candy store on Fayetteville Street that he ran for the next 57 years.[197] The candy store acted as an open forum among Raleigh's citizens and visitors who gathered to discuss the news of the day. In the capacity of candy store owner, Royster, known as a "philosopher, student, thinker, and musician," would join in to listen and talk. Royster's gregarious personality, as well his candy, "must have been powerful draws." Attaining Royster's confidence in Caraleigh made for a popular addition to Caraleigh's public perception of prosperity.[198]

V.C. Royster's burial was conducted at the Oakwood Cemetery.[199]

William Augustus Linehan (1862–1931). W.A. Linehan was among the first stockholders in the Caraleigh Cotton Mills and Land Development company.[200] Linehan, "a full blooded Raleighite," was elected a director of Caraleigh in 1891, and similar to F.O. Moring and J.R. Chamberlain, Linehan was a director of the Raleigh Banking and Trust Company, which was comprised of men whose leadership was "progressive, yet conservative."[201] News of Linehan's passing in 1931 brought remembrance of his being "one of Raleigh's best known citizens," and a "most prominent" businessmen of the capital city.[202] For over four decades, Linehan led the Cross & Linehan Clothiers Company which was succeeded by his son, also W.A. Linehan.[203] The elder Linehan was buried at the Oakwood Cemetery.[204]

David E. Everett (1846–1919) was elected by Caraleigh stockholders to be one of Caraleigh Cotton Mills' directors in 1897. A native of Goldsboro, North Carolina, Everett spent half a century in the profession of dentistry, 44 years in Raleigh. Everett served[205] as the president of the Raleigh Dental Society and was a charter member of the North Carolina Dentists' Association.[206] Remembered as a "gallant Confederate veteran," Everett enlisted at age fifteen in the Confederate States Army and served until the end of the conflict.[207]

A testament to Everett's allegiance to the New South Creed can be seen through his leadership role in creation of the "Worth Bagley Monument," in which Everett was the treasurer for the monument's committee.[208] Worth Bagley, born in Raleigh in 1874 to a prominent Raleigh family, was a naval officer aboard the USS *Winslow* during the Spanish-American War and was the first American to die during this conflict on May 11, 1898. Bagley's martyrdom in 1898 was framed as a symbol of a reunited nation, since it was the first war since the Civil War where the South shed native blood for the United States.[209]

After 1865, Everett studied at the Philadelphia College for Dentistry and Surgery and graduated in 1868, proceeding to practice dentistry in Wilmington, North Carolina, and then in Memphis, Tennessee, before relocating to Raleigh in 1876. After a short sickness, Dr. Everett was taken to Rex Hospital where he died. His earthly remains were interred in his hometown of Goldsboro.[210]

Alexander Quarles Holladay (1839–1909) was the first president of the North

Carolina College of Agriculture and Mechanic Arts, spending ten years at the head of the institution. He was a director of the Caraleigh Phosphate and Fertilizer Company in 1895.[211]

Born and reared in Cherry Grove, Spotsylvania County, Virginia, Holladay studied languages, philosophy, and law at the University of Virginia in 1857 and traveled abroad in 1859 to study at the University of Berlin.[212] When the War between the States began, Holladay came home from university studies and volunteered in the state militia at the rank of private and soon afterward was commissioned a second lieutenant of infantry and artillery, and later became aide-de-camp to General Braxton Bragg.[213] Holladay took part in numerous battles early in the war but was soon sickened with typhoid fever. After recovering, Holladay rejoined the Confederate Army and remained "to the end, receiving his parole from General Sherman" in April 1865.[214]

After the war, Holladay formed a law practice with his father in Richmond and served two terms in the Virginia senate, 1871–75. By 1877, Holladay had left the field of law for a career in education and, in 1889, became the first president of the newly created North Carolina College of Agriculture and Mechanic Art (now North Carolina State University).[215] The main building of the college during its initial years of operation was later renamed in Holladay's honor.[216] Holladay contributed to the

Faculty of North Carolina College of Agriculture and Mechanic Arts group photograph, 1892, now known as North Carolina State University (University Archives Photograph Collection. Oversize photographs [UA023.030], Special Collections Research Center at NC State University Libraries).

fulfillment of the New South Creed as an investor in Caraleigh, and more importantly, as the president of what is now North Carolina State University in Raleigh, where his leadership reflected credit upon the institution with each graduating class that contributed to the "great army of education people in the State."[217] "Colonel" Holladay's final resting place was in Raleigh's Oakwood Cemetery.[218]

Charles Boudinot Root (1818–1903) was named a director of the Caraleigh Cotton Mills in 1894.[219] A native of Massachusetts, Root descended from one of the "oldest and distinguished" families of New England.[220] Root moved to Raleigh in 1837 and was a business partner with Bernard Dupuy, both skilled silversmiths and craftsmen.[221] Eventually, Root became sole owner, rising to become a "leading" businessman in North Carolina.[222]

Root was a longtime public servant and served the city of Raleigh and Wake County in numerous capacities; notably he was appointed mayor of Raleigh during and immediately after the Civil War, "having been elected to that office by the Democratic Party, of which he has ever been a firm adherent."[223]

While northern by birth, Root embraced the fundamental values of the Confederacy, including slavery as seen in an advertisement that Root placed, "Negroes for Hire," in December 1864.[224] Root was one of nine vice-presidents in Wake County's Southern Rights association, a group that enthusiastically called for North Carolina's secession from the union of states and North Carolina's entry into an "immediate alliance with the States of the Southern Confederacy" in April 1861.[225] The aldermen of the city elected Root as mayor of the capital city in 1861 upon the resignation of Mayor William Harrison, who joined the Confederate Army as an officer in the "Raleigh Rifles."[226]

In 1865, Root was again appointed mayor pro tem, and in this capacity advertised a "Free School for White Children" in Raleigh to be administered under the auspices of the American Union Commission, an organization from New York, whose goal it was to "aid in the restoration of the union" through various methods, one of which was "popular education."[227]

In 1867, Root ran for mayor but was defeated.[228] As he had done before the Civil War, Root focused mostly on business activities as president of the Raleigh Gas Company and as an executive officer with the North Carolina Mutual Life Insurance Company with R.H. Battle.[229] Oakwood Cemetery was C.B. Root's final resting place.[230]

Edward Chambers Smith (1857–1940) was a director of Caraleigh stockholders via election in 1900.[231] Born in Murfreesboro, North Carolina, E.C. Smith graduated from Davidson College in 1881, and after studying law at

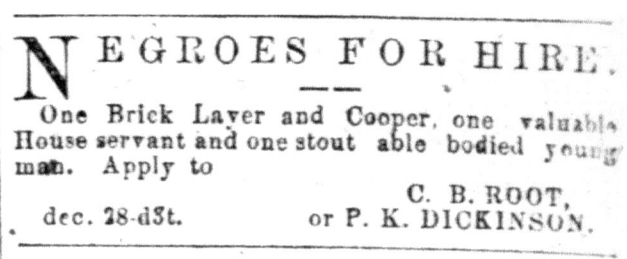

Slave owners could generate income by temporarily leasing their slaves' labor in a system known as hiring out. The 1864 advertisement in the *Daily Confederate* newspaper shows that C.B. Root hired out his slaves. Charles Boudinot Root (1818–1903) was appointed mayor of Raleigh during and immediately after the Civil War (*Daily Confederate* [Raleigh] December 28, 1864).

the University of North Carolina and the University of Virginia, was, in 1883, admitted to the bar and served as a lawyer until deafness compelled his retirement.[232] E. Chambers Smith was the chairman of the Democratic Party's State Executive Committee from 1890 to 1892 and was among the founders of the Young Democratic Clubs five decades before his death. E.C. Smith was, along with his father Chief Justice W.N.H. Smith, a supporter of Peace College, serving on its board of trustees for a number of years. E. Chambers Smith served as leader of a number of organizations: chairman of the North Carolina Fisheries Commission, member of the State Board of Improvements, director of the finance committee of the North Carolina railroad. The Kappa Alpha Order was the only strictly Southern fraternity in Southern states in 1912, and Smith served as its "15th Knight Commander" from 1901 to 1912 and from 1915 to 1916.[233] And when the Kappa Alpha Fraternity divided its territory into districts in 1912, the states of North and South Carolina were named the "Ed Chambers Smith Province" of the fraternity.[234]

As chairman of the Democratic Party's executive committee in 1892, Smith presided over the party's meeting that announced its official platform and proved to be a unifying, respected leader during a fractious period.[235] And, at the same "harmonious meeting," Smith started proceedings with "a ringing speech," which emphasized to the audience of 3000 that all present "were Democrats and called for unity."[236] After Smith's attempt to brook party divisions, former Governor Thomas J. Jarvis gave an hour-long speech where he "called on men of all shades of opinion: Alliancemen, St. Louis Platform men, and Third Party men to unite in the great fight against the enemy, 'the Republican Party.'"[237] The Democratic Party's platform that Smith helped create, kept true to the New South Creed's goal of Southern economic resurgence, continued native rule of the state, and avoidance of any federal action that would hinder the reestablishment of white supremacy. In reaffirmation of Democratic party goals, nine points were aimed at promoting the state's economic growth; it called for silver coinage in currency and increase of currency, a refutation of President McKinley's Tariff, an end to the increased taxation of cotton, the end of national banks, and a graduated income tax. However, in the first point of the party's platform, the Democrats addressed continued fears of "a race war" in the state and any possible federal action.[238]

> We likewise denounce the iniquitous force bill, which is not yet abandoned by the Republican party, but is being urged as a measure to be adopted as soon as they regain control of the House of Representatives, the purpose and effect of which measure will be to establish a second period of reconstruction in the Southern States, to subvert the liberties of our people and inflame a new race antagonism and sectional animosities.[239]

Alongside N.B. Broughton, Smith was named to the Democratic Party's "Central Committee" representing Wake County in 1900.[240] In that same year, further recognition of Smith arrived with his attendance at the annual birthday celebration of "Thomas Jefferson, the great Democrat" that was held in Washington, D.C., with other "leading Democrats of the nation."[241] For those seeking the governorship, Smith's endorsement for gubernatorial elections was valued. In 1908, E. Chambers Smith gave his support to fellow Caraleigh executive Ashley Horne for governor, saying of Horne that "if there is a more loyal Democrat, I have not heard of him."[242]

Frank O'Kelly Moring (1845–1920). F.O. Moring was born to a family of prominent merchants and planters in Morrisville, North Carolina, a town near Raleigh.[243] Moring led in the establishment Caraleigh Cotton Mills as its first secretary and treasurer in 1891, as well a director in the "Caraleigh Phosphate and Fertilizer Company."[244]

After his services as "a boy soldier" in the Confederate Army, Moring became one of Raleigh's leading citizens as a farmer, banker, businessman, and alderman in Raleigh.[245] In 1866, with the Civil War concluded, Moring moved to Raleigh where he was employed in the wholesale grocery business and became a known commission merchant, heading the firm Pool and Moring. Moring was elected president of the Southern Colored Goods Association in 1904.[246] F.O. Moring also served as an alderman in the City of Raleigh between 1882 and 1887, when significant changes were implemented to the city's water system and streets to keep pace with Raleigh's growth.[247]

Moring was, in the 1880s, a member of the Watauga Club, a group of middle-class reformers who championed progressive ideals directed towards economic and social improvement of North Carolina.[248] The Watauga Club totaled about 18 men and included Josephus Daniels and Walter Hines Page, the son of Caraleigh director A.F. Page. The Wataugans believed their state's "backwardness" had much to do with illiterate whites and African Americans.[249] Publicly supported education, according to Wataugan philosophy, would rectify the two problems in a growing industrial South. For whites, schooling would teach "discipline and conformity to authority, thus producing a literate and disciplined work force."[250] For freed slaves and their progeny, Wataugans thought that schools would provide a means by which whites could control blacks; schoolhouse paternalism would replace the institution of plantation style paternalism that was lost with emancipation. This philosophy informed Governor C.B. Aycock's advocacy for education for black students as well as white, seeing universal public education as a tool to control their black population.[251]

Josephus Daniels (1862–1948) was born in Washington, North Carolina. Daniels's direct relationship with Caraleigh was in advocacy for causes that he and Caraleigh executive Alfred A. Thompson supported.[252] On several occasions, Daniels spoke directly to audiences at Caraleigh to support education, temperance, and the Democratic Party.[253]

His father, also named Josephus, was a Confederate shipbuilder who was killed before his son was three. As a young man, Daniels worked picking cotton, clerking in a drug store, and in

Josephus Daniels, 1862–1948 (Harris & Ewing, Library of Congress).

a printing office, the latter of which led to a lifelong career in newspaper publishing. While Daniels was a bar-approved lawyer as of 1885, he never actively practiced law. Daniels' party loyalty helped him win the 1887 election as printer-to-the-State, which he held for four, three-year terms. When his newspaper endeavors became unprofitable, Daniels petitioned members of President Grover Cleveland's administration for assistance and was subsequently given positions in the United States Department of the Interior until 1895. It was while Daniels was in Washington, D.C., that he purchased Raleigh's *News and Observer* and merged it with the two other newspapers that he unabashedly used to support the Democratic Party's campaign of white supremacy in the 1890s and early 1900s.[254]

Under Daniels's aegis, the *News and Observer* prospered, becoming the first newspaper in the world to have more subscribers than the city's population in which it was based.[255] Daniels' adroit writing skills did much to embed New South Creed ideals in the minds of many. One example was the 1898 death of Daniels' brother-in-law, Ensign Worth Bagley, during the Spanish American War. The battle death was viewed to be of particular significance because, as Colonel William H.S. Burgwyn stated, "It is truly an extraordinary coincidence that North Carolina should lose the first soldier in 1861, and now the first in the present war [against Spain]."[256] Daniels's reporting on Bagley's outdoor funeral ceremonies at Capitol Square in downtown Raleigh artfully emphasized symbols of national unification, while simultaneously summoning noble allusions of the Lost Cause, in near-spiritual tones.

At the foot of George Washington statue the nearby "United States flag draped over the quaint old building state capitol building" rested Bagley's body, lying in state, "exultant in the sweet wind from the south" that awarded extraordinary approval that was "typical of the pride of this great nation in the thrilling valor of this youth from the Old North State."[257] Following the funeral services at Capitol Square, thousands of people lined the streets to observe the funeral procession that carried Bagley's casket to the Historic Oakwood Cemetery, where thousands of citizens had taken their places along the way and on hills overlooking beautiful Oakwood. It seemed that the entire city was mourning, with places of business closed and a sense that there was no "desire except to gather about the center of the common heart" of the event at hand.[258]

Raleigh's Oakwood Cemetery, the final resting place for a thousand or more Confederate soldiers, was the logical burial ground for the hometown hero in the late 1800s, an integral component part of the state's religious-like record of service and sacrifice. Bagley's interment at the cemetery was skillfully and emotionally conflated with the sacrifices of the Confederacy.

> Down the little hill, all knew so well, over the little rock bridge, the bridge of sighs to many a home, around the bend along the gentle slope, a gentle climb, there was the spot, the spot where his gallant father, Maj. W.H. Bagley of the Confederate Army, lies, and where rest the dust of his honored and distinguished grandfather, Governor Jonathan Worth ... the sad rites were said.[259]

Daniels' lifelong leadership in the state's Democratic Party led to his appointment to important positions in the national government. Daniels used his influence to support presidential candidate Woodrow Wilson in the election of 1912, and for this, Daniels was appointed Secretary of the Navy from 1913 to 1921. In this role, he

The George Washington Statue at the State Capitol, Raleigh, North Carolina, was dedicated on July 4, 1857. The statue is encircled by a low gridiron fence, flanked by two small cannons and in close proximity to statues of former governors of North Carolina Zebulon B. Vance and Charles B. Aycock (photograph by the author).

notably appointed a young future president, Franklin Delano Roosevelt, his assistant secretary. As navy secretary, Daniels eliminated beer and wine aboard naval vessels. Etymological legend has it that the phrase "Cup of Joe" started when sailors drank coffee in obedience to Josephus Daniels' alcohol proscription onboard warships. Daniels was encouraged, but refused, to run for the governorship of North Carolina in 1932. Daniels did support his old assistant secretary of the navy, Franklin Roosevelt, for president. For his support, Daniels was once again rewarded, this time with the post of United States ambassador to Mexico, which he held until 1941.[260]

Alfred Augustus Thompson (1852–1920) A.A. Thompson was the mayor of Raleigh from 1887 to 1891 and was president of Caraleigh Mills from 1898 until his death in 1920.[261] Born and reared in Chatham County, Thompson relocated to Raleigh where for over four decades, his leadership of numerous state "public and

Historic Oakwood Cemetery was founded in 1869 and is close to the State Capitol in downtown Raleigh. Oakwood is the burial ground for many of Caraleigh's founders, as well as over 1,300 Confederate and two Union Soldiers (photograph by the author).

Dedicated in 1907, the Ensign Worth Bagley Monument stands in Raleigh's Capitol Square (photograph by the author).

private enterprises" influenced the state's economic, political, and social development.[262] His time as mayor of Raleigh occurred during a "turning point in the history of Raleigh" where it grew from a small corporate municipality to a "great growing city."[263] An indicator of Thompson's stature in Southern society was his being referred to as "Colonel," a public show of respect among Redeemers, even if they never enlisted for military service.[264] A.A. Thompson was widely regarded as "a virile business man" who stood at "the front rank of North Carolina business men."[265]

A man of reputedly of "exalted character," Thompson occupied a revered place in the Democratic Party, with his two terms as Raleigh's mayor assisting in the "Rescue of Raleigh from Republican Rule" and restoration of native white rule.[266] Raleigh's mayoral responsibilities included serving as judge and jury of the Raleigh's courts. As judge, Mayor Thompson was said to have "held the scales of justice so evenly that alleged offenders against the law got a square deal, whether that was what they wanted or not."[267] Thompson gained a reputation for being "honest, competent and reliable," attributes that made him a leader in business, political, and social activities thereafter.[268] Thompson garnered a broad base of esteem throughout the state and the South that was credited to his "wisdom and splendid business judgement."[269] For example, in 1903, A.A. Thompson was the president of three textile operations: the Raleigh Cotton Mills, Neuse River Cotton Mills, and the Caraleigh Cotton Mills, of which he had "been for years president" and "a large owner."[270] While the average annual salary in the United States in 1900 was $449, A.A. Thompson was earning $4080 annually, a sum earned from the three mills he led.[271]

Thompson's reputation spanned across the entire state, but it was best known in Raleigh where he was regarded as one of the "most forceful orators of the capital," whose voice was "frequently heard from the rostrum."[272] In 1893, Thompson was elected to the presidency of the "Commercial and Industrial Association of North Carolina."[273] In 1897, Thompson was cited as being the president of the Raleigh Electric Company and along with several other Caraleigh officers, director of the Commercial and Farmers Bank.[274] In 1901, Thompson was appointed member of the North Carolina Good Roads Association and[275] Governor Craig appointed him in 1914 to the state's railroad freight commission.[276] In 1915, "Col. Alf Thompson" was also president of the North Carolina Cotton Growers Association and was thought to be among the "distinguished men" from around the country, according to Mayor T.L. Kirkpatrick of Charlotte. While saluting Thompson and other "mill captains," Kirkpatrick asserted that

A.A. Thompson's gravestone at the Historic Oakwood Cemetery (photograph by the author).

2. Raleigh's Most Reliable and Substantial Men 61

they were the "the barometers of the economic life" and the hub in the industrial and commercial growth of the state's prosperity.[277]

Raleigh's first Chamber of Commerce was created in Thompson's mayoral office in 1888.[278] According to the *News and Observer*, 300 or more of "Raleigh's best citizens" arrived at Mayor Thompson's office to solidify a plan of action to lure business investment, attendees included numerous future Caraleigh Mills leaders—T.H. Briggs, N.B. Broughton, W.G. Upchurch, R.H. Lewis, and C.B. Root.[279] The chamber's "immediate goals included establishment of a cotton mill, an increase tobacco sales, and low taxes, and improvement of streets and roads."[280] Among the body of men assembled were "young and vigorous businessmen," as well as "our old, respected, venerable pillars" of the city, all of whom demonstrated that "Raleigh was on her mettle" and had been "unreservedly aroused and awakened on the subject of her industrial growth and development."[281] The meeting hashed out details over its constitution, election of officers, and their president's vision for progress.

At this meeting, T.H. Briggs motioned for a minor name change from the "Raleigh Chamber of Industry" to the "Raleigh Chamber of Industry and Commerce," but his request failed.[282] F.B. Arendell requested that rules for membership be emended to say that "all worthy white male citizens," as opposed to "all worthy male citizens" was approved.[283] After several other matters were discussed and voted upon, N.B. Broughton recommended that the organization be established permanently, and he called for the creation of a committee to "retire and recommend officers."[284] The three-man committee included "Messrs. N.B. Broughton, Ashley and Carter."[285] W.H. Pace nominated Mayor Thompson to be the organization's first president, but Thompson declined, saying that he would rather see other "citizens of Raleigh elected to the position."[286] At the conclusion of the meeting, R.S. Tucker, a Confederate veteran and leading businessman, was named the chamber's president. The first vice president was A.A. Thompson, and W.G. Upchurch was the second vice president.

The initial speech of the organization's first president emphasized his dedication to the greater prosperity for his "native city" and the "advancement all interests which may result in a permanent advantage to and be worthy of this, the capital city of the State."[287] Continuing, Tucker underscored the first article in their constitution, which called its members to "foster and cherish all our enterprises," adamantly urging that "no stone [should remain] unturned that will be to our advantage and to the prosperity of the city."[288] Tucker cited that Raleigh had, in the past, lacked unity in achieving industrial progress and argued that "the active cooperation of the solid men of the city, in order to give confidence and stability and to assure success to any projected enterprise, remembering that a little leaven of activity only is required to leaven the whole loaf."[289]

"Colonel Thompson's" penchant for leadership afforded him an advantageous position, seated at the table of power in Raleigh that extended to newspaper reporters and editors who facilitated Thompson's ability to shape "matters relative to the development of the state."[290]

Regarded as one of the most important men in the state, Thompson's political connections worked to ensure Caraleigh's birth and financial ascendancy.[291] Thompson's prestige was acknowledged in the news stories of Caraleigh's creation, helping to explain how Caraleigh's history had been remembered and forgotten. Reporters demonstrated veneration of Thompson's authority, acknowledging his statewide prominence, as captured in one newspaper excerpt in 1893:

> As was easily expected, the press gave him full attention, and the immediate action of the Press Association was such as to greatly encourage him and the entire Commercial and Industrial Association in making further attempts to develop every resource of the State through organized effort.[292]

The adulatory treatment that Thompson and the rest of Caraleigh's titans of industry commanded assured that their shared values were impressed upon Caraleigh, especially in the case of temperance and white supremacy. Both Josephus Daniels and A.A. Thompson were "temperance men," as were other dignitaries who came to Caraleigh to warn residents about the dangers of the "devil's own drink."[293] Caraleigh's Baptist church founders—N.B. Broughton, J.T. Pullen, and Thompson—stoked the people's enthusiasm for prohibition to crowds that sometimes overflowed the capacity of meeting places in the mill village.[294] Josephus Daniels publicly urged Raleigh's citizens to disavow saloons, as did J.T. Pullen. The talk of alcohol dispensaries were equally abhorrent, according to Thompson, because they only "educated the appetite [for alcohol] ... of Raleigh." The *North Carolinian* provided extended commentary from Thompson on the subject.

> Thompson maintained that "twenty-three churches in Raleigh are open two or three times a week. Saloons are open all the time except about four hours of a day. There are 2300 children in public schools. The twenty-three are open to learn them to drink." Thompson added that the saloons help no businesses in Raleigh except three: "the county home, the insane asylum, the penitentiary."[295]

Although the cause of temperance was popular with Caraleigh's supporters and founders, there were others who were fond of "the demon, strong drink."[296] In fact, the mere rumor of a "blind tiger" at Caraleigh in 1898 inspired great indignation.[297] One incensed resident responded that Caraleigh was populated by "law-abiding citizens" only, and scolded the *Raleigh Times* for making such a scandalous accusation: "I will guarantee there is no blind tiger in or near Caraleigh, nor has there ever been. Those who drink whiskey can get all they want uptown, where all the police and detectives are."[298]

And in 1903, the *News and Observer* reported that any land sold from Caraleigh's original tract of 200 acres prohibited "the manufacture or sale of liquor," a clause present "in the first deed" of Caraleigh's land.[299] In fact, Henry H. Stanton's purchase of Caraleigh land in 1893 was permitted "upon the express condition that no vinous, malt or spiritous liquors of any kind shall ever be manufactured or sold there" by him or his heirs.[300]

But the "irresistible plea and argument for prohibition" preached in Caraleigh, proved resistible to some.[301] Caraleigh, a designated location to register voters for the statewide "Prohibition Election" in late May 1908 was successful statewide, but proved a failure for Temperance forces in Caraleigh.[302] The statewide vote saw the city of Raleigh vote to ban alcohol, but not so in the rural areas of Wake County, where Caraleigh's vote count was 32 votes for prohibition and 66 against.[303]

When Republicans and Democrats fought for control of the state between 1898 to 1900, "Colonel Thompson" advanced the Democratic Party's racially driven agenda of the era.[304] A statewide action to reverse the "republican-negro rule" was carried out that resulted in the 1898 Wilmington Race Riot and the passage of an amendment to the state's constitution in 1900 disenfranchising African Americans in North Carolina.[305] When Wake County Democrats met in 1898, Thompson used his "magnificent" oratorical abilities that "had the undivided attention of the delegates at the 1898 Wake County Democratic Party convention" during the vigorous debate about the absorption of Populists into the Democratic Party who had joined forces with Republicans to unseat Democrats from power in 1896.[306] Making clear that he was a "straight Democrat," Thompson expressed disapproval of "joining hands with a lot of people who were responsible for the present disgraceful state of affairs" that caused Democrats to lose power to African Americans who had attained positions of authority throughout the state.[307] In attendance at the state's 1898 Democratic Party Convention were E. Chambers Smith, N.B. Broughton, and Josephus Daniels, all of whom voted to abide with the Democratic Party's racially driven political agenda:

> Whereas patriotism, as well as devotion to the principles of the Democratic party direct, and good sense as well as good will dictates that allow who agree that white supremacy and good government and white metal are paramount issues before the people should work together in the upcoming campaign....[308]

A.A. Thompson was chairman of Wake County's Democratic Party's Convention and delegate to the state convention in 1900, where he presented a report that had been unanimously adopted and which he read aloud "after careful consideration."

> Resolved by the Democratic party of Wake County in convention assembled:
> 1. That we congratulate the people upon the restoration of white supremacy and good government.
> 2. That we endorse the proposed constitutional amendment... [designed to deny African Americans the right to vote].
> 3. That the battle cry in the coming campaign shall be "White Supremacy" ...[309]

The vindictive energies of the Democratic Party received wide support from many of Caraleigh's directors and investors.[310] With Thompson's stature in the Democratic Party, and his terms as "chief executive of the City of Oaks," the former mayor used the vast network of the state's leading citizens to buttress the power of the oligarchs who controlled Caraleigh's textile mill, phosphate plant, and village.[311] Being outside of Raleigh city limits, Caraleigh was without authentic elected representation in municipal government; however, so long as Thompson was Caraleigh's de facto representative in Raleigh, his presence reassured Caraleigh's supporters that the mill and its village operated according to Democratic Party philosophy.

For Caraleigh, Thompson's relationship with some of the state's most powerful men bore significance in how the mill village indoctrinated their workers. Josephus Daniels and A.A. Thompson, both dedicated and celebrated leaders in the state's Democratic Party, often partnered often in leadership duties.[312] And concerning African Americans, Alf. Thompson and Josephus Daniels agreed. Daniels stated in 1899 that "the only certain way to ensure white supremacy is to eliminate the ignorant negro vote, the only certain way to secure permanent good government by the party of the White Man...."[313]

Thompson's death in 1920 was lamented in the *News and Observer* as the loss of a commanding figure in the capital city and of one of Raleigh's "best mayors."[314] In his honor, Thompson was buried in Oakwood Cemetery and a Raleigh school was dedicated in his name in 1923, the "A.A. Thompson Elementary School," for white children only, as racial mores demanded; the school remained in operation until 1971.[315]

3

African Americans at Caraleigh

The juxtaposition of a textile mill and a fertilizer plant at Caraleigh on Maywood Avenue demonstrated the rules of racial hierarchy in action, where African Americans did not work in the textile mill itself, but at the nearby phosphate and fertilizer plant.[1] Employment at Caraleigh's fertilizer plant was seasonal, "for a few weeks or months,"[2] a type of work that constituted a "typical Negro job," sometimes dangerous and providing little "steady employment."[3] Caraleigh's cotton mill messiahs brought into being a labor structure that resisted the drift towards racial equality between the poorest of whites and African Americans. The white farm families who came to Caraleigh worked in the less dangerous textile mill and African Americans in the phosphate and fertilizer plant.[4]

Though researcher Gunnar Myrdal found that while "white workers were paid a low wage" and were dependent upon the mill owners, "they could at least be offered the consolation of being protected from Negro competition."[5] Myrdal's perceptions were showcased at Caraleigh, with its mill welfare programs designed to aid in the white workers' well-being, whether physical, social, moral, or intellectual; thus, mill engendered programs working in assistance of its white workers extended beyond a paycheck to civic, social, and religious activities, which, of course, mill directors choreographed. For the "natural leaders of the South," posited journalist Gerald Johnson—cotton mills were "not a business, but a social enterprise."[6] Throughout the South, cotton mills were a manifestation of social, economic, and racial standing.

Ulterior motives besides financial gain inspired the creation of the South's new industrial order. Professor, journalist, and writer Gerald W. Johnson in 1925 maintained that early mill men constructed textile factories to rescue poor white farm families who were "swiftly sinking to the Negro's standard of living," a situation that vexed mill captains who viewed themselves part of "a master class."[7] Highly conscious of their sense of moral superiority and incumbent responsibility to their kinsmen, Johnson thought that southern cotton mill owners, men who would not have allowed slaves to starve twenty years earlier, built cotton mills in a dutiful act of civic and social compassion for destitute white farmers.[8]

Raleigh's Anglo-Saxon Pride

In Raleigh, Caraleigh's advocates found fertile ground to perpetuate an antebellum social order, replete with "deep class division and awful caste exploitation," as Paul

M. Gaston described existed throughout the South.⁹ Many of Caraleigh's founders openly championed white supremacy, one of those "old ideals," in W.J. Cash's words, that failed to decay after the Confederate defeat. Even during the South's mechanized textile boom, Caraleigh showed that it, had yet to alter its agricultural philosophy to industrial conditions, especially where attitudes of race were concerned.¹⁰ Caraleigh Fertilizer plant's advertisement carried forward a common antebellum stereotypical attitude that slave holders held about their slaves, as being submissive and childlike, in agreement with planters' "projections, desires, and biases."¹¹

The state's visceral social, racial, and political climate of the 1890s and early 1900s was ubiquitous. In 1892, only a few months after Caraleigh commenced operations, Raleigh celebrated the centennial of its founding with parades, speeches, and festivities at the city's center. Kemp P. Battle, a well-known lawyer, railroad businessman, University of North Carolina president, and historian gave a speech to mark the occasion,¹² calling the event a "happy day," with "no sighing over the past" because "the present was joyous with glad faces and the future looked to with fond hopes."¹³ After Battle's allusion to sectional reconciliation, his description of Raleigh's past revealed the city's racially biased values, saying that Raleigh was in possession of a "pure" and "Anglo-Saxon" whiteness:

> With pure English blood on both sides in our veins, and with an ancestry which, for a hundred years has known no home but North Carolina, we did feel a pride in scope and character of the celebration of the hundredth birthday of this Anglo-Saxon city. And so long as Anglo-Saxon pride and spirit remain with our people, there will be no backward step in the grand march of progress.¹⁴

Caraleigh Phosphate and Fertilizer Works postcard advertisement, undated ("Compliments of Caraleigh Phosphate and Fertilizer Works, Raleigh, N.C." Durwood Barbour Collection of North Carolina Postcards [P077], North Carolina Collection Photographic Archives, Wilson Library, UNC–Chapel Hill).

Caraleigh's architects, several of whom were central to Raleigh's Centennial celebrations, used the New South Creed as a template to move forward on the "grand march of progress" while maintaining the South's racial status quo.[15] Historians Michael D. Schulman and Jeffrey Leiter pondered whether the social "stratification system that developed in the post–Civil War South" was a reappearance of the pre–Civil War "plantation-based class and social structures" with "power and privilege" in the hands of the new industrialists, instead of the plantation class.[16] Caraleigh's example confirms the findings of another historian—Jay R. Mandle—that found the plantation system was reborn in the cotton mills, with "relative positions in the stratification system remained" unchanged, although the "roles of specific groups changed."[17] For "owners of capital," the Southern cotton mill boom presented an opportunity for Raleigh's oligarchs to increase their wealth at the expense of indigent workers: the landless poor white farmers and their families who fled the farms to the cotton mills. The former slaves and their descendants, disallowed from working inside the cotton mills, were relegated to only seasonal employment at Caraleigh's fertilizer and phosphate plant, and women and children, who remained dependent and powerless under the thumb of patriarchy. The Civil War had destroyed slavery and the essence of antebellum economic, social, structures, but postbellum arrangements "had much in common with their predecessors," according to Schulman and Leiter.[18]

Lewis Hine's Images and Caraleigh

Visitors who walk in the hallways of the Historic Caraleigh Mills condominium complex encounter enlarged black-and-white photographs plastered on its walls. Some images show decades old photos of Caraleigh Mills, others depict cotton mill workers laboring or standing in front of textile machines. The pictures of workers, all of whom were white, were not of laborers in Caraleigh Mills. The photographer responsible for the images, Lewis Hine, was a significant figure in the history of social documentary photography in the United States in the early 1900s. Hine's pictures show white workers—children and adults, both male and female—but few, if any, of African Americans working in mills.[19] The choice to put Hine's images on the walls at the Caraleigh condominium complex represents an honest effort to preserve a sense of textile mill history with visual reminders of the South's cotton mill campaign and perhaps provoke questions from viewers: Why are all the pictures of white workers? Do the pictures provide an accurate portrayal of Caraleigh? Were these images a well-intentioned misinterpretation? Why are there no images of African Americans in Caraleigh's hallways? Did Caraleigh have African American workers?

From the 1880s to 1910s, depressed agriculture conditions motivated farmers, most of whom were poor and white, to migrate to cotton mills for work in North Carolina. Throughout the South, African Americans were rarely employed in mills because of segregation requirements,[20] which disallowed African Americans and whites to work alongside in mills, even in unskilled positions, because it was believed that such an arrangement would pose a threat to white dominance.[21] Newspapers confirm the African American presence at Caraleigh, and these were mostly pejorative in tone. The reportage of two funerals of Caraleigh directors, however, provide

Historic Caraleigh Mills condominium complex hallway, 2020 (photograph by the author).

glimpses of attitudes toward race relations. For instance, at the 1895 funeral of W.G. Upchurch, Caraleigh's first president, it was reported that his "casket was borne by six colored friends of the deceased," with all six African American men named individually: a small but dignified gesture.[22] This was in contrast to what happened at the conclusion of J.R. Chamberlain's funeral, when "four masked figures in robes of the Ku Klux Klan appeared at the grave, placed at the head of it a cross of flowers and paused for a silent prayer. Then they departed in a waiting automobile."[23]

Caraleigh's treatment of African Americans was in line with the widespread philosophy of white supremacy popular in North Carolina in the late 19th century which held that "the negro race is essentially a race of peasant farmers and laborers" predestined for serfdom and that education for blacks would "only unfit him for work."[24]

While the Caraleigh phosphate and fertilizer operation was touted for its success, its laborers were mentioned only when they went on strike or were injured. By 1916, the Caraleigh Phosphate and Fertilizer plant was Wake County's largest business, and black workers comprised the majority of its labor force of around 125 men.[25] In 1907, the *Raleigh Times* reported that "about one hundred negroes who were employed at the acid pit walked out, after making a demand for higher pay."[26]

While there were undoubtedly health hazards for white workers at Caraleigh, the number of injurious accounts about African Americans at the phosphate and fertilizer plant far outnumber those of white workers. Newspaper reports of deaths and serious injuries at Caraleigh corroborate the seminal research of historian Jacquelyn Dowd Hall and her coauthors about Southern cotton mills in general, that the "dirtiest and heaviest work went to black men."[27] In 1907, for example, the *Charlotte Observer* reported that a "negro named Matthews" was "badly mangled" when he was "caught in a shaft at the Caraleigh Fertilizer factory."[28] In 1908, "four negroes" died while relining the chimney where sulfuric acid was made, succumbing to inhalation of gasses.[29] In 1914, a "colored laborer," Luke Hill, perished when "caught in the machinery [that] runs day and night all the time." Both of Mr. Hill's legs and arms were broken, having been "caught in the shafting ... before the machinery could be stopped," the *Chatham Record* disclosed.[30] And in 1917, another "colored" employee, James Williams, of the Caraleigh Phosphate Works "lost his arm by amputation" after he was "terribly mangled" at the mill.[31]

Employment for African Americans at Caraleigh held little attraction; however, they were essential to complete the "very important" work in the "acid pit," part-time work in dangerous conditions, with low pay and public scorn.[32]

Historian Holland Thompson wrote in 1906 that "in the South, the right of the negro to earn a living by any sort of manual or mechanical labor has been recognized as a matter of course." Black men "work beside whites without question" in a number of instances, but "the working of negroes, particularly negro men, beside white women within walls would not be tolerated." Holland tied this intolerance to what was thought to be the "unspeakable crime" of possible sexual relations between black men and white women, as Thompson explained:

> No association which might permit the possible lessening of the negro's deference toward white women would be allowed. It is a fixed belief, not susceptible to argument, that daily contact and associations, might tend to make the negro bolder and less respectful. For this reason, the only negroes employed directly in the Southern textile industry are a few outside the mill proper, serving as laborers, draymen, firemen; and a smaller number engaged in some of the preparatory processes.[33]

While Holland Thompson's work provided some examples of successes and failures in the employment of African Americans in Southern mills, he concluded that requiring white operatives to work alongside "negroes would be a dangerous experiment from a social standpoint" and that in 1906, given the "state of the public mind ... indiscriminate employment" was "unthinkable."[34] In *The Mind of the South* (1941), Wilbur J. Cash observed that during the first decades of the 20th century, "the cotton-mill worker was likely to fear and hate the Negro even more than the poor white on the land."[35]

The antebellum Southern "paternalistic habit," as W.J. Cash put it, of a highly stratified social hierarchy carried over into the new industrialization era. It was understood that it was the right of the former slave-owning, planter class to "instruct and command" those below them.[36] This inspired a "social solidification of the land," perpetuating the "strait-jacket conformity," "intolerant of dissent," that predominated in the South and was exemplified at Caraleigh.[37] In the context of the period from 1892 to 1930, this meant that Caraleigh's hierarchy of power would maintain the status quo, with poor whites, African Americans, and labor unions remaining obedient to the mill directors' orders.

By 1906, Holland Thompson recognized that relations between mill workers and their employers statewide had been on the wane when textile employers seemingly grew more "businesslike, and the operative lost his rural habit of mind."[38]

Accompanying this change was a growing sense of "class consciousness slowly developing among the workers" that would bring momentous results.[39] Caraleigh's history confirmed Holland Thompson's predictions, as tensions between labor and management became hostile at the phosphate plant.

The 1907 Phosphate Plant Strike

African Americans at Caraleigh worked at the phosphate and fertilizer plant, which was referred to as the "acid pit."[40] In 1907, low wages and dangerous working conditions fueled labor unrest at Caraleigh's phosphate plant.[41] This was especially true in the years leading up to the First World War, years favorably portrayed in newspapers for the "extensive plant of the Caraleigh Phosphate and Fertilizer Works," where the plant, already described as "immense," had been enlarged to increase output and profit.[42]

The 1907 troubles began with Claud Evans, whom a reporter characterized as a "strange and well dressed negro" who reportedly fomented a strike.[43] The superintendent of the Caraleigh Phosphate and Fertilizer plant, J.J. Dye, said that he "ordered" Evans to leave the factory, having observed Evans "prowling around and talking to the men." When Dye confronted Evans again, he reportedly replied, "I will leave when I d—n please. I have as much right in here as you or any other man." Evans stated that "Mr. Dye had been bulldozing negroes enough already and that he was going to put a stop to it." It was then, when walking toward the office, that Dye turned and saw Evans following him, with "his knife open," and swearing "vile oaths."[44] Evans attacked Mr. Dye, who drew his own blade and proved "too quick" for Evans, cutting an "ugly gash" in Evans' shoulder.[45] Soon after this combat, "about one hundred negroes who were employed at the acid pit" walked out of work.[46] Within two days, the general manager, J.R. Chamberlain, reported that the back of the strike was "about broken," because management had secured a "sufficient number of additional laborers" to work for the old wage of $1.10, instead of the strikers' demand of $1.35.[47]

African American presence at Caraleigh has been ignored in the chronicles of the state's history, but many of Caraleigh's founders have been widely celebrated. The value of a historical product, whether a primary or secondary source, cannot be debated without looking at both the context of its production and the context of its consumption.[48] Whether in newspapers, books, pamphlets, a Southern readership wanted to read reports of economic success, the rehabilitation of its defeated Confederate heroes, and the punishment of its former slaves, as well as of their descendants, whom they had been forced to emancipate. The elements of Caraleigh's historical narrative, including its silences, preceded the creation of Caraleigh itself.[49] The newspaper sources that comprised public understanding of Caraleigh prior to its initial closure in 1930 were part of the propagandistic visions of a resurrected South. Reporters and editors, such as Josephus Daniels, bequeathed full-throated support for Caraleigh's constructed place in North Carolina's history. In a lengthy review of Caraleigh's mills and fertilizer works, Josephus Daniels gushed forth fawning praise:

3. African Americans at Caraleigh

> ...the Caraleigh Mills Company has become an honor to the North Carolina metropolis. Long may it flourish and prosper, ever adding to the industrial standing of Raleigh is the ardent and sincere wish of the writer.[50]

Thus, the primary sources concerning Caraleigh and their founders "set the cycle of silences" about its shortcomings, which historians subsequently perpetuated.[51] The narrative of Caraleigh was largely "premised on previous understandings."[52] The "distribution of archival power," as Michel-Rolph Trouillot, author of *Silencing the Past*, framed it, did not favor African Americans and later creation of historical products.[53] This phenomenon greatly limited archival artifacts necessary for historical research about the African American story at Caraleigh; thus, the racial strife of Jim Crow profoundly shaped and rendered Caraleigh's black voices buried and silent for later researchers. White supremacy shaped the tenor of newspaper reports about Caraleigh, but these comprised the few primary sources available to later historians.

The few mentions of Caraleigh's African American workers were pejorative, with news reports of insubordinate black workers serving to reaffirm racial fears of whites reading about "100 Negro Workers Demand More Pay."[54] For white reporters and the white readership, the simple rhetorical cure to this situation was to "repress the unthinkable and to bring it back within" the truth they wanted to believe. Trouillot believed that "human beings tend to force reality within the scope of these beliefs" and "within the realm of acceptable discourse."[55] In keeping with the racial zeitgeist of the era, the preferred news was that "the backbone of the strike among acid pit laborers" was nearly broken.[56]

4

Raleigh's Pure Water Question[1]

Mayor Alfred Augustus Thompson dealt with Raleigh's access to clean water before Caraleigh was constructed. In 1888, it was suggested that the roadmap for Raleigh's march to progress depended on three important "improvements."[2] First was "perfect sewerages," followed by "good streets," and then "good county roads."[3] Two years later, the importance of water appeared in Mayor Thompson's annual report, urging vigorous action to make Raleigh a town of diversified industries, with access to "cheap water" to attract new industries.[4] However, in the same 1890 report, Mayor Thompson expressed concerns about the Walnut Creek watershed that was, in his opinion, "very defective."[5] Two years prior to the opening of Caraleigh Mills, water resources derived from Walnut Creek, just south of Raleigh, appeared, at best, questionable.

The *State Chronicle* touted two of Mayor Thompson's accomplishments as among the most significant in Raleigh's history. The first was "the completion of and putting in operation the Raleigh Water Works," which was "accomplished early in 1887."[6] Thompson's "second great achievement" was the "construction of the Raleigh Sewer System."[7] Years later, in 1907, Thompson maintained that water-power was pivotal to the growth of Raleigh.[8]

Caraleigh's Healthy Location

Caraleigh Mills and its nearby Phosphate and Fertilizer plant were situated next to Walnut Creek, and the health and sanitary conditions at Caraleigh received mostly praise throughout Caraleigh's first 38 years of existence. The *Morning Post* cited that Caraleigh was "one of the most successful, substantial, and progressive cotton factories in the Southern states" in 1899; the same article cited Caraleigh's mill workers as proof of "success and progress," depicting them as a "a sturdy, healthy and happy-looking lot" who wore "a picture of contentment on their countenances."[9] In 1904, Josephus Daniels of the *News and Observer* visited Caraleigh and proclaimed that the village was in a "healthy location" populated with "healthy, robust people, who seemed to enjoy life."[10]

In 1917, the *Charlotte News* described Caraleigh's location as sitting on "gently rolling hillsides affording the finest kind of natural drainage,"[11] adding that Caraleigh's management was "deeply interested in the well-being of operatives," as its "record of health has been good since the mill was first started."[12] In 1919, the

Southern Textiles Journal credited Caraleigh Mills' management for the "bright, happy, intelligent looking" workers who were provided homes "wired for electric lights" with water that was supplied from "deep wells" to ensure "its purity, and all have septic toilets."[13] The 1923 *Southern Textiles Journal* similarly extolled the sanitary conditions at Caraleigh, which prevented "any menace to the public health of the village."[14]

Stories that could tarnish what historian Moses Neal Amis in 1902 called the "justly proud" reputation of Raleigh's beloved Caraleigh were overlooked, with Caraleigh's environmental failures less powerful than the belief in the "eminent ability and intelligent management" of Caraleigh's architects.[15] Broadus Mitchell explained in his book, *The Rise of Cotton Mills in the South*, that enthusiasm for textile factories in the South "may best be caught in newspaper items," while news of cotton mill failures were avoided.[16]

Caraleigh Mills was at the center of several waterborne calamities in its first four years that endangered the health and well-being of residents of the mill village and the populace of Raleigh. While there were a few candid, and accusatory, lines of newspaper coverage that assigned culpability to Caraleigh's founders, these were suffocated in seas of laudatory stories of Caraleigh, written in admiration for those on a mission to lead Raleigh in economic recovery. Cathy L. McHugh's scholarship in *Mill Family: The Labor System in the Southern Cotton Textile Mill Industry, 1880–1915* found that mill families were often unhealthy prior to arrival in a mill village, with health problems being rooted on the farm and transplanted to the mill village.[17] But Caraleigh's example stands in contradiction to McHugh, because the distressful water-centered health problems of Caraleigh were not transferred to the village; they were created there.

Submerged beneath years of congratulatory reports about Caraleigh, followed by decades of less than robust historical analysis, were the tales of Caraleigh's twin environmental disasters of 1892 and in 1894. These events showed that in the race to achieve profits, Caraleigh's investors and directors were willing to pay a steep price. The first incident stemmed from a fire at Caraleigh's phosphate plant in August 1892 that endangered water supplies for the entire city of Raleigh for over a hundred

Girls' Club at Caraleigh Mills, 1923 (*Southern Textile Bulletin*, Vol. 24, no. 17 [June 21, 1923], 152–153).

years.[18] The second incident, during the summer of 1894, resulted in the "loss of many lives" at Caraleigh and threatened end operations of the mill. At least 90 of its 100 employees were sickened.[19]

Water at Caraleigh

The Caraleigh Mills Cotton Mills building on Maywood Drive sits at the bottom of a hill, in a flood plain.[20] Exploration of land within a two mile radius Caraleigh in 2020 shows that Walnut Creek and its tributaries have been extensively dredged, canaled, and irrigated to control the potential flooding, but these water controlling features were not present in the 1890s. Walnut Creek sits just behind Caraleigh Mills and where the phosphate and fertilizer plant had once stood, a situation that proved dangerous for its workers and for the entire city of Raleigh. First, Caraleigh's location in a flood zone made its residents susceptible to typhoid and malaria. For example, 27 years after Caraleigh's operations started, the *News and Observer*, in 1919, reported that Caraleigh Mills' management had paid for the "draining of a large swamp area near their mill in order to relieve the village from an onslaught of the mosquitos which were found to be breeding in large numbers in this area."[21] Second, the capital city's early water system originated from Walnut Creek in the area of Caraleigh, creating a scenario that saw the introduction of toxins into Raleigh's drinking water for many years.[22]

Caraleigh's founders in the 1890s ignored the potential waterborne health problems of placing the cotton mills and phosphate plant in this low-lying area. The Walnut Creek Sporting Club foresaw that its fishing hobby was in danger. A few months prior to the opening of Caraleigh Mills and its phosphate plant, the fishing club had made "arrangements" to fish in another pond and forego its lease of the waterworks pond, expecting that the fish there would "be killed by the sludge from the acid works at Caraleigh."[23]

Accusations of the abuse and neglect of mill workers from northern newspapers appeared validated when Caraleigh's operatives and their families came "down sick with fever" in 1894.[24] Those who fell ill were said to be located "in a valley, very near Walnut creek."[25] Some observers believed that both the company's textile mill and village were built on a site that was "badly chosen from a sanitary standpoint,"[26] that put the mill and the workers homes in a "flood plain," an area susceptible to flooding from nearby rivers, creeks or streams.[27]

Public Health and Water: Prelude to Disaster

In 1886, six years before Caraleigh Mills opened for business, the North Carolina's State Board of Health believed there was a statewide lack of concern about clean water that was dangerously "backward."[28] Contaminated drinking water throughout the state was registered among public health officials as "one of the commonest and most persistent sources of disease and death with which we have to combat."[29] In the case of Caraleigh Mills, its directors failed to protect its workers, despite being having been warned.

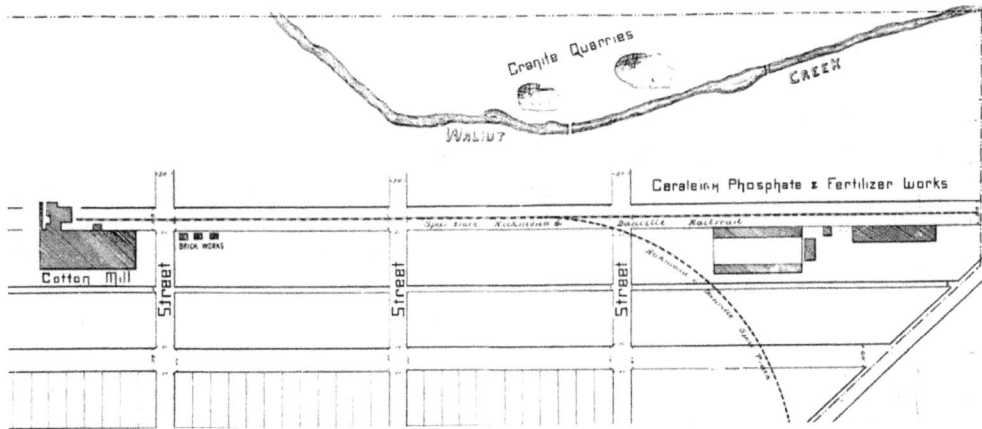

Map showing the locations of the Caraleigh Cotton Mills and the Phosphate and Fertilizer Works in south Raleigh (Wake County, North Carolina, Register of Deeds Tammy L. Brunner, BM1885-00152).

C. Vann Woodward's conclusion about Southern cotton mills was that when it came to care for the textile workers, the "profit motive did not necessarily preclude the philanthropic motive, but it does seem to have outweighed it in some instances."[30] Woodward's statements were corroborated by the professional opinions of Dr. James McKee about Caraleigh Mills. In 1889, Raleigh's aldermen created the local Board of Health and McKee, who was also the County health superintendent, was named its first president.[31] McKee asserted that "no regard was paid to health or hygiene [of the workers] when the Caraleigh Mills were built there."[32]

The modern idea of improvements in public health were undertaken in England's "Great Sanitary Awakening" during the early 1800s and influenced similar actions across the Atlantic Ocean in Massachusetts and later in North Carolina.[33] This was visibly reflected in the state's creation of the North Carolina Board of Health by the General Assembly in 1877.[34] In its first two years, North Carolina's Board of Health published two significant reports about water sanitation. Authored by William Cain of the University of North Carolina, "Disinfection, Drainage, Drinking Water, and Disinfectants" and "Sanitary Engineering" offered details about the rudimentary analyses of the state's drinking water.[35] Professor Cain stated that typhoid, diphtheria, and certain enteric diseases were "common in North Carolina due to bad wells, foul yards, privies and cess pools tainting the air with their gases."[36] Cain maintained that "whether we accept the germ theory or not, it is admitted that drinking foul water and breathing impure air" was "dangerous for humans."[37] Cain argued that the state should "follow the natural instincts and avoid polluted air and water, especially as North Carolina can afford the pure articles in such abundance."[38]

Drinking water and sanitation may have been of great concern throughout the nation in the late 1800s, but North Carolinians displayed a persistent attitude of apathy about topics related to hygiene and sanitation, ubiquitous among the public and physicians alike. This phenomenon was exacerbated with the recovery of the state's economy from the Civil War and Reconstruction that resulted in a population increase, leading Professor Cain in 1880 to predict that cities would soon demand water of purer quality "than can be supplied by wells and springs now used" and would seek to adopt public water supply systems.[39]

In 1886, in line with Professor Cain's prediction, Raleigh acted to create a community water system for its growing populace. For Raleigh, the most obvious water source was Walnut Creek. But officials were skeptical of Walnut Creek's water. According to David H. Howell's 1989 *Historical Account of PUBLIC WATER SUPPLIES in North Carolina*, Walnut Creek already contained drainage from one-fourth of the nearby town of Cary, the "excrement of about one hundred people being cast daily upon the watershed in close proximity to the stream."[40]

On August 24, 1886, Raleigh's Board of Aldermen met in special session to discuss a plan for drinking water and sewage systems that would accommodate the "present population of Raleigh," and for nearby areas that would eventually be added to the "future city."[41] During the meeting, opinions differed about which water source should Raleigh obtain its supply. Dr. Richard H. Lewis of Raleigh, an early public health advocate and leading health official in the state between 1892 and 1909,[42] believed that since Walnut Creek was located "below the insane asylum" (later named the Dorothea Dix Hospital), it was "contaminated by sewage from the insane asylum."[43] Lewis expressed concern about the possible hazards of this water for Raleigh's consumption, water that would later be used by residents of Caraleigh Mills.[44] Lewis believed that Walnut Creek "was doubless [sic] contaminated by sewage from the insane asylum."[45]

Another expert, Dr. W.B. Phillips, of the State University, agreed with R.H. Lewis's concern about Walnut Creek and recommended using water from "Peach Tree and Jack's Branch, near Milburnie."[46] Phillips believed that the thousands of gallons of sewage from the "asylum" that poured into Walnut Creek made it impossible for filtration systems to remove the "dissolved impurities from the water."[47] Added concern was generated about well construction for public drinking. The city's aldermen favored the use of publicly accessible and shared drinking water wells, called "gang wells," for residents to obtain water, but there was disagreement about this, too.[48] A Doctor Dabney maintained that "there could be no certainty that driven wells were not contaminated by surface water" from Walnut Creek. This also made it likely that there would be cross-contamination among nearby wells. Nevertheless, Dabney alluded to the possibility that filtration systems might render Walnut Creek water usable.[49]

At a September 9, 1886, Board of Aldermen meeting, concerns were raised over the purity of Raleigh's water. Dr. R.H. Lewis opposed Raleigh's use of Walnut Creek water, saying that "in times of drought, it would not provide enough water" and that he "feared contamination and further diminution as the lands were cleared."[50] Alderman F.O. Moring, a central figure in the founding of Caraleigh Mills, as well as the phosphate plant, understood the concerns over Walnut Creek water, as well as the implications of the use of the land in and around the creek. Moring stated that "the matter of purity of [the] water supply was one which [would] require constant attention and care."[51] A week later, the aldermen heard a report from the county board of health regarding a suggested course of action for the city to take to attain a pure water supply. The health professionals urged that there must be "careful chemical and microscopical analyses" of water sources and that these results should be added to their "medical knowledge" and "personal investigation" in order to arrive at a "positive and accurate opinion," in response to Raleigh's water supply questions.[52]

In 1887, a civil engineer published a study entitled *Dangers of Shallow Wells*. The findings showed, with few exceptions, that Raleigh's drinking water came from private wells located within house lots or from public wells on street corners.[53] Rainwater was noted to be the safest for consumption in rural areas and small towns because it was the "purest and best for all household uses."[54]

Complicating matters was that knowledge about the causes of malaria and typhoid in the late 1880s was incompletely understood among physicians and the general public. A researcher argued that there was "considerable evidence" that "in many cases malaria is due to the character of well waters."[55] Statewide sanitation evaluations in the late 1800s found that private wells and bathrooms (privies) indiscriminately intermingled their water sources, declaring "bad water," to be "one of the most efficient agents in spreading disease."[56]

In the years prior to the deadly summer of 1894 at Caraleigh, there were numerous reports, both official and unofficial, about water problems in the Walnut Creek area. Expert testimonials further asserted that communal wells in the area of Walnut Creek were liable to be "contaminated by surface water."[57] Nevertheless, the state's chemist conducted tests of the water and reported that the water was "of the purest" he had "ever examined."[58] The report failed to mollify the public criticisms of those who argued that waste drainage from the asylum ran directly into Walnut Creek, and that it joined the sewage from inhabitants above Rhamkatte Road (now Lake Wheeler Road), creating a "stench extremely disagreeable" and obvious to anyone within half a mile of Walnut Creek.[59]

Caraleigh was outside of Raleigh's city limits; however, because of Caraleigh's nearness to Walnut Creek, the city's water source, the mill community's water too was under the legal aegis of "health authorities of the city and county"[60] to exercise "due surveillance" to "police and protect" the watershed of Walnut Creek tributaries.[61] Raleigh and Caraleigh shared concerns about Walnut Creek's water system, making Caraleigh's water problems, Raleigh's water problems.

Summer of 1892: The Fire

On August 18, 1892, one of the largest fires in Raleigh's history broke out at the Caraleigh phosphate plant. The explosion of a lamp ignited a larger blaze that caused hundreds of tons of sulfuric acid to spill onto the soil.[62] The fire that destroyed the Caraleigh Phosphate and Fertilizer warehouse started in what the *State Chronicle* described as the "mammoth" acid chamber, which measured 250 feet long and 60 feet high.[63] The "acid house," used for creating sulfuric acid, was "totally burned."[64] The phosphate plant had a $5,000 water system with seven hydrants and a pump, but use of the hydrants was stymied when the fire disabled the pump, leaving the firefighters to depend upon gravity-fed pressure from a 10,000-gallon water tank atop the manufacturing mill. Further complications arose in the struggle against the conflagration. First, the "engine" that could have "supplied water for the fire service" was useless because the engine was in the building where the fire started. Second, the Raleigh firefighters' hoses could not connect to the lone available hydrant because the threads on the Raleigh hoses and the Caraleigh hydrant did not match. Furthermore, the single hose on site attached to the one hydrant was too "near the burning building," forcing the "men who were handling" the hose to retreat, leaving the hose itself to be burned.[65] By midnight on August 19, the entire building was destroyed, and more than 400 tons of sulfuric acid spilled "almost immediately over the water supply pipe" which provided water to the city from the Raleigh Water Company.[66] Not only was the pipe contaminated, but the soil also became supersaturated with sulfuric acid which permeated into the water table, polluting the city water supply.[67]

Soon after the fire, Raleigh residents complained about ill-tasting water, compelling officials to conduct chemical and bacteriological tests. The tests revealed high sulfuric acid content in the water and additional tests showed that the acid content gradually diminished over time.[68] Another test, conducted on September 24, 1892, revealed that there was "no acid," in the water. Dr. McKee stated officially that the "water supply from Walnut Creek to the city of Raleigh" was "pure and wholesome, free from pollution."[69] Seven years later, Raleigh's *Morning Post* reported that citizens had "quit drinking city water," because of its "disagreeable taste," and had the effect of causing "considerable nausea" and vomiting.[70] Even before official state tests provided proof, the public's "prevailing impression" was that the Caraleigh Phosphate Works was to blame for dumping its industrial waste "down on the banks of Walnut Creek near the Caraleigh Mills."[71] Apparently, many in and around Raleigh avoided drinking water and sought other safer liquids of an alcoholic consistency. This was an embarrassing irony for many of the Caraleigh leaders, who were at the vanguard of banning alcohol. The *Morning Post* headline characterized the rancid water problem as a "Setback for Temperance."[72]

During a special meeting of the Board of Aldermen in 1899, six years after the fire of 1892, the Committee of Physicians investigation concluded that Raleigh's water, supplied by way of the Caraleigh Phosphate Mills, was contaminated with sulfuric acid.[73] The pollution was rooted in "either the 1892 fire or the tipping over of a large vat in 1898," according to a historical account of Raleigh's fire department.[74] Raleigh's water, the physicians told the *Raleigh Times*, was "injurious to health, and unfit for domestic use." Although the water was "causing disordered digestion and bowel disturbances," the water was not considered "dangerous to life." To guarantee the "permanent purity of Raleigh's drinking water," physicians recommended relocating the water supply pipe that ran through Caraleigh to a safely distant area.[75] Caraleigh escaped official remonstrance. The *Morning Post* reported that the water was polluted with "intestinal bacilli," superseding worries about chemical contamination of drinking water and removed Caraleigh's Phosphate and Fertilizer plant from culpability.[76]

The city of Raleigh instructed the Raleigh Water Company in March 1899 to "immediately change the present course of their intake pipe [at Caraleigh]" to avoid any possible "contamination from … the vicinity of the Caraleigh Phosphate Works." It took more than a century for the site of Caraleigh's fertilizer and phosphate plant to be officially recognized as being dangerously polluted. The plant located at the 1600 to 1750 block of Wheeler Road made the National Priorities List in 2004 and was considered among the most seriously polluted sites, according to the federal Environmental Protection Agency (EPA) and North Carolina's Department of Environment and Natural Resources.[77]

According to the EPA, a review of historical data concerning the cleanup efforts at Caraleigh "prompted an investigation in June of 2004."[78] The investigation of the site found lead levels of "more than 5,000 parts per million in some soils," including "arsenic as high as 253 ppm. The EPA recommends remediation for lead levels above 50 ppm and arsenic above 1.5 ppm."[79] This recommendation resulted in the removal of 4,500 tons of contaminated soil, leaving an excavated site two feet deep that was then covered with clean soil and plans to build a greenway on the site.[80] The EPA's "removal action" at the Caraleigh fertilizer plant started in 2004, with the goal to stabilize the site that posed an "imminent and substantial threat to human health or the environment."[81] A 2006 EPA report concluded that the Caraleigh Phosphate and Fertilizer Works facility had used lead-lined acid chambers in the production of various fertilizers. As a result of the 1892 fire, the sulfuric acid released at Caraleigh continued to leach into Raleigh's water supply "in great volumes each time it rained."[82] The great fire at the Caraleigh Phosphate and Fertilizer plant was only the first instance in the 1890s whereby the health and lives of citizens in Caraleigh and Raleigh were endangered in the quest for productivity, efficiency and profit.

Summer of 1894: Epidemic

About two years after the great fire at Caraleigh's phosphate plant, Caraleigh's existence was again threatened by the "loss of many lives" because of "typhoid and malarial fevers."[83] Some of the state's most noteworthy figures in the state visited Caraleigh investigate, John T. Pullen was one, another was Governor Elias Carr who blamed Caraleigh's poor location for the outbreak of sickness, stating that "the site of the settlement was very badly chosen."[84] Also accompanying the governor was the state health inspector, R.H. Lewis, and James McKee, Wake County superintendent of health who agreed with Carr's opinion. McKee said that he "always held it a most unfortunate location,"[85] with both the company's textile mill and village being built on a site that was "badly chosen from a sanitary standpoint."[86] But others pointed to the poorly built workers' homes, impure water, poor ventilation of workers' homes, and a reservoir pond that the nearby Water Works Company maintained.[87] The accusation of unsanitariness was partially based on Caraleigh's proximity to Walnut Creek, putting the mill and the workers homes in a "flood plain," an area susceptible to flooding from nearby rivers, creeks or streams.[88] This contributed to the conditions that caused Caraleigh's operatives to be subjected to possibly contaminated water.

Indeed, a visit to the Caraleigh Mills Cotton Mills building on Maywood Drive in the year 2020 makes it obvious that the textile plant sits at the bottom of a hill, in a flood plain.[89] Further exploration of land within a quarter-mile radius of this location also shows that the area has been extensively dredged, canaled, and irrigated to control the numerous streams and tributaries that branch off of Walnut Creek, which sits just behind Caraleigh Mills and was where the phosphate and fertilizer plant had been situated.

The housing Caraleigh provided its workers was also subject to criticism. The *Evening Visitor* reported on July 5, 1894, that "ever since the houses have been occupied there has been considerable sickness, but of course nothing like the state of affairs now, when in every house some one [sic] is sick."[90] Fatal illnesses were reported at Caraleigh as early as May 1894, but by July, conditions had clearly worsened.[91] That summer, McKee inspected homes at Caraleigh and reported that the homes were "badly ventilated." But, McKee also asserted that that Caraleigh's water, having been "chemically analyzed" was "unusually pure," but a "biological examination," also was in the process of being conducted.[92]

While the public statements from powerful men castigated the judgment of Caraleigh Mills' founders, newspaper reports shifted blame to Raleigh's Water Works Company "for allowing filth to be emptied" in the southern part of Raleigh and its suburbs, resulting in "many deaths."[93] The effects of "bad drainage" formed the basis of a "just complaint" in April 1894 from those who lived along Walnut Creek.[94]

> Two sewers empty into it. At times, when the pumps at the waterworks are running the stream is full; then there is quite a space of when there is almost no water, and the ill-smelling mud is acted upon by the sun, producing any amount of malaria ... the result is a regular epidemic of chills and fever ... found to prevail in no less than sixteen families.[95]

In the summer of 1894, lawyer F.H. Busbee stood before the Wake County Board of Commissioners, representing "persons living on Walnut Creek" and argued that the sewers that connected to Walnut Creek and its numerous ponds, swamps, bogs, marshes, and other tributaries were bringing "a great accumulation of filth" that rendered the area south of Raleigh dangerous and maintained that "water works pond ought to be drained and abandoned."[96] The very flat lands drained and channel of the creek "straightened as far as Eatman's old Pond ... the open sewer from the insane asylum must be made closed," and that the sewage from the penitentiary should connect with the asylum sewer, which should be "built through Tucker's meadow."[97]

Word spread quickly that summer of 1894. Newspapers reported Caraleigh's misfortune of "the Caraleigh sufferers,"[98] summoning the citizens of Raleigh to provide "prompt and generous" aid to those who were "down sick in bed with fever."[99] Raleighites responded with lawn parties and concerts to benefit the "unfortunate people at Caraleigh Mills."[100]

By the final week of July 1894, newspapers were reporting that the sickness at Caraleigh Mills had "greatly abated" but that much costly work remained to be done to stop the suffering at the mill village.[101] First, the pond was "to be drained."[102] Then, Caraleigh's homes were to be cleared of their occupants. The houses could "be fumigated and ventilated," because they had not been "built in a proper way."[103] One "prominent physician" believed, according to the *Evening Visitor*, that the reason the sickness was "so prevalent and hard to stop was because when several people were sick in the same house or when a death occurred, it was impossible to properly disinfect the house."[104] Another thought was that "every mill or factory should have an infirmary" where workers could convalesce in a "well-ventilated" building and thereby "give a chance to thoroughly disinfect the houses" of those sickened.[105]

Fevers and Chills: Typhoid and Malaria

Many Raleigh citizens speculated in 1894 and 1895 that the condition of water in and around Caraleigh was the cause of malaria and typhoid. Neither the general public nor medical professionals clearly understood diagnoses and treatment for both diseases. Typhoid was better known in the medical community than malaria in 1894, but malaria was still "a difficult disease to detect and control," according to historian Michael P. McCarthy, with medical experts in disagreement "about the best way to prevent" malaria.[106]

Typhoid was widespread throughout North Carolina in the late 1800s, with 35 counties reporting cases of typhoid in 1888. Although the threat of typhoid fever was common in the late 1880s, typhoid remained a danger well into the 20th century.[107] The sanitation connection to typhoid and other enteric diseases was slowly becoming clear to public health officials who reported in 1889 that "cholera and typhoid fever … are contracted in the majority of cases through the ingestion of infected food and drink, especially the latter. Hence, when diseases are present, it is a safe plan to boil the water used for drinking purposes."[108] In May 1889, North Carolina health officials declared that it was an "established fact that polluted drinking water is the primary cause of typhoid fever."[109] And further stated that "'pollution usually comes from the drainage of privies, sink drains, barnyards, and other nuisances into the family' drinking well."[110]

The year 1880 was significant for deciphering the nature of the typhoid. That year German scientists identified the bacteriological culprit, the typhoid bacilli. As with malaria, the medical community and the public were slow to accept the new findings about the disease. Traditionalists firmly supported the idea that typhoid was caused by miasmas, meaning "atmospheric conditions or vapors that rose from filth."[111] For decades, the miasmist believers remained skeptical that typhoid was caused by typhoid bacilli. Justification for their belief was that it was difficult to detect typhoid microbes in a given sample of drinking water, and that even minute amounts of typhoid microbes were capable of triggering an epidemic. This hesitancy often proved deadly. Typhoid can be contracted through the bodily waste matter of an infected person or through the ingestion of contaminated food or water. Typhoid can also spread through hand-to-hand contact. Nevertheless, the bad air theory of the miasmists persisted. For example, one newspaper explained in 1901 that typhoid "gains entrance to our bodies chiefly in the milk and water we drink, which comes from infected sources," but that "a rarer method is by inhalation of infected air."[112]

The microorganism associated with typhoid attacks the intestinal tract, resulting in diarrhea, vomiting, subsequent dehydration, and "fevers as high as 106 degrees."[113] In severe cases, patients could experience seizures, coma, and death. Typhoid did not discriminate among its victims, affecting both the rich and the poor, the famous and the unknown. While in North Carolina, the Wright brothers both contacted the disease. After Wilber Wright ingested infected shellfish, he died in 1912. His brother Orville got typhoid when he was 25 but survived and lived until 1948.[114]

Despite the scientific discoveries made by 1880, miasmas had long been considered the culprit behind both typhoid and malaria. The North Carolina Board of Health's 1885 publication *Sanitary Engineering* described miasmas as "malarial poison."[115]

> It is generally believed that all damp places, as most ponds, marshes, swamps, river bottoms subject to overflow, etc., portions of which along the banks, are alternately wet and dry, are such as originate malarial poison, and must continue to originate it so long as such conditions hold. The occasional overflow of salt water aggravates the evil, as also the

accumulation of leaves, decaying wood, etc., especially where thick vegetation causes a stagnation of the air, with dense shade. It is obviously correct then to cut down such vegetation immediately around the damp locality, drain it and put it under cultivation. If the rise and fall of the water, in the pond or marsh, alternately covers and exposes much of the banks—i.e., if the banks are not vertical, or made so,—then the body of water must be entirely drained off, if possible; otherwise the injurious decompositions due to wet soils will continue to go on and breed malaria. It is found the winds can transport malaria some miles. It is best not to cut down open forests at a little distance from the damp localities, as they intercept the malaria to a considerable extent.[116]

The epidemic of poor health in Caraleigh in 1894 was during a transitional period for the scientific understanding, prognosis, and prevention of both diseases. Dr. McGee visited "most houses" at Caraleigh in the summer of 1894 and "found typhoid and malarial fevers there."[117] During the year after Caraleigh's epidemic of fever, physicians expressed disagreement in public testimony as to "the causes of malaria at Caraleigh."[118] A patient's sickness and symptoms were reported as a set of symptoms including fever, chills, malaria and typhoid. The description of the type of sickness, as well as the cause, varied according to the source. One source asserted that typhoid fever was caused by inadequate housing at the mill and its ill-chosen location.[119] Another contended that the cause of typhoid was the "filth … [that] emptied near Bledsoe's grove and Holmen's mill."[120] Caraleigh was nearly forced to shut down because of the outbreak of malaria and the fever, which was attributed, according to experts, to its poor location. This location was described as being "extremely malarial" in 1894.[121]

1895: Walnut Creek and Its Tributaries

A year after the outbreak at Caraleigh, the Raleigh municipal government took the Water Works Company to court for causing the deadly "chills and fever" at Caraleigh and south Raleigh.[122] Undoubtedly, this litigation was politically awkward for Alfred A. Thompson, the president of Caraleigh Mills and former mayor of Raleigh whose administration had been lauded for the construction of the Raleigh waterworks and sewer system. Now, with the public health problems, both of these systems were under scrutiny.[123] The legal battle, highly anticipated according to Wilmington's *Weekly Star*, included "a brilliant array of legal talent pitted against one another."[124] At the center of the 1895 case was the question of whether a pond maintained by the Water Works Company was the origin of the sickness at Caraleigh and south Raleigh.[125] The subsequent investigation and 1895 courtroom hearing included testimonials from nearby residents, city officials, and experts on contagious disease. Their statements were, the *News and Observer* opined, conflicted "from beginning to end," which underscored the still-developing scientific understanding of the causes of malaria.[126]

Typhoid, "the dread of rich and poor alike," was better understood in 1895, but not completely.[127] In 1880, Karl Joseph Eberth discovered the germ that caused typhoid and that its entry into the human system was through the drinking of infected sources, namely "milk and water."[128] But the causes of malaria remained mysterious. For thousands of years, the science of malaria asserted that its fevers in humans were caused by miasmas, or unhealthy smells or vapors that rose from swamp land and entered into humans through the respiratory tract or skin. Hence the etymological root of the word malaria, "bad air."[129] The discovery that mosquitoes were responsible for malaria occurred in 1897. North Carolina health officials hinted at ongoing research but also continued to make room for archaic understandings of the disease:

> If a micro-organism is the cause, as is now conceded, and its habitat is fermenting organic matter in the soil, it is certainly a reasonable conclusion to arrive at that the entrance could be more readily effected through the mouth and the digestive tract than by either lungs or skin. Going further, [a] professional medical publication stated that it is well known that the system succumbs more readily to malarial influences while fasting; doubtless this is explained by the fact that the microorganism has to reach the alkaline intestinal tract before developing its pestilential manifestations and this is more easily done through an empty stomach than a full one, with the protective influence of active gastric digestion.[130]

In 1897, science reported that parasites, namely mosquitoes, were the vectors of the malaria disease.[131] In 1899, during another court case about malarial conditions of Walnut Creek, one physician testified that the theory about the malaria had "changed in some material respects in the last few years. Some scientists thought that malaria was found in impure drinking water and others that malaria was caused by the mosquito."[132] The discussion during the 1895 court case about malaria in and around Caraleigh reflected the scientific ambivalence.

One resident who lived on Rhamkatte Road, about 1,900 yards from the Water Works Pond, claimed no health problems, but observed that "the brickyards near Caraleigh—were full of water most of the time" and that the yard contained five or six acres [filled with] water that had "a scum on it." Various experts offered sworn testimony that "whenever the surface soil in a malarial district is disturbed there is a source of malaria." Others believed that draining the water around Caraleigh would cause malaria. Still others opined that "it would be better that the pond stand as it is, than to drain it."[133]

G.L. Kirby, the superintendent of the North Carolina Insane Asylum, testified that "female inmates" who were exposed "to the breezes from the water works pond," had been seriously sickened with "malarial troubles," while the male inmates, who were healthy, had not. Kirby went on to admit that the theories regarding the cause of malaria were "not necessarily defined." Some scientists thought that malaria would not cross water because it would be "absorbed by the water," while others believed that malaria was "most often introduced through the atmosphere by inhalation."[134] Still others considered that, from water, "malaria rises more rapidly at night than in the day time," but that it rises "in the hot sun." Kirby noted that the people who lived "in this climate near mill ponds" had the "general experience" of "chills and fever" because of the environmental factors of "heat and moisture, and vegetable matter."[135]

Expert witness Dr. J.A. Sexton treated patients in the southeast section of the city who suffered from "chills and fever," which he believed came from both the Water Works pond and nearby mud flats.[136] Sexton thought that eliminating the pond would not remove the source of the sickness, because he erroneously testified that "malaria chiefly gets into the human system through the atmosphere" via inhalation.[137]

Dr. James McKee also took the stand as an expert witness. McKee was the

Raleigh city superintendent of health and, prior to that, the Wake County health superintendent. He testified that the "land along [Walnut Creek] was very marshy, conducive to malaria; if there were no pond, conditions would remain as they now are, there would be chills and fevers." McKee posited that the unhealthy conditions in the area south of Raleigh antedated the Water Works Pond. He visited the sick at Caraleigh in the summer of 1894 and had found "typhoid and malarial fevers there."[138] He claimed that the disease was caused by "unsuitable clothing, improper food, and unclean [living] quarters." That McKee's criticisms directly impugned the founders of Caraleigh was unmistakable.[139]

> conditions of Caraleigh Mills were calculated to contaminate the water at the mills; no regard was paid to health or hygiene when the Caraleigh Mills were built there; he [Dr. Mckee] doesn't think the water works pond affects the health of the operatives at the Caraleigh Mills.[140]

When cross-examined, McKee maintained that "heat, water, and vegetable matter in a decaying state produce malaria."[141] He also said that the land below Fayetteville Road was "not hygienic" and to Holleman Road was "unsanitary."[142] These conditions existed in the area of Caraleigh prior to existence of the Water Works Pond. Dr. O.J. O'Hagan, a physician from Greenville, North Carolina, concurred with McKee's estimation, testifying that "the site of Caraleigh Mills" was "badly chosen."[143] Furthermore, O'Hagan's personal visit to the workers' homes led him to blame the poor water supply and ventilation that augmented the "malarial effects of the adjacent swamps." A juror queried O'Hagan as to how malaria enters the human body: "Principally through the breathing organs," O'Hagan responded, "but often through drinking water. When the ground begins to crack and open up, the exhalations of the earth are more unhealthy than at any other time." In the end, O'Hagan argued that the swamp around Caraleigh, not the Water Works Company pond, was the primary cause of the malarial outbreak.[144]

The *News and Observer* reported in January 1895 that Caraleigh residents were eager to see the "Raleigh Water Works drained," hopeful to no longer be subjected "to the sickness and loss of life caused by the pools and ponds there."[145] But the residents would have to wait until November 28, 1895, for the Water Works Company to have its pond drained. Statewide news reported that it had been "pretty satisfactorily shown"—in spite of contradictory testimony at the trial—"that the pond was the cause of the fever epidemic at Caraleigh Mills last year."[146] The investigation that summer ushered in the implementation of a "much needed sanitary reform" in the area.[147] The court concluded that the pond the Water Works Company maintained had become a public nuisance, endangering public health in Caraleigh and South Raleigh during the summer of 1894. The final legal remedy that centered on the rancid water around Caraleigh worked, unknowingly, to address the root of the waterborne source of the sickness.

1899: Walnut Creek's Water, Redux

A subsequent, "stubbornly fought," court case in 1899 further illuminated waterborne concerns surrounding the same "small sluggish stream"—Walnut Creek.[148] The

News and Observer described it as one of "the very greatest moments in the city of Raleigh's legal history."[149] In 1899, Bart N. Gatling sued the City of Raleigh for $4,000 in damages, based on his claim that the city sewer emptied into Walnut Creek in proximity to his land, thereby creating a health hazard and diminishing his property's value, as the *North Carolinian* reported.[150] In addition to the loss of a third of his plantation's value, Gatlin argued that the sewer caused him to suffer from "chills" and "malaria" and that he was "threatened with typhoid," in addition to enduring "the odor of sewerage."[151] The city's response did not refute the unhealthfulness of the area around Walnut Creek. Instead, the city maintained that the "swamps, stagnant marshes and mud pits" caused the nuisance, not the sewer, per se.[152] The stakes of this court hearing were high for the city. If Gatling prevailed, "a precedent would be set and half a dozen other suits would be started by men who were in exactly the same position" and would "have the same ground for an action."[153] Additionally, the city would be "compelled to extend its sewer much farther down the creek," which "would mean the expenditure of many thousands of dollars."[154]

Fred W. Mahler testified that until 1893, he lived about "two and one-half miles outside the city" and about a "half a mile from the creek."[155] He moved from the area at the advice of a physician, because he had developed "malaria and was threatened with typhoid."[156] It was additionally noted that "workers living on the place were also sick."[157] Mahler believed that the city's sewer system threatened "the health of the place." He asserted that for a year or two after the sewer was established, "we didn't notice it, then it began to get worse and worse."[158] Another witness stated that during the summer, when the water was low, it was "insufficient to carry off the volume of sewerage."[159] Witnesses in agreement with Gatling believed that "if all obstacles and hindrances to the flow of water were removed," it would help matters.[160]

When cross-examined about the cause of malaria, Dr. Hines ruled out fecal matter. Instead, he pointed to "the creek and the marshes and the decaying vegetable matter" in their waters.[161] When asked if there was "an excess of fecal matter in this creek ... would it in your opinion cause malaria to a family a mile away?"[162] The physician retorted, "I don't think so. It may cause typhoid fever, but not malaria ... *some* think it can be communicated by the mosquito."[163] He thus argued that clearing the land "around malarial swamps" would disturb it and was calculated to "increase the prevalence of malaria."[164] Dr. J.A. Sexton, who testified in 1895 in agreement with Hines, maintained that "the vegetable matter" that passed through the sewer would "unquestionably, in its decomposition, generate malaria. The other matter would not cause malaria."[165] He concurred that the "clearing of the lands along the stream had conduced [*sic*] the spread of malaria."[166] Dave Holland, a resident who lived a quarter of a mile from the sewer, disagreed and said that the "odor from the sewerage was distinct," and the sewage resulted in "chills and fever from July till nearly Christmas."[167] Another witness concurred, positing that "before the sewer was put in, we had good health. Now we are sick nearly all the time."[168]

A.A. Thompson, a former mayor of Raleigh, and one of at least half a dozen inspectors sent out to look at the sewer and creek waters, reported, as relayed by the *State Chronicle*, that he saw no evidence of sewer deposits on the land and "no odor until he came within twenty feet of the sewer."[169] Other "inspectors reported similarly: 'only a faint odor with no refuse deposited on the land'; 'no odor till within eight feet of the mouth of the sewer ... no solid matter in the discharge of the sewer ... the water discharged almost clear.'"[170] Dr. James McKee also argued, in the city's defense, that marshes were "productive of malaria" and that even if waste from the sewer line was present, malaria was never "supposed to be caused by fecal matter."[171] He insisted that "the mud holes on the creek, the stagnant water and dying vegetation are productive of malaria."[172] The testifying doctors all agreed that sewerage would not cause malaria, though it would "cause typhoid fever."[173]

Gatling's suit against the city of Raleigh ultimately failed because the jury believed that the plaintiff had not been injured "by the negligent and unlawful construction or management of the defendant's sewer."[174] The resulting headline in the news was that the sewer "did not cause malaria."[175] Similar to the poisoning of Raleigh's water caused by the 1892 fire at Caraleigh's fertilizer plant, and the illnesses incurred during the 1894 summer at Caraleigh, the complaints of the suffering of average citizens in 1899 fell upon deaf ears. The powerful men associated with the city, or Caraleigh, or both, evaded culpability for their actions, whether intentional or otherwise.

Historiographical Considerations

According to historian Brent D. Glass, one achievement of North Carolina's industrial cotton barons was their "ability to live up to the expectations of Victorian values by projecting an image of social responsibility and paternalistic control."[176] This pattern, according to Glass, had "eluded challenge by journalists and historians well into the twentieth-century."[177] Glass did mention that there were some criticisms found in "several private sources."[178] The same elements of Caraleigh's story provides evidence that, in part, refutes Glass. The July 5, 1895, edition of the *Evening Visitor* reported Governor Carr's opinion that blamed Caraleigh's poor location for the sickness of its workers.[179] The July 12, 1895, issue of the *News and Observer* provided court testimony that Caraleigh's leaders enabled workers to live and work in harmful conditions that were seemingly designed to poison the water at Caraleigh without care for the health of the laborers.[180] In the same article, a witness believed that Caraleigh was culpable for sickness among workers in 1894 because of unsatisfactory clothing, food, and insanitary housing.[181]

Contrary to Caraleigh's officers who claimed to be the noble protectors of their workers, these newspaper accounts tarnished that image. After the Water Works Case concluded in 1895, the *News and Observer* published a whole page entitled *The Capital City's Tribute to The State's Milling Interests* that featured Raleigh's three mills: Raleigh Mills, Pilot Mills, and Caraleigh Mills. The news article about Caraleigh gushed effusively with praise for the "wisdom" of its founders and declared that the "coining of the word Caraleigh from the names Carolina and the Capital City ... forms an important epoch in the industrial history of the State and the South."[182] While there had been some criticisms of Caraleigh's founders publicly pronounced, contrary to Glass's supposition, there were also large-scale, pro-mill propaganda articles. When reviewed in juxtaposition, the volume of mill propaganda news feature stories dominated the few sentences of criticisms buried in lengthy news articles about Caraleigh's founders.

An embellished narrative of Caraleigh's progress in newspapers and industry journals confirmed the opinions of Walter Hines Page, who was always "suspicious of the extravagant claims made by Southerners," asserting in 1909 that "nobody tells the whole truth about institutions."[183] Instead, Southerners instead preferred to "accept traditions and formulas and to repeat respectful formulas."[184] The veracity of "New South propaganda sheets" and "glowing reports" found in Southern newspapers also left Lewis H. Blair, a Confederate veteran and postwar economics expert, skeptical.[185] After touring the South, both men failed to see the expected industrial utopia about which they had read. Instead, they discovered great disparity between reported economic progress and reality. Blair expected to see a region that was "enjoying a veritable deluge of prosperity," but concluded that New South propaganda was inaccurate, lacked objectivity, and was "mischievous and misleading."[186] A similar conclusion could apply to Caraleigh Mills. But any prolonged discussion of Caraleigh's water-quality disasters would cast an unwanted shadow upon Caraleigh's esteemed founders and endanger the South's quest for "glorious material and industrial triumph."[187]

> ...to doubt the current charming presentations of Southern growth and prosperity is to bring down anathemas upon one's head. What! the South not prosperous. Impossible they cry; and the individual who questions is an idiot.[188]

In the New South context, "failures and bankruptcies were seldom recorded" and "the inevitable trend had to be upwards."[189] Presenting Caraleigh in anything other than a favorable light was indubitably unpopular.[190]

Caraleigh's historical silences seemed a constant force, as the "New South" narrative eclipsed accusations of alleged mismanagement that resulted in death among the cotton mill's operatives.[191] What was forgotten, or ignored, during both the 1895 and the 1899 court cases involving waterborne woes in the southern part of Raleigh was the 1886 report from Dr. Phillips, a "professor of chemistry at the university," who had directly discussed the "condition of the water supply for the city of Raleigh from a chemical standpoint."[192] From August 19 to August 26, 1886, Phillips had made firsthand observations and gathered data about the waters in and around Walnut Creek from seven miles out leading to Raleigh, including Rhamkatte Road; Phillips concluded that the creek "would furnish enough water for a city two or three times as large as Raleigh" but that it was "not the quantity of water but the quality" that made him think that Walnut Creek was "unsuitable as a source of water to be used for domestic purposes" ... adding that he believed "that Walnut Creek water would be a dangerous water for such purposes."[193] Dr. Phillips argued that Walnut Creek was too short and muddy of a creek and filled with debris from land under cultivation, including manure.[194] Phillips advised against using Walnut Creek, reporting that drainage from city garbage and refuse made contamination of wells in the area likely.[195] If that was not enough, Phillips said that sewage from Dorothea Dix discharged in the area above Rhamkatte Road and nearby "water closets, bathrooms, barns and stables" made Walnut Creek water non-potable and unhealthy. When he ambled through the area, Phillips found Walnut Creek "almost impassable from nastiness" of sewage, with an "extremely disagreeable stench."[196] Walnut Creek's water had one sole benefit, said Phillips: its nearness to Raleigh. The professor admitted that he did not submit an analysis of water as evidence in his report, because he had not been asked to make one; other tests had been conducted, but Phillips did not believe the limited number of tests adequate evidence either one way or another.[197]

The 1910 Raleigh Chamber of Commerce published another exemplar of anemic objectivity in its promotional booklet that advertised the capital city's accolades in "commercial, financial, educational, and manufacturing development."[198] Print space was made for a description of the Wake Water Company, which started in 1886 as a business venture, and was incorporated in November 1901, being redubbed the Wake Water Company. A description of how Raleigh obtained its water was included:

> The water is pumped from Walnut Creek, a never-failing creek of pure water, a few miles south of the city. The entire stream and its source are carefully patrolled so as to prevent any fouling of the water, and the low death rate of Raleigh is sufficient evidence as to the purity of the water supply.[199]

Caraleigh shared numerous connections with the Raleigh Water Works, which was reconstituted in 1901 as the Wake Water Company. A.A. Thompson was listed as the vice-president of the "Raleigh Water Company in 1899," and the "principal owners" of the Wake Water Company included Caraleigh's founders, N.W. West and Julius Lewis.[200] Lewis was president of the Raleigh Water Works for 25 years until the city of Raleigh purchased it, reforming it as the Wake Water Company.[201] The purpose for the reformation of the Raleigh Water Works, via sale to the city, was to change of ownership and give "the stock a better market value," thus reducing the liability of stockholders, who had been the same owners of the Raleigh Water Company. Beyond the obvious financial benefit to these men, another was to make the water company a home-owned enterprise.[202] Previously, the *New Berne Weekly Journal* reported, more than half of the company's stock had been owned "by persons in Dayton, Ohio."[203]

The *News and Observer* editorialized in July 1895 that the Caraleigh epidemic court decision that demanded removal of the water works pond was "inconsequential," with all of the other nuisances and disease producing elements along Walnut Creek.[204] Presciently, the editorial called for Walnut Creek to be "canalled and dredged," along with the "bogs and marshes that surrounded Caraleigh Mills."[205] In doing so, the "debris, filth and sewage from the asylum, penitentiary and city pass off at once instead of being left to float leisurely down, rotting in the sun, and scattering germs and disease along its route."[206] While Raleigh's leading newspaper was clamoring for improvements to benefit the public weal, another newspaper, the *Wilmington Messenger*, noted Caraleigh Mills' leaders apparent unwillingness to engage in the court case on behalf of their sick employees.

> Though the owners of Caraleigh Mills were deeply interested in the drainage matter, which was decided here this week, they took no part in the prosecution and contributed no funds. For this they were severely scored by counsel. Last year at one time it seemed that they would have to stop work by reason of the sickness of nearly all their employes [sic].[207]

Caraleigh's founders, who were among the owners of the Water Works, showed little energy in attacking the Water Works for the sickness of its workers in 1894. To what degree Caraleigh's and the Water Works' associations influenced legal decisions about the epidemic at the mill remains unclear.

Whether purposeful or accidental, reports in the *Bulletin of the North Carolina*

Board of Health (hereinafter BNCBH) in July and August 1894 revealed misinformation about the severity of conditions at Caraleigh. Wake County's July entry, submitted by Dr. McKee, reported just "six cases of typhoid fever [and] Malarial fevers [that] have prevailed, notably at Caraleigh Mills, two miles from the city. The Walnut Creek flats, upon which the mills have been erected, are in an unsanitary condition and efforts are being made to correct it. Public buildings in good condition."[208] Newspapers in early July contradicted this report, claiming that there were "in all 30 cases yesterday."[209] To explain this discrepancy, Dr. McKee responded that "there are more cases than are reported. Some of the doctors are as careless about reporting contagious and infectious diseases as they are about reporting births. There is an ordinance imposing a fine for such neglect and I intend to have it enforced."[210]

The August 1894 editorial in the *BNCBH* spoke, in veiled fashion, of events in Caraleigh, as well as the attitude of the mill operatives toward sanitation measures. Neither Dr. McKee, nor Caraleigh, were mentioned by name, but there was little doubt that both were the topics of editorial remarks:

> The almost invincible indifference of the masses of the people [to practicing public health] is most discouraging. Not long since in a conversation with a very intelligent physician of large experience and accurate observation on the necessity for the people of a certain settlement scourged with typhoid fever, whose water supply had been shown by bacteriological examination to be infected with the bacteria of the human intestine, to boil their drinking water, he remarked, "They would rather die than to boil their water," and we were forced to admit that he was probably right.[211]

Consequently, science trumped what appeared to be the legal conclusion that blamed the Water Works Pond. In 1894, bacteriological studies, as discussed in the *BNCBH*, analyzed Caraleigh's drinking water "from the lower well and the lower spring at the Caraleigh Mills" and demonstrated its "strong contamination with fecal matter."[212] Despite this bacteriological difference, later scientific discovery confirmed that *bacillus coli communis* could cause "the typhoid symptom complex" in those infected.[213] Its symptoms were easily clinically confused with symptoms of malaria, chills, and fever.

The 1894 incident at Caraleigh was significant in the state's public health history because it reinforced to state health officials the inescapable fact that there was bacteriological contamination of drinking water. This could only be definitively ascertained through the science of bacteriology, a subject in which state health officials lacked expertise to detect oncoming waterborne incidents and the infection sources. To ameliorate the situation, the Marine Hospital Service offered to train state health officials at its laboratory in Washington, D.C. A free six-week course of instruction was made available in practical sanitary bacteriology, including the bacteriological examination of drinking waters.[214] The fever outbreak at Caraleigh may have had ripple effects, as evidenced when the state changed its procedures in dealing with possible outbreaks of typhoid fever in the state's 1895–96 Biennial Report from the Board of Health. This report announced that the state had "made arrangements for bacteriological examinations of suspected drinking water," to locate and confirm "the origin of typhoid fever, and [to check] its further spread in more or less epidemic form," though in individual, or "sporadic cases."[215]

The case of Caraleigh in 1894 raises questions over why there were inconsistent reports of both malaria and typhoid. At least three factors explain late-19th-century physicians' inability to quickly diagnose patients. First, the two diseases could, at the outset, at least, exhibit similar symptoms. As the North Carolina Board of Health described it, "certain diagnosis in the early stages of many cases of typhoid fever has been a stumbling block in the management of this most serious and widespread disease until quite recently."[216] With the development in 1896 of a "serum test" that required one drop of a patient's blood for analysis, a microscopic analysis would "settle the nature of the 'simple continued fever.'"[217]

The second factor is that medical understanding of both diseases was evolving, with numerous discoveries being made in the 1890s and early 1900s. While the causes of typhoid became better understood in 1894, the causes of malaria remained largely unknown until 1897. For instance, in 1895–96, state officials recommended that North Carolinians boil their water prior to drinking, to prevent malaria. The health authorities believed that ingestion of the water was the direct cause of the malaria, not the mosquito. North Carolina's Board of Health reported in their 1895–96 report that it was "a matter of common observation that, in families using boiled water, those who, for some reason, do not drink it have been known to have malarial attacks while others escaped."[218]

The third factor that hampered accurate diagnoses was that individual testing for typhoid was not yet available in 1894–95. Water testing depended on the financial ability, or willingness, of district and state health officials to do it. North Carolina's Board of Health investigated the typhoid testing problem at length and admitted that public prevention efforts were costly, raising the question, "Can we afford to save typhoid victims?"[219] The government acknowledged that typhoid was preventable and made educational efforts to instruct the public in how to prevent it.[220] Yet, despite these efforts, the report argued, the public's "almost invincible indifference" toward practical hygiene only exacerbated the typhoid situation.[221]

As mentioned, the governor and health officials publicly criticized Caraleigh's poor choice of location and the conditions of its mill houses. Caraleigh Mills nonetheless eluded official blame in both the 1895 and 1899 court cases. The 1895 court case blamed the Water Works Company pond as "the cause of the fever epidemic at Caraleigh Mills" in 1894.[222] In the 1899 case, Caraleigh was barely mentioned. When Caraleigh was mentioned by name, the mill was excluded from any possible culpability in polluting Walnut Creek with a chemical dye. The argument was that the "dye that the Caraleigh Mills turns into the creek is copperas and acts as a disinfectant." However, copperas has become regarded as a hazardous material, harmful to humans and aquatic life, not to be washed in a sewer.[223]

By 1895, clean water in the state was recognized as a serious matter, with the North Carolina State Board of Health declaring that it had a responsibility to act as "a disinterested body whose only concern is the protection of the health of the people."[224] Concomitantly, it summoned the legislature to award it "mandatory powers" to control "all public water supplies" on behalf of the people.[225] The people had a "right to demand that their lawmakers should provide means" of access to "pure water."[226] The Board of Health reasoned that it would be the most trustworthy body for this endeavor:

> [I]t should not be left up to the water companies themselves, most of which are private corporations whose principal stockholders are often non-residents, chiefly interested in dividends. But even where the works are owned by the city itself the management cannot be counted on as the best always, owing its influence of political considerations.[227]

Silence from the Start

Numerous studies in the late 1880s of the water around Caraleigh revealed that the dangers of pollution around Walnut Creek were ignored, with Caraleigh's leadership choosing to expose their workers to the most ruthless consequences of industrialization.[228] In 1890, Mayor Thompson had voiced concern about the "laws protecting the watershed of Walnut Creek," which he thought "very defective."[229] The desire to proceed with the construction of Caraleigh, despite forewarned dangers, proved too powerful for Caraleigh's directors to resist. The fulfillment of *noblesse oblige*— the inferred duty of the privileged to act generously and nobly toward the less privileged—fell woefully short.

After the typhoid outbreak in the summer of 1894, and the subsequent court case in 1895, news of the sick at Caraleigh received ample coverage in newspapers, as did criticisms of Caraleigh's directors. Discussion of the contamination of water at Caraleigh has remained glaringly absent from the state's history, and from the few studies about Caraleigh, in particular. This should be an unsurprising outcome for members of the state's "progressive plutocracy."[230] Among them, a former mayor of Raleigh, a future gubernatorial candidate, several Civil War heroes, and numerous leading businessmen. Clearly these men had the motive and means to ensure that continued negative news of Caraleigh Mills in public discussions was quashed. This was especially important when the discussions involved the politics of clean water and the prospects for land values in south Raleigh. Public talk of south Raleigh's water problems was disassociated from Caraleigh. Soon forgotten, Caraleigh's shortcomings were buried underneath propagandistic stories of the mills' valiant successes in conjunction with the South's economic rebirth.

In November 1895, the *News and Observer* published a "Cotton Mill Edition" which projected "The Capital City's Tribute to the State's Milling Interest," including the Pilot Mills, Raleigh Cotton Mills, and Caraleigh Mills. Unmentioned were criticisms of Caraleigh founders in 1894 over the location of the mills, which the governor and others had publicly blamed for the epidemic of fever. Instead, a healthy dose of Southern patriotic praise was heaped on the "wisdom" of Caraleigh's leadership, despite public fault-finding of the Caraleigh's captains.

> The promoters of Caraleigh Company had faith enough in the future of Raleigh and North Carolina to build in the suburbs of the city an enterprise that is a credit to the South; and they had foresight enough to possess themselves of a large body of suburban land, the steadily increasing value of which will, as the city expands amply reward them for their labors and fully demonstrate the wisdom of their investment.[231]

In 1897, Raleigh's *Morning Post* trumpeted Raleigh's location as a "sure Klondike for Capital without the danger of death" because of its congenial climate and soil.[232] The same article extended the claim with its description of Caraleigh, a textile mill that had built housing for their operatives and provided them "the best of care and attention."[233] In 1904, ten years after Caraleigh's summer of epidemic, Josephus Daniels' *News and Observer* published "A Great Day at Caraleigh," an article that continued the silence about that dreadful summer of 1894. Prominent statewide leaders celebrated that day, which incidentally was Confederate Memorial Day. The leaders extolled the values of "religion, education, and patriotism" in speeches to Caraleigh's school children. Of the numerous speakers, two of particular significance included the "Hon[orable] A.A. Thompson, president of the Caraleigh Mills Company," who presented the village school with an American flag; and "Josephus Daniels, editor of the *News and Observer*, [who] presented the Bible to the school."[234] The subsequent article in Daniels' newspaper held to the historical silence about 1894:

> Caraleigh is a prosperous mill village ... on every hand there is evidence of prosperity. The people in this town take great pride in their homes, and a neater, cleaner village can not be found anywhere. The people of this town enjoy a good public school, have a church, several stores, and a more contented and happy people would be hard to find. It is a healthy location, and one only has to see that they are a healthy, robust people, who seem to enjoy life.[235]

A Washington, D.C., newspaper in 1912 sang Caraleigh's praise for providing "liberally for its employees with housing and a school."[236] Weeks prior to the United States' formal entry into the First World War in 1917, the *Charlotte News* reported that Caraleigh Mills was "doing much for the betterment of its people" and took measures "to put the mill community in healthy and sanitary conditions."[237] Knowingly or not, the author explicitly papered over the tragic events of two decades earlier. The author added that Caraleigh's management was "deeply interested in the well-being of operatives," as proven by its "record of health," which "has been good since the mill was first started."[238] The memory of 1894 crossed the threshold of silence into amnesia. Clearly, the Caraleigh Mills Company wanted to bury memories of the outbreak of "fever" from 1894.[239] Insofar as potential waterborne health problems were concerned, as the *Southern Textile Bulletin* would put it in 1923, the "attractive mill village" prevented "any menace to the public health of the village" with water supplied from "deep wells" and "septic toilets" for "all."[240]

For nearly a century, Harriet L. Herring's 1929 *Welfare Work in Mill Villages* has been an essential work for historians and students of North Carolina textile mills. Herring mentions Caraleigh twice, and makes no reference to the summer of 1894.[241] Herring reported that in 1919 that Caraleigh's "acting executive" had for "many years personally carried on something of a health education and sanitation campaign" at Caraleigh.[242] The Caraleigh executive employed a "general community worker" who expanded efforts in the mill community to educate Caraleigh's residents in basic sanitation and healthful living.[243] These lessons included "efficient rubbish and garbage removal" and "orderly yards and clean streets," which provided visible evidence of the "success of the program."[244]

Herring's second mention of Caraleigh hints at a criticism of the mill. She discussed the mill's lackluster experience with the homeownership of mill cottages among its workers. Caraleigh "had always sold lots to employees, upon which they build ... as they please or can."[245] But Caraleigh's young were often disinterested, choosing not to follow "the example of thrifty parents." Of course, this was not the fault of the mill, according to Herring's source at Caraleigh. Rather, it was because the young were "indifferent workers or citizens or simply preferring to move."[246] This led Caraleigh to buy lots at market value, whenever a property was for sale "since it is quite near the mill."[247] Perhaps memories of 1894 galvanized revulsion to homeownership at Caraleigh. The waterborne health danger was unalleviated because, in part, of the Mills' location, at the bottom of a hill, where a malodorous muck from Walnut

Creek surrounded the mill and its cottages. Interestingly, an 1899 *News and Observer* article reported that Caraleigh provided "adorable" suburban houses for its workers, "owning to its high and excellent location."[248] Josephus Daniels' newspaper was clearly complicit in historical malfeasance, because Caraleigh is hardly situated on an elevated position.

A movement of Southern self-appraisal emerged in the 1930s in both academic and literary that acknowledged the mistreatment of first generation of textile workers.[249] Rural sociologist and lifelong University of Chapel Hill professor Samuel Huntington Hobbs, Jr., postulated in 1930 that labor troubles in North Carolina were likely to persist unless conditions changed.[250] While not naming any particular mills, Hobbs' pithy observations mirrored Caraleigh's experience with company housing in unsanitary conditions and substandard working situations:

> In the textile industry, for example, the chief local problem is the corporate ownership of the homes of mill workers. This is a peculiar condition not without possibly grave consequences.... But we may expect labor troubles along with our growth as an industrial state. The second generation [of mill workers] will not be as complacent as the first generation of industrial workers has been. ... It is possible to have fair capital profits along with healthy, wholesome, and prosperous labor conditions.[251]

The memories of the acid spill in 1892 and the epidemic in the summer of 1894 at Caraleigh were buried. There was little left for posterity to do but read a confirmation of silences in the historiography of Caraleigh. Four previous historical studies of Caraleigh were undertaken before the present book: "Caraleigh: A Forgotten Mill Village," written by an unnamed author[252]; Daniel L. Watkins's "Caraleigh: Raleigh's Cotton Mill Village"[253]; "Caraleigh, Survey Area XVI," unnamed author, a typed, seven-page manuscript located in the North Carolina Archives, Historic Preservation section, 1991[254]; and an 18-page *National Register of Historic Places Registration Form*.[255]

"Caraleigh: A Forgotten Mill Village" made no reference to water-quality problems at Caraleigh during its first decades of existence.[256] But it provided a favorable review of the mills' location: "There could be no better spot to situate such a mill since there was easy access" to railways tracks.[257] The anonymous author's sole acknowledgment of environmental concerns referenced "Walnut Creek, which ran along beside the mill and could be used for dumping waste, such as dye from the mill," to which was offered the disclaimer, "of course this was before the emphasis on ecology." The manuscript makes no reference to the 1892 fire at the phosphate and fertilizer plant, or the summer of sickness in 1894.

In 2000, University of North Carolina graduate student Daniel Watkins successfully submitted his master's thesis entitled *Caraleigh: Raleigh's Cotton Mill Village*. Compared to previous works, Watkins' work was the most significant and thorough study of Caraleigh. Nevertheless, the Watkins thesis continued the historical silences of the mill and its village, with the founders of Caraleigh named, but otherwise not analyzed in any great detail. There were few insights given about the "Caraleigh Phosphate and Fertilizer Works," which was acknowledged with two interviewees reporting that one's grandfather had worked there as a manager. Nothing was mentioned regarding the plant's African American workers.

Watkins did not examine Raleigh's significant water centered events at Caraleigh

Modern water management features abound along Walnut Creek in the area of Caraleigh in 2020. The picture shows Walnut Creek at the intersection of South Saunders Street and Interstate 40, about a mile from Caraleigh Mills (photograph by the author).

A scene along Walnut Creek on the Greenway about a mile from Caraleigh Mills (photograph by the author).

in the 1890s but found that "getting water" remained a challenge for Caraleigh residents in the 1930s and 1940s. His omission can be understood, because Watkins' stated goal was to tell the history of the "residents of Raleigh's Caraleigh community" via the oral interviews of "twenty-nine long-time and former Caraleigh residents," none of whom were born before 1900; and of those interviewed, only seven had worked in any textile mill at all.[258]

In his discussion of the mills' history, Watkins included details about the cotton mills' water systems for "dyeing operations," toilets, and "wash rooms," as well as a water system with "hydrants outside the building" and "1,000 feet of hose for use in case of fire."[259] Also included was a discussion of Caraleigh's residential water use. It was recalled that the company drilled wells "near company houses periodically along the streets."[260] In total, there were estimated to have been seven wells drilled, thereby requiring dozens of Caraleigh residents to share well water. Some residents also drilled their own wells behind their homes. Either way, it was a daily household chore to carry water "from the nearest water pump."[261]

It was not until the 1930s, according to Watkins, that Caraleigh "families gradually added running water to their homes."[262] Watkins reported that Caraleigh residents used water barrels "to catch rainwater" from rooftops, a practice that Harriet Herring's research found provided a rich environment for mosquito breeding and subsequently malaria.[263] These conditions were responsible for diminished productivity in textile mills in the early 1900s.[264]

The passage of time obfuscated access to those few primary sources critical of Caraleigh, with reports of suffering, death, and pollution concealed beneath reports filled with plaudits. Watkins's work excludes Caraleigh's history of contamination of Raleigh's water system and events in the summer of 1894. At the time of Watkins study, many of the mill workers from the earliest era of Caraleigh's life, from the 1890s to the 1920s, simply were not present. The likelihood of stories from those earliest years of Caraleigh being passed down through oral tradition was further squelched during the eight years that Caraleigh was shuttered during the Great Depression, 1930 to 1938. When the mill reopened in 1938, Caraleigh's first generation of workers had likely "gotten jobs out of the textile mills or moved to other mills."[265] Daniel Watkins' gaps in research can be further attributed to the lack of early digitized newspapers not as widely accessible in 2000 as they have been made by 2019–2020. Digitization of newspapers started in the 1990s and early 2000s, thereby limiting accessibility for researchers to make robust use of newspapers from Caraleigh's early years.[266]

The 1991 "survey" of Caraleigh's historic land and housing development included a narrative that mentioned Walnut Creek and the "many streams that meandered through [the] pastural and sylvan lands" of Caraleigh. These natural resources, the survey continued, were "tapped as Raleigh's main supply of drinking water."[267] But tellingly, the survey recognized the political clout of the "former mayor of the city," Alfred Augustus Thompson, and how he utilized the "location of the creek to his advantage as president of the Caraleigh Mills."[268] Thompson and Caraleigh's investors had nothing to gain from remembering the dark chapters of water pollution at Caraleigh. However, the creation of "a historical product" must take into account the "context of its production and the context of its consumption."[269]

In the 1890s, news stories of the Walnut Creek's water catastrophes provided some publicly uttered criticisms. These pejorative utterances were soon overshadowed with lengthy newspaper columns trumpeting Caraleigh's successes, serving to suffocate any culpability on Caraleigh's responsibility in dumping acid into Raleigh's water supply, or sickening its own workers. Reports that cast doubt on the "wisdom of the investment" at Caraleigh were diluted in the rhetorical ocean of hyperbolic boosterism for Caraleigh. The *News and Observer* called Caraleigh "a credit to the South," an undertaking that was "propitious and destined to keep pace with the rapid development of the new industrial South."[270] The cause of the 1894 outbreak of sickness was disputed and blamed on the Water Works Pond.

Recollection of the troubles at Caraleigh in 1894 emerged in 1938 when the *News and Observer* published a paper that Dr. James R. Rogers read to the Raleigh Academy of Medicine.[271] Rogers, a Raleigh native born in 1866, practiced medicine in Wake County from 1893 until his 1940 death. In his obituary, Rogers was saluted as the city's oldest physician.[272] Rogers recalled in 1938 that Dr. Richard H. Lewis had "steered" him through dealing with the "very obstinate" epidemic of "typhoid fever" at "Caraleigh Hill."[273] Rogers treated Mrs. Sarah Jones and "her family of five or six children," all of whom were sick, in bed, with typhoid fever, except for Mrs. Jones who had what was described as "walking typhoid."[274] Prior to the full recovery of the Jones family, Rogers treated "about 90 other cases."[275] The origin of the fever, according to Rogers, was "an abundance of colon bacilii" found in "an old well on the hill at which all the employees secured their drinking water."[276] Dr. Rogers employed a "simple and inexpensive" remedy that "practically cured every case on Caraleigh Hill,"[277] that included supplying boiled water to every house in the community, twice a day.[278]

The publication in 2008 of K. Todd Johnson and Elizabeth Reid Murray's *Wake: Capital County of North Carolina, Vol. II, Reconstruction to 1920*, is an indispensable resource for the history of Raleigh and its county. Johnson and Murray's work included a paragraph that relied on Dr. Rogers's account of events at "Caraleigh Hill around the turn of the century," although Dr. Johnson did not mention the date of his experiences at Caraleigh.[279] Consistent with Johnson's 1938 article in the *News and Observer*, the 2008 history of Wake County did not mention the mill owners or the Water Works Pond, the latter of which was found legally culpable for Caraleigh's 1894 outbreak of sickness.[280]

A paragraph about the Caraleigh Phosphate and Fertilizer Works was included in *Wake: Capital County of North Carolina, Vol. II, Reconstruction to 1920*. The entry included the function of the factory, its connection to the cotton mills' founders, the fire, and its being "Wake's largest single enterprise" by 1916. However, when discussing the details of the fire, readers were assured that the "loss was covered by insurance."[281] Johnson and Murray's encyclopedic review of Wake County's history ends in 1920, but unmentioned were the fears expressed throughout Raleigh in the late 1890s and early 1900s that toxins from the 1892 fire at Caraleigh had contaminated Raleigh's drinking water.[282]

These oversights were the fruits of the industrial promoters whose publications overlooked numerous reports about Caraleigh's less than ideal location in the 1890s and, afterwards, failed to hold Caraleigh's founders accountable for any purported irresponsibility. The details of faded memories of sickness and death in and around Caraleigh Mills were conveniently forgotten with few exceptions. Raleigh's historical record of the environmental disasters at Caraleigh in the 1890s have remained only meekly mentioned and largely unexamined chapters in the history of south Raleigh.

But there were other health problems in Caraleigh besides typhoid and malaria.

Caraleigh's Pickle Eaters and Dirt Eaters

When the *Brooklyn Daily Eagle* newspaper in 1902 reported the research findings of Dr. Charles Wardwell Stiles, a zoologist with the Bureau of Animal Industry of the Agricultural Department, it earned irate responses from Raleigh textile owners. Stiles' research "among the poor whites or 'crackers' of the Southern States" led him to deduce that the newly discovered germ produced symptoms akin to "chronic malaria," sapping vitality and inspiring "abnormal cravings of appetite which have produced the 'dirt eaters' and 'pickle eaters' of unusually squalid sections of the South."[283]

Josephus Daniels considered Stiles' findings yet another example of "misinformation about the character and conditions of the operatives in Southern mills," the amount of which, argued Daniels, comprised more than he could "ever hope to correct."[284] The news of Stiles's assertions perturbed Caraleigh Mills secretary, F.O. Moring: "What is meant by it I cannot begin to imagine. The presence of 'pickle eaters' is entirely new to me though I have heard of 'dirt eaters.'"[285]

Moring's disbelief revealed that he was unaware of the scientific findings of Charles Wardell Stiles who had established in 1902 that the hookworm infection was a widespread phenomenon throughout all the Southern states.[286] People who ate soil as a part of their diet were referred to as "dirt eaters," as well as clay eaters, sandlappers, and pickle eaters. Research has concluded that the act of dirt eating was a consequence of iron deficiency, as well as being a practice thousands of years old, often passed down through generations.[287] Colonial and antebellum physicians had documented geophagy, the eating of soil, among suffering African American slaves on plantations that had caused extreme sluggishness and discolored pale skin. While it was thought that the habit of geophagy should be ended, some physicians believed that clay eating resulted from iron deficiency in the body.[288] Enslaved Africans likely brought hookworm to the region in the 1600s, carrying the eggs in feces. Once deposited in the South's soil, the hookworm eggs were able to thrive in the warm, sandy soils, eventually hatching into larvae. Exacerbating the spread of hookworm was the frequent lack of sanitary facilities that allowed the eggs to sit in an open environment permitting hatched larvae to burrow into bare human feet, creating the perception that was inherent to the South.[289]

Hookworm was ubiquitous at the Caraleigh settlement in 1904, as one visitor described it:

> The cases could be seen before the treatment began. Of all the listless, pathetic, don't care people on earth, they are the limit. The doctor made them all over again. When he finished with them there was such a renaissance, a rebirth of mind and body, that really they were not like the same folks at all. And yet, thymol and salts did it all.[290]

Stiles approached the Rockefeller Foundation in 1909 and convinced them to create the Rockefeller Sanitary Commission for the Eradication of Hookworm, which subsequently launched a "crusade to save the South" from hookworm.[291]

The head of North Carolina's state board of health, W.S. Rankin, asserted in 1909 that it was "hard to go into a crowd and not discover ... persons with this debilitating disease; one which saps alike the body and soul."[292] The description of the disease from the "Academy of Medicine" seemed an affront upon the South emanating from the North, once again.

> Not only does this disease lead to chronic anaemia but to a general enfeeblement of mental and physical activity and moral perversions. A young adult may appear to be only a child. The appetite is perverted and as a result those afflicted may become addicted to the habit of clay-eating, earth-eating, sand-eating, pickle-eating, and various other perversions of appetite. ...the proverbial laziness of the Southern "cracker" is shown to be caused by the affection.[293]

Walter H. Page, previously mentioned as a proponent of the New South philosophy, had also gained a reputation for being a critic of his home state's shortcomings. A "gadfly of philanthropy," Page urged the Rockefeller Foundation to bankroll a crusade to implement large scale actions to end hookworm in the former Confederacy that would be a "panacea for the South's ills," believing that "for the first time, the main cause of their long backwardness" was removable.[294]

The Rockefeller Foundation's initial surveys discovered that up to 43 percent of those Southerners surveyed were infected with hookworm, and in other areas rose to as much as ninety percent, or more.[295] The Rockefeller Foundation inspired "campaigns" to eradicate hookworm, beginning in 1909 and ending in 1914, with a plan of attack to educate and treat those sickened and eventually transfer these duties to state and local health entities to continue the work.[296] Rockefeller Foundation's anti-hookworm program did not extinguish hookworm from the South, and it continued to be a presence in the region; however, in the 1930s and 1940s, it was acknowledged that hookworm was noticeably diminished and less severe than it had been previous to the Rockefeller Foundation's arrival.[297]

5

Mill Patriarchy and Child Labor

Researchers of Southern mill workers found that the majority lived in small company-owned villages. Half of these villages by 1916 did not have running water, sewer connections, or electricity, but labor shortages and mill profits inspired a multitude of improvements to attract and retain workers.[1] In a pattern of attack and reprisal, northern criticisms of mill villages were responded to with hyperbolically defensive reports of their improvement.[2] Exaggerated amelioration of life in Caraleigh's village antedated the World War I years, though starting well after the calamities of 1892 and 1894.

Caraleigh sparsely invested in "village betterment" projects for its workers during its first two decades of existence.[3] The *Charlotte News* reported in 1915 that Caraleigh was slow to build up "a very attractive town" and had yet to provide those "things of amusement and convenience," but predicted improvements for workers via "welfare work" were to come as soon as practicable.[4]

In *Welfare Work in Mill Villages: The Story of Extra-Mill Activities in North Carolina*, Harriet Herring described welfare work as "all or any activities of a company for the comfort and well-being social, moral, intellectual, or physical of its employees, carried on by the efforts of the owner and manager personally, or by volunteer or specially employed workers."[5] The difference between social work and welfare was that in social work, there was no connection with the employer.[6]

Welfare work at Caraleigh commenced in 1915 with a "rousing meeting" celebrating the start of company sponsored programs for village enhancement activities.[7] It was with "stirring music by the village band of fourteen pieces" that Caraleigh's workers "got in line for village betterment." Lena Rivers Smith, the welfare agent for the North Carolina Cotton Manufacturers Association, commenced Caraleigh's welfare efforts, addressing the crowd with how she thought "the activities of the Caraleigh people ought to be directed."[8] Caraleigh's operatives in 1915 welcomed paternalism, and pledged allegiance to the same.

Around the turn of the 20th century, southern textile mill owners were accused of mistreating workers and were the subject of fierce criticism from northern reformers. These admonishments were countered in the 1925 article "Service in the Cotton Mills" by Gerald W. Johnson, who refuted the one-sided characterizations of Southern mill owners, who were described as criminals, eligible to be "hanged."[9] Johnson argued that cotton mill men hardly fit the mold, because they financed a broad array of welfare activities for their laborers, ranging from housing, social clubs, churches, drug stores, athletic teams, and more; pavements and community morals were "looked after with equal assiduity."[10] Johnson asserted that tradition informed Southern cotton mill managers' desire to avoid abuse of their workers, because the mill men retained "something of the old slaveholder's spirit" to look after "his people with the passionate energy that characterized the care of the ante-bellum aristocrat for his Negroes."[11] From Johnson's estimation, Northern investigators who came south and raised a "hideous outcry" about conditions in the mills and their villages ignored the welfare work conducted at the expense of the mill to benefit laborers.[12]

Caraleigh's owners exercised their influence over workers through many extra mill activities, the implementation of which controlled the village and its inhabitants according to a hierarchical framework of authority, adhering to a stratified racial system of dominant and subordinate races. This familiar antebellum pattern of traditional authority, otherwise known as paternalism, permitted Caraleigh's leaders and supporters to be "involved in the everyday activities of workers' lives" in a way that strengthened the "organic bonds between workers and employers."[13] Besides shaping attitudes about racial mores, another effect of the "heavy hand" of cotton mill paternalism was the prevention of "workers from mobilizing and protesting."[14] A petite example of how paternalism tried to undermine potential labor unrest at Caraleigh was displayed in an 1899 article in the *News and Observer*.

> The pic-nic [sic] given to the employees by the owners of the Caraleigh Cotton Mills yesterday was an event to be commended. Capital and labor have common interests, and it is pleasant and fitting to see this fact appreciated by both. The management of Caraleigh have done a graceful and pleasant thing. It is an example that other mill owners might wisely follow.[15]

Caraleigh's pattern of paternalism recruited mother nature to influence its workers and project an image of health and harmony to the public.[16] A sylvan setting was encouraged at Caraleigh, with management's providing for "prizes" for the "best kept yards," and with gardening activities, the latter of which was a cotton mill tradition rooted in the agricultural origins of textile mill workers.[17] Harriet Herring's scholarship found that of the 322 mills studied in the late 1920s, most mill housing provided garden space as means of providing food and adding space between houses.[18] But Caraleigh's emphasis on horticultural pursuits went beyond Herring's findings, where floriculture extended into propaganda, publicizing the village's healthy conditions.

Although Caraleigh's village was not "destitute of flowers," mill management further incentivized horticulture, promising prizes to village families who grew the "nicest gardens" and the "handsomest flowers."[19] In 1915, a yearly floral fair was planned and predicted to develop into "a part of the social life of the village."[20] The next year saw the "Caraleigh Flower and Garden Contest" that reportedly created much "rivalry among the residents" who vied for top prizes for best vegetable gardens and attractive flowers.[21] The event inspired the development of a "civic spirit" in the village where mill families took "great pride" in making their homes attractive "with all sorts of flowers."[22]

The 1916 floral event at Caraleigh—ostensibly about ornamental flowers, healthy gardens, and pretty homes—also showcased the mill village's "cleanliness and sanitation" to visiting dignitaries, W.H. Booker of the State Board of Health and "Dr. D.H. Hill," who had just stepped down as president of the "A. and M. College."[23] The village's sanitary conditions were not listed as a category for judgment in Caraleigh's "Flower and Garden Contest," but they were certainly considered. W.H. Booker commented that "it was a real pleasure I assure you to serve on your committee to judge gardens and sanitary conditions around the homes at Caraleigh."[24] Booker complimented the "good people" of Caraleigh, a "progressive" community "on the wide awake," with an "industrious spirit" where "practically all residences, particularly in the closely built up section," had "sanitary toilets of a type rated by government officials at nearly 100 per cent."[25]

In addition to flowers, trees played a role in Caraleigh's propaganda campaign. When Caraleigh's decision-makers decided to plant trees to provide shade around the mill, they avoided "the usual maple or elm" and instead chose pecan trees. Besides shade from the sun, the selection of pecan trees, Caraleigh's management reasoned, would give occasional nourishment, act as a management tool to control its "doffer boys," young males ages 12 to 14, and provide a modicum of moral instruction.[26]

> The doffer boys will be taught to protect and conserve thee trees and when the trees begin to bear [nuts] it is Mr. Briggs idea to furnish boxes to the boys in which to stow the nuts where they will be kept until the Christmas holidays and then every child in the village will be given a share of them as a holiday gift from the doffer boys. This is a new idea and one at which some of those who have had trouble in raising young trees around a village will be skeptical, but I believe it will work. My idea is that many a man can be kept out of a crooked path if some one trusts him.[27]

Besides pecans, Caraleigh's mill welfare provided age appropriate amusements for its child workers, or "doffer boys." As reported in 1915, Caraleigh's management converted the area around the mill into a "playground for the children," with swings, whirling and "acting poles, where the doffer boys found great amusement when they are not in the mill."[28] In the shadow of the mill, Caraleigh's playground was said to be "always alive with little children."[29] A similar story was parroted in the June 1916 *Industrial Development and Manufacturers' Record* about Caraleigh's welfare work that started about "a year or more ago" with the creation of a playground for its "young people" and that these comforts gave "the overseers" assurance, thereafter, that they were "never troubled as to the whereabouts of the doffer boys."[30]

Caraleigh's mill welfare programs extended to its sponsorship of athletics, in corroboration with statewide trends where mill support of athletics formed a significant part of mill welfare from the 1890s to the 1920s and were of "distinct community value," as great as education.[31] Caraleigh's community support rollout in 1915 included the creation of athletic activities for boys and girls. There were "basketball and tennis courts" for "larger girls," both of which were "expected to become a leading sport as there are many of the girls in the mill who belong to the teams in the city schools."[32] Mill sponsored baseball teams were ubiquitous in the South from the 1890s to the 1920s, eclipsing other mill supported athletics, because it was a primary means of recreation during the summer months, as well as a source of pride for cotton mill communities.

The degree to which mills supported their teams varied, but before 1915, company assistance given to baseball teams mostly meant financing the tools of the game: bats, balls, and possibly uniforms.[33] Despite baseball's popularity in Raleigh in 1892,

Caraleigh children in 1923 enjoying the company created playground (*Southern Textile Bulletin*, Vol. 25 [June 21, 1923], 152–153).

with "baseball fever" noticed among the city's youth, public discussion of a Caraleigh baseball team appeared to be a decade behind other nearby mills, with both the Raleigh Cotton Mills and Pilot Mills having baseball teams in 1896.[34] It was not until 1910 that the Caraleigh Mills team was reportedly a "strong team," defeating "their old time rivals—the Pilot Mills."[35] Caraleigh's team must have been intimidating in 1910, as the *News and Observer* thought that the team would "make all in this territory knuckle under their supremacy on the diamond."[36] And when the City Baseball League was formed in 1915, the Raleigh Playground Commission counted Caraleigh as one of its six teams, with players "between 14 and 18 years old."[37]

Up until the late 1920s, most mill baseball teams played on vacant fields owned by the mill. By 1929, many mills' involvement increased with the construction of fenced-in baseball diamonds with grandstands, charging admission fees to watch games.[38] Some mills even hired workers based on their ability to play the sport. Caraleigh's initial lack of support for a baseball team was because of its lack of "a suitable piece of land for a baseball park,"[39] but by 1910, Caraleigh had a baseball team that played their games on a nearby field. When the owners disallowed the children from playing on this field, Caraleigh "leased a place and a baseball park has been started for the young men."[40]

Mill-sponsored musical bands were an important part of many mill communities, although they were far fewer in number and less often worker initiated when compared to baseball teams.[41] While the cost of instruments and worker mobility often undermined the sustainability of most mill bands, Caraleigh's band lived a long life, becoming a point of pride and entertainment. Caraleigh resident Frank Farlow recalled in 2000 that the "splendid Caraleigh Band" gained a reputation for making many mundane occasions more pleasant than they otherwise would have been.[42] Recognized as a success, the Caraleigh band was valued as an essential element of the mill's identity that contributed to the community's morale.

Caraleigh's management provided the band's support for decades, which was called upon to play at events both large and small: auctions, political rallies—for Democrats and Republicans—dances, barbecues, tax rallies to support public schools, and baseball games.[43] Mill workers in 1907 of the "Caraleigh Mills

Silverine Band," comprised of "eighteen to twenty mill operatives," gave the "officers of the mill" a "serenade" in demonstration of their appreciation for new uniforms and instruments.[44] The "Caraleigh Society Hall" filled to capacity when political candidates spoke to the people of Caraleigh, with the assistance of their "excellent brass band...."[45]

Caraleigh's band celebrated statewide temperance victories. In 1907, Caraleigh's band played "stirring and patriotic music" at the forefront of a Raleigh procession of "hundreds of voters," who bore "banners of prohibition and torches" as they "surged through the streets shouting the glad news that King Alcohol had been vanquished" in the Capital City.[46] To mark the end of the First World War, Caraleigh's band marched in Raleigh's victory parade and performed to an audience of 75,000 citizens, "from homes both humble and palatial," who "expressed admiration" for the state's returning "warriors" with "lusty yells, frenzied waving of hats, and vigorous handclapping."[47]

Company-provided housing for mill workers was of paramount importance when it came to mill welfare programs. To naysayers, southern textile mills thought that workers' housing settlements paralleled a system akin to medieval feudalism, whereby the mill owners possessed "near absolute power as lords of the manor" in the villages.[48] In 1919, an article in the *Southern Textile Bulletin* detailed conditions for Caraleigh's workers as "made pleasant" through management's providing its workers "more than a square deal," characterizing Caraleigh as having enjoyed "continually growing and improving conditions in the plant and in the village."[49] Caraleigh's population was "something like 600," with the company having built 125 houses with fifty of them owned by these "thrifty people."[50]

All of the houses were "well built," and electrified, with some made of wood "frame, others of brick," with water that was supplied to all homes via "deep wells, thus insuring its purity and all have septic toilets."[51] Pictures displayed Caraleigh residents "civic pride" and care of their cottages, streets, pavements, and gardens that were "kept in a neat sanitary manner."[52] A community house—for social club meetings, social affairs, and public meetings—was constructed at company expense to carry out welfare work. In front of the mill, a playground for the children was constructed with swings and see-saws. In the back of the mill, the company constructed a

Salvation Army Children's Band Instruction at Caraleigh, August 1937 (used with permission of the *News and Observer* [Raleigh] and the State Archives of North Carolina).

bath house with tubs, baths, hot and cold showers, and dressing rooms: all free of charge for Caraleigh employees.[53] The push to ameliorate living and working conditions at Caraleigh included rewarding mill-approved, positive behaviors. For example, in 1919, North Carolina's "Bureau of Infant Hygiene of the State Board of Health" taught the public about the "dangers of flies" and encouraged children to wage war on flies.[54] In this contest, two "pupils of the Caraleigh School each won $1.50 for leading in the fly swatting contest in Wake County."[55]

Harriet Herring visited Caraleigh Mills in the late 1920s and interviewed its superintendent, who had "for many years personally carried on something of a health and sanitation campaign."[56] Caraleigh's appearance made a favorable impression upon Herring.

> Mr. Briggs could give me no estimate on the village cost, but it must be somewhat larger than ordinary because of the amount of sanitary work they do. It is the first village I ever saw that had trash cans on the street—neat galvanized cans and not a one I saw was overflowing, nor had any trash or garbage or rubbish around it showing they are emptied often. His sanitary force serves all the houses in the village whether they are mill owned or not—for garbage, toilet, etc.[57]

When it came to the health of its employees, Caraleigh's leadership had ample motive to forget about its past shortcomings. Even prior to the nation's entry into the First World War in 1917, which exacerbated an existing labor shortage in North Carolina, the continued creation of new textile mills inspired competition among mills to attract and keep operatives.[58] With the expansion of textile mills and thousands of potential employees off to serve in military uniform, mill owners realized that more than just adequate wages were needed to attract and employ potential mill workers. To help address labor deficiencies, mill managers engaged in "welfare work."[59]

Herring found in 1925 that there were ten mills in the state that permitted its operatives to participate in Metropolitan Life Insurance Company's program, which provided a full-time nurse. Caraleigh was one of the ten that enlisted a "Metropolitan nurse" to attend to mill workers' healthcare.[60] Caraleigh's experience corroborates Jennings Rhyne's conclusion that the differences among mill villages incentivized and attracted mill families, thus galvanizing mills to engage in "welfare work."[61]

While textile mills started to provide health care for workers in the early years of the 20th century, hospitals and physicians still were not readily accessible and rules regarding illness or disability were less than sensitive. In 1999, Caraleigh elderly residents Faye Senter and her sister Ruth Wilkins recalled that "back then, all the babies were born at home. Grandma would always go to the daughters…" to oversee the delivery of newborns.[62] Another resident, Hannah Messer, posited that "when women worked in the mill, they had to come home to nurse the babies. So the mill would let them off long enough to come home and feed the babies. Then, they'd go back to work."[63]

In many textile communities, the company employed a community worker to organize and promote a broad range of activities to buttress community morale, increase solidarity, and improve overall quality of life.[64] Community workers' activities were broad in scope and ranged from visiting ill workers, organizing theatrical plays, or starting a sewing class for children. Women, unwed mothers, and girls most often took advantage of recreational and educational club initiatives. Boys tended to seek out athletic coaches or the bandmaster and other male-led activities organized by their fraternal order, which in Caraleigh was the Junior Order of United American Mechanics (Jr. O.U.A.M.).[65] Harriet Herring's discussions with Caraleigh's manager in the 1920s included Caraleigh's experience with its community worker:

> She had women's clubs, girls' clubs, recreation, visited families especially sick to give instructions as to household problems, carried on vigorous health campaigns which Mr. Briggs had done to some extent before but made better headway now that he had someone to head it up. They used a cottage fitted up for work, in part of which she had a little model housekeeping arrangement.[66]

In 1921, the *Greensboro Daily News* reported, and favorably reviewed, Caraleigh's first community fair that the Woman's Club organized and conducted in the community hall. Under the direction of Caraleigh's community worker, the fair exhibited patchwork quilts, gardening, sewing, cooking, knitted goods, and handmade dolls.[67] One "very attractive booth" showed each stage of mill production that started with raw cotton, proceeded through the processes of dyeing, spinning, weaving, and ending with finished cloth. The "thrifty housewives" were noted to be "mighty good cooks," with biscuits, muffins, cakes, and candies. And despite a challenging spell of "heat and water famine" that summer, "proudly displayed" glass jars packed with fruits and vegetables revealed the wherewithal of Caraleigh's women. Caraleigh's Woman's Club consisted of about 100 women who held monthly meetings to plan programs and listen to invited speakers. Hailed as a "decided success," the stated objective of the 1921 fair was to put "new life and zest" into the mill village with their first, but not the last, "big constructive" venture.[68]

Researchers of textile mills have found that a choice of language that emphasized familial relationships among textile employees indicated systemic paternalism, a linguistic touchstone denoting fatherly oversight within a mill community. The family metaphor often used in the mill village pointed to paternalistic management practices that provided for workers' needs, left workers dependent, and concomitantly muted their self-autonomy.[69] Caraleigh's mill-centered community developed a familial linguistic pattern that corroborated the scholarship of Jacquelyn Down Hall who recognized the theme of family used during hundreds of oral interviews of southern cotton mill workers.[70] Daniel Watkins' interviews of Caraleigh residents from 1995 to 2000 found a pattern of familial language used when Caraleigh residents described themselves and their fellow mill village inhabitants.[71] When speaking about older people they knew, Caraleigh residents referred to them as "aunt" or "uncle," and if one achieved notoriety, as was the case with Rommey Glover, one of the state's first highway patrolmen in 1929, he was described as a one of "Caraleigh's sons."[72]

Caraleigh Baptist Church

Churches were the most common form of welfare activity in North Carolina cotton mills,[73] as the church was a centerpiece for many mill-sponsored social activities and moral instruction. Caraleigh's church experience corroborated the mill experience in the rest of the South, where religion permeated cotton mills and their villages from the start.[74]

Organized religion at Caraleigh began with the First Presbyterian Church that organized a "Sabbath School" on Caraleigh Mills grounds in 1892 and subsequently held revivals that lasted weeks. But the Baptist denomination left a more lasting imprint on the village, with[75] John T. Pullen organizing "cottage prayer services" that later developed into the Caraleigh Baptist Church, born on June 2, 1904.[76]

Besides mill owners, three other noteworthy Raleighites were responsible for growing the "missionary station at Caraleigh Mills" to the Caraleigh Baptist Church.[77] Caraleigh church's "Founding Fathers" included Needham B. Broughton, the 1902 president of the North Carolina Anti-Saloon League and a one term state senator; his nephew, John M. Broughton, the "first native of Raleigh elected Governor of North Carolina in 1940"; John T. Pullen, banker, author, and philanthropist, who was a deacon at the nearby Fayetteville Street Baptist Church.[78] Pullen financed the church building's construction, after the president of Caraleigh Mills, A.A. Thompson, provided the land.[79] Church lore documented the conversation in its history: "As the little mission grew, a need developed for a building. Pullen declared, 'Get me the land and I'll get you the building.' Alf. Thompson, President of the mill company heard of the proposal. His company furnished the lot, and Pullen was as good as his word; he furnished the building."[80] The initial church building was located on Park Avenue, later renamed Gilbert Street, and in 1924, a new church sanctuary was constructed on Green Street and still used in 2020.[81] From 1904 to 1943, the church held one Sunday evening service and struggled to stay open because of a lack of funds, partly because of the "low wages of its members."[82] Nevertheless, the church paid for its own expenses, and obtained funds for a local orphanage, and funds to support home, state, and foreign "missions."[83]

Christian religious beliefs undergirded cohesive relationships between mill workers and their employer. The Caraleigh Mills company permitted church members to donate money to the Caraleigh Baptist Church directly through payroll deduction.[84] By the strengthening of religious worship, mill owners developed a nexus for reinforcing the ideology of hard work and "clean living."[85] Caraleigh Baptist Church's "eavesdropping committee" acted to monitor immoral behavior, with punishment for wayward members that included expulsion from "fellowship in the church body."[86] In July 1905, one member was expelled from the church for an unnamed infraction, but public repentance, "asking the church to forgive him," resulted in restoration of church fellowship.[87] In another instance, one congregant was cited for use of "intoxicating" drink, another for the use of "profane language," and a "sister in the church was dismissed for admitting that she had been dancing."[88] Absence of any male church member from "two consecutive church conferences" would initiate an "investigation as to why" and a visit from "the deacons" to confront the recalcitrant.[89]

Caraleigh's Baptist church supported conservative efforts since its start, a trend that continued for decades: In 1948, the church asked county officials to cease the issuance of licenses to sell alcoholic beverages[90]; in 1956, they opposed, on constitutional grounds, a proposal from the Roman Catholic Church that they operate a new county hospital then under construction[91]; in 1957, Caraleigh joined other churches to oppose the "permitting of dancing in Baptist Colleges," voting to disallow donations to colleges that allowed dancing, "especially Meredith College and Wake Forest

College!";[92] in 1959, the church protested a bill in the North Carolina Legislature that would have legalized gambling. The early decades of the church, especially during the 1940s to the 1960s, saw the "church filled with many families whose children married and stayed within the church...." But by the 1980s, young people left without replacement.[93] The church's symbiotic relationship with the mill and its "operatives" largely ended when the mill closed in 1930, at the outset of the Great Depression. Nevertheless, Caraleigh's Baptist church continued to serve its parishioners in the 21st century and has remained an important part of the community.

Junior Order of United American Mechanics

Besides Caraleigh's Baptist church, the Junior Order of United American Mechanics (Jr. O.U.A.M.) was one of the "focus points in the community's life."[94] The Caraleigh branch of the "Junior Order" was instituted in 1903 and named the Walnut Creek Council No. 55, using a frame building as it headquarters on the 200 block of Maywood Avenue.[95] Despite being a northern organization, the Junior Order's ideology aligned with the values of Caraleigh's leaders.[96] Admittance to the Junior Order was available to white, native-born American men who professed "a belief in a Supreme Being," were opposed to a union of church and state and were "not engaged in liquor traffic."[97] North Carolina's branch of the Jr. O.U.A.M. started in 1890 and by 1905 possessed "the second largest membership of any secret order in the state."[98]

Membership in the Junior Order was a selective process that reflected mill hierarchy, with membership usually consisting of skilled workers, foremen, and managers. Inclusion enhanced the social standing and future job prospects in the mill.[99] The Order of United American Mechanics was born in Philadelphia in 1853, and it formed a junior organization as a way to prepare young applicants before they joined the main organization.[100] In 1885, the Jr. O.U.A.M. became its own "independent, secret, native American, patriotic, beneficiary" organization, retaining most of the characteristics of its original parent order, including its guiding philosophy, symbols, and system of organizational governance.[101] As its own organization, no longer a preparatory organization for a parent organization, the Jr. O.U.A.M.'s use of the word "Junior" no longer bore reference to the ages of members and the word "Mechanics" no longer referred to the occupations of its membership. Nevertheless, the organizational goals remained unchanged from its original founding:

> To maintain and promote the interest of Americans and shield them from the depression effect of foreign competition; to assist Americans in obtaining employment; to encourage Americans in business; to establish a sick and funeral fund; to maintain a public school system of the United States of America, to prevent sectarian interference therewith, and uphold the reading of the Bible therein.[102]

With the support of the state and influential Raleigh citizens, the Jr. O.U.A.M. in Caraleigh also influenced the minds of the village's children. May 10, 1904, state dignitaries and prominent members of Raleigh society participated in ceremonies honoring the village's branch of the Junior Order and Caraleigh's school.[103]

Josephus Daniels, editor of Raleigh's *News and Observer*, presented the Bible to Caraleigh's school, and gave a speech that buttressed the values of the

Junior Order. Daniels emphasized the importance of "reading the Bible in public schools," maintaining that "every wise statute of government was based on the Bible" and that the Bible's "law was superior to civil law." For these reasons, Daniels "wished" that the Bible "was read in every school in North Carolina."[104] Following Daniels, the superintendent of Raleigh's city public schools, E.P. Moses, reiterated Daniels' emphasis of the Bible's place in public schools, adding an indirect reference to the Civil War, with the placement of the "flag of this country ... on the eve of Memorial Day ... had cemented and united the country and we were now living under one flag."

B.R. Lacy, North Carolina's state treasurer, spoke to the gathered audience and described the Junior Order as "the noblest and truest of any organization" that stood for education and patriotism, with its "foundation stone the Christian religion."[105] Also present was A.A. Thompson, president of Caraleigh Mills, who presented the American flag to the new school and gave a short speech that extolled the ideals of patriotism, dutiful morality, and a fastidiousness work ethic: "...we must first make ourselves worthy of the flag ... each and every one was each day weaving a flag. While weaving a flag, if we should put in a bad piece, like they do in the mills, we pull it out." Continuing, Thompson rhetorically asked, "How many stars do you propose to put into the flag?" asserting that the flag was the "glory of the nation."[106]

In the presentation of a "beautiful flag and Bible, handsomely bound" to commemorate the school's opening, J.Y. Joyner, the superintendent of North Carolina Public Schools, "delivered a magnificent address" where he praised the Junior League's emphasis on education.[107] When Joyner finished speaking, A.A. Thompson arose and declared that "the children of Caraleigh now had an opportunity to secure an education" and pledged "the Caraleigh Company would" ensure its continued support for the education of its children.[108] The confluence of dignitaries from Raleigh, the state, and the Caraleigh Company made clear the Junior Order's role as an extension of the mill's authority to the Caraleigh Community.[109]

The Junior Order remained "popular" in Caraleigh for decades thereafter, maintaining its tradition of supporting education that continued after the mill's closure in 1930. Caraleigh resident Doris Joyner recalled that she walked each day two miles to school and back, never missing a day or being late for class and "the Junior Order gave us a gold pen for not missing a day. They were really behind education."[110] The Walnut Creek Junior Order No. 55 also "supported two orphanages for the children of its members." And when a Caraleigh employee "was killed by a car walking to work at the Caraleigh Mill on Maywood Avenue," the Junior Order ensured that the employee's children were placed in an orphanage.[111]

Membership dues for the Junior Order were affordable for the most skilled workers and management. Mill village leaders' participation in the Junior Order yielded a tacit improvement of one's standing.[112] The hierarchy within textile mills was transparent and pronounced with membership in the Junior Order: "weavers ... held themselves above one who spins; a man who fixed looms, above a card hand; and so on." Mill families who kept up appearances, that is "self-respecting and decent and clean," were appraised to be of a "higher standard" than those who were content to live on a "backstreet" or "way down the end of the row ... and allow the house and children and premises to remain dirty."[113]

Education at Caraleigh

Some textile industry experts maintained in the early 1900s that an education was largely unnecessary to become a cotton mill operative, but an operative with a trained mind could be a more efficient worker. This sentiment was reflected in Raleigh schools opening day attendance report showing both mill villages of Pilot Mills and Caraleigh with the lowest number of students attending in either the white or "colored schools" in 1907.[114] Despite the mixed messaging about education, many mills provided schools for the more "ambitious boys and girls" who wished to pursue their studies further.[115]

While North Carolina's school crusade from 1901 to 1910 provided an arena for Progressive Era Southern women to participate during an age of growing activism and assertiveness, men led Caraleigh's educational effort.[116] The initial effort at education at Caraleigh was with John T. Pullen's establishment of a night school in 1897.[117] And two years later, "the school committee decided yesterday to give Raleigh township three additional schools" one of which included "primary schools for white children ... located at Caraleigh"[118]

A permanent school at Caraleigh operated from 1903 to 1980. In 1924 a new school building at Caraleigh was built and dedicated to Miss Eliza Pool.[119] Pool was a distinguished educator and was named North Carolina's most outstanding teacher in 1926, representing North Carolina at the Philadelphia Sesquicentennial Celebration.[120] The Eliza Pool Park, dedicated in 1996, was where the Eliza Pool School stood from 1924 to 1980.[121] The village of Caraleigh was not officially annexed into the City of Raleigh until December 31, 1957, but Caraleigh's school was always part of the Raleigh school system.[122]

The 1903 founding of the school at Caraleigh provided another example of mill paternalism that paralleled the Baptist church and the Junior Order at Caraleigh. Just as the Caraleigh Mills Company provided land for the Caraleigh Baptist Church, they also contributed a rent-free building that contained three rooms for a school of five grades in 1903. In 1904, Caraleigh Mills donated land, as well as $500 for a school building, provided that it obtain a commitment from the School Board of Raleigh Township to provide matching funds. In addition to the money and land, Caraleigh gave the school a piano. The new 1904 school building, known to residents as the "Green School," stood on the corner of South Saunders Street and Gilbert Street, the location where the Caraleigh Furniture would later occupy.[123]

In April of 1908, State School Superintendent James Y. Joyner, newspaper editor Josephus Daniels, and City School Superintendent F.M. Harper, spoke at an education rally at Caraleigh, hoping to inspire support for a school tax.[124] Despite the efforts of the noteworthy speakers, most mill workers at Caraleigh were less than enthusiastic about educating their children in the first decade of the new century. The employees of Caraleigh Mills, and incidentally, Pilot Mills, gave the fewest votes in support of taxes for schools, and they "actually cast more votes against the school tax."[125]

The city initially provided "horse-and-buggy transportation" for teachers to the school but, in 1915, the school later upgraded teacher transportation from Raleigh to Caraleigh with a Model T Ford.[126] In 1916–17, an additional room was provided for the fifth grade, and when pupils completed the fifth grade, they were sent to the

Centennial School for the sixth and seventh grades; high school education was provided on West Morgan Street.[127]

Despite the attention that was sometimes given to Caraleigh's school children in 1912, the school suffered from lack of funding. The April 3, 1922, the *News and Observer* featured Caraleigh in an article about a county-wide school bond vote to improve township schools. The Caraleigh's school, which had been described in 1917 as a "modern graded school," was five years later described as needing improvement[128]:

> The Caraleigh School houses 119 students in three poorly equipped and exceedingly uncomfortable rooms. The building is heated by stoves that smoke constantly. The children near the stoves are too hot and those near the windows were too cold. An increase in enrollment of thirty-five percent in ten years indicates the popularity of the school. Unlike the Pilot Mill School, this one [the Caraleigh School] is owned by the Township.[129]

One Caraleigh resident, Doris Joyner, recalled the Green Street school in a 1999 interview: "Yeah, I went through the fifth grade down there. It was only through the fifth year. It was wonderful. It had big rooms with a big pot-bellied stove to heat and a water cooler to get water from—three rooms, two rooms to start with and another room added."[130] Following completion of the fifth grade, Caraleigh students had to walk to school in Raleigh each day—two miles to school and two miles back. Joyner attended the Centennial School in Raleigh on the corner of South Street and Fayetteville Street, for sixth and seventh grade, and eighth grade at Raleigh High School at the corner of Salisbury Street and Morgan Street. Joyner recollected that she and her brother had "never missed a day and was not tardy." For this, the Junior Order awarded both with a gold pen in recognition.[131]

Caraleigh students transferred to the Hugh Morson High School in Raleigh, named for a longtime educational leader in 1924 but not opened until 1925.[132] Caraleigh children who made the transition from the school in Caraleigh to Raleigh schools found it difficult for a number of reasons. Of course, the walk was a daily ritual that was recalled with little fondness. Caraleigh resident Joyce Phipps started high school in 1930 and when asked how she got there, she vigorously replied: "Walked! Walked! ... We walked fast." The pedestrian journey to school, Phipps remembered, started at 7:15 in the morning took 30 to 45 minutes, to ensure punctual arrival for the start of class at 8:30 a.m. Another resident reminisced that weather rarely changed this school routine: "Winter time, snow whatever, that was the way they got to school—walking."[133]

Child Labor

Similar to other textile plants in the state, Caraleigh employed children in their mill and saw little need to hide it. The July 2, 1899, *News and Observer* described Caraleigh's pay scale.

> This mill gives daily employment to 250 people, and its pay roll amounts to between $1200 and $1500 a week. The employees receive from $1.50 (children) to $9 a week. The foreman—there are three in the mill—get $18 a week. Many young girls earn $6, $7, $8 a week.[134]

5. Mill Patriarchy and Child Labor

North Carolina's transition from farm to industry in the late 1800s and early 1900s amounted to a "transfer of families instead of by individuals from the county to the town."[135] The paradigm shift was a "radical change" whereby families had to "learn how to live in towns and to adapt themselves to their surroundings."[136] Since children worked on farms, it was reasoned, they were also expected to work in the mills. Historian Holland Thompson maintained that the idea of disallowing children to work developed only when a community "ceases to think in terms of agriculture."[137] In the nascent industrial years for the state, child labor grew into an ethical and social "problem."[138] Opponents of child labor laws believed that legislative restrictions would hamper industry and "turn back the tide of progress ... throw children into idleness" and leave them to "play on the streets and become demoralized."[139]

For example, in 1910, there were more than 107,000 tenant and share cropping farmers, most of whom were white, which represented 42.3 percent of all farmers. This was more than twice the amount in 1880.[140] For these farmers, as well as for owner-operator agrarians who were in persistent peril of economic failure and loss of land, the option of employment as a wage-earning textile mill worker offered some hope of accumulating wealth of some sort, rather than bankruptcy. The low wages, long hours, and unregulated use of female and child labor in the mills permitted the textile capitalists to earn handsome profits from the 1890s to the 1920s.[141] North Carolina, in the late 1800s and early 1900s, was both "the leading textile state" and as where "the proletarianization of white farmers and their families was most extensive."[142] This changing agrarian situation in the state provided a rich source of wage earning, non–farm owning, laborers whose only possession of significant material value was the pay earned from their labor.

W.J. Cash commented that wages in mills were termed a "family wage" because low wages necessitated work from "every member of a family," father and mother, and "the woman who was about to become a mother," as well as children. State newspapers in 1900 reported that "the evil of employing young children" in North Carolina's cotton mills was "generally recognized," but that sole blame did not belong to the mill owners; it would be a "gross injustice," one newspaper argued, to "denounce them for its presence," for there were many skilled mill workers who refused work "unless their children were also employed."[143] Cash admitted that if one asked any person in "a Southern mill town today" about working in the mills, "you are likely to hear a tale of their having gone into the mills so young that they had to carry about boxes on which to climb in order to reach the spindles they tended. At six, at seven, at eight years, by ten at the latest, the little boys and girls of the mill families went regularly to work."[144]

By 1915, the cotton mill became an essential component of North Carolina: "The state is North Carolina, and 'our industry' is the cotton mill."[145] The "cheap labor advantage" was at the heart of southern cotton mill profits.

Wanted Immediately!
20 GIRLS
For the Spinning Department
APPLY AT THE
CARALEIGH MILLS.

Caraleigh advertisement (*Raleigh Times*, April 5, 1898).

So, when anti–child labor advocates scolded North Carolina for its allowance for wide use of child labor, critics were met with stiff resistance from mill owners, workers, and from the families who worked in the mills.[146] Child labor laws were passed in several states by 1907, but in other states, such as Alabama, North Carolina, South Carolina, and Virginia, anti–child labor advocates recognized that improvement was needed, because cotton mills "employed the greatest number of children" and thereby represented the "greatest hazard to the growth and development of future generations."[147] In 1906, historian Holland Thompson admitted that an accurate count of the number of children who worked in North Carolina's textile mills was "difficult to ascertain," but that regardless of statistics, in person observation "shows extensive employment of children."[148]

A 1918 report about "Child Labor in North Carolina" stated that compulsory education laws required children to attend school for four months but provided no "satisfactory machinery for enforcement," with enforcement throughout the state left to just one man. On paper at least, the state's child labor laws protected children from factory work until the "ripe old age of 12."[149] Caraleigh Mills utilized child laborers who were aged 10 to 12.[150] Caraleigh resident Nannie Mae Hussey Smith was interviewed in 1999 and stated that her mother, born in 1900, started in the mill when she was 11 years old and was so short that she "stood on a box to work at the mill."[151] The *Raleigh Times* published a letter to Santa Claus from a child working "in the mill" on December 24, 1909, stated that he was a "smart little boy" wanting "a big drum and candy and nuts and fruit."[152] The *News and Observer* reported in 1919 that a "10 year old employe [sic] of the mill" had been arrested for theft.[153]

In 1899, a proposed law to ban child labor in Georgia provoked public discussion and comparison between labor practices in Georgia and North Carolina.[154] One investigator, "Mrs. Richard A. Ellis," had inspected mills in both states and believed that conditions for mill workers were "much better in North Carolina than in Georgia."[155] In 1899, Mrs. Ellis visited 20 or more mills in the Carolinas, including Caraleigh, where she found a level of "comfort, intelligence, and good moral standards" among mill workers that was wholly absent in Georgia. Ellis thought that a mill in Durham, managed by W.A. Erwin, was the "best managed mill."

On the topic of child labor, Ellis summed up Erwin's labor practices: "When a man comes with his family and asks for employment ... he [Erwin] will employ him and the robust children who are over age 12 at once, and that if the younger ones have learned to read and write by the time they are 12 (or the delicate ones 14) he [Erwin] will also employ them." Erwin "did not allow children under 12 years of age in the mill," preferring instead that they "go to school" and become "intelligent operatives" and "virtuous citizens." A voice in agreement with Erwin's philosophy of child labor was "Mr. Moring, of Caraleigh Mills" who was "quoted as entertaining the same sentiments."[156] Despite Moring's alleged indifference for child labor, Caraleigh Mills employed children, with the younger children working as "Spinners and Doffers" and "girls and boys over sixteen" trained to "learn cotton mill work."[157]

A child labor investigator who visited Caraleigh was Irene Ashby, "a young English girl of social standing," who inspected Southern cotton mills from 1900 to 1901 for the American Federation of Labor. Ashby intended to draw attention to the abhorrent conditions in the mills and inspire legislation that would restrict the employment of children.[158] Ashby toured two dozen cotton mills and deduced that the evils of child labor in southern cotton mills were not the fault of Southern manufacturers, but rather on "the Northern capitalist."[159] Ashby pointed out that child labor was banned in the North but pursued by them for the profits that "cheap labor" would yield for their investments in southern textile mills.

Prior to the opening of Caraleigh, southern cotton mill operations were noted for their high rates of return to investors. In 1882, investors earned anywhere from 22 percent to 75 percent in profits; however, this evidence highlights that the lackluster pay of mill workers were what made the investor's profits possible and ensured that workers did not partake in this "profitable venture."[160] In her fierce condemnation of Southern child labor practices around the turn of the century, Irene Ashby appealed to Southern racism hoping to convince investors to "take a determined stand against child labor" citing their de facto embrace of what she considered white slavery.[161]

> While the children of poor whites are working the factories poor negro children are attending schools that millions of northern capital are expending annually to maintain, and this, when an educational qualification will soon be required of voters. The only possible way to secure the supremacy of whites is to assure the education of whites.[162]

Accusations that the profits of cotton mills came off the backs of children were dismissed in North Carolina, because "children under 12 years of age" were, it was argued, not employed. But at Caraleigh, there was an age-based pay differential where younger workers were paid ten cents a day, compared to older workers who earned approximately 12 to 13 dollars a week.[163]

Textile industry publications dismissed the alleged exploitation of child workers in Southern cotton mills. The *Manufacturers Record* in a 1916 response to critics argued that the mills were fast improving, had made "wonderful strides" within the past few years, but that there were a few mills that were "not in step with the times." It was these few "isolated" mills that "sensational writers" chose to unfairly represent "in pictures that have gone into public print purporting to be typical of Southern mill conditions."[164]

A 1918 National Child Labor Committee (NCLC) report stated that North Carolina possessed an "absence of adequate child labor legislation," with little enforcement of any such existing laws. For example, state law protected "children to the ripe age of 12" and entrusted the "inspection of manufacturing establishments and prosecutions for violations to one man—in a state which, in 1910, employed 9,303 children under 16 in 281 cotton mills alone!"[165] Acting in loco parentis, Southern cotton mill owners were viewed as workers' caretakers, as their social benefactors who employed a form of paternalism that received growing condemnation as each year passed in the early decades of the 1900s. Historian George B. Tindall captured this phenomenon in his magnum opus, *The Emergence of the New South*:

> From the beginning of the century, the mills had come under a siege of criticism that developed an image of the mill baron as a greedy and dictatorial exploiter of women and children. During the 1920s, another cycle of criticism focused upon the theme of a mill village isolation that threatened to develop an [sic] hereditary helot class.[166]

Despite its assertions otherwise, the state's insincerity in enforcing child labor laws was clear. North Carolina officials resented outside groups from "interfering" with the state's cotton mill industry and asked for the "names and addresses of [the] various children of whom Mr. Hine had spoken...."[167] The state's welfare committee's intransigence towards the NCLC's findings was in line with "North Carolina cotton-mill men in defending their right to manage their own affairs." The NCLC recognized the Tarheel State's antagonism toward eliminating child labor, saying it was "odd the state stands alone among all textile states in the country as having no state inspector to aid the Manufacturers' Association in enforcing the law," and that while state law had already set a maximum age of workers at 13, North Carolina's 1910 census indicated 4,003 children working in the mills who were under 14. Of all the states, North Carolina had the highest number of children working under age 14, despite being the only Southern state with "an age limit higher than twelve."[168]

Lewis Hine was a New York City school teacher who became an investigative reporter for the National Child Labor Committee.[169] In the first two decades of the 20th century, Hine employed photography to document working conditions of child laborers.[170] In 1915, Hine accessed 16 North Carolina cotton mills—none of which were Caraleigh—and found more than 50 children that he judged to be from 10 to 12 years old, and in addition to these, 23 children told him their ages as follows: seven workers under ten years of age; three of 10 years of age; six of 11 years of age; and seven of 12 years of age.[171] Hine's work confirmed the open secret that child labor was used in the state, but the phenomenon was controversial in 1915 and the subject of much scrutiny. While there has been no indication that Lewis Hine ever visited Caraleigh Mills, Hine's photographs of child labor have been prominently displayed throughout the halls of Caraleigh Mills, forcing inhabitants of "the mill" to visually confront the sordid history of child labor in the state.[172]

The hallways at the Historic Caraleigh Mills condominium complex are lined with images of the textile mill and cotton mill workers (photograph by the author).

6

World War I to the 1920s

World War I was a cataclysmic event with global effects that started in Europe in 1914 and ended in 1918. While the United States did not officially join in combat operations until 1917, the conflict's effects were felt economically before America's entry and afterward. For much of the South, especially Caraleigh, cotton was central to its economic well-being. The war initially disrupted the global cotton trade and prices nosedived below ten cents a pound. A year later, cotton prices noticeably started to rise again, and eventually cotton reached 30 cents a pound. Ultimately, World War I stimulated the economy of the Southern states.[1] The best years for cotton were from 1917 to 1919, when cotton prices averaged 27 cents a pound.[2]

Production operations ran day and night during the war at Caraleigh Mills and its Phosphate plant.[3] Sizeable advertisements in the *News and Observer* were placed by those wishing to purchase Caraleigh stocks, and stock traders reported that Caraleigh Mills stock were "as good as you can get."[4] Caraleigh had surplus profits to help the war effort and engage in extra mill improvements that would attract workers and improve their standard of living, notably with the company's installation of a "sewer system" to provide sanitary septic sewage outfits for operatives' residences in 1916.[5]

There were a few Caraleigh residents who served in uniform during World War I. One was Robert M. Cook and another, Private Sam Williams, who died in 1934 and was buried in Bunker Hill Cemetery, the company's graveyard.[6] Caraleigh's support for the conflict was most visible in its participation in Liberty Bond drives and other indirect activities to bolster the Allied cause of defeating the Central Powers.[7] Caraleigh's village and mill also showed support via the "purchase of War Savings Stamps," Liberty Bond drives, and food conservation activities.[8] When the Fourth Liberty Loan drive to support World War I proclaimed that it had reached its $500,000 goal, it noted that $20,000, the second largest contribution, came from the Caraleigh Fertilizer and Phosphate Works.[9]

When President Woodrow Wilson pledged United States' support of the Allied effort in April 1917, he called for each citizen, especially those in the South, "to plant abundant foodstuffs, as well as cotton" ... in support of those "fighting for their liberties and for our own."[10] This food-focused war effort "included the matter of food conservation."[11] Caraleigh Mills and Raleigh Mills "employed a whole-time home demonstration agent" to comply with the "food conservation propaganda all over the State."[12] A canning house was constructed in a "cool spot and screened where canning, preserving, jelly making, drying and pickling" was taught three days per week; instruction and the cans were provided "at no expense to the employees."[13]

In January 1918, a "great accomplishment of women and girls in this State…" was reported when 51,575 women in "canning clubs" throughout the state who preserved five million cans of food, yielding a profit for the war effort of more than a million dollars.[14] By June 1918, numerous cotton mills were petitioning the North Carolina Agricultural Extension Service for the support of more "trained women as home demonstration agents."[15] The addition of home demonstration agents in 1917 for the war effort at cotton mills denoted a "new phase of the food conservation movement where patriotic women were lauded for their contributions to the war effort, including twenty-three women from Caraleigh who canned 1500 containers of food."[16]

In the early 20th century, there was frequent movement from mill to mill among textile workers thought to be detrimental to the war effort.[17] Mill owners from "Caraleigh Mills, Pilot Mills, and Raleigh Mills paid for a full-page advertisement in the August 22, 1918, edition of the *News and Observer* appealing to itinerant mill workers' sense of patriotism and the power of the federal government to compel 'any man now employed in useful war work to stick to his job.'"[18] Doing so, according to the Department of Labor, was "a patriotic and intelligent duty to your country."[19]

Caraleigh's Post–World War I Years

There were substantial changes in the decades during and following World War I in the textile industry in North Carolina. The war created increased demands for textiles and phosphate based products; however, conflict between labor and management diminished textile industry profitability through the 1920s.[20] For Caraleigh, the end of World War I and the arrival of the "Spanish Flu," marked the start of a foreboding period of economic lethargy that antedated the start of the Great Depression by nearly a decade. The "once flourishing mill" of Caraleigh withered in the postwar economic climate that "was well underway in 1920."[21]

One sign of financial trouble was that the company started selling some of its land as a cemetery by 1925.[22] Burial plots, with space enough for six graves, sold for ten to eighteen dollars. The deaths of a number of Caraleigh's patrons, none of whom were buried at Caraleigh's Bunker Hill Cemetery, also signaled decline. The most significant death was that of the politically connected president of the mill, Alfred Augustus Thompson, who died in 1920.[23] Caraleigh, once the concern of the state's top tier business and political leaders—such as Needham B. Broughton, Josephus Daniels, John T. Pullen—was of little concern to the state's leadership. The end of the 1920s were worse than the start of the decade. The Great Depression that started in 1929–1930 would exacerbate an already desperate situation for Southern cotton mills; and for Caraleigh, the decade of the 1930s was punctuated with the mill closing operations from 1930 to 1938.[24]

The "Spanish" flu hit North Carolina hard from 1918 to 1920. From July and November 1918 alone, the state lost 13,644 citizens.[25] By March 1920, physicians reported that the flu "epidemic" was diminishing, with two North Carolina doctors stating that "at its height, they attended as many as 50 sufferers in a day," but lately "could count only 15 to 20 cases of the disease in their practice."[26] The sickness appeared most dangerous to those between the ages of 20 and 40. Steps

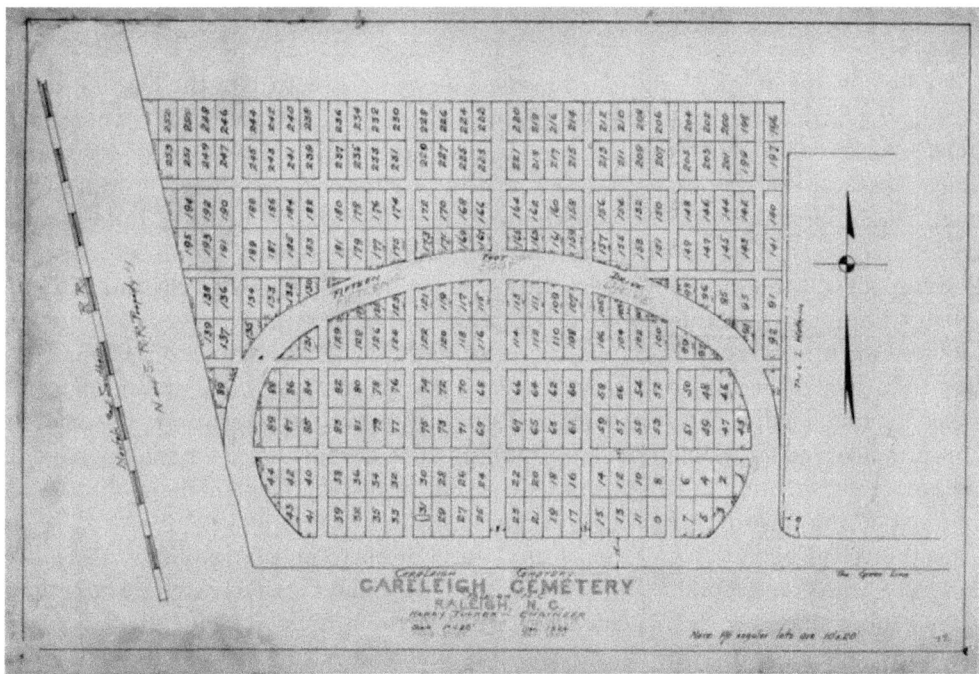

The 1924 map for the Caraleigh Cemetery, located on what the Caraleigh community members called Bunker Hill (Wake County, North Carolina, Register of Deeds Tammy L. Brunner, BM1924-00072).

taken to limit the spread of the disease included the disallowance of gatherings of people. Schools, church services, and funerals were closed. Daniel Watkins's indispensable 1999 interviews of Caraleigh residents provide firsthand accounts of those years.[27]

Doris Joyner, who was born in 1909, recounted the flu years:

> During the epidemic of the flu they had a soup kitchen. Miss [Evie] Morgan [212 Maywood Avenue] had a big iron pot she used for washing. She had her washing done at home by colored people. They would make big pots of soup in that big pot. They made that soup and take it to the homes where people were sick with the flu. In my house, it was my daddy and brother who were very sick with the flu. They would go to the homes with the soup, but they would not go inside.

Wesley Watkins was interviewed and discussed the death of his mother:

> First day of August 1918, I was four years old. Ruby [his sister] was two. Over there on Rhamkatte [Road] where we lived there was three women right in a row died within a week of each other. That was before they knew what the flu was and anything. Because there's three that died right there together; now people talk about the flu in the wintertime, but this was summer.

Hannah Messer remembered the loss of lives:

> Well, a flu epidemic came through,—Aunt Leila—Daddy's twin sister died. Momma said there were just so many sick that the City of Raleigh or Wake County would just send a nurse out with a wagon type thing with nothing but soup for them. Just feed them soup. Momma said there was hardly a house that it missed. It was such an epidemic.

Labor Troubles, 1914–1920

The conclusion of World War I marked a critical juncture in the history of the Southern textile industry, resulting in diminished market demand for textile products.[28] Across the South, the response to less profitability was to reduce workers' wages, extend their working hours, and the introduction of updated, more efficient machinery. These postwar changes in the mill industry resulted in increased conflict between profit-seeking mill owners and second-generation mill laborers. The impact of economic downturn did not become fully felt until the fall of 1920, when Caraleigh's workers, aligned with the United Textile Workers of America, agitated for union recognition and improvement of their working conditions with less-than-fruitful results for the striking laborers.[29] Caraleigh was a nonunion workplace, as was most of the state's manufacturing operations. By design, the South's "progressive leaders" during the late 19th and 20th centuries advertised the state to manufacturers willing to relocate as an oasis for profit-seeking capitalists who sought non–labor union workers willing to accept low wages.[30]

There had been disagreements at Caraleigh between management and labor before World War I, notably in the 1907 Phosphate and Fertilizer strike and in January 1914, when 50 weavers staged a strike over the practice of "docking" weavers' pay for producing "inferior cloth." The 1914 strike, unlike what happened in 1907, was resolved via settlement between the workers and management.[31] But Caraleigh's labor strike in 1920 was more visceral in tone and in conclusion.

Between 1919 and 1921, labor Union membership increased across North Carolina, as did the frequency of worker walkouts and strikes demanding better pay and improved working conditions via collective bargaining. The *News and Observer* reported December 25, 1919, that textile workers at the Pilot Mills went on strike and had declined management's offer of a 20 percent raise, with "no recognition" of the workers' union.[32] Six days later, it was reported in the *News and Observer* that Union mill workers at Pilot Mills and management later reached an agreement with striking workers to negotiate a contract "embodying all the terms of settlement" and recognition of their union; but soon thereafter, management denied the agreement, leading workers to start a "second strike," because union workers claimed they had been "double crossed." Additionally, it was reported that Pilot Mills management hired armed guards and placed them inside the Pilot Mills plant and in their mill village. Legal proceedings were started against striking Union workers at Pilot Cotton Mills but the case never was fully taken to court when management and workers reached a compromise agreement.[33]

In the same December 31, 1919, edition of the *News and Observer*, it was noted that workers at the Caraleigh and Raleigh Mills had also asked for legitimate recognition of their union. Unyielding, A.A. Thompson's response "emphatically denied" the union's right to exist in either workplace.[34]

About five months later, Union members at Caraleigh Mills went on strike in May of 1920, demanding the recognition of their union organization. There was disagreement over the number of Caraleigh's employees who were members of the union. The United Textile Workers of America, Picara Local No.1262, said the striking workers comprised 75 percent of Caraleigh's workforce, while Caraleigh's management said it was only 40 percent.[35]

The Pilot Cotton Mills employees, after a two month strike, were operating under the same type of agreement that was being asked for at Caraleigh, while union employees at the Raleigh Cotton Mill were afforded the right of committee representation without a recognized written agreement. W.D. Briggs, Caraleigh's secretary and treasurer, believed that it was unnecessary to negotiate with Union leaders at Caraleigh, because Caraleigh had only improved workers' conditions since the first year of World War I:

> ...since 1914, we have voluntarily advanced wages three times what they were at that time; the working hours have been reduced five hours a week without any reduction in pay; house rent has not been advanced one penny and still remains largely at $1.10 and $1.35 a week for three and four room houses with electric lights and garden space.[36]

The Caraleigh strike ended badly for its Union employees in 1920 when Justice of the Peace J.E. Owens issued ejection orders for 23 of the 115 striking workers from company housing. Execution of the ejectment order was carried out on June 28, 1920, an event the *News and Observer* mockingly headlined as "Moving Day" for Caraleigh's mill employees.[37]

The strike had created hostility between non-union and striking workers. Briggs stated that "the feeling [of resentment] of the sixty percent who remained at work toward the forty percent who struck is so strong that the mill would lose the sixty if the forty were taken back."[38] During the strike, Caraleigh management employed a "special detective" to investigate the strike at Caraleigh to provide "daily reports to the superintendent of the mill and headquarters of his company."[39] Hostility between striking workers and management were revealed in the reports; nevertheless, Caraleigh's leadership admitted that it was, and had been, willing "to treat with the operatives about any question which came up from either individuals or committees from the workers," and it recognized the "principles of collective bargaining"; however, it did not believe that the "workers should be dominated by influences outside the mill."[40] Thus, when the "Constable" arrived to enact the ejectment orders, he "fanned the flames" of anger further when the police deputized "eight or nine" non-striking Caraleigh operatives to assist in removing their former coworkers from their homes.

> Babies were moved out in their cribs, stoves with dinner ready for the cooking were put into the street, beds were dismantled, in a hurry and set out of doors....[41]

Threats and acts of physical violence ensued as deputized Caraleigh employees carted household belongings to the street. One of the evicted "struck one of the deputized officers in the back with a stick," and another "used abusive language toward another."[42] One woman quipped, "ain't that a black eye to Caraleigh," while pointing toward a cooking stove on the sidewalk, along with a "bed, trunk, bureau, and table beside it."[43]

The next day, "a United States flag, raised with proper ceremonies..., flapped lazily in the breeze" over the gathered crowd and around two tents set up for "the homeless twenty three."[44] The tents proved inadequate to cover people and their "household goods" that were piled partly "in the gutter." But "splendid relief" arrived with the donation of a larger tent from "a defunct carnival show."[45] The striking Caraleigh's families soon left their street-side encampment to pitch their tents "on the property of relatives and friends" in Raleigh.[46] Countering the appearance of heartlessness, Caraleigh Mills' manager said that the eviction orders could have been actuated two weeks prior to June 28, but Caraleigh Mills had declined so that families could have sufficient time to vacate. And, a few families suffering from sickness, were not required to immediately depart from their homes.[47]

Labor disputes in the mills during the 1920s brought increased national and international scrutiny of the South's textile industry, adding more ignominy to what critics already held as a disreputable institution. To many critics of cotton mills, Caraleigh's strike confirmed that "the horrors of southern capitalism" were present in Raleigh, corroborating similar experiences throughout the South in the 1920s and 1930s.[48]

7

The Great Depression Era to World War II

The Great Depression was the most devastating economic catastrophe in the history of the United States.[1] Starting in 1929 and lasting an entire decade, Americans experienced an unprecedented downturn with unemployment rates well over 20 percent and persistently above 10 percent throughout. Household incomes abruptly diminished, resulting in inadequate access to nutrition, housing, and medical treatment. The economically disastrous period triggered social and psychological stresses contributing to increases in ill-health, suicides, homicides, and lower rates of fertility.[2]

The 1933 inauguration of Franklin Delano Roosevelt as president of the United States marked the start of the New Deal initiating his strategic plan to end the Great Depression via a swarm of federal government programs. The New Deal relief programs helped society move towards the pre–Depression era, healthier, more normal demographic patterns of live births, sickness, and overall health.[3]

The Great Depression was marked with the closure of Caraleigh Mills on or "about July 1, 1930."[4] Judge W.C. Harris placed the company under the temporary receivership of W.D. Briggs to ensure the orderly liquidation of Caraleigh Mills' assets.[5] Along with the loss of Caraleigh's jobs, there was also an end of mill-sponsored welfare. This concerned the citizens and philanthropic organizations, and eventually New Deal federal assistance would try to fill the welfare work-vacuum for Caraleigh's poor throughout the 1930s.

Yet, years before the start of the Great Depression, there were indications of unhealthy conditions at Caraleigh. For example, a dental clinic was permanently established in 1922 where "scores of children" who "otherwise would not or could not have had dental work done."[6] The dentistry performed at Caraleigh was described in patriotic terms as "a practical effort toward the saving of the teeth, and health of the nation."[7] Dental work, admittedly, was important to the health of children, but so, too, was "the hot school lunch, supplemented with a glass of milk, ... [which] was most needed in the mill and village schools."[8] Visitors to Caraleigh in 1922 noted that 82 percent of the children seen suffered from "one or more defect" associated with "malnutrition."[9]

And as might have been expected, the mills' closing brought added "hardships for many of the people of the Caraleigh area...."[10] One chronicler of Caraleigh opined that "never again would she regain her former status in the processing of cotton."[11]

The closing marked the end of an era for the mill and the village, which led to several other multifaceted challenges to Caraleigh.[12] The wages earned from the mill were gone, and, for good or bad, also gone was the paternal institution that had attempted in the 1890s to mollify the "shock between the life on the farm and at the mill."[13] Another loss for Caraleigh was its voice in Raleigh's political halls of power that had, to one degree or another since its birth, given Caraleigh some level of representation. Caraleigh's voice in Raleigh's city government was squelched for nearly two generations, from 1930 to 1973.[14]

As the nation entered the first year of the Great Depression, newspapers reported that about 20 of the 200 unemployed mill families were desperately "in need of food" and unable to "find work in another place."[15] After Caraleigh Mills closed in 1930, "200 families" who were dependent upon work in the mill were unemployed. But by August, the majority of these families found employment elsewhere, with "around 25 families" dependent upon charitable organizations.[16]

Watkins' study of Caraleigh estimated that "the people of Caraleigh were better prepared for the tough Depressions days" because their "farming roots allowed them to feed themselves and share with others around them," as their agrarian tradition of growing their own food had become a mill village tradition.[17] Watkins interviewed 29 individuals between 1995 and 1999 who had experienced the Great Depression in Caraleigh. One interviewee mention "that their family had a garden, hogs, and chickens," with milk often gotten from a nearby neighbor and during the summer, "everyone foraged for food," often picking blackberries in nearby woods, but even "with gardens, hogs, chickens and cows, times in Caraleigh were still hard."[18]

But not every family grew their own food supply at Caraleigh. A small example of the level of desperation was the report of a rash of chicken thefts that occurred at Caraleigh between November 30 and December 1, 1937, and the subsequent arrest of six "chicken stealing" criminals ages 14 to 17, and one young adult age 23, to criminal action.[19] Homeless travelers along the nearby Highway 15A (now South Saunders Street) often would knock on the door, asking for food and water; this made Caraleigh residents aware of their "actual better fortune than some."[20] While the Caraleigh community benefited from self-sufficiency, they also received aid from the federal and state government sources, as well as from numerous charitable organizations in Raleigh.

Caraleigh and the New Deal

Franklin D. Roosevelt's expansion of federal government to provide employment opportunities assisted Caraleigh.[21] In the early 1930s, the villagers at Caraleigh disliked President Herbert Hoover, but they favored Franklin D. Roosevelt, with his New Deal programs that often were referred to by three or four letter acronyms, such as the Works Progress Administration (WPA) and the Civilian Conservation Corps (CCC). Tyree Watkins, who lived in Caraleigh during the Great Depression, recalled that villagers "were put to work" in New Deal initiatives … "building roads and all that sort of thing."[22] Some Caraleigh residents joined one the earliest New Deal job creation programs, CCC.[23] Tyree Watkins recalled that his brother, Archie Watkins, worked as a "trailblazer," building the Blue Ridge parkway just outside of Asheville, North Carolina. He and his group would survey, mark, and cut down trees while plotting the route that the parkway would take along the mountains.[24] Wesley Watkins also joined the CCC, remembering that for "about six months," he was "up in the mountains," building trailways for log trucks and that "each boy got to keep $5 of their pay" and the rest of the pay was sent home to their families.

Daniel Watkins' interviews of Caraleigh residents who lived there during the Great Depression noted that it was difficult to determine who worked for which New Deal program, because "people in Caraleigh lumped New Deal agencies all under the WPA umbrella."[25] Nonetheless, Watkins concluded that Caraleigh residents took advantage of New Deal opportunities. Several interviewees recalled family members working in a "cannery that was established in Caraleigh at the old Caraleigh School." Others mentioned sewing rooms, where uniforms were made "for the Army or CCC people" in one, and in another, "...people worked making quilts and clothes to give to the needy people."[26] Caraleigh resident Robert Senter got part time work with the National Youth Administration (NWA). Designed to assist young Americans in high school and college students, Senter recalled that he worked in the Hugh Morison High School chemistry lab after school cleaning for a set number of hours per week to earn extra money.[27]

Two of the more significant New Deal programs in the Raleigh area that impacted Caraleigh included the construction of the new Raleigh Waterworks, as well as the Raleigh-Durham Airport.[28] The Public Works Administration (PWA) that was created in 1933 to finance federal and nonfederal construction projects of public benefit.[29] The PWA particularly assisted workers in construction and related industries who suffered heavy job losses during the Great Depression. The PWA provided support to state and local applicants with grants of up to 45 percent and loans of up to 70 percent of project costs. From 1933 to 1939, the PWA helped in the construction of a majority of the nation's new educational facilities, its sewage disposal plants, 35 percent of its hospital and public health facilities, and 10 percent of all roads, bridges, subways, and similar engineering structures.[30]

On the edge of the Caraleigh community, just across the street from the Eliza Pool School on Fayetteville Road, was a significant New Deal project in the Raleigh area, the construction of the new waterworks plant.[31] By May of 1938, Raleigh had outgrown its Water Works complex constructed in 1887. City officials entertained three possibilities to fix the situation: the first, postponement of creating a new water facility until absolutely necessary; the second, cut off water supplies to non-incorporated areas of the city to reduce strain on the existing water supplies; the third, use funding from the federal government's Public Works Administration (PWA). The latter came to fruition with a PWA grant for 45 percent of the $700,000 cost for the new plant and its improvements to the water supply system.[32]

Work started on the new Raleigh Water Works plant in July 1939 following plans and specifications prepared by Raleigh engineer William C. Olsen, one of the preeminent designers of municipal water plants in North Carolina during the 20th century. In June 1940, Raleigh mayor Graham Andrews dedicated the new Water Works in the name of Ernest Battle Bain who had a four decade association with the city's water supply starting in 1897 with the Raleigh Water Company. The new plant was built on the same site as the old Raleigh Water Works and incorporated parts of it into the new plant. The E.B. Bain facility was Raleigh's first modern treatment system and the lone source of treated water during the city's post–World War II development boom between 1940 and 1967, but remained in use until 1987, operating in conjunction with a newer, more distant water plant on the Neuse River. The Raleigh City Council declared the E.B. Bain Water Treatment Plant a Raleigh Historic Landmark in 1997.[33] The designation was based on the E.B. Bain Plant's technological advances that significantly aided Raleigh's development in the mid–1900s, as well as its architectural attributes, being among the foremost examples of Art Deco style in Raleigh, possessing "a surprising level of architectural detail."[34]

Caraleigh residents worked on New Deal construction improvements to the Raleigh-Durham Airport.[35] In 1936, the *News and Observer* reported that WPA supervisor Truman Miller was making an inspection tour of "15 proposed airport projects in North Carolina" and by[36] August 1941, North Carolina had been approved for $1,168,000 for construction or improvement of six of the state's airports, including Raleigh-Durham.[37] Raleigh's portion of the funds for the Raleigh-Durham airport was described in 1941 as a mere portent of what was "slated to be one of the largest and finest airports in North Carolina."[38]

Depression Era Welfare Aid

Because Caraleigh was outside the city limits of Raleigh, there was no legal requirement for the city to spend their funds on Caraleigh; however, it was reported that the Wake County Welfare Department was looking after the "Caraleigh situation" with added funds from "Community Chest officials."[39] Additionally, a number of the city's charitable organizations and private citizens stepped up to provide

The Ernest B. Bain Water Treatment Plant was used from 1940 until 1987 and is a Raleigh Historic Landmark (photograph by the author).

Caraleigh the help it needed. In June 1930, the William G. Hill Masonic Lodge "voted unanimously to increase the annual donation for supplying milk to undernourished children at Caraleigh Mills school for the year."[40] During the Christmas of 1930, the Junior Woman's Club of Raleigh saw to it that "forty children of Caraleigh Mill were served lunches for one week...."[41] A letter of thanks from Caraleigh expressed appreciation to the Women's Club for the provisions of hot lunches and requested added aid. In response, the Junior Club responded by "also sending one pint of milk daily to a young girl suffering pellagra and a quart of milk daily to a tubercular patient ... [and] a baby crib to a family, which was without necessary number of beds."[42] In March 1931, the Raleigh Rotary Club provided "45 families of Caraleigh Mill workers" garden seeds.[43]

June 1931, the *News and Observer* reported that parent teacher associations were involved in extensive "welfare work" for the children in Raleigh.[44] The Welfare Committee of the Raleigh Council Parent-Teacher Associations gave their annual report that showed 32,515 lunches had been served, 33,302 pints of milk served, in addition to food, medical services, and clothing. Welfare work was carried out at the Eliza Pool School where "hot soup for forty children was taken to the school every day for practically the entire term."[45]

Entertainment was also donated to lift the spirits of Caraleigh's poor. February 1931, the Raleigh Civitan Club donated "$10 for a row of tickets at the play to be given by the Raleigh Junior League for the benefit of undernourished in the Caraleigh community."[46] On February 14, 1931, Raleigh's Junior League performed "Beauty and the Beast," in which arrangements were made for "the children of the Caraleigh and Pilot Mills" to be in attendance.[47] On December 23, 1931, Mrs. R.C. Upchurch entertained an "old fashioned box party" to raise funds to care for two especially needy Caraleigh families at Christmas.[48] The members of the Junior League of Raleigh sponsored two plays for the benefit of the milk fund, entertaining over 600 children from Caraleigh and Pilot Mills who attended as "special guests."[49]

The financial hardships in Caraleigh were documented in the "People's Forum" section of the *News and Observer* on August 13, 1934,[50] with discussion about a proposed change to the state's constitution that would exempt from taxation homes and small farms of up to $1000. In his support for the measure to assist the poor, Dr. J. Edward Kirbye, pastor of the United Church in Raleigh, cited one Caraleigh family's experience:

> In the winter of 1932, I was asked to go to the home of one of our mill families. The family consisted of a father, mother, and one son. In our chapel at Caraleigh, it had been noted that they were absent from the services. They had always been very faithful members of his group. On reaching this home, I found that their absence from church had been due to lack of clothing. The family had been saving during the years that each had worked in the mill and had been able to get a modest home with about one-half acre of ground for a garden. The mill had closed the year before and they were dependent now for subsistence upon this garden and such odd work as they could get. There was little employment and the food supplies were very meager in the home. After taking care of the clothing matter the father said the one of the great questions was how to pay the $16.50 in taxes which were past due upon their home. Then he went to a drawer and showed me savings of $6.50 which were to be used toward the $16.50 tax debt. The family had been willing to go without clothing in order to save every cent possible to meet the tax. If the proposed new Constitution of North Carolina had been in effect the situation of this worthy family could

have been remedied. However, it was remedied by a gift and the taxes for the year paid. J. Edward Kirbye, Raleigh N.C.[51]

Throughout the 1930s, baseball and softball leagues were organized and funded through Raleigh's Young Men's Christian Association (YMCA) and the WPA. George Washburn, director of the playground and recreation for the local YMCA, directed organization of softball leagues for men and women in the Caraleigh community in 1935, with stated motivations to realize the benefits of developing a healthy sense of sportsmanship and another to combat the "prevalence of infantile paralysis."[52] The federal aid was appreciated in Caraleigh, but Raleigh's municipal officials were less than enthusiastic. When the WPA indicated that they planned to drain "lowlands in the Caraleigh village," the *News and Observer* reported that because Caraleigh was not within the city limits, although in Raleigh Township, the drainage project had not been included in "the city commissioners preferred list."[53]

Raleigh's indifference to helping Caraleigh was observed when the city's decision makers found little interest in continuing their support of recreational programs for poor children. On June 15, 1937, city officials and "recreational-minded citizens" went on a "sightseeing" tour to nine city playgrounds; these included "five white and four Negro," one of which was Caraleigh's.[54] The nine locations were Boylan Heights, Thompson School, "the playground behind Washington High School," Caraleigh School grounds, the Mary Talbert House, Manly Street Church, Deveraux Meadow, Fred Olds School, "Oberlin School for Negroes."[55] The visit to Caraleigh described as such: "A rhythmic band at the playground on the Caraleigh School grounds entertained the visitors, and was a small example of the varied program, from checkers to softball, undertaken there."[56]

The tour of playgrounds was hoped to inspire support for additional funds from the city commissioners for the "wise use of leisure" time for children. The day-long event culminated with a dinner meeting attended by the Raleigh Recreational Commission. At the dinner, Dr. Harold Meyer, professor of sociology at the University of North Carolina and director for the southern district of the Works Progress Administration, declared that Raleigh failed to "support a lively recreational program."[57] Municipal decision makers were uninterested in funding recreational play, as evidenced in "startling" financial figures of comparison among North Carolina city budgets: Asheville $48,000; Durham $41,000; Greensboro $28,000; High Point $24,000; Raleigh $3,000.[58] In addressing Raleigh's financial reluctance, Meyer maintained that increased support for "supervised play" would galvanize the inherent preventive powers of recreation for youth, resulting in diminished "juvenile delinquency and crime."[59] It was claimed that the total withdrawal of Federal funds for workers at the city playgrounds would result in the curtailment of many recreational activities unless the city financially committed more fully. But Meyer's pleas in June 1937 fell upon deaf ears.

When the City Commissioners failed to meet a 40 percent sponsorship contribution required to maintain WPA recreational aid, the Caraleigh School playground was closed in November 1937.[60] When Caraleigh parents petitioned Mayor George A. Iseley of Raleigh to restore playgrounds to their community, the mayor's response was negative. The mayor cited financial strain and the fact that Caraleigh was "outside the city limits" and therefore ineligible "for any direct appropriation for such a program."[61]

Caraleigh, the Salvation Army and the News and Observer

Caraleigh's poor were initially ineligible for aid from the Salvation Army in Raleigh because charity's rules disallowed "funds for out of town work."[62] Despite the rules, Captain R. Hoekstra, leader of the Raleigh post of the Salvation Army, beseeched the citizens of Raleigh for donations to support "relief work in the village" of Caraleigh.[63] In the end, Hoekstra was successful in securing aid for Caraleigh, but not before his characterizations of Caraleigh published in the *News and Observer* inspired outrage in the mill village.

Demeaning portrayals of Caraleigh in Raleigh's newspapers were not unprecedented. From coverage of the typhoid epidemic in the summer of 1894, to rumors of a "blind tiger" alcohol establishment in the village in 1898, Caraleigh residents grew to mistrust Raleigh's reporters. The tradition of suspicion persisted into the 1930s, with the *News and Observer* again accused of misrepresenting the Caraleigh village, causing Caraleigh's citizens to mock the *News and Observer* moniker of "Old Reliable."[64]

In the first week of 1930, the *News and Observer* published interviews with Captain Hoekstra of the Salvation Army intended to encourage public donations for

Salvation Army Daily Vacation Bible School, Caraleigh, around 1937 (used with permission of the *News and Observer* [Raleigh] and the State Archives of North Carolina).

Caraleigh's poor, not publicly humiliate and anger Caraleigh's residents. But all of the aforementioned were achieved. Caraleigh residents denied that they were "starving and destitute" and indignantly denied that desperation in their community "led several hungry girls into harlotry," labeling the accounts of prostitution of Caraleigh girls an "unwarranted lie."[65] So "affronted" were the Caraleigh residents, they refused to accept aid from the Salvation Army.[66]

Hoekstra responded that his previous comments concerning "harlotry" at Caraleigh were misunderstood: "I did not say that any of the girls in the village had fallen," but instead intimated that "conditions were so bad that many of the families were actually suffering from hunger and that I was afraid for what may happen to the girls if relief was not secured."[67] The situation was resolved when the Walnut Creek Council No. 55 of the Junior Order's appointed a "committee to see that the injustice to the community was corrected." This reconciliation led to the Salvation Army receiving enough donations to "begin relief work" in the village and feed "around 25 families" which were "dependent on the relief agency."[68]

The honor and chastity of mill girls was a long-held, sensitive subject throughout the South. A Southern promoter and historian of the textile industry, Holland Thompson, criticized depictions of unsavory behavior of mill girls in the 1905 novel *Amanda of the Mill*. Thompson found the book to be an erroneous display

Members of the Caraleigh Teen-Age Girls Club at Pullen Park, Raleigh, North Carolina, June 1938 (used with permission of the *News and Observer* [Raleigh] and the State Archives of North Carolina).

of ignorance, or misrepresentation of facts for salacious literary effect.[69] Thompson remarked that North Carolina's mill workers married young, thereby making sexual indecency uncommon.[70] Continuing, Thompson added that female workers in many mills self-policed impropriety through an "unofficial committee for the protection of social purity."[71] Ladies labeled sexual deviants faced banishment, with the possibility of eviction for themselves and their entire family from company housing.

Marie Van Vorst's 1905 novel, *Amanda of the Mill*, was interpreted in the South as a literary attack on the "matronly reserve" of women and working conditions in the mills.[72] While the novel was set in South Carolina, reviewers throughout the South rose to defend the bulk of factory girls in North Carolina who were reportedly sinless. The *Concord Daily Tribune* in North Carolina applauded the author's "splendid style" in telling the story, but thought it inaccurate, opining that "such conditions as are shown in this story do not, we think and trust ... exist now."[73] Conversely, a Los Angeles reviewer thought Van Vorst accurately portrayed "the oppressions of the 'poor white trash.'"[74]

The *New York Times* review of the book said the author "paints with a strong hand the terrible life in the mills, its women dirty, sodden creatures, the men brutalized; pitiful little children working through the night shifts for a pittance."[75] Another New York newspaper, *The Sun*, called it a "curious mixture of grim realism and florid melodrama; an up-to-date problem novel" with overused "repetition of the horrors" that faced "the white slaves" in cotton mills.[76]

Senator Lee Overman of North Carolina feared that Senator Beveridge of Indiana heard the Van Vorst novel's suppositions as fact when Beveridge appeared to recruit some details from the book to support his proposed child labor legislation. The *Concord Daily Tribune* further editorialized that conditions in the mills, as set forth in the book, were "untrue," and that these had animated Senator Beveridge's mind with "very false ideas as to conditions in the South."[77]

Caraleigh residents cried foul once again when the *News and Observer* on November 10, 1937, published several pictures of children at the Caraleigh School Daycare nursery. An accompanying caption claimed that "40 percent" of Caraleigh's children were "under-nourished" because many parents were underemployed, unemployed, or both parents had to work, making care for children a desperate challenge.[78] Some of the children in the pictures, it was explained, were from homes where both parents were jobless, but their children were "given one good meal a day from funds supplied in part by the Community Chest. Otherwise, they would die of slow starvation."[79]

The report of starving children provoked anger from 36 residents of Caraleigh who claimed that the images and story of "suffering and half-starved" children was "a gross misrepresentation."[80] In response, the newspaper explained that the story and photographs were published to assist the Community Chest, not offend the Caraleigh Village. Caraleigh's citizens demanded correction of the inaccuracies.[81] Feeling maligned and unfairly singled out, the mill villagers argued that Caraleigh was not the lone section of the county or city with hungry, undernourished children. Citing that Raleigh schools, without exception, has a free milk and lunch list that included some of the wealthiest areas of Raleigh whose children were unable to purchase food necessary for nutritious diets.[82]

Because information obtained about Caraleigh was not taken from a cross-section of their village, residents claimed that overeager reporters needing information for "slum clearance feature stories" led to fallaciously insulting stories.[83] Instead, residents argued that the sources about conditions in Caraleigh were from "a few relievers and 'downtown observers.'"[84] Caraleigh's leaders maintained that the same percentages of undernourished children existed Raleigh, not just Caraleigh.[85]

Caraleigh's community felt attacked when other generalizations about them published in the *News and Observer* included that Caraleigh children were repeatedly visitors in delinquent courts and that mill residents accepted charity when they did not need it. Especially irksome was one reporter's opinion that the Caraleigh playground, which had been closed, "meant more than church to this community."[86] A local history written in the 1970s opined that the loss of employment at Caraleigh's mill, along with the insensitive newspaper coverage, had a unifying effect in the Caraleigh village:

> Perhaps it was at this point where Caraleigh residents became so proud for this sense of pride in the community [that] can be sensed in the neighborhood today. In the 1930's this pride might have been the only salvation they could hold on to. It could have been this fierce determination to prove the newspapers wrong which helped them survive the times and hardships which were inflicted on them.[87]

Work During the Great Depression

Just as Caraleigh families had pooled their resources together when working in the mill, the family tradition of mill labor persisted into the 1930s, when all family members combined their earnings. For some, the Pilot Mills Cotton Company, located north and to the east of Caraleigh, kept many at Caraleigh employed. One taxi driver recalled that he "would pick up as many as he could get in the taxi … [and] charge very little a week" to take Caraleigh residents to the Pilot Mills.[88] By 1937, though, Pilot Mills provided the only bus service to Caraleigh when it chartered a bus to transport workers, three times a day, to and from work.[89] But the vast majority of Caraleigh adults by 1930 obtained "jobs out of the textile mills or had moved to other mills."[90]

By 1940, only 47 of the 580 adults who lived in Caraleigh Village were employed as textile workers. The death of the mill in 1930 was psychologically traumatic to a people whose "…'sense of the past' was determined by working in the mill."[91]

Although child labor had been discontinued in mills by the 1930s, kids contributed to the family income with smaller jobs. Nannie Mae Smith recalled that during the Depression, "many kids had to work," as she did because her mother was a widow, working to support herself and three small children. Working children under age 16 needed a permit; Smith remembered needing one.[92] Smith was old enough to babysit for families where both parents had jobs, and also got "a job working at Woolworth's on Saturdays" working the "candy counter selling candy and peanuts" earning $1.25 per week.[93] When recollecting her childhood experiences during the Great Depression, Smith's son would say that she was "crazy for working" for such meager sums of money. But Smith retorted that if she quit, "there would have been 25 people waiting to take the job."[94]

7. The Great Depression Era to World War II

Golf provided entertainment and income for some families in Caraleigh during the Depression. There were two golf courses within walking distance from Caraleigh, the Carolina Pines Golf Course and the Raleigh Golf Association, with railroad tracks from the Norfolk-Southern Railroad providing a path for Caraleigh boys to both courses.[95] Caraleigh resident William Phipps remembered that "We boys would go out and caddie and try to make 50 cents during depression times. I've walked that railroad track a many a time across that trestle (over Walnut Creek) going to the Carolina Pines Golf Course."[96] The boys would sneak onto the golf course at night, wading into the water holes in bare feet to locate lost golf balls so they could sell them back to the clubhouse. Robert Senter recalled his childhood golf activities, saying that the price obtained for the retrieved golf balls depended on its quality. About being a young caddie, Senter said that "we didn't get but 60 cents for carrying that bag for 18 holes. No! 50 cents, the golf course took a dime for insurance."[97] Youthful experiences as golf ball hunters and caddies produced at least two professional golfers from Caraleigh, brothers Tommy Card and J. Percy Card.[98] Tommy rose to become the Head Pro at the Carolina Country Club for three decades, and Percy eventually became the "Head Pro at Cheviot Hills Golf Course in Raleigh" and a lifetime member of the Professional Golfers' Association.[99]

In July 1931, the effect of the Raleigh Golf Association's reduction of membership fees led to favorable outcomes, even for Caraleigh. The golf club increased its membership, improved the quality of its "18 greens," expanded its facilities and created an increased demand for caddies. Practically "all of the course's caddies were recruited" from Caraleigh.[100] "One of these Caraleigh caddies was 'a 15 year old young man' who was 'badly handicapped by a bad club foot.'" Despite the debility, the teen endeavored to "earn a living" as a caddy at the local golf course. Talk of this hard-working caddy led to an orthopedic surgeon's examination who advised that he could "correct the crippled foot." Raleigh Kiwanis and Rotary Clubs agreed to pay for surgery and any extended hospital care that resulted in success.[101]

Traveling circuses and various exhibition shows used Caraleigh's grounds to encamp and entertain crowds from Raleigh and surrounding areas in the 1930s and 1940s. Shows filled with "thrilling acts" kept the "thousands of spectators on the very edge of their narrow board seats" occurred so often at the mill village that Caraleigh's name and circuses became synonymous: "Caraleigh Mills Show Grounds," "Caraleigh Circus Lot," "Caraleigh Circus Grounds,"[102] In 1933, The Ringling Brothers and Barnum and Bailey's circus brought the "biggest and most elaborate circus to Raleigh yesterday with its 31 tents, 1600 personnel, 1000 menagerie animals including 50 elephants, 27 camels, 27 zebras 700 horses." The news augured that Caraleigh Village and adjacent property owners would "reap a harvest" from parking fees.[103] Ringling Brothers and Barnum and Bailey were but one of the numerous entertainment groups who came to Caraleigh: In 1934, the "Russel Brothers Big Three Ring Circus," and the "Tom Mix Circus" in 1936.[104] Also, in 1940, the "Johnny J. Jones Exposition" encamped at Caraleigh for six days with its "22 riding devices" for thrill seekers to enjoy.[105]

In September 1941, the "Cole Brother's Combined Circus" arrived at the "'Caraleigh circus grounds,' boasting a long list of stars of the circus" to thrill Raleigh circus fans. The famous boxer Jack Dempsey, "ex-king of the heavy-weights," was featured as leader of the opening spectacle, the "Pan Americana" and rode in on a "beautiful dapple-grey Kentucky stallion at the head of the inaugural pageant, with 'a cast of 263 persons, three herds of elephants, a girl ballet of 60 dancers, hundreds of horses and animals.'"[106]

Schooling During the Great Depression

The Eliza Pool School at Caraleigh ended at the sixth grade, and students then were expected to walk the two miles to the Hugh Morson High School which started in the seventh grade. From the 1930s to the early 1940s, many Caraleigh children were compelled to choose between school and work, with many opting to work. In 1999, William Phipps recollected that he "quit school early" and "took a job painting and hanging wallpaper, stuff like that. Eliza Pool [sixth grade] is as far as I went. I was making a little more money than the average man, because I was working a trade."[107] The decade saw options for students in having to walk to school, when groups of four or five students would combine their resources to take a taxi to school, "ten cents a day to go and come back."[108] Caraleigh parents petitioned Raleigh for bus service for students. In the early 1940s, the Carolina Power and Light Company (CP&L) provided bus service for students in the mornings and afternoons each day. But the necessity of boarding the bus after school meant that students could not participate in extracurricular activities.

The transition from the smaller Eliza Pool School building to the Hugh Morson High School in Raleigh was not only logistically challenging, but it was also intimidating for Caraleigh students. Caraleigh residents who were students in the 1930s recalled that the level of academic rigor proved difficult, as was the mixing of students from more affluent families with Caraleigh students. School-aged children from Caraleigh came from a close-knit, isolated village that was racially, religiously, and economically homogeneous. The interaction of Caraleigh kids with students from other parts of Raleigh provided their "first real understanding that they were poor."[109]

The principal of Caraleigh's grade school made a public appeal in the *News and Observer* for many of her students who were "barefooted" and unable go to school during frigid temperatures of the winter of 1936.[110] For readers, description of Caraleigh's children, ages six to 13, painted a grim picture of deprivation for readers, with students who went "barefooted through the snow" and some of the older girls able to "brave the sub-freezing weather in the flimsiest of cotton."[111] The principal outlined student needs that included underwear, coats, sweaters, emphasizing that looks were unimportant. Also, it was requested that footwear with good soles were especially needed, but worn-out shoes would do little good, because "none of the children's families" had funds for repairs.[112]

Recalling that many "didn't have money to buy things," Caraleigh children often wore clothing that was handed down from relatives: "Joyce Phipps talked about the only coat she had was handed down from her aunt. Ruth Wilkins mentioned that she only had one skirt, and Nannie Mae Smith talked about having only two dresses [that] her mother made."[113] Another resident reminisced about the use of old flour sacks, purchased for five cents each, to make dresses, pants, sheets and pillow-cases: "I have made many a dress for 30 cents."[114] Wearing clothing not as nice as the other students made Caraleigh's students feel inferior, as one Caraleigh student recalled: "Some [students] were so ugly to us. They made fun of everything you did. We had nothing. I had two dresses that Momma had made. It was different in Caraleigh; so many people at home were the same, everybody tried to help. I hated every day I was there. I dropped out of school at 10th or 11th grade. I got a job at Eckerd's Store at the soda fountain."[115] Another Caraleigh resident who was a student at Hugh Morson remembered that "we stood out; people knew where we were from."[116]

Depression Era Despair, Morality and the End of Temperance

The emotional strain endemic in the 1930s resulted in destructive behaviors among some of those in the mill village. Some harmed themselves, others engaged in criminal activity, or formed an abusive relationship with alcohol. One day in 1932, Caraleigh resident James Joyner who had unsuccessfully tried to find employment for three years, despite a "wide search" for work became so "despondent" that he decided to end his search at his brother's home on Summit street in Caraleigh, when he carefully placed a blanket on the floor, rolled one blanket into a pillow, laid down and "fired a .32 caliber bullet through his right temple."[117]

From Caraleigh's start, efforts were made to dissuade villagers from consuming alcoholic beverages. In 1903, it was reported that any land sold from Caraleigh's original tract prohibited "the manufacture or sale of liquor."[118] In 1937, the Caraleigh Baptist Church requested that state authorities prohibit the sale of intoxicants within a half mile of Caraleigh's Baptist church.[119] Disdain for alcohol was hardly a Caraleigh phenomenon. Twelve years prior to the 1920 national Prohibition law via the Eighteenth Amendment to the Constitution of the United States, North Carolina in 1908 became the first among Southern states to disallow the making, selling, or distributing of alcohol.[120]

There was statewide support to ban booze in 1908, as shown with 62 percent of the state's voters accepting the alcohol ban. But in 1933, when the Eighteenth Amendment to the United States Constitution was repealed with the Twenty-First Amendment, the state's 1908 prohibition law remained in effect. In 1933, thirty-six states agreed to repeal the Eighteenth Amendment, but North Carolina was not one of them. The state voted 300,054 to 115,482 against ratification of the Twenty-First Amendment.[121] It was not until 1935 that the state legislature granted a local option to 18 counties, districts, and townships to have their own local liquor laws.[122] In 1937, the state's legislators passed the Alcoholic Beverage Control bill that established the State Board of Control, known as the North Carolina Alcoholic Beverage Control Commission, which started operating liquor stores selling distilled spirits. The state law enabled individual counties to decide to allow for the sale and manufacture of alcohol within a county's jurisdiction. And despite its history, Caraleigh had become less than a fortress of temperance in 1933, according to one observer.

Raleigh resident W. White, in a letter to the editor in May 1933, observed sentiment of "general jubilation over the advent of beer," with politicians and legislators "joyfully hailing the arrival of beer, when everyone knows it means the incoming of the old liquor business that once cursed our land."[123] White was also disgusted with the "paramounting beer propaganda" published in newspapers that treated with levity the legalization of beer consumption in 1933. Continuing in remonstrance, White heard "that in Caraleigh, there was a general debauch all Saturday night. Poor people out of work and suffering for food must now have their misery aggravated by what little money they have squandered for drink."[124]

Gradually, North Carolina discontinued its own prohibition of alcohol with beer and light wine sales permitted soon after the end of national prohibition, with an optional county liquor law implemented in 1937.[125] Caraleigh's residents often made the police blotter for violations of state laws governing alcohol before and after the national end to prohibition. For example, Foster Maye, a white man from Caraleigh Mills, was arrested in 1933, for having possession of two gallons of liquor in his car and charged with "possession and transportation."[126] News in 1934 documented many alcohol related events, such as "Liquor Den Broken Up" in Caraleigh,[127] and in the same year, "a young white man of the Caraleigh section was found guilty of possession of 29 gallons of liquor."[128] Dave H. Pope, former chairman of the Wake Board who also represented the City of Raleigh on the County Board of Commissioners, had resigned from this position to run a "filling station business" at Caraleigh. It was Pope's behavior at Caraleigh that compelled his wife to file for divorce, charging Pope "with associating with women of ill repute, excessive use of intoxicants and cruelty to herself and their child."[129]

World War II

The United States entry into World War II started with Japan's bombing of Pearl Harbor on December 7, 1941, and ended in 1945 with Germany's surrender on May 7 and Japan's capitulation on September 2. As had occurred in both small and large towns throughout the country, the war affected all of Caraleigh's residents. In the late 1990s, Caraleigh residents proudly recollected that "Caraleigh did its part" during World War II, especially with its young men who performed military service.[130] "Boys would graduate [from school] on Friday, and they left [for the military] on Monday."[131] Tyree Watkins looked back on joining the war effort, saying in an interview in 1999 that "I was drafted and went to the Post Office and they pulled thirty men out of the group that was up there that day to go to the Marine Corps. The rest of us went into the Navy."[132] Special church services were held at Caraleigh's Baptist church to honor service men of Caraleigh.[133] The Caraleigh Women's club, including mothers and wives of military men, dutifully kept vigil during the war by going to church to pray for their sons and husbands.[134] The church at Caraleigh kept a display board that represented each person in service, and changes were made each time a servicemember was listed as missing-in-action or killed.[135]

There were approximately 580 people over age 18 living in Caraleigh in 1940. During World War II, approximately 50 of Caraleigh's young men served in all branches of the military and three making the ultimate sacrifice for their nation. Second Lieutenant J.B. Morgan, a bombardier in the Army Air Force, was killed in action on October 9, 1943, during combat operations.[136] Private First Class R.D. Gay died of wounds received during combat operations in Austria on May 5, 1945, only two days before German forces officially surrendered.[137] Corporal Orrell's death in service was listed as DNB (died non-battle), which included sickness and accidents outside the combat area.[138]

Caraleigh children supported the troops in various ways. Thomas Joyner, a young boy in Caraleigh during World War II, said that students collected scrap iron for the war effort. In the yard of the Eliza Pool School, there was a pile of scrap iron "10–15 feet high and 20–30 feet across at the base."[139] And because the South became a major troop training area during World War II, Caraleigh residents would often see troops moving to and from Fort Bragg in Fayetteville, North Carolina. Residents watched troops make transit along Highway 15A through Caraleigh: "I remember all us kids getting out there along Highway 15A watching the Army convoys come by. I mean about every fifteen minutes another convoy would come by. A lot of time, they'd stop; we'd carry apples and all that stuff out there to them; they'd give us stuff."[140]

Wartime regulations were supported in Caraleigh in two of Caraleigh's stores— Senter Grocery and Mrs. Riley Grocery, both of which publicly proclaimed their cooperation with the "National Nutrition Program."[141] Participating stores were recognizable with display of a red, white and blue window seal, letting "Mrs. America" know she was shopping at a store that lived "up to Uncle Sam's great Nutrition Program!"[142] Under the direction of the Office of Price Administration (OPA), food and other important commodities were subject to price controls and rationing to ensure that needed resources were available to support the war effort. At home, the rationing of sugar, gasoline, shoes, and more prevented hoarding by the wealthy or the less honest. Caraleigh resident Pauline Horton recalled:

> You were issued a coupon book each month with so many coupons for each meat so many for sugar and so many for flour and coffee and everything. We had several older customers who quit trading with us because we wouldn't sell them some of those items without stamps. They just didn't understand how it worked. We had people come from all over everywhere; they'd find out you had a little piece of beef or pork. You could buy pork on the black market if you were willing to take a chance. People would find out a certain place had sugar or whatever and everybody would flock in to get some sugar or some pork or whatever it happened to be.[143]

Despite the war, instances of lawlessness at Caraleigh furthered south Raleigh's reputation as a location to find misbehavior, for those who sought it. Contributing factors that revived Caraleigh's erstwhile criminal behavior included alcohol intoxication, the violation of wartime regulations, as well as an increased number of service members visiting Caraleigh. A court of law in 1942 declared that Whitaker's Place, located in Caraleigh along Highway 15 A, be "padlocked" and closed, because it was a public nuisance. The "'bootlegging' joint" had engaged in the "unlawful sale of intoxicating liquors at all hours of the day and night," attracting large crowds.[144] Apparently, this had gone on for some time, as it was noted that the owner, George Whitaker, had several previous convictions for the same infraction.[145]

Air raid drills and mandatory blackouts were enforced in Caraleigh. One resident remembered that blackouts required "window shades" to be drawn, "cars were to pull off the road and turn off lights, railroad trains were to pull down shades on passenger cars and substitute white lanterns for their taillights, and factories were forbidden to operate night shifts unless blackout conditions could be maintained."[146] In 1942, two Caraleigh men were charged for violating air raid ordinances, one for refusing to take cover during an air raid drill, and the other for driving off after "being parked by a warden" during an air raid drill.[147] Clarence Henderson served as air raid warden for Caraleigh until he resigned because of his conviction for violation of blackout regulations in 1943.[148]

A United States Marine from the New River Marine base was shot at Todd's Café one night in 1943. Lillie Pearce, waitress and gun shooter at the café, told the Sheriff that the incident started when the marine and his companions "demanded beer after the 11:30 beer-curfew." Her refusal to provide more beer, Pearce said, compelled the marines to aggressively approach her "around the counter," at which time she shot the marine.[149]

Historians largely agree that World War II sparked economic growth throughout the United States, the scale of which was among the most significant in the nation's history.[150] To working people, the war's effects were clear: twenty percent of the population was employed in the military, causing the unemployment rates to dramatically diminish from 14.6 percent in 1940 to 1.9 percent in 1945.[151] That World War II ended the Great Depression was recognized at Caraleigh, as Tyree Watkins saw it:

> The whole United States benefited from the war. They may not agree, but before the war broke out there were rough times. People couldn't get work, salaries weren't anything and after the war broke out, things started. After the war that's when it really picked up. All the adult people went back to work building automobiles and machinery and industrial stuff, things just exploded.[152]

And in the early years of the war, there were indicators of urban expansion of Raleigh's city limits foreshadowing a more permanent and official union between Raleigh and Caraleigh. In 1942, a post office substation of Raleigh opened at Horton's store on Maywood Avenue in Caraleigh. The Raleigh City Commissioners, while working with the Walnut Creek Council No. 55 of the Junior Order of United American Mechanics (JOUAM) of Caraleigh, approved the renaming of streets in Raleigh, Caraleigh, and other communities to dispel confusion caused by streets sharing the same, or similar names.[153] In 1944, the Raleigh City engineering officials, while working with Caraleigh's JOUAM, created a "workable system" of house address numbering for the village.[154] For years, it was explained, organizations such as the Carolina Power and Light Company and the Southern Bell Telephone Company were confused by streets in Caraleigh and Raleigh with the same names and houses in Caraleigh on the same street in sharing the same address number.[155]

8

Old Mill, New Owners

1938–1943: Raleigh Mills Company

The Great Depression silenced Caraleigh's spindles in 1930, but hope of renaissance arrived in 1937 when New England textile enterprises increased their "southward migration" in search of cheap labor.[1] Conflicts in Europe and Asia inspired in the 1930s resulted in a "war-bred textile boom" in Southern mills, many of which "had all but given up the ghost" of a cotton mill revival.[2] But Caraleigh's reopening was delayed when the expected arrival of new, Northern-based, occupants were delayed by the disastrous "big wind" that devastated "parts of New England" in 1938.[3] Known as the New England Hurricane, it was one of the deadliest and most destructive tropical cyclones ever experienced in Long Island, New York, and New England.[4]

Caraleigh residents, long tired "of rumors" that Caraleigh Mills would "again hum with industry," were told operations would start on January 1, 1939, with the production of "upholstery materials, plushes, casket coverings, and other materials."[5] Estimates were that the new Northern textile concern at Caraleigh would employ 300 and eventually expand to 700 people,[6] welcomed news to the "few residents" in the "almost deserted village of Caraleigh."[7]

Both Northern and Southern newspapers suggested that the South's allure to outside business interests was rooted in the South's small town "low wage centers," where workers were "poorly paid" and endured "poor living conditions," thereby enhancing the profit for manufacturers.[8] Conversely, J.T. Anderson, industrial engineer for the Department of Conservation and Development, asserted that the new industries relocating to North Carolina were lured by the state's multitude of "natural advantages."[9]

The Raleigh Mills Company made little impact upon the Caraleigh community. The company's operations at the Caraleigh Mills building indicate continued delays until the end of 1941. One report stated that the work "to renovate Caraleigh Mills," which had been "idle for the last 10 years" was slated to begin on November 10, 1941.[10]

1943–1951: Premier Worsted

"Premier Worsted Mill," owned by the Lawton Company, took over the Caraleigh Mills building during World War II, in 1943. Wartime demands created logistical and manpower shortages for the company and postwar labor disputes also proved challenging in an industry that was believed "essential."[11] In 1944, the company operated at about 25 percent of its capacity and employed around 225. It reported that a "wartime labor shortage" had caused the use of an insufficient number of workers, but it augured the need for 650 to 700 employees.[12] When in full operation Premier Worsted at Caraleigh produced about 9,000 to 10,000 pounds of yarn a week, and production was predicted to reach 40,000 pounds weekly, with raw yarn then converted into finished cloth and used in the creation of men's suits.[13]

In 1949, the Textile Workers Union of America, CIO, sued Premier Worsted for unfair business practices because the company discharged four employees for union activities. The decision of the National Labor Relations Board (NLRB), as reported in May 1949, required that Premier Worsted reinstate dismissed workers "and reimburse these employees for wages lost." Additionally, the company was mandated to "post immediately in conspicuous places notices stating that they will not in any manner in the future interfere with the rights of employes [sic] to organize and conduct the affairs of their union."[14] There was resistance to the NLRB decision; in June of 1950, the United States Circuit Court of Appeals for the fourth circuit responded to a "petition for enforcement" and directed the "Premier Worsted Mills of Raleigh to honor the NLRB's earlier decision to rehire, with back pay, the four employees who were found to have been 'discriminatorily discharged.'"[15] The court noted that there had been ample evidence presented "of surveillance of union activities, of interrogation of employees as to union membership and threats of economic reprisal engaged in by supervisory employes ... acting for the employer."[16] When Premier Worsted closed by the summer of 1951, the American Woolen Company announced its plan to expand southward with the purchase of the old Caraleigh building, described as being "a large, airy building with plenty light" and about "110,000 square feet."[17]

1951–1955: American Woolen

The American Woolen Company was the "largest textile company in the United States when it announced in July 1951 that it purchased the 'old Premier worsted Plant,'" hoping to start operations by the end of 1951.[18] Predicting that the plant would create 500 jobs at Caraleigh, extensive renovations to the mill were implemented that included a new roof, updated electrical fixtures, and fresh paint.[19]

But the company's arrival was ill-timed, because of the increased popularity and production of synthetic fabrics that started replacing those made of wool. So, after about five years, the American Woolen Company left Caraleigh.[20] Described in 1954

Unidentified workers in Caraleigh Mills, 1955 (courtesy Frances Collins).

as "cash rich but business poor," the American Woolen Company was beset by mergers with competitors and reorganization from within.[21] American Woolen Company's arrival in Caraleigh had little impact on the village.[22]

1956–1999: Fred Whitaker Company

The Fred Whitaker Company (FWC), a Philadelphia-based business, bought Caraleigh in 1956 to dye and process and dye synthetic fibers, rather than process wool. The FWC was a major wool supplier during the first half of the century in Philadelphia and had earned a reputation for innovation and competitiveness, while being service oriented.[23]

From the end of World War II to 1957, the textile industry was "hard pressed" to achieve profitability, as evidenced by over "500 liquidations" of textile firms. While the number of mills and employees diminished, modernized plants and machinery resulted in increased production. Textile products' "share of the consumers dollar" sharply decreased, thereby informing an unfavorable outlook among many in the textile industry that were resigned to the downward trend "for at least some years to come."[24]

Employees at the old Caraleigh Mills plant. Viola Suggs stands on the far right with two unidentified workers in 1955 (courtesy Frances Collins).

A Fred Whitaker Company sign remains in the Historic Caraleigh Condominium complex (photograph by the author).

The Fred Whitaker Company belief that its "'spirit of inventiveness' could be transplanted to and co-commingled with the talents and hard work of the Caraleigh Mill people..." was rewarded. The Whitaker Company plant at Caraleigh developed an "innovative way of dyeing yarn, the 'Spacedye'" process. Revolutionizing the carpet industry, the Spacedye process was patented in 1961, resulting in the Whitaker Company's expansion with the 1963 creation of another mill in Roanoke, Virginia, dedicated to the Spacedye process. Afterwards, the Caraleigh location "continued to produce many products including 'garnetted fiber, staple fiber, nylon pellets and ... industrial nylon yarns.'"[25]

When the company announced its closure in 1999, there was clearly a love for the spirit of Caraleigh and its community that owners since 1938 did not express as fully as FWC: "For some 44 years, FWC and its associates have kept the old 'Caraleigh Mill' alive and running. Sometimes jumping and hopping, sometimes limping slightly. But always running." Fred Whitaker Company closed its plant on Maywood Avenue on or about October 8, 1999.[26]

Fred Whitaker Company employees at Caraleigh, undated (State Archives of North Carolina).

9

In Raleigh's Orbit

Caraleigh's Place in Raleigh's Growth

In 1952, Raleigh's City Council created of a one-mile zoning area outside the city's limits that included Caraleigh. With this, Raleigh would dictate Caraleigh's development. Although the mill village technically remained a separate entity apart from the capital city, Raleigh officials ordered the expansion of Caraleigh's land usage to include both industrial and residential development.[1] Despite this, the economic descent of Caraleigh continued unabated.

The fruits of Raleigh's economic expansion between the 1930s and the 1960s were not so fully enjoyed in south Raleigh as they were in the city's northern zones. Cumulatively, Raleigh experienced a distinct development pattern characterized as "slow but steady growth in population and physical size" that peaked in the 1960s.[2] The city's expansion was rapid between 1930 and 1960, with a population increase of 151 percent, a 376 percent boost in land area, and a rise in employment of 134 percent. Raleigh's 1960 population more than doubled the 1940 population and tripled the city area. Between 1920 and 1960, the city expanded mostly to the north and west, and the state's capital city became an important financial center, with retail trade increasing fivefold during the 1950s. Wholesale business made Raleigh a leading distribution center, and while manufacturing jobs in 1960 comprised only 9.3 percent of Raleigh's total employment picture, it too enjoyed robust increase in the 1950s.[3]

Raleigh's development was enabled with its position in the easternmost portion of the "Piedmont Crescent," a number of small-to-medium-sized cities situated in a semi-circular fashion that extended west and south from Raleigh to Greensboro, Charlotte, and through to South Carolina.[4] Raleigh was connected to these cities via a network of railroad and federal interstate highway systems. The cities spread along the transportation lines feeding into one another, creating a chain of urban development, with no single metropolis playing a dominant role. Of the North Carolina cities involved, Charlotte possessed the largest population in 1960, numbering 201,564. Greensboro's population stood at 119,574, followed by Winston-Salem with 111,134, and Raleigh's 1960 population was 93,931.[5]

Raleigh's evolution between 1940 and 1960 followed main transportation routes to the north, south, east, and west, but more to the north and west. The expansion of needed roadways, or Raleigh's arterial facilities, influenced Raleigh's human geography and economic development, and subsequently affected Caraleigh. Caraleigh, located on the south side of an intra-arterial area of the city, was at the center of road access to metropolitan Raleigh.

Because the northern and western sectors of Raleigh flourished between 1940 and 1960, these parts of the city attracted "status-seeking" citizens with higher incomes for a variety of reasons, including land of a higher elevation and availability of more open spaces of property.[6] Residents of north Raleigh, who were mostly white, consumed more land per family, averaging four to six houses per acre.[7] Prospects for profit with real estate purchases in north and west Raleigh attracted further investment.

James Wesley York, real estate developer in Raleigh, for example, strategically created a complex housing development of garden apartments and single-family homes encircling the newly opened shopping center in west Raleigh, Cameron Village.[8] The housing plan was designed to assure cash flow to cover the shopping center's initial costs.[9] Cameron Village was claimed to be the world's first planned shopping center, a significant event in the history of consumerism that highlighted west Raleigh's status in 1949.[10] While officials cited the center as part of the city's "parade of progress,"[11] Caraleigh's progress in 1949 was less of a parade and more of a crawl, with Caraleigh adding street signs and address numbers in order for residents to have mail service for its "381 residences and businesses."[12]

In comparison to other parts of Raleigh, the residents to the south and east of downtown lived in more congested conditions that were an "almost solidly Negro zone."[13] East Raleigh had more than 90 percent of the city's African American population, concentrated in less than 6 percent of the city's land area, all "within walking distance of the city center." South Raleigh and the downtown district grew into an area that attracted lower-income residents who were known to live in "rented and dilapidated houses with poor household facilities."[14] Denizens of these houses tended to be "roomers—some unmarried, and others married but not living with families."[15]

An abundance of state-owned land in south Raleigh factored into the city's settlement patterns and population spread between 1940 and 1960. Educational institutions, public institutions—such as Dorthea Dix—parks, playgrounds, water reservoirs, in addition to prisons, dynamite storage facilities, rock quarries, and the "Negro residential area have repelled the spread of white population."[16] Furthermore, geographer Chittaranjan Pathak in 1964 cited that the "lack of streets and other facilities, inherent poor drainage, and a lack of higher ground have inhibited the growth of population" of south Raleigh.[17] The areas of north and west Raleigh, in comparison, enjoyed a pattern of population density that was more evenly distributed along the main transportation systems than in the inter-arterial sections to the south and east of Raleigh, where Caraleigh was located.

A result of World War II, according to economists, was that the nation experienced the creation of a more balanced distribution of wealth, forming ideal conditions for an advanced consumer economy; in the state's capital, these postwar benefits were enjoyed more fully in north Raleigh, as opposed to Caraleigh in south Raleigh that would enjoy a much smaller slice of the postwar economic pie than the rest of the city.[18]

Margaret Ruth Little's research in *Getting the American Dream for Themselves: Postwar Modern Subdivisions for African Americans in Raleigh, North Carolina* revealed that there were far more subdivisions built in north Raleigh as opposed to south from the 1940s to the 1960s. Eighteen subdivisions—three African American and 15 white—were south of downtown Raleigh, with Western Boulevard serving as boundary of the south side of the city. Areas north of downtown Raleigh had a total of 50: one African American and 49 white.[19] The story of Raleigh's Madonna Acres subdivision and its creator John W. Winters clarifies development trends in Raleigh from 1945 to the 1960s. While Winters worked as a skycap in 1957 at the Raleigh-Durham airport, he realized that "developers were expanding the city to the north and west but paying little attention to predominantly black southeast Raleigh."[20] So Winters purchased 13 acres of land, platted it in 1960, and named it after one of his daughters Donna. The Madonna Subdivision was the first black subdivision in the city created for African Americans by a black developer.[21]

1956: "Tell the people in Caraleigh..."

During the two decades following World War II, Americans experienced a rise in prosperity unparalleled in its history, resulting in increased marriage and birth rates, and consumer demand for housing for newly formed families. With greater availability of construction materials and the birth of federal home loan programs, a home building frenzy commenced throughout the nation to sate the repressed housing demands of veterans and their families that lasted through the 1960s.[22] Raleigh's housing construction, inactive for two decades because of the Great Depression and World War II, was galvanized for both black and white residents.[23] For a large number of African Americans, poverty remained a reality; however, income for black residents increased 40 percent during World War II and by another 50 percent in the 1950s, creating opportunities for some African American families of the middle-class to seek suburban home ownership.[24]

Raleigh's population in 1950 was around 66,000 people, with African Americans comprising one third of this total. Racially restricted residential home purchase rules and segregationist land use practices persisted, despite the *Shelley v. Kraemer* Supreme Court decision in 1948 that eliminated race-based property covenants.[25] This was true throughout North Carolina and the state's capital, with many white communities pledging continued allegiance to racially divided lifestyles, evident in Raleigh's subdivisions, elements of its downtown core, and a large share of areas just outside the city.[26] Beyond facing the usual financial and logistical challenges that home buyers encounter, African Americans in the 1950s contended with deeply embedded racist attitudes from those apprehensive about new black housing communities.[27]

Andrew Wiese's *Places of Their Own: African American Suburbanization in the Twentieth Century* found that black communities in the South grew with new housing construction on the outskirts of cities or on the borders of existing African American neighborhoods. In recognition that many Southern whites wanted to maintain the racial status quo associated with housing segregation, Southern middle-class blacks desired respectable housing separated from poor and working-class blacks.[28] And many of those newer black housing communities, even if built just outside city limits, were soon annexed, following a region-wide trend of absorption in the 1950s and 1960s.[29]

In 2006, historian M. Ruth Little maintained that the "first planned postwar subdivision for African Americans was Rochester Heights, laid out in 1957 near Garner Road adjacent to the planned Beltline."[30] The *News and Observer* reported in November 1959 that the "Biltmore Hills housing project for Negroes" was being built, immediately south of the Rochester Heights subdivision. Rex Burnham, who worked under E.N. Richards and Associates and was in charge of the project, mistakenly stated that the Biltmore Hills subdivision represented the "first effort made to provide housing for Raleigh Negro families of average income."[31]

Largely because of racially charged protests from Caraleigh's residents in 1956, what would have been Raleigh's first planned subdivision for African Americans was rejected. Caraleigh was a racially and geographically isolated enclave in south Raleigh when Raleigh's postwar suburban expansion made the possibility of a planned African American community to be constructed nearby. Racial antipathies in Caraleigh were aroused on August 29, 1956, when E.N. Richards submitted plans to the City Planning Department for a housing development on 44.4 acres of 117 housing lots "for Negroes" in southeast Raleigh.[32] The three bedroom, one bath houses of brick veneer were to be financed through federal home loan programs, the Federal Housing Administration (FHA) and the Veterans' Administration (VA).[33] Hostility to Richards' plans was partially based on his call for an eastern outlet road to nearby highways that would run through Caraleigh, and the mill village's collective belief in racial segregation.

On September 14, 1956, the Raleigh City Council received petitions from those opposed to plans for an African American housing development on South Saunders Street, with copies of petitions, addressed to R.L. Penny, owner of the land, and E.N. Richards, the developer for the project. The petitions expressed opposition from residents of Caraleigh, as well as adjacent neighborhoods, to the creation of a housing subdivision for African Americans "near Caraleigh" with over 1200 signatures and a "threat to use dynamite if necessary to block" it.[34] These were received by the City Council to provide them with "information and guidance."[35] The enumerated signatures were listed as such: 530 from Carolina Pines, Parkland, Hertford Village, Fairview Acres and 687 from Caraleigh and Fuller Heights. Along with the signatures on the petition came a textual response, as reported in Raleigh's African American newspaper *The Carolinian*:

> The petition notes the area "is overwhelmingly occupied by persons of the white race with at least 99 per cent of the inhabitants being of the white race." It also stated that "there are many areas in or near Raleigh which are predominantly of the Negro race, which areas would be many times more desirable to all citizens of both races than the subject area." The petition continued: "While the undersigned citizens are desirous of maintaining good race relations, they are nonetheless strong believers in the principle of separation of the races in residential sections." The petition concluded by asking Penny and Richards to abandon the project and warned "that construction of the project would undoubtedly jeopardize the good prevailing relations now existing between the white and Negro races."[36]

Caraleigh citizens requested a public hearing with the City Council, but Raleigh's Mayor Fred B. Wheeler disagreed, saying that "we don't have any right to hold a hearing on it. The race issue has no business before the Council."[37] City Manager W.H. Carper responded, too, saying that the "city cannot designate areas by race," and

Councilman W.G. Enloe added that "I don't think we should have a racial debate up here."[38] In response, Paul R. Jervay, the owner and editor of Raleigh's African American newspaper, *The Carolinian*, lambasted both Caraleigh and Raleigh's City Council:

> So the residents of Caraleigh do not want a Negro housing development near them. Their spokesman Willis P. Holding has been quoted as saying that 500 residents of that area are in opposition to the proposed Negro project. On the other hand, Mayor Wheeler is quoted as saying he doesn't want any race matters brought before the City Council. We feel that this matter should be brought before the Council and decided once and for all with white people moving into and virtually taking over areas that were once all-Negro it is highly presumptuous to say the least, for a group of white people here to say they will oppose a Negro housing project anywhere.[39]

Jervay, an outspoken opponent of racial segregation, accused Raleigh's City Council of practicing racist policies that "crowded out" African Americans from the city, denying them "space in which to breathe and live."[40] Jervay "prayed" that the City Council would "tell the people in Caraleigh and everywhere else that Negroes are citizens, too, and have the right to live in and own decent homes."[41]

By the end of the first week of October in 1956, the protests and suggested alterations to his plan from City Council, Richards informed Raleigh's City Council that he had abandoned his plan to construct a residential subdivision for African Americans.[42] Mayor Wheeler believed that Raleigh needed more "housing for Negroes" but did not think that Raleigh's City Council was the "place for it."[43]

1957: Raleigh's Annexation of Caraleigh

In 1957, several "outlying areas" of Raleigh were slated to be annexed by the capital city, but a "strong opposition" was heard from Caraleigh, Hertford Village, Coley Forest Ridge Road area, and Bellevue Terrace.[44] A few weeks before the December 31, 1957, public vote to decide on annexation, the opposition was in "high gear" casting doubts upon the success of the city's expansion proposal. On the first day 286 people registered and "of these, 170 were counted at Caraleigh" where opposition was strongest.[45]

Jack Coss, the Raleigh's Assistant City Manager, distributed informational leaflets that explained the benefits of annexation: "fire protection, police service, garbage collection, street lights, school patrol, street maintenance and cleaning, and parks and playgrounds."[46] The cost of partaking in "progressive growth" would come at an estimated cost of "$1.38 per $100 real and personal property assessed valuation"; this price seemed much too high for many of Caraleigh's villagers who were bitter because of their belief that the city had neglected and scorned them for too many years.[47] Following "bitter campaigning" in Caraleigh, the annexation vote of December 31, 1957, with 233 voting for and 186 against, Raleigh absorbed Caraleigh village. This added "575 acres of land and 1,923 Caraleigh folks" to the area known as Raleigh.[48]

One Caraleigh resident recalled that the annexation was practical because for many decades, residents maintained the village and not relied "on the city for assistance," but were "no longer physically able" to clean "out ditches" and repair the

Balloting at Caraleigh for Raleigh's annexation of the mill village, 1957–58 (State Archives of North Carolina).

roads.[49] Some of Caraleigh's residents believed that annexation "definitely benefited" from police and fire services from Raleigh, but many of the promised fruits of annexation were slow to arrive.[50]

By the early 1970s, two decades after annexation, many problems with Caraleigh's "sewer, water, fire protection, and storm drainage" remained ignored.[51] For example, in 1959 city officials told Caraleigh resident Bruce Jefferies to expect city sewer service "within 60 to 90 days," compelling Jefferies to hold off on the installation of a septic system of his own and instead opted to have a "modern bathroom installed in his house."[52] But when city officials did not follow through on their promises, Jefferies and other residents at Caraleigh were left to do as their forebearers had done, rely on the "outhouse" or privy. With backyard outhouses "near overflow," and existing septic systems failing, the response to complaints about the awful odor were met with this answer: "dig another hole."[53] Caraleigh's annexation in 1957 brought frustration among mill village residents who believed that there was "no real answer" to the problems of the old mill village.[54]

Despite the annexation of 1957, Caraleigh residents did not feel as though they were a part of Raleigh. A sense of separation—physical, social, economical, and political—fueled Carleigh's sense of ostracism.

> The predominantly white, blue-collar town has been cut off from the rest of white Raleigh by the black Southside area on the north and east and by the physical barrier of Walnut Creek on the South and Dorothea Dix Hospital on the west.[55]

Nanny Clark sits on her porch on Maywood Avenue across the street from the Fred Whitaker Company in 1974 (State Archives of North Carolina).

According to the *News and Observer* in 1974, Caraleigh residents believed that these racial and geographic barriers limited the village's growth potential, resulting in "little new residential building" compelling young workers to move to other areas.[56] W.A. Horton explained Caraleigh's bleak situation in 1974 in this way.

> Caraleigh is more or less a rural area ... [where] most people know each other and there has been a lot of intermarriage. These people distrust all types of government. They don't have much education and they don't have much money ... the people in this community are even worse off than the blacks. The blacks have a little political clout now.[57]

Horton's insights touch upon some of what philosopher Ivan Illich had to say about modernized poverty, whereby dependence upon institutional care has added a dimension of "helplessness" and "psychological impotence" for people to "fend for themselves."[58] According to Illich, "the poor have always been socially powerless," and at Caraleigh, the dissolution of their paternal overseers heightened this realization between 1930 and the 1970s.[59] Caraleigh's operatives and their families, as underpaid dependents of the Mill from 1892 until 1930, were abandoned at the start of the Great Depression. The paternalistic care that mill executives and their investors exerted upon Caraleigh's workers created a real sense of dependence. This institutional reliance, predicated on corporate profits, combined with operatives' inadequate "schooling," bequeathed Caraleigh residents with a feeling of collective powerlessness and a loss of personal potency.[60] Political, economic, geographic, and social structures appeared to align against Caraleigh.

Caraleigh's perception in Raleigh was captured in a 1975 newspaper article:

> South Saunders Street has never been confused with Glenwood Avenue. Glenwood Avenue has always meant majestic trees, comfortable neighborhoods and an exclusive

country club where some of the city's elite discuss their putting game over afternoon cocktails. South Saunders Street is auto body shops, barbecue eateries, warehouses, and bars where blue collar workers down their beers while listening to country western tunes. To many of the residents of the working class neighborhoods off of South Saunders Street, such as Caraleigh and Fuller Heights, there has never been any doubt about which side of the city the bread is buttered on.[61]

Although the Fred Whitaker Company, which operated inside the old Caraleigh textile building, was busy "around the clock" in 1974, churning out many bales of synthetic materials, the company's good fortune did not salve the sting of Caraleigh's sense of inferiority.[62] In years past, the noise of "the great machines" in the mills signaled good prosperity for the village, but, in the early 1970s, many residents feared that the Caraleigh village was slowly perishing.[63]

In a sad irony, the death of the mill was reflected in the Company's graveyard located just across Walnut Creek. When Caraleigh started to sell burial plots on its own land sometime in the early 1920s, residents were told that the burial area would be cleared and a road and bridge built, so relatives could visit the graves of loved ones. By the early 1970s, the cemetery on Bunker Hill was overgrown with thick vegetation, without a road or functioning bridge. There was a railroad trestle, a precarious walk over the creek, offering the only path. Residents interviewed in 1974 included Nanny Clark, "an old woman, 73, small, in well-worn clothes" who recalled that "My daddy got about four or five lots…. Daddy is buried up there, and so is my aunt."[64] Winnie May Womack shared that she had two children buried on Bunker Hill and complained that there was no way to get up there: "I'd like to see it cleared up…. Caraleigh promised they would do it. But they went bankrupt. I surely would like to see it cleared up."[65]

From 1930 until the early 2000s, the combined macroscopic forces of inequity conspired against Caraleigh. In its first few decades' existence, Caraleigh was celebrated as a gem in Raleigh's crown of success, only to devolve into a "poor and powerless" part of the capital city.[66] But Caraleigh became of official interest to Raleigh's elected officials with annexation starting in 1958. Previously demonstrated concern for the mill and its village was predicated on profits for those who had a vested interest in its success. And when the profits ended, so did any authentic care for Caraleigh's denizens. Thus, access to benefits from the city came through unofficial channels by way of its founders, providing the mill village de facto political voice in Raleigh's city government.

The 1920 death of the mill's most powerful caretaker, A.A. Thompson, and the mill's closing at the start of the Great Depression in 1930, made Caraleigh an orphaned community of no matter to Raleigh. Caraleigh's situation, in terms of human geography and physical location, compounded its diminished status.[67] W.A. Horton, proprietor of Horton's Cash Store on South Saunders Street, stated that "there's nobody on this side of town who has any political clout." Caraleigh's population was—as a blue collar village filled with the undereducated and moneyless—made to feel that they were "the stepchildren of the city," abandoned outcasts with a deep "distrust" for government.[68]

The philosophy of white supremacy taught to the South's children in the early 1900s showed signs of life in the 1970s with Carleigh's support of George C. Wallace, governor of Alabama and candidate for president of the United States, embodied resistance to the civil rights movement of the 1960s and 1970s.[69] A change in presidential primary rules saw North Carolina hold its first presidential primary election in May of 1972 whereby the candidates were subjected to a popular vote. After the votes were tallied, George Wallace was the clear winner, beating former North Carolina Governor Terry Sanford with more than 100,000 votes.[70]

During presidential primaries in 1976, Wake's Republican voters gave Ronald Reagan a 58 percent victory over Gerald Ford; the county's Democratic Party awarded Jimmy Carter nearly 66 percent of their votes over Alabama Governor George C. Wallace, who earned 34 percent of the votes. Jimmy Carter was victorious in every Raleigh voting precinct, except two: "the heavily blue-collar precincts of Caraleigh and Carolina Pines, located off South Saunders Street, which went to Wallace."[71] Decades after Caraleigh's village had been tutored in the tenets of white supremacy, its lessons echoed in later generations.[72]

Caraleigh Neighborhood Association

Rachel Carson's 1962 book, *Silent Spring*, sparked public unease about ongoing environmental pollution of the land, air, water in the United States, resulting in an uptick in popular interest and call for action. The heightened awareness reached a crescendo by 1970 that affected nearly all aspects of American society, both public and private. During President Richard Nixon's administration, the Environmental Policy Act was signed on January 1, 1970, soon leading to the creation of the Environmental Protection Agency (EPA) and the Occupational Safety and Health Administration (OSHA). The first Earth Day event was held on April 22, 1970. New ecologically oriented organizations formed that were large and small, across a wide geographic spectrum that were local, statewide, national, international in scope.[73]

The Caraleigh Neighborhood Association (CNA) organized in 1974 was started during this era of environmental revolution with goals to preserve and beautify the community, while enhancing quality of life for residents.[74] To achieve their objectives, the CNA cultivated alliances with various environmental and neighborhood organizations, as well as with political candidates and elected officials.[75] The CNA was particularly active in the HANDS organization, Home and Neighborhood Development Sponsors (HANDS). W. Clyde Greenway, the public relations director for Sears, Roebuck for the Southeast region, started HANDS in 1957. Greenway's vision was to combat the "blight" that was slowly weakening the nation's cities.[76] The City of Raleigh became the pilot city for the HANDS program. With guidance from the City, the Sears, Roebuck and Company, and the Raleigh Garden Club, ten small, neighborhood HANDS groups were organized during its first year, growing to 40 clubs by 1982.[77] The philosophy of the HANDS organization was to energize and assist garden clubs to lead in community enhancement, environmental improvement and beautification.[78]

For decades, the CNA worked with HANDS towards a "clean, green, and beautiful" Caraleigh and Raleigh.[79] They organized neighborhood clean-up campaigns and participated in city-wide efforts, landscaped gardens in the village, created "Yard-of-the-Month" award.[80] The group called for the city to pave Caraleigh's streets and encouraged home beautification actions.[81] The CNA received grant money from the Wake County Beautification Committee in January 1976 that paid for two Caraleigh road signs welcoming visitors, as well as crepe myrtle trees, shrubs, and tulip bulbs.[82]

Caraleigh residents' gave ample energy in the 1970s and 1980s to enhancing the village's floriculture and appearances, it spent more much time fighting various rezoning efforts thought threatening to the life of the Caraleigh community.[83] A pillar of the CNA's philosophy was that the mill village's survival should see "no additional commercial or industrial zoning."[84] The CNA's activities led to Caraleigh's earned reputation for having an abundance of civic pride that was "hard to beat."[85] During its first years, the CNA reportedly spent more time at City Hall combatting zoning cases, determined to prevent Caraleigh's "erosion" while pursuing its "right to remain a community as free of industry strangulation as possible."[86]

Examples of Caraleigh's 1970s political networking included two fierce advocates of neighborhood activism, Isabella W. Cannon and City of Raleigh Councilor Miriam P. Block. In 1977, Cannon became the first female mayor of Raleigh and first woman mayor of a state capital city, which put her in the national and international spotlight. After announcing her candidacy for mayor, Cannon made her first public appearance at a monthly CNA meeting.[87] Miriam P. Block served as a City Councilor from 1973 to 1988 and was regarded by the CNA as Caraleigh's "one genuine friend, who without fail was always attentive and responsive" to the community's needs.[88] Miriam Block and the CNA supported the mission of the HANDS organization that reflected the era's spirit of environmentalism with a sense religious zeal. The dedicatory prayer at the HANDS dinner in Raleigh on May 28, 1976, revealed a strong sense of eco-theological values, as seen in a copy of the prayer which Miriam Block mailed to the CNA after the event:

> Our Father in Heaven—
>   Tonight, we thank you for these people gathered here—the gardeners of Raleigh—who willingly work and study to keep and create natural beauty, who do so much to improve our environment, to keep America green, and to beautify our landscape. ...[89]

Caraleigh residents in the 1970s-1980s followed a national strategy of "downsizing," whereby neighborhood groups used zoning rules to stymie unwelcomed development.[90] This tactic limited the construction of apartment complexes and further commercialization of the mill village.[91] When one Caraleigh property owner in 1976 tried to have nearly four acres of land on Moring and Prospect Streets rezoned from residential use to industrial, she ran into fierce opposition. Her neighbors argued that Caraleigh already had areas zoned for industrial

Isabella Cannon thanked volunteers soon after her historic election in November 1977 as mayor of Raleigh. The illustration from the bottom of the letter illustrates the spirit of the post–Vietnam War years (Caraleigh Neighborhood Association papers, author's collection).

use, further cited that the city council earlier approved residential zoning in Caraleigh "to give the neighborhood a chance to survive as a residential area."[92] Caraleigh neighborhood activists believed that if zoned for more industrial use, industry would smother Caraleigh to the point that residents could no longer "call themselves a community."[93]

The Capital city's rapid growth in the 1970s and 1980s incurred slow-moving traffic circulation problems, especially along the narrow roads leading to the city

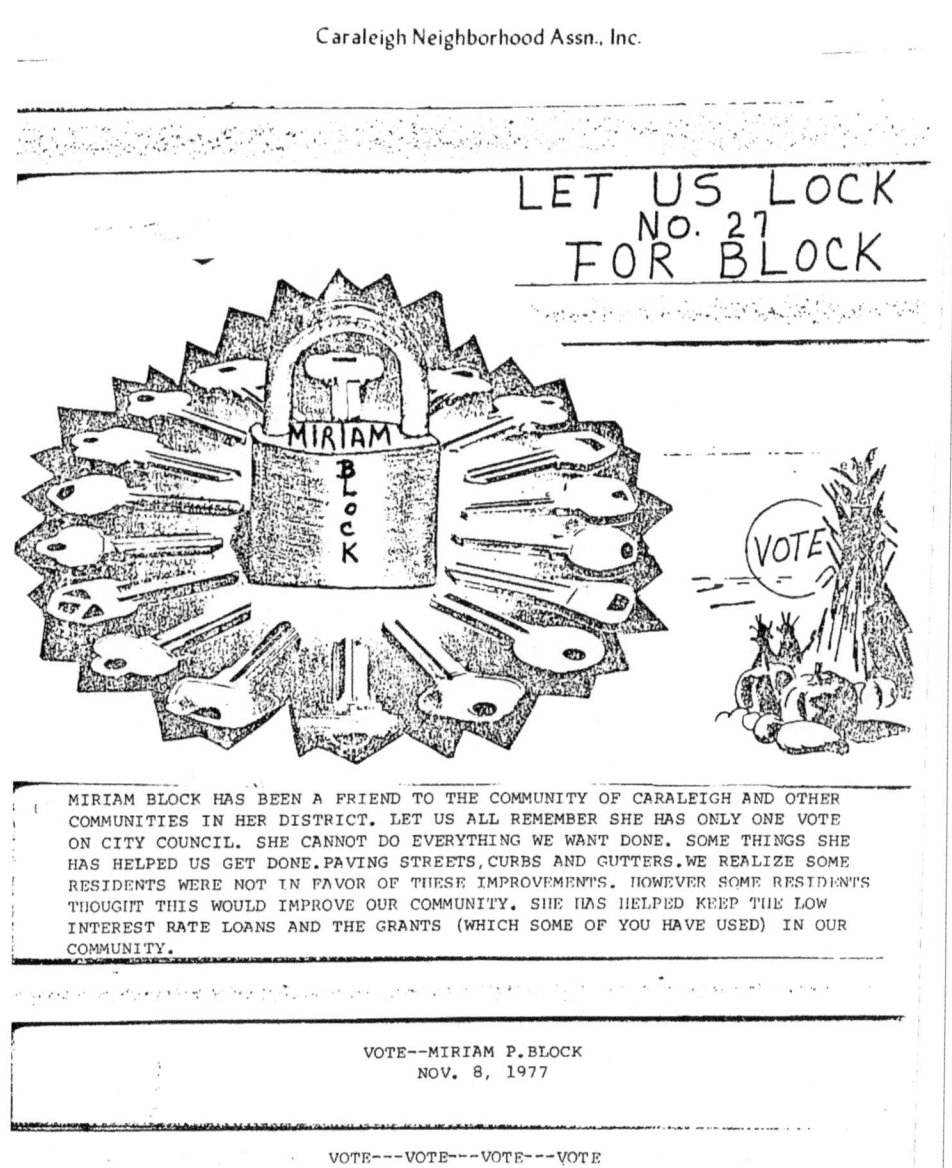

A political support flier showing support of the Caraleigh Neighborhood Association for Miriam Block in her reelection efforts of 1977 (Caraleigh Neighborhood Association papers, author's collection).

from the south.[94] Starting in 1975–1976, Caraleigh residents raised opposition to the state's plans to increase and extend traffic flow from downtown Raleigh with the creation of the Dawson/McDowell Street road extension to South Saunders and the widening of South Saunders Street to link up to the nearby Raleigh Beltline, Interstate 40.[95] Caraleigh's dissent was rooted in the widening of the 1.2 mile stretch of South Saunders Street from two lanes to six, because South Saunders ran through the middle of Caraleigh.[96] Residents feared that expansion of South Saunders Street would exacerbate Caraleigh's physical dissection with increased traffic, disrupting of homes and businesses, and endangerment of children playing.[97]

A proposed alternative was to connect McDowell and Dawson streets' traffic to Wilmington Street, but state highway officials estimated this would be more costly, at $10.4 million, as compared to South Saunders Street option of $8.7 million. Highway planners admitted that using South Saunders Street would negatively impact Caraleigh, but they favored the Caraleigh route not only because of its less-expensive price tag, but also for its access to the new highway beltline, Interstate 40, which was still under construction in 1976.[98]

The Raleigh Beltline was initially conceived in 1951, with planning starting in 1957 and its first section of 12.7 miles completed in 1964. The segment involving the Beltline's connection to South Saunders Street started to become a reality in 1982 and was not completed until 1987.[99] A 1982 report maintained that revamping of South Saunders Street allowed the North Carolina Department of Transportation to compel 74 Caraleigh property owners to sell their land, homes, and businesses. A 1986 newspaper article stated that "14 businesses, five single-family houses, two apartments, eight duplexes and eight miscellaneous buildings fell to the bulldozer."[100] Horton's Cash Store on the corner of South Saunders Street and Maywood Avenue was a notable casualty, with the store "taken" by the state in 1982 and closed.[101] The store served Caraleigh's community from 1937 to 1982. During its final years, Horton's store mainly served Carleigh's small population of elderly residents, but this was not always the case. Just after World War II, Horton's was a thriving full-service grocery requiring nine full-time butchers and was the Caraleigh Rural Post Office until 1972.[102]

Caraleigh property owners who were in the path of the South Saunders Street widening were told to vacate their land by January 1982; however, months of delays with the start of road construction aggravated already present feelings of angst among the displaced. But Caraleigh residents realized that they had little choice but to accept their luckless fate. The 1981–1982 Project Report for the Caraleigh Neighborhood Association (C.N.A.) did not mask the community's frustrations.

> The community accepted the fact that the South Saunders Street extension project was forced upon us and were resigned to beginning [to] look forward to its completion. The project, or rather the State of North Carolina, unnecessarily forced two elderly couples to relocate when, in fact, they probably could have finished living out their lives in the home they loved so dearly. The only neighborhood business that actually benefitted the neighborhood was forced to close. This action has understandably been a disappointment and is not a popular subject. We will be a little happier when the debris that has accumulated on the now State owned property is removed.[103]

Years of road construction along South Saunders community "terribly embarrassed" the community, because it "created an eyesore" that "blighted" the image of their neighborhood and the city of Raleigh.[104] The plant manager at the Fred Whitaker Company, which was housed in the original Caraleigh Cotton Mill, corroborated the CNA's view of the state's road construction on South Saunders Street: "I think it's probably going to be good for the city of Raleigh, as far as getting traffic in and out. But it hasn't been kind to the community ... but that's the price of progress."[105] Ninety-year-old Caraleigh resident T.H. Stroud disagreed. A former employee of Caraleigh Mills cotton plant who was forced to move from his home on Summit Avenue, Stroud said, "I think it's a good idea. It's improving the place. I think it'll be a lot of help to motorists. And we'll be able to get to town quicker, at least."[106] Mildred Flynn, a longtime resident of Caraleigh and a leader of the Caraleigh Neighborhood Association, was bitter about the road construction. Flynn countered that Stroud's opinion was in the minority and that "the state and the city just did what they wanted" and failed to listen to neighborhood protests.[107] Nevertheless, despite years of aggravation over road construction, the Caraleigh Neighborhood Association donated $300 to the city for added landscaping and floral beautification of the median on South Saunders Street in Caraleigh.[108]

When road construction finished in July 1987, traffic flowed into Raleigh and out of the capital city along the enlarged South Saunders Street. To the mill village residents, it once again appeared that Caraleigh was a necessary casualty for the Oak City's prosperity, sacrificed upon the altar of Raleigh's improvement. In compensation, city and state officials maintained that increased vehicular traffic "could generate development in the south and southeast sections of the city."[109]

Miriam P. Block and the Citizens' Revolt: 1973

In Miriam Block's 1973 election to Raleigh's City Council, Caraleigh found a substantive, supporting voice. Block was elected to Raleigh's City council during what was proclaimed to be a "citizen revolt," whereby seven new council members were elected and installed: two African Americans, one of whom was Clarence E. Lightner, Raleigh's first black mayor, a woman, a minister, a college professor, an architect, a retired fire chief, and a tax lawyer, who was Jewish.[110] Most of these new council members, considered as more progressive than their predecessors, possessed a favorable attitude towards neighborhood and environmental concerns.[111] For Caraleigh, Block's win was significant because she was their representative in District D, giving Caraleigh representation in Raleigh politics, absent since the death of A.A. Thompson in 1920.[112]

Many in North Carolina's capital believed that Raleigh's political structure was dysfunctional. From the 1890s to the 1920s, Raleigh's municipal government was synonymous with the city's Chamber of Commerce; both entities were dominated by wealthy business interests that gave little attention to parts of the city filled with poor residents.[113] Caraleigh, for example, had unofficial representation in the form of its powerful founders who were often both business leaders and city officials. Raleigh's governmental arrangement favored local oligarchs that conceived Caraleigh, a setup whereby municipal leaders were elected to at-large seats, chosen mainly by powerful petty aristocrats with little or no public input.[114] But Raleigh's imbalanced method governance changed with the adoption of the district system in the early 1970s that divided the city into five political districts.[115] Miriam P. Block had called for this because it compelled "closer contact with constituents" and allowed potential candidates of modest means to run for office.[116] Unlike the political era of A.A. Thompson, the district system allowed Miriam Block to put "neighborhood interests over backroom politics."[117]

Miriam J. Preston Block (1920–2005) was born and reared in Mattoon, Illinois, and attended the Mattoon school system, then Eastern Illinois University and later the University of Illinois. In 1941 Miriam married William Joseph Block and around 1957 their family moved to Raleigh.[118] Miriam Block was an elected member of the Raleigh City Council for five terms from 1973 to 1985.[119] It appeared to many that Block rose quickly from 52 year old housewife to an imposing political powerhouse. But such criticisms failed to recognize that for years before her 1973 election, Block had carefully cultivated a wealth of political capital as a neighborhood activist.[120]

In 1962, Block fought the construction of a shopping center that residents in Southwest Raleigh opposed; over erosion problems, Block was "firmly against" added development around the ecologically sensitive Lake Johnson area.[121] Block also advocated for passage of the 1969 Southside Urban Renewal bonds and the 1971 water and sewer bond campaign. Perhaps Block's most politically advantageous involvement was with the West Raleigh Civic Association formed in 1969. The organization, filled with university faculty from such middle class subdivisions as Kentwood and Cardinal Hills, started over concerns about the Kent Road public housing project, later turning its energies on problems of urbanization in the Lake Johnson area.[122]

Before winning election in November 1973, civic organizations had twice strongly supported Block's appointment to fill vacancies in the

Miriam P. Block was an elected member of Raleigh's City Council for five terms from 1973 to 1985 (State Archives of North Carolina).

City Council, but Block was snubbed both times. Civic groups cried foul not only because they backed Block, but that both appointment decisions were made behind closed doors, in secret meetings, where the council members' selection choice was made without public input.[123] Block viewed both of these instances as symptomatic of a sick city council comprised almost entirely of developers and businessmen, people who stood to financially "gain for their business interests during their term in office."[124] Block proclaimed that Raleigh needed officials who would "concentrate on public needs."[125]

The land developers were wary of having Block in office because of her opinions about land development in Raleigh, which she believed to be mismanaged. Block called for adherence to comprehensive land plans so "the city can grow intelligently," believing that such "long range planning has been woefully inadequate in Raleigh."[126] Block ran for office as a reform candidate, campaigning for improved land-use planning to control urban growth, in opposition to special interest influence in city hall that hid their actions behind a veil of governmental secrecy. Block expressed confidence in her ability to win in a fair election, partly because she was already an established community organizer by 1973. A councilman, in Block's opinion, needed to possess a "depth of knowledge" of the area they wish to represent, as well as its problems, "something she said her three opponents do not have."[127]

Block did not assume victory in November 1973 as evidenced in her conducting the most intensive campaign of all the other candidates. Added to her hard work was her involvement in numerous organizations. Block's organizational affiliations and leadership included the Democratic Party chairman of precinct 41, Democratic Women of Wake County, the Eleanor Roosevelt Club, Girl Scout leader, Sunday School teacher, tutor in English as second language and a tutor in the Wake County School System.[128] Block's husband was head of the political science department at North Carolina State University, undoubtedly a source of support for her political actions.[129] This amounted to a long-range strategy that propelled Block to victory over her opponents in 1973 by a crushing margin of nearly four to one.[130]

Even after her November 1973 first term victory, Block continued to strengthen and expand her political base of support. Dutifully, Block addressed constituent complaints, making it a practice to call and talk to ten constituents each evening, and she frequently attended speaking engagements at garden clubs and other community groups.[131] Once in office, Block filled city boards successfully with members of the West Raleigh Civic Association. Added to the planning commission were Thomas Perry and Paul Moore. Perry, of North Carolina State University (NCSU), was a soil scientist and Moore, a realtor; to the Greenway Commission, Richard Volk and Conrad Miller, both of NCSU, were also added. Volk was a soil scientist and Miller a horticulture professor.[132] When Block made her appointments, the West Raleigh Civil Association became a noted political force and accusations of political patronage were made against Block. In response, Block said that she disliked the term "patronage" because it implied some sort of political payoff. Block argued that her appointments were made because those men were "very talented."[133]

During her Raleigh political career, Block built a network of supporters that would spark envy in other politicians.[134] Block's "meticulous labors in her political vineyard" made her appear a nearly unbeatable force in Raleigh politics.[135]

> Raleigh City Councilwoman Miriam P. Block doesn't smoke fat cigars. But Mrs. Block is the closest thing this city has seen in recent years to a ward politician; spinning a web of intricate ties throughout her sprawling Southwest Raleigh district and practicing a local version of patronage politics.[136]

Block projected a less than ferocious demeanor that did not mirror her political power, causing opponents to underestimate her.[137] Douglass Matthews, Block's main opponent in the 1973 election, was less than impressed with Block upon meeting her. When campaigning door-to-door, residents warned Matthews about the formidable Mrs. Block, predicting "little chance" of victory. Expecting to come face-to-face with a "political spellbinder," Matthews said he met instead a "soft-spoken" woman who "talked hesitatingly, often back-tracking to find the right word."[138] Until the voting results came in, Matthews thought that Block was overrated. Block won 2197 to 766.[139]

During her first term in office, Block stood up for policies of better city planning, the creation of citizen involvement programs, and increased neighborhood preservation. Businessmen viewed Block's political platform as anathema to their goals. In 1975, Amedo DeAngelis was another political opponent for Block to vanquish. DeAngelis, a native of Reading, Pennsylvania, moved to Raleigh in the 1950s on a football scholarship to North Carolina State University and graduated in 1958. DeAngelis returned to Pennsylvania but in 1963 returned to Raleigh where he started restaurants, opened the South Hill's Twin Cinema, and a coffee shop in Rex Hospital.

From the outset, DeAngelis underestimated Block, saying that "a woman's place was in the home" and not in business or political leadership. In response, Block "mimeographed the newspaper article that quoted DeAngelis and passed it out at the polls during the Oct. 14 primary."[140] Backpedaling, DeAngelis clarified his misogynistic utterance saying that he was referring to "mothers of children under age seven" and not to Block, per se. Going further, DeAngelis maintained that "when I compare a housewife with a businessman, the businessman could do a better job on the city council."[141]

Block's supporters for reelection included the West Raleigh Civic Association, Boylan Heights Preservation and Restoration Society, Caraleigh Neighborhood Association, and the Community Coalition, which was the political arm of the city's neighborhood groups. During her first two years in office, Block "pushed through the rezoning of large portions of her district—action requested by the neighborhood groups to keep out unwanted development in areas such as Lake Johnson, Caraleigh, Carolina Pines, Robinwood, Boylan Heights, Fuller Heights, and Fairway Acres."[142]

DeAngelis devalued Block's community groups, painting them as "cliques" filled with academics who lacked business acumen.[143] Block dismissed accusations that the city council inhibited Raleigh's economic growth between 1973 and 1975: "I don't think it can be validated in any way. The slowdown in construction in Raleigh (due to the economy) has been less than in other cities."[144] Mrs. Block promised that if reelected in 1975, she would "support the use of some of the federal Community Development anti-slum money in the Caraleigh, Nazareth and Method communities of Southwest Raleigh."[145] When Block defeated Amedeo R. DeAngelis with a vote tally of 1,975 to 966, a coalition of Raleigh business owners called for a change to the district system of electing city council members, arguing that it had created an "anti-business" climate, detrimental to the city's prosperity.[146]

Miriam Block was Caraleigh's voice in Raleigh for the village's "poor and powerless."[147] In explanation of her philosophy, Block claimed that there was conflict of interest in Raleigh's government; "many council members in the past have not excused themselves from votes on issues in which they had a monetary interest."[148] Although Block did not provide specific examples to her argument, the full history of Caraleigh presents a sterling example of supporting evidence for Block's argument.[149]

Caraleigh founder and former Raleigh Mayor A.A Thompson and Councilwoman Miriam Block were at once similar and dissimilar. Thompson's death in 1920 was also the year of Block's birth. Both were members of the same political party, albeit a Democratic Party whose philosophy of governance had changed by the 1970s, most notably in its early 1900s policy of racial antipathy towards African Americans. Both Block and Thompson also had opinions about Raleigh's water and its relationship with phosphate.[150] Thompson supported the widespread use of phosphorus to create fertilizers for farmers to enhance their nutrient deficient soil; conversely, Block called for reduced use of phosphates, advocating a ban on phosphates in laundry detergents as an environmental protection. While warning audiences about the dangers of laundry detergent that included phosphates, Block would sometimes hold her favored visual aid, a "very white shirt washed in non-phosphate detergent."[151] Both Thompson and Block made Caraleigh a priority, but for different reasons.

During her first term in office, Councilwoman Block requested the council to begin a large-scale street resurfacing project to repair the "pothole-laden" roads in Caraleigh.[152] Caraleigh "has not had a road resurfaced since it was annexed into the city in the late 1950s."[153] The other Council members were ambivalent because the resurfacing of the entirety of Caraleigh would have doubled the city's yearly resurfacing budget. Block compromised and proposed resurfacing only some of the streets: Green, Summit, Gilbert, Prospect, Maywood, Pantops, Thompson, and Moring streets.[154] When Block was accused of "pork barrel politics" in getting Caraleigh's roads paved in exchange for political support, Block quipped that Caraleigh had such a small population that vote-getting was not her motive.[155]

Block's encouragement of citizen activism and organization into community groups galvanized Caraleigh to action. The 135 members of Caraleigh's Neighborhood Association led a cleanup campaign that resulted in dozens of pickup truck loads of trash being hauled out of the neighborhood, with "17 old cars" removed and "14 houses" repainted.[156] Caraleigh residents were encouraged to maintain their lawns with "Yard of the Month" contests for the most improved lawn[157]; a Caraleigh newsletter was started and distributed; a community goal was discussed to create a sign announcing to motorists who were entering Caraleigh.

Raleigh's growth in the 1970s and 1980s resulted in increased road construction leading to the city and added rezoning requests of land in Caraleigh; residents saw these as existential threats that would fragment and imperil their "way of life" deteriorating the "body and soul" of Caraleigh.[158] Caraleigh and other neighborhoods fought losing battles against commercial and industrial zoning and road expansion in the 1970s and 80s.[159]

Charles Craven, a columnist with the *News and Observer,* described Caraleigh in 1979 as an "old pleasant neighborhood threatened by the building of a superhighway," because Raleigh's growth had created traffic situations that begged for relief.[160] The traffic situation had changed from 1949 when the Caraleigh community protested the "proposed re-routing" of Highway 15A, a major travel artery, "from their section of the city."[161] The city responded in 1979 with a plan that had three options. Options one and two would have had little to no effect on Caraleigh; plan three, however, was perceived as an existential threat to the "essential character" of the mill village.[162] The creation of up to eight lanes of traffic to reduce traffic problems in the south-central portion of Raleigh, as well as the addition of a median that "could," it was argued, "create a sense of barrier" for drivers and pedestrians.[163] The city's proposed remedy for "congestion and delay for through motorists" was to alleviate existing traffic buildup and to "accommodate traffic demand to the year 2000."[164] The proposed widening of the pavement on Saunders Street from 44 feet to 88 feet also included mitigation measures for pedestrian disruption at Caraleigh; there would be a "signalized" crosswalk at the intersection of Maywood Avenue and Saunders Street.[165]

One of the seven Caraleigh businesses that were to be directly impacted was "Horton's Cash Store" that had served the people of Caraleigh for four decades, 25 years of which were at a location planned for the road widening project. Horton contended that elimination of his grocery store would "create a hardship for the community, especially the elderly and disabled." Caraleigh Neighborhood Association, consisting of about fifty families, echoed Horton's sentiments saying that road expansion would divide their neighborhood and "ruin the community."[166] On Caraleigh's behalf, Miriam P. Block maintained that "Caraleigh was a thriving residential and business area before 1900. Some of its residents are second and third generation homeowners and taxpayers..." and that "it has been a good place to live, a cohesive and friendly neighborhood where people are on a first name basis and who share interests in everything from for [sic] the children, churches, the streets and even the trees and flowers.[167] This type of residential neighborhood is scarce and valuable."[168] Citing her historical perceptions of Caraleigh prior to 1900, Block petitioned the city planners, saying "please don't ruin the homes of the people of Caraleigh. They were here first." Block's history of the Caraleigh community was a bit of a stretch in accuracy since the area where Caraleigh was constructed in 1892 was described as mostly "fertile farmlands."[169]

Nevertheless, Block believed that because Wake County's population had mushroomed, bringing with it "morning and evening traffic" that was nightmarish, especially "at McDowell, Dawson, Lenoir, Saunders, Cabarrus Streets," something had to be done.[170] To Wayne L. Horton's argument that the expansion of South Saunders Road would "cut in half" Caraleigh's community with added "lanes of 45 mph traffic," city officials reminded Horton that Caraleigh was "already traversed by Saunders Street," therefore there was no new division.[171] Going further, officials declared that option three was best for the city of Raleigh, and that the road widening project's effect on the community of Caraleigh, which was "neither clearly growing nor deteriorating," would not destroy the "essential character of the neighborhood."[172]

Over the years, the land in and around Caraleigh has provided interesting reminders of Raleigh's past. Lake Wheeler Road, which forms Caraleigh's western boundary, was constructed in 1771 as a military road for British troops to combat the Regulator uprising. Lake Wheeler Road originally was named "Ramsgate Road," but later corrupted into "Ramcat Road."[173] The word "Ramsgate" was associated with a road that the Canterbury Pilgrims in England traveled upon. Over the last few centuries, Lake Wheeler Road has also been known as "Ramsgate Road," "Rhamkatte Road," "Tryon Road," "Asylum Road," and "Holly Springs Road."[174]

At one point, when workers in 1891 were grading a portion of Rhamkatte Road for passage of a railway line to Caraleigh, an explosive blast was necessary to cut through granite-laden earth.[175] After the smoke cleared, a serpentine casualty was discovered, a "striped snake, 17 foot long, with a spiked tail and perfectly blind."[176] Workers cut open the dead snake to find "the red coat of a British officer" from the Revolutionary War, swallowed over a century earlier. Of course, this may be just a tall tale. But later relics dug up from Caraleigh's earth have proven more believable.

Wake County Coroner Marshall W. Bennett inspects bones from a Civil War era grave recovered in 1960 at the intersection of Maywood Avenue and South Saunders Street (used with permission of the *News and Observer* [Raleigh] and the State Archives of North Carolina).

During the Civil War, there were 11 Confederate artillery batteries encircling Raleigh in preparation for defense against any invading forces. One of these artillery batteries was located at the future site of Caraleigh. The Confederate artillery around Raleigh was unused, though. Union troops entered Raleigh after the city had surrendered, allowing General William Tecumseh Sherman to make a bloodless, dress parade procession.[177]

Union troops bivouacked on Caraleigh's high ground, overlooking the city. Rumors about soldiers' graves in Caraleigh were confirmed in 1960 when city workers were excavating the earth for a sewer line at intersection of South Saunders Street and Maywood Avenue. The remnants of a coffin and the bones from its occupant were found, suspected remains of a Union soldier, "a Yankee."[178]

The state's Farmers

Market sits across Lake Wheeler Road, just short walk from Caraleigh Mills. Before moving to its present location in 1990, state officials permitted metal detector enthusiasts to search for historic artifacts. Because the area was occupied by 17,000 Union troops, the amateur archaeologists dug up relics such as uniform buttons, buckles, and minie ball bullets.[179]

10

1980s–2020s: From Sow's Ear to Silk Purse

The pace of improvement in Caraleigh took place slowly over the final decades of the 20th century, incrementally but noticeably. Residents recalled that Caraleigh's neighborhood was long considered a "tough" place, but that the ameliorative change began in the mid–1970s when the city paved its streets and residents started "fixing up their homes."[1] Another glimmer of changed appeared with the appearance of a "For Sale" sign in the yard of a home on Maywood Avenue in 1985. The Caraleigh Neighborhood Association's records characterized this as a "situation most unusual," because property sold at Caraleigh had "never actually gone through the real estate dealer route."[2] Caraleigh residents noticed in 2010 that changes were afoot in the mill village, leading the *News and Observer* to ask, "Is it gentrification?"[3]

The term "gentrification" has suffered from overuse to the point of transmutation, according to Dennis E. Gale, author of *The Misunderstood History of Gentrification.* Gale thought that the

> definitional promiscuity, of the word gentrification had rendered its meaning muddled and inexact. In popular culture and academia, gentrification has come to be applied to nearly slightest instance of perceived urban improvement: the creation of museums, aquariums, hotels, music halls, coffee houses, bike paths, and more.

Gale restores sharp edged clarity to the word that had been dulled by overuse.[4] His understanding of gentrification was rooted in the neologism that British sociologist Ruth Glass developed when observing the transformation of old housing in inner-city London neighborhoods in the 1960s. Gale's review of gentrification, according to Glass:

> "gentrification," denoted not the random or occasional improvement of older city properties but, rather, a more or less systematic and continual process leading ultimately to the nearly complete conversion of a neighborhood's physical, economic, and social character. In short, gentrification was not merely ameliorative; it was transformative.[5]

In the 1970s and 1980s, researchers used phrases such as "neighborhood resettlement" and "neighborhood revitalization" but later adopted Glass's "gentrification" when describing similar phenomena in North America.[6]

Glass's theory upended Homer Hoyt's widely accepted "Filter Theory" about the lifecycle of homes in inner cities. The Filter Theory posited that as homes get older, they structurally deteriorate and their value depreciates, along with their functional utilities, such as their electric systems, bathrooms, kitchens. Older housing *filters down* economically to attract lower income residents as renters, or owners. Conversely, newer housing would attract middle and high income families who were *filtering up* the socioeconomic ladder. Hoyt's outlook was reinforced with the increase in roads, highways, automobiles, and mass movement to the suburbs in the United States after World War II. Hoyt maintained that middle class families would seek better homes to avoid "blighted areas in the midst of cities" that were "jungles of crime" and training grounds for miscreant behavior.[7] The Filter Theory asserted that older homes and neighborhoods after about fifty years should be replaced with newer homes. This presumed pattern of housing obsolescence, widely accepted by the people who determined neighborhood and housing investment and expansion actions, was not favorable to older communities such as Caraleigh. The death of Caraleigh's patrons—however abusive—along with the national decline in the cotton industry in the 1920s, followed by the Great Depression, further compounded Caraleigh's squalid status, and was assuredly within the paradigm of Hoyt's Filter Theory. And of course, Raleigh's method of municipal elections only exacerbated Caraleigh's seemingly crushing troubles. But the beginning of an authentic gentrification process awaited Caraleigh as a new millennium approached.

To reduce confusion about the process of urban growth, transformation, and decline, Gale described the elements of "embryonic gentrification,"[8] used to denote the gentrification process in the United States that emerged around 1915 and lasted until the 1980s.[9] Embryonic gentrification included the localized improvement of older housing by do-it-yourself homeowners in a neighborhood where new construction was uncommon. The genesis of an area's embryonic gentrification was made possible by the availability of existing homes for rehabilitation that required lower costs and skill levels to undertake compared to building a new home. For the residents of neighborhoods whose older houses showed glaring signs of obsolescence and disrepair, restoration was an affordable, manageable option in comparison to new home construction.[10]

Often proceeding at a sluggish pace, a neighborhood's nascent journey of authentic gentrification proceeded attract the attention of real estate speculators who would buy and sell, or rent, properties for sizable profit. The embryonic gentrification process proceeded to gain institutional approval from entities such as banks and insurance companies, thus reversing previous trend of decay in the neighborhood. Typical large-scale renovations often occur with the renewed use of vacant "properties such as mills," warehouses, and factories for new residential or commercial ventures.[11] In full bloom, a gentrifying area shows signs of increased investment, rather than disinvestment and deterioration, rising property costs, and upward socioeconomic transition in the population of newcomers.

Caraleigh's journey to gentrification largely followed Dennis E. Gale's paradigm. At first, "no one wanted to live" in Caraleigh, a neighborhood remembered as a "red light district" in the early 1970s, where many of its poor denizens made a living by any means: gambling, prostitution, or even selling liquor by the drink from their own houses.[12] Filled with a number of "street people" who openly demonstrated their substance addictions on Caraleigh's streets, the old mill village appeared an unlikely candidate for real estate investment.[13] Caraleigh's slum reputation started to slowly diminish starting in the 1970s, ushering in changes to the village and the state's capital city.[14] Raleigh's Gilded Age entrepreneurs saw cotton manufacturing as the impetus for development in lands south of Raleigh's city center in 1892, but a new generation of real estate entrepreneurs risked their wealth to take advantage of opportunities in Caraleigh.

Raleigh's Housing Woes and Caraleigh's Revival

James (Jim) Gerardi and Betty Gerardi, residents of Caraleigh since 1974, recalled that Caraleigh was considered a rough area. An area filled houses that were so cheap, they were practically "given away."[15] The Gerardis recalled that when they first moved to Caraleigh in their early 20s, they "were very poor."[16] Nevertheless, the couple thought that they needed a home for their new family, so they purchased one of Caraleigh's aged and enfeebled homes, and proceeded to rehabilitate it. This was the start of the couple's habit of buying and refurbishing other existing homes in Caraleigh throughout the 1980s and 1990s. Jim Gerardi recalled that he also relocated a number of older homes from other parts of the city and moved them into several of Caraleigh's vacant lots.

Betty and James Gerardi stand in front of their Caraleigh home in 2021. The Gerardis revived the boarded-up and condemned home in 1974 and have lived in it since (photograph by the author).

The start of Caraleigh's gentrification was with James and Betty Gerardi in 1974, when they engaged in do-it-yourself improvements of older houses in Caraleigh, where new construction was uncommon. When asked about the cause of Caraleigh's turnaround towards improvement, Jim Gerardi thought the overarching reason was its proximity to Raleigh, which led to the road widening of South Saunders Street from two lanes to six lanes in the 1980s. The Gerardis were at the forefront of Caraleigh's gentrification process, but others followed, such as William J. Dumont, someone whom Jim Gerardi regarded as "an asset to the neighborhood."[17] Although not a resident of Caraleigh, Dumont bought, revived, and rented properties on a larger scale than the Gerardis.[18]

Economic growth in mid–1980s escalated housing costs in the Triangle: Raleigh–Durham–Chapel Hill. By 1986, Raleigh was experiencing an acute shortage of available housing for both rich and poor residents.[19] Housing in the wealthier northern suburbs of Raleigh was expensive and competitively priced. And even in the low-income housing areas, there was a dearth of available homes, where there was high demand but little supply.

It was noted that city regulations pertaining to low-income housing did little to help improve underdeveloped parts of the city, where there was little concern for identifying substandard housing and requiring landlords to make needed repairs. Recommendations were many, but one proposal was that the city motivate builders to repair and construct homes in under-developed neighborhoods; this prescription augured the transformation of Caraleigh and a plan of action for William J. Dumont.[20] *News and Observer* reporter Josh Shaffer recorded William J. Dumont's observations of Caraleigh in 1994, which confirmed that the mill village's diminution that started in 1930 continued to the 1990s.

> He saw beer drinkers on porches, tossing cans into the yard. He saw rotting roofs and plywood-covered windows. He saw worn out people on worn down streets. But he also saw the shadow of a special neighborhood in those broken-down bungalows. Decades ago, Caraleigh was a place of blue-collar pride. Residents helped run the machines of the textile mill on Maywood Avenue, and everybody knew everybody else's name. Dumont wanted that again.[21]

Dumont's first purchase of Caraleigh property in 1994 led to dozens more, earning him a reputation for being among Raleigh's most "well-liked" landlords.[22] Dumont's strategy and practice of buying dilapidated properties, upgrading them, and ejecting troublesome renters, inspired wide praise. By 2010, the police, politicians, and longtime Caraleigh families recognized William J. Dumont as the catalytic force that revived "the South Raleigh mill village one bungalow at a time."[23] Dumont explained that institutional lenders refused to loan him money to buy houses in Caraleigh because of its unsavory reputation; and when banks did finally offer him loans for homes in Caraleigh, it was only after Dumont made renovations to the property in question.[24]

Homeownership usually marked neighborhood improvement; however, Dumont achieved progress in Caraleigh via property rentals. Three examples showcase Dumont's property management tactics:

> In September and October [2010], police arrested the people living at 163 Maywood after finding opium and cocaine. So Caraleigh's community watch approached Dumont and he bought the place. Today he is restoring the columns that graced the front in the old mill days.

At 135 Maywood, an elderly couple needed to move but nobody would buy their 875-square-foot house with the kitchen linoleum torn down to the bare wood. Dumont paid $54,000 in cash for it—"A bank wouldn't give you a mortgage on that thing," he said—and today he's not just refurbishing the kitchen. He's building an addition out back."

At 127 Maywood, Dumont bought the house strictly because his tenants next door were complaining about the noise. [Don't] "Bother my tenants," he warns.

With genial and practical property management style, Dumont won the hearts and minds of the people of Caraleigh and subsequently attracted future investment in the area.

In addition to Dumont's efforts, other options were pursued to alleviate Raleigh's housing shortage, one experiment included allowing prefabricated homes to be placed on single lots in existing neighborhoods.[25] A quarter acre of city-owned land in Caraleigh on 125 Prospect Street—a weedy lot that had sat undeveloped for three decades—was selected for locating a manufactured home as a demonstration. The use of factory-built, low-cost, modular housing that could be readily moved into a neighborhood would require changing city zoning codes; doing so, would have been the first use of manufactured homes in the Raleigh-Durham Triangle.[26] Debates ensued over the summer and winter of 1999 over the structural quality and aesthetics of locating prefabricated homes within the city. Some Caraleigh residents approved the inclusion of manufactured homes in their neighborhood because several homes were deteriorating and a couple had been abandoned.[27] Despite "strong neighborhood support in Caraleigh" for inclusion of manufactured-homes in areas already populated

William J. Dumont consults with Dionacio Barajas in 2010 at a home they were renovating. Starting in the 1990s, Dumont bought and refurbished dozens of old mill houses in the Caraleigh neighborhood (used with permission of the *News and Observer* [Raleigh]).

with "traditional or stick-built homes," Raleigh's Planning Commission voted against the proposal in October 1999.[28]

But just a month later, significant changes to the language of the city ordinance persuaded the city council to reverse their earlier vote, allowing for inclusion of manufactured homes in Raleigh's city limits.[29] Great pains were taken by the Manufactured Housing Institute and Raleigh's Urban Design Project to ensure that their prefab home in Caraleigh looked similar to other homes on the street.[30] Caraleigh's experience at the vanguard of modular home use was a noteworthy event in the history of housing in the Triangle area. The modular home on Prospect Avenue was hailed as the first new home created in Caraleigh in three decades. This may have been the perception, but Wake County public records reveal that at least one new home was built in the Caraleigh neighborhood in every decade from the 1900s to the 2010s.[31] Nevertheless, the impression that Caraleigh was a less than vibrant part of the city remained.

The Caraleigh Furniture store, in business for over five decades, illustrated socioeconomic changes in south Raleigh when it closed its location on South Saunders Street in 2000.[32] Eighty-two-year-old Leon Rose recalled that when his father first opened the store in the 1940s, Caraleigh was at the "end of the bus line" and "South Saunders was just two lanes" of traffic.[33] The longtime Caraleigh business was one of four Raleigh area furniture stores that closed, reflecting macroscopic industry trends whereby larger national furniture retailers entered formerly local and regional markets.[34] Macroscopic market pressures alone did not compel Caraleigh Furniture's closure; there was also the owner's desire to retire, his son's disinterest in assuming leadership, and the increased value of the property in Caraleigh that promised profit by either selling the land or leasing the store's location.[35]

North Carolina's textile industry, profitable in the late 1800s, started a steady decline by the mid–1920s that continued to the Great Depression and persisted throughout the 20th century. From 1975 to 1985, the state's textile industry shrank by 28 percent. The subsequent mill closings threatened obsolete mill buildings with destruction.[36] As of 2001, Caraleigh was one of three late-19th-century mills in Raleigh that remained and was the "largest extant late nineteenth century industrial building," standing out "as a well-preserved example of an increasingly less common type of significant industrial building."[37]

When the Fred Whitaker Company (FWC) closed down its operations at the 160,000-square-foot Caraleigh Mills textile building in October 1999, hopes for a quick sale of the Caraleigh site failed when the potential buyer could not obtain financial backing for its plan to convert Caraleigh into a condominium complex.[38] It seemed that the dark and empty brick Caraleigh Mills building, once considered the pride of Raleigh, would enter the 21st century an unlikely candidate for investors' attention. But a second, and successful, attempt at Caraleigh's resuscitation awaited.

Vaughn King's Challenges at Caraleigh

In November 2001, Barney Joyner, owner of the Joyner Realty, purchased Caraleigh Mills' 15 acres of land and its 160,000 square foot building for $1.4 million

10. 1980s–2020s: From Sow's Ear to Silk Purse

Developer Vaughn King talking on his cell phone outside Caraleigh Mills, August 2002. Because of the historic value of the building, home buyers could obtain tax credits and a 50 percent reduction in property tax (used with permission of the *News and Observer* [Raleigh]).

dollars.[39] Joyner partnered with Vaughn King, owner of King's Building and Development, to renovate the Caraleigh Mill building into "120 condominiums and about 30,000 square feet of office space" at a cost of $17 million dollars over a two year period.[40] The central goal was to create affordably priced condominiums at around $112,000, which was about half the cost of a new Wake County home in 2001.[41] King was the leader in the transformation of the Caraleigh Mills building into a usable, livable space that he hoped would enhance the city's economy and help alleviate ever problematic traffic woes. The *News and Observer* opined approvingly that the mill was not "much to look at now, but it could be just the silk purse south Raleigh needs."[42]

Joyner and King advanced a plan of action that would result in what the *News and Observer* called a "Mill reincarnation" with several robust "selling points."[43] Joyner argued that "the location alone," so close to downtown, would sell the project.[44] Still, King and Young's planned conversion of the red brick mill buildings—conveniently located near Interstate 40, inside the beltline between South Saunders Street and Like Wheeler Road—had its detractors who were concerned about building upscale housing in an otherwise disreputable part of the city.[45]

Caraleigh project supporters cited the ongoing call for core development in Triangle area cities to reduce traffic on over-crowded roadways; therefore, with Caraleigh's closeness to North Carolina State University's Centennial Campus and downtown Raleigh, Caraleigh would help diminish Raleigh's traffic "crush" during peak hours.[46] The case for Caraleigh was undoubtedly assisted with the successful

The main Caraleigh Mills building just prior to conversion for residential condominium use. Notice that most of the windows had been bricked up (State Archives of North Carolina).

mill-to-condo precedent that had already taken place at the "The Village at Pilot Mill north of Peace Street" just north of downtown.[47] The *News and Observer* expressed support for Caraleigh's resurrection, editorializing that it was logical, safe, and a "wise use of resources," that once initiated would be the "downtown area's largest residential project."[48] Caraleigh, the newspaper maintained, would give a boost to the local economy, reduce traffic, and result in "a little more life on city streets after 5 o'clock...."[49] One challenge to building in south Raleigh was its long-held reputation as "a working class" area in a "slum" environment; a clear acknowledgment of this was Vaughn King's plan to include "a gate and a guard on duty 24 hours a day" at Caraleigh, but resident Jack Finley of Raleigh never recalled "a guard, just the gate," while another pioneering resident, Eleanor Jones, remembered that "for a couple of weeks only three units were occupied ... [but] there was a kind old man guarding the mill" who had once "worked at the mill."[50] A 2001 description of Caraleigh was part of the application process for "National Register of Historic Places" that noted "a concrete drive leads into the mill complex from Maywood Avenue past a one-story frame building that serves as an office and guardhouse. A chain link fence surrounds the mill property, with a gate at the drive."[51]

Vaughn King believed that living in a building over a century old refitted with modern apartments would make the condos unlike any other residential community in the region.[52] The *News and Observer* succinctly captured Vaughn King's vision for Caraleigh Mills resurgence: "Our main thing is the product—its location, the look, the amenities."[53] And of the numerous advantages that Caraleigh Mills condos would boast, King's resourcefulness would capitalize on the historic significance of

Caraleigh when he led the effort to have Caraleigh's inclusion on the National Registry of Historic Places in 2001; Caraleigh's historic official acknowledgment from government authorities resulted in tax reductions from state, local, and federal government for homeowners, presenting condominium homeowners with a strong incentive to buy, saving Caraleigh condominium owners thousands of dollars of taxes.[54]

The Caraleigh Mills condominium complex was one of the first preservation efforts in the Triangle and the state to spread the benefits of the reduced tax credit historic preservation programs to individual home buyers, instead of corporations who previously were the most likely beneficiaries from state and federal tax breaks for undertaking large preservation projects.[55] The director of the Historic Districts Commission for Raleigh, Dan Becker, believed that tax savings incentives were needed to spark growth, in evidence stating that "Glenwood South wouldn't be anything without the historic preservation tax credits."[56]

In the process of rehabilitating Caraleigh, 60,000 square feet of buildings were extracted to create an open courtyard in between the two main buildings. But the buildings retained their original maple flooring, thick beams and, of course, its two-inch thick brick walls; the bricks, which were made in a kiln behind the mill, spoke to the uniqueness of Caraleigh for Vaughn King: "You can see the actual fingerprints from the bricklayers in almost every brick." Besides the brick walls, there was original maple flooring and stunning windows, with no two units being identical to one-another, because each possessed their own architectural features. Amenities at Caraleigh include a fitness center, conference room, swimming pool, playground for children, and two fenced-in dog parks, one for smaller dogs and another for larger canines.

Caraleigh Mills was comprised of several buildings built over time between 1891 and the 1950s. The initial 1892 Caraleigh building construction was two stories. The first floor was used for weaving and the second floor for spinning. The building stood on a 325 by 100 foot main block, on a raised foundation of stone, boasting walls of brick, an Italianate structure, with a monitor roof. Full two-story pilasters defined the narrow bays that were the width of the windows. The top of each pilaster had a small solid, curved bracket at the base of a shaped rafter end serving to project the full depth of the roof's overhang.

Behind the 1892 main building, on the South side, were smaller spaces that occupied a two-story addition created around 1900 to 1910 that measured approximately 80 feet by 300 feet. The 1900–1910 building was also made of brick and possessed "twelve-over-twelve

The plaque denoting Caraleigh's placement on the National Register of Historic Places (photograph by the author).

The courtyard at Historic Caraleigh Mills, 2020 (photograph by the author).

segmental-arched windows," featuring a corbelled brick cornice that lacked the pilasters. The 1900–1910 building's first floor was used for "beaming" and "warping" was done on the second floor. Later in the 20th century, this 1900–1910 addition was used as office space, bathrooms, a repair shop, and kitchen. There was also a four-story water tank tower constructed onto the south elevation of this 1900 building section; a remnant of this tower still projected above the roofline in 2000.[57]

During the third building campaign around 1910, a brick two-story, L-shaped wing was constructed onto the west end of the original building and the 1900 addition. A fourth major building campaign occurred ca. 1919, when a large brick wing was built onto the east end of the 1892 building and the ca. 1910 furnace and machine shop addition. This section has a shallow gable roof, rectangular and metal. A brick one-story warehouse, measuring "59 feet by 104 feet" was built to the southeast of the mill building in 1919. The warehouse possessed weather-boarded walls, sliding wood doors, and an interior that was one open space where raw goods were likely stored.[58] During the late 1950s, a final building campaign took place with one-story concrete block additions. These had flat roofs of varying heights and were constructed onto the east and west wings of the building, and a concrete block wing was added to the 1919 warehouse building, standing to the southeast of the 1892 structure. These 1950s additions had neither windows, nor decorative finishes.[59]

Caraleigh's pre–1950s additions retained their diagonal wood floors and two wood staircases that were found in the 1892 section and in the 1910 "finishing" and "warping" building. In 2000, it was found that the exposed brick walls had been painted several times, and the original metal sliding doors that allowed access between the various sections remained intact. The ceilings and roofs of the large

Overhead view of Historic Caraleigh Mills taken from the northeast corner of the building complex, looking in a southerly direction (courtesy Christopher E. Sauls).

open areas were found to be supported with rows of evenly spaced square posts. The new, 1950s parts of Caraleigh had exposed block walls with floors made of poured concrete.[60]

The century old construction in Caraleigh's buildings presented numerous multi-faceted challenges and spatial constraints: mechanically, architecturally, and electrically.[61] Specifically problematic were the "fixed floor-to-floor height" and "fixed column locations" that made "'routing the ductwork' and placement of electrical equipment" difficult.[62] These imperatives needed to be met to comply with the "egress corridor to doorways" building and safety codes.[63]

In the 1880s and 1890s, fire insurance companies influenced the design of textile mills, calling for Gilded Age mills to utilize slow-burn construction methods and materials—brick and thick wooden beams—to reduce damage from potential fires. Brick outer walls bequeathed solidity and prestige to the company's image, and it was fireproof. Three to four-inch hardwood floors, and interior buttressing of massive wooden timber, if ablaze, burned more slowly and permitted fire-fighters to get water into the building. Other fire-retardant features included a tower that contained a water tank which supplied water, an emergency sprinkler system, and firewalls and doors that were tin-clad.[64]

On May 25, 2001, Caraleigh was placed on the National Registry of Historic Landmarks. In December 2002, King succeeded in getting Caraleigh Mills recognized as an historic landmark with the state.[65] In state recognition was a noteworthy incentive to potential buyers because historical recognition meant that an individual condominium owner would enjoy a 50 percent property tax reduction. The Caraleigh complex had already been placed on the National Register of Historic Places, which also granted condo owners additional federal tax credits; however, the reduction in property taxes also included preservation rules from the U.S. Department of the Interior's standards that also governed the rehabilitation of historically significant buildings. If the National Park Service or the North Carolina State Historic Preservation Office thought these rules were being ignored, then the tax credit incentive could be ended.[66]

The new residents of the Caraleigh building were mandated to preserve its historical character. The implementation of this mandate conflicted with modern building plans, notably with safety and energy efficiency considerations that cannot always be incorporated into century old materials and construction methods. Following the necessary historic preservation regulations was made less onerous with the adoption of the North Carolina Rehab Code (NCRC) for renovation projects; this plan worked in agreement with the International Building Code (IBC), but made meeting preservation standards less demanding.[67]

Raleigh's mayor, Charles Meeker, viewed the North Carolina Rehab Code "as a big plus for the older areas of the city and trying to get things renovated." The Caraleigh project manager for Integrated Design out of Raleigh, Mark Valand, admitted that he faced numerous design and construction obstacles with the century-old building that started with determining the anatomy of the structure. For Valand, the NCRC "did some things ... that were very favorable," and they believed that the NCRC was "perfectly suited for historical structures" such as Caraleigh Mills.[68]

The Code "opened up the door to be more lenient" in working around fixed structures that necessitated creative solutions previously disallowed. For instance, Valand cited "use existing stairways that the (IBC) might not allow you to use."[69] Despite the benefits, the reality was that preservationists had to deal with historic preservation officials at the state and federal levels. Failure to meet the preservation standards risked losing tax deferral recognition. Vaughn King asserted that preservation officials did not want to see walls covered with gypsum board and metal studs in order to get a layer of added insulation; instead, "they want to see the exposed brick."[70]

Another bellwether for preservationists was maintenance of the original wood. King recognized the imperative to keep the "original floors" if they were at all salvageable: "Anything that's salvageable you have to restore and keep it original."[71] But Caraleigh's hardwood floors proved to be no simple matter. The floors required a lot of "special drilling tools." These tools were needed to drill through one-inch-thick "maple with a four-inch by 12-inch tongue and groove flooring underneath" that was often filled with old nails that destroyed many drill bits.[72]

Nevertheless, the nail-filled wood was easier to deal with than getting through the solid-granite foundation walls that were 11 feet thick. These walls did permit the concealment of piping and wires, but their exposure assisted in keeping Caraleigh's industrial look. This was also complemented with paint to strengthen the industrial appearance, said Jeffrey Johnson, senior principal engineer for the Raleigh-based company Bass, Nixon & Kennedy Inc. (BNK).[73]

Joseph Sechler, a lead engineer at the Caraleigh renovation, believed that the concealment of the heating, ventilation, and air conditioning (HVAC) equipment was a more formidable problem; because, with typical condominiums or residences, there would be a crawl space to hide equipment and run ductwork, or there would be an attic space, and Caraleigh Mills possessed neither. The crawl space beneath the building disallowed placing the HVAC equipment there, because the Caraleigh building was in a flood plain. Without an attic, or a basement area, there was the option of the roof.

One plan was to build closets atop each unit and add dropped ceilings to contain the equipment, as well as adding some of the HVAC along walls in units. The National Park Service denied the dropped ceiling proposal, because "they wanted to maintain the open full height of the existing space throughout," maintained Valand. A compromise was reached where a few dropped-ceiling areas were created to conceal some mechanical equipment and, at the same time, maximize floor space use. Concomitantly, numerous spaces in units have exposure from floor to the existing roof that proved satisfactory to National Park Service preservation requirements.[74]

Perhaps the most striking of features at Caraleigh Mills' condominiums are the 20-foot high ceilings and 11-foot high arched, multipaned windows, originally intended to provide mill operatives with light and ventilation. In 2000, it was determined that most of the second-floor windows had maintained their "original segmental-arched twelve-light upper sash and twelve-light bottom sash."[75] The first-floor windows, however, along with a few on the second floor, were either bricked over or had some added louvers inserted. Despite this, those windows' form and size remained apparent in 2000.

Caraleigh Mills' condominiums include 20-foot-high ceilings and 11-foot high arched, multipaned windows, originally intended to provide mill operatives with light and ventilation (photograph by the author).

For Vaughn King, window preservation was critical to maintaining its historical appearance, but matching the original window details was not easily accomplished: "You can't just go to Lowe's and buy new windows," said Tim Simmons, the senior preservation architect at the Restoration Branch of the State Historic Preservation Office in Raleigh.[76] Simmons maintained that half of the windows at Caraleigh needed to be replaced, frame and all, which required the services of a millwork company that could construct historically accurate windows. Much of the glass in the salvageable frames also needed to be replaced. The original glass of single-pane construction was an inefficient window, by today's energy conservation and insulation standards. The National Park Service shied away from replacing the single pane glass, afraid that it would compromise the historical look of the mill, but after negotiations with State Historic Preservation Office, a compromise was reached whereby double pane, insulated glass was allowed for the sake of energy efficiency, as long as a good faith effort was made to maintain the look of the original windows.[77]

King was a visionary who understood the potential in a building that was described as dingy, dirty, dark, and musty; instead, King saw "a fantastic piece of property." Along with the tax credit benefits and its 14.5 acre location inside the beltline, a downtown condominium seemed "pretty awesome."[78] King's nearly two year effort ended successfully with Caraleigh renovated into 84 condominiums in 2003 at a cost of $14 million dollars.[79] Joseph Sechler artfully summed up the rebirth of Caraleigh's mill building in this way: "Basically, an old shoe was going to get tossed out and we polished it up, put it on, and we're going to take it to the dance."[80] Caraleigh Mills' rebirth caused people to reconsider south Raleigh as more than simply a slum to be avoided. The Sir Walter Raleigh Awards were established in the early 1980s to honor outstanding contributions to the city's appearance and livability. Caraleigh Mills was named among the winners in 2004 in the Residential category for its "conversion and rehabilitation of a former south Raleigh industrial building into residential space."[81] In 2005, Caraleigh's condominiums ranged in price from $169,000 to $460,000 and ranged from 940 square feet to 2000 square feet.[82] By 2005, 64 out of 84 "luxury condos" at Caraleigh's gated community had been sold.[83]

The Final Frontier

In 2015, the *News and Observer* proclaimed south Raleigh to be "downtown's final frontier," an area slower to redevelop and gentrify than other parts of central Raleigh.[84] Houses in the area sold for much less than $100,000, while real estate prices in other downtown areas surged.[85] Prominent among entrepreneurial businesses to stake their claim in south Raleigh was the Trophy Brewing & Pizza Co., which purchased 2.5 acres of land for 2.3 million dollars, just 200 or so paces from Caraleigh's cotton mill condominiums on Maywood Drive. Trophy's executive officers planned to include a large brewing system, a small bar, kitchen, garden and more. David Meeker, one of Trophy Brewery's partners, believed that their location and quality beer would attract downtown residents, visitors to the State Farmers' Market located across the street, as well as those in the younger demographic residing and working in the areas surrounding Caraleigh.

A scene inside the Trophy Brewery on Maywood Avenue, with employee Mariah Hachmeister at work in July 2021 (photograph by the author).

David Meeker added comments in 2015 that reinforced the belief that Caraleigh had been left behind during Raleigh economic advancement in previous years:

> The west side and the north side, I feel like, are developed—and the east side has all this young energy, and I feel like the south side is going back in time.... There are older folks living in the neighborhoods. Most of the homes have not been renovated. There's some of the old-school character—neighbors caring about neighbors. The folks who have lived in some of those neighborhoods and are involved with the neighborhood association have literally been there for 40 years.[86]

In 2004, Caraleigh resident Mildred Flynn lobbied City Hall for assistance with reigning in the open drug trade and rundown housing in Caraleigh, partially a result of Raleigh's neglect of the neighborhood. Flynn believed that "south Raleigh had little meaning to people outside the neighborhood" and was thought of differently when compared to "Southeast Raleigh" with its traditionally black neighborhoods closer to downtown, or "southwest Raleigh," which was filled with student housing abutting North Carolina State University.[87] Specifically, Flynn requested that the Caraleigh neighborhood be included in the Southeast Raleigh Assembly, a city-appointed group of business leaders and community activists focused on challenges in areas east of South Saunders Road and downtown.

In 2004, Flynn repeated a sentiment that had been held among residents at Caraleigh for decades: "We're not in Southeast Raleigh, and we're not in Southwest Raleigh. Sometimes I feel like we're out here all alone because we're south Raleigh."[88] But by 2015, Flynn's skepticism turned towards optimism because of new life at Caraleigh and increased property values. She thought favorably of Trophy Brewery's location on Maywood Drive, and though not a beer drinker, Flynn saw that Trophy helped Caraleigh transform into a place that was "really hoppin'."[89] Despite a ferocious tornado that briefly tore through Caraleigh in 2011, property values increased between 2010 and 2015; nearly 50 homes in the half-mile area around her home had sold and new residential home developers moved to build in south Raleigh.[90]

Richard Johnson and his wife Amy Goodale, owners of the CitySpace Homes firm, seized the moment at Caraleigh in 2015, when they started building 57 single family houses next to the Caraleigh Mills building and across the street from the Trophy Brewery on Maywood Avenue.[91] CitySpace Homes—recognizable for their eye-catching tall, skinny, and colorful appearance—referred to as "folk vernacular," were envisioned by Johnson to be part of Raleigh's "second warehouse district."[92] With a strategy that targeted underutilized lots of land in historic neighborhoods on the downtown periphery, the entrepreneurial instincts of Goodale and Johnson were validated when their homes started selling before being advertised.[93]

Caraleigh's smokestack is visible between a group of CitySpace Homes. Recognizable for their eye-catching tall, skinny, and colorful appearance, the homes have been referred to as "folk vernacular" architecture (photograph by the author).

Raleigh's Southern Gateway Corridor Study: 2017

The Southern Gateway Corridor Study Final Report (SGCS 2017) was the result of years of multidisciplinary investigation, analysis and evaluation of the economic potentials of south Raleigh.[94] Starting in the summer of 2013 and ending in 2017, the SGCS 2017 findings included input from community residents, outlined the process, analysis, framework ideas, and development strategies for ameliorative action to achieve the primary goal: "to implement improvements and transform this district into an area worthy of the title, Raleigh's Southern Gateway."[95]

Caraleigh sits in Raleigh's Southern Gateway district, a corridor of land three miles south of downtown Raleigh, with streets defining the district's boundaries. The northern terminus starts at MLK Boulevard, extending south to the intersection of South Wilmington and Tryon Roads; Lake Wheeler Road marks the district's western limit and Hammond Road acts as the eastern border.[96]

The SGCS report, in 2017, theorized that the Southern Gateway district possessed several stellar advantages, as well as a number of shortcomings, that could be built upon and magnified for the economic benefit of Raleigh and the entire Triangle Region. Another observation was that a superior skyline view of the city could be gained when driving into Raleigh along South Saunders Road, but gave a disparaging account of the adjacent neighborhoods and land along this approach which lacked "a cohesive character and identity."[97] The advantages of the Southern Gateway area included its proximity to downtown Raleigh and the future Dorothea Dix Park, a mixed housing construction that reflected historic character and modern, high-quality construction, and particularly exceptional access to Interstate Highway 40 and the rest of the Triangle Region. Additionally, SGCS 2017 noted that residential neighborhoods north of Interstate 40, including Caraleigh, saw increased private and public reinvestment that resulted in two major branches of the Capital Area Greenway system which increased accessibility to the State Farmers' Market and Dorothea Dix Park, all of which were close to Raleigh's downtown center and within walking distance from the Historic Caraleigh Mills Condominium property.[98]

The strategic plan for the Southern Gateway established four localized centers within the corridor that were to be "focus areas of development," one of which was "Old Saunders" in which Caraleigh was situated.[99] Caraleigh was characterized as an area ripe for growth and conservation opportunities. The strategic plan for the Caraleigh area of the Southern Corridor called for design guidelines that conserved and supported the village's character, "while allowing for appropriately scaled growth," where investors could repurpose old warehouses and raw spaces to entice entrepreneurs.[100]

> It would be advantageous for these businesses, such as tech shops, brewers, alternative/indoor farming, to be located close to downtown and yet in an area that also presents opportunities for inexpensive, perhaps forgotten spaces in which to build new businesses and a community.

The Southern Gateway report predicted a bright future for Caraleigh. However, it also verified that for Raleigh's benefit, Caraleigh had been sacrificed, "eroded by a lack of investment and the overwhelming focus on the transportation needs of commuters and visitors to downtown Raleigh from outlying areas."[101]

The SGCS 2017 market analysis of south Raleigh found that land use was mostly commuter-oriented, strip-mall-style commercial development, resulting in many underutilized or undeveloped parcels of land.[102] Other factors that dampened investment market interest included physical barriers such as railroads, vehicle roadways, the floodplain, and public perceptions of south Raleigh being a crime-filled zone. The Southern Gateway Study's suggested prescription to remedy south Raleigh's ills called for public and private partnerships that would be critical to "catalyzing major projects in these areas."[103]

Downtown South: 2019

For the Caraleigh Community, the Downtown South project appeared to mark the end of the mill community's abandonment and isolation from Raleigh. In June of 2019, North Carolina business leaders John Kane, Billie Redmond and Steve Malik announced the "Downtown South" project, an ambitious public-private partnership with a goal to achieve a renaissance for south Raleigh, on 55 acres just beside Interstate 40 and South Saunders Street. The three visionaries pledged $1.9 billion of their own money to the Downtown South project that would ultimately envelop Caraleigh.

Making concise use of visual language, John Kane described that their project aimed to take the southern edge of downtown Raleigh and stretch it to Interstate 40. The renovated area would act as a "new hub of activity in downtown Raleigh" about one mile from the Raleigh Convention Center.[104] Downtown South was slated to include a 20,000 seat stadium, 1.6 million square feet of office space, 1200 hotel rooms, 1750 multi-family residential units, 125,000 square feet of retail and restaurant space, and high rise buildings. Promotional details about Downtown South's connectivity to the Triangle Greenway system, Dix Park and the State Farmers' Market, made Caraleigh uniquely a centerpiece community in the design of Raleigh's restructured southern gateway.[105]

If achieved, Kane asserted, Downtown South would turn the southern entrance to downtown Raleigh into a "dense, mixed use–urban entertainment district" that would be unique to Raleigh.[106] A prominent real estate developer since 1978, Kane declared that their plans would be a "game-changer" for the capital city and for an area of Raleigh that "has not had the love that it needs, and we are trying to give it that love and that investment."[107] Kane drew comparisons between the people of south Raleigh and those who lived in the area of his North Hills project, where demographics were starkly different in educational and income levels. When speaking of south Raleigh, Kane asserted that "this is a part of the city that we all need to support."[108]

Businesswoman Billie Redmond said that "the value of real estate is driven by use," and that the land to be used for Downtown South was underdeveloped, underutilized and unpopulated, so nobody would be displaced because of the project.[109] Redmond—owner of Trademark Properties and among the top twenty CEOs in the Triangle—outlined the economic benefits of the Downtown South project, where development planned would provide space for housing, working, live entertainment, and easy access to the city's bus line. Redmond maintained that Downtown South's development of unused land and uninhabited land, after adding $1.9 billion of investment over a 15 year span would add "a lot more money to state coffers for use" with the addition of thousands of jobs, $5.6 million to state income taxes and $1.6 million dollars in sales taxes.[110] While the economic benefit would accrue to the entire state, Wake County and Raleigh would especially gain; Wake County with $2.7 billion, the creation of 5900 sustainable jobs, and the addition of $3.7 million in tourism related tax revenue per annum. And perhaps most stunningly, property taxes on the formerly underused land would increase from $140,000 to $20 million annually.[111] Redmond thought all the elements for growth were present in the Downtown South project:

> Our demographics are good, our growth is solid, our employment numbers are good. That's a market dynamic that we should take advantage of today. It's really important that we also move that to south Raleigh. As Steven [Malik] and John [Kane] have both said, it's time to spread the growth in ways that are really good for economics for every citizen in Raleigh. We create a walkable community that's tied to downtown and major traffic corridors through the bus transit system, and it means that there's opportunity for all, which means at the end of the day means equity, equitable wealth.[112]

Steve Malik, who gained notoriety as the force behind North Carolina's youth-to-soccer club and the owner of both the North Carolina Football Club (NCFC) and the North Carolina Courage women's soccer teams, agreed with Kane and Redmond. In 2017, Malik tried to rally support for Raleigh's soccer team to be added as an expansion team to Major League Soccer and to have a stadium created in the Halifax Mall area of downtown Raleigh. When support for this effort evaporated, Malik made another push for a stadium to act as central component of the Downtown South project.[113] Malik believed that Raleigh was overdue for a respectable athletic venue, stating that of the five largest cities in North Carolina, Raleigh was the only one without a stadium and was likely the largest city in the South without a downtown stadium.[114] Malik added that "we currently have 14,000 players in our youth club plus 25,000 of their parents, and that's just a snapshot. If you go back to the 40-year history of soccer in this community, the level of support for a project like this is off the charts."[115]

In agreement, John Kane saw the stadium as "the stimulus needed to make Downtown South a viable alternative for development."[116] And while Malik wanted a home for his soccer teams, both Kane and Malik confessed that having a professional team, or teams, was not an essential requirement for the Downtown South project's success, because the venue could host hundreds of other events including concerts, festivals, and other sporting functions in a location designed to move traffic in and out of the area when conducting large festivals.[117]

Malik's previous efforts to gain support for an athletic stadium led him to go on what he described as a "two year journey of listening" to people in the Raleigh community. In reflecting on his audio odyssey, Malik found that people overwhelmingly supported the creation of added entertainment options for downtown Raleigh. For quantifiable proof, Malik pointed to a national firm's poll findings that gauged support for the downtown Raleigh entertainment district plan; the poll's conclusions underscored broad public support from all demographic categories, with 75 percent of those polled expressing support.[118] Malik noted that the area south of downtown Raleigh was an opportunity zone, a 2017 tax designation Congress created to encourage long-term investment in economically disadvantaged urban and rural communities throughout the country.[119]

Echoing the overtures of John Kane and Billie Redmond, Malik pointed out the socioeconomic disparity between north Raleigh and south Raleigh, and in so doing, struck a reparational tone.

> And the jobs and economic impact of this project are clearly what polled well and what this part of town needs for economic equity. I think that for us to be a progressive city and take our next step in the national landscape, we need this. The time is now to get that done, and we have an opportunity to do what has never been done here before.[120]

Conclusions

Through the slowly evolving process of gentrification that started in the mid–1970s, Caraleigh demonstrates metamorphic renewal in 2020 of physical, economic, and social dimensions.[121] The roads are paved, old houses continue to be revived and new homes built; businesses prosper, and new ones arrive; the income of its residents is no longer limited to employment at the mill.

Caraleigh's population started to racially diversify with available and affordable housing attracting newcomers in the 1990s. While two percent of the state's population was described in 1999 as Latino, Caraleigh reportedly had a large Hispanic population in 2004, and of its 2,229 residents, two-thirds were white.[122] But in 2020, waves of new residents continue to arrive in Caraleigh, bringing a population that appears younger, more affluent, and racially diverse than it was before 1970.

Caraleigh's birth embodied many of North Carolina's late 19th-century progressive trends that were interwoven with memories of the Civil War and Reconstruction.[123] A geographically isolated industrial mill village that mirrored aspects of plantation culture, Caraleigh's founders—the enlightened "white elite" of society—imbued residents with their values and ideas.[124] Mill directors and their appointees sought control of their laborers' behaviors through the company-supervised work, housing, church, graveyard, school, and social organizations.

During Caraleigh's first few decades, the power of the state's "most progressive citizens" instilled and reinforced Caraleigh's social, economic, and political structures.[125] The ideas of Caraleigh's well-heeled elites lived on longer than the mill but withered away with the passage of time. Although Caraleigh's textile operation and the fertilizer plant closed operations during the Great Depression, two instances demonstrate the shared racial verities of the mill owners continued in the minds of Caraleigh's residents. The first was the protest against locating a housing subdivision near Caraleigh in 1956 and the second was the Caraleigh community's 1976 presidential support for George Wallace.

From its inception, Caraleigh's wealthy creators careless resolve took advantage of the state's cheap labor advantage to attain profits and ignored repeated warnings about locating Caraleigh in a floodplain. Yet, the state's Raleigh-based patricians proceeded in the process of plundering Caraleigh of its human capital on the pretext of statewide economic restoration, regardless of environmental or social repercussions.[126]

Caraleigh was incrementally orphaned as profitability in the textile industry decreased after World War I, with concern for Caraleigh disappearing in 1930. Being outside the city limits of Raleigh provided a reason for city officials to deny Caraleigh support during the Great Depression. Despite the best efforts of Raleigh's charitable organizations and individuals in the 1930s to assist Caraleigh, resentment only grew in Caraleigh. In the heart of south Raleigh, Caraleigh's residents were made fully aware that they were on their own, ostracized and cast aside by the "great white men" of the state whose individual narratives remained untarnished by their misdeeds Caraleigh.[127] As recently as 2010, longtime residents of Caraleigh remembered that they always felt snubbed by white-collar Raleigh.[128]

Profitability for the textile industry in the United States grew more competitive as the 20th century progressed. The newer occupants of Caraleigh's old textile building between 1938 to 1999 never attained the stature of the institution of origin. In the final decades of the 1900s, the southern textile industry failed to compete on a global scale, when manufacturers who were lured to foreign nations with low-wage workers.[129]

The restructuring of Raleigh's City Council's election to the district system in 1973 gave Caraleigh a caring voice in Miriam Block. Besides inspiring community spirit and involvement in betterment activities, Block drew attention to forgotten promises about municipal services—noticeably with roads and sewage—that the city made to Caraleigh during its annexation campaign in 1957. However, Block could not stop the forces of Raleigh's growth that increased the dissection of Caraleigh's community with the widening of South Saunders Road.

Caraleigh and the south Raleigh gentrification process started in the 1970s, thanks to the financially savvy entrepreneurs Betty and James Gerardi; it continued in the 1990s with William J. Dumont, and in 2003 with Vaughn King. The Gerardi family bravely started the process of renewal when nobody else dared. William Dumont's aggressive and risky investments in Caraleigh's properties, along with his humane method of property management, inspired others to invest in Caraleigh. Vaughn King's arduous task of refitting the old Caraleigh textile mill into a condominium complex proved successful, but a financial gamble. The efforts of all four people revived the heart of south Raleigh.[130]

Change in Caraleigh continue to accelerate, as evident with the release of the Southern Gateway Corridor Study in 2017 (SCGS 2017). The multidisciplinary study found that investment in south Raleigh would be not just potentially profitable, but restorative in undoing the decades of automobile driven development that had nearly erased Caraleigh. This sentiment was reinforced in 2019 when the leaders of the Downtown South project emphasized the goal of economic parity for south Raleigh, that part of Raleigh which had not experienced economic gains that the rest of Raleigh enjoyed in previous decades. Whether Downtown South will be the new catalyst for south Raleigh remains to be seen.

The Southern Gateway Corridor Study of 2017 was tantamount to an admission of Raleigh's collective culpability for Caraleigh Community's slow and grinding devolution that began in 1930. The authors of SCGS 2017 prescribed that planners should be mindful of the character and scale of the Caraleigh community with any new development proposals, declaring that "special consideration should be given to protect and complement the historic character of the adjacent Caraleigh neighborhood."[131] With Caraleigh's history, one that has hitherto been largely ignored, this question must be asked: what parts of Caraleigh's history should be protected, exactly?[132] Besides the Caraleigh textile building itself, which Vaughn King was credited

Overhead view of Caraleigh Mills taken from the south side, looking north, with downtown Raleigh's tall buildings visible at the top right. On the left edge, a few newly constructed CitySpace Homes sit, close to Caraleigh's swimming pool (courtesy Christopher E. Sauls).

Built in 1929, this Caraleigh home on Maywood Avenue is destroyed for new development in August 2021. The neighboring home, the roof of which can be seen behind the truck, was built in 1910. None of the original 1890s mill homes in Caraleigh remain (photograph by the author).

for having recognized as a historical landmark, which other elements of Caraleigh's history should be conserved and reused?[133]

Caraleigh's creation, demise, and renaissance is steeped in irony, because the forces of wealth and political power—the same which had for over a century used, abused, shunned, dissected, and disregarded Caraleigh—were now among the same calling for the re-creation of the mill village and south Raleigh.[134] A prosperous dawn appears emergent in south Raleigh and Caraleigh. The death of disinvestment in this area proclaimed in 2019 may well develop more thoughtfully than in the 1890s.

Chapter Notes

Preface

1. Aaron Sánchez-Guerra, "In Ongoing Hearings, Residents and City Staff Say Downtown South Plans Need to Slow Down," *News and Observer* (Raleigh, NC), November 02, 2020.
2. Anna Johnson, "Raleigh's Downtown South Proposal Gets 'No' Votes. but Can the Project Survive Them?" *News and Observer* (Raleigh, NC), December 8, 2020.
3. "Boom in Real Estate," *Morning Post* (Raleigh, NC), August 13, 1899.
4. Colleen Quigley, "Advocates Speak Out on Potential Effect of 'Downtown South' on Nearby Raleigh Residents," Oct 28, 2020. CBS17.COM. https://www.cbs17.com/news/local-news/wake-county-news/advocates-speak-out-on-potential-effect-of-downtown-south-on-nearby-raleigh-residents/.
5. "Raleigh Downtown South—How Will It Affect the Environment?" *Interfaith Creation Care of the Triangle (ICCT)*, https://interfaithcreationcare.org/downtown-south-project/.
6. Henry Hinton, "Talk of the Town 103.7 FM," December 7, 2020. See recording of show at 15:40–15:45 https://wtibfm.com/?p=1820.
7. Piia Varis Ico Maly, "The 21st-century Hipster: On Micro-populations in Times of Superdiversity," *European Journal of Cultural Studies*, August 18, 2015. https://doi.org/10.1177/1367549415597920.
8. Joseph A. Amato, *Rethinking Home: A Case for Writing Local History* (Berkley: University of California Press, 2002), 3.
9. Amato, *Rethinking Home*, 5.

Introduction

1. EPA Announces the Availability of the Administrative Record for Caraleigh Phosphate and Fertilizer Works Removal Site in Raleigh, N.C., Release Date: 04/03/2006. https://archive.epa.gov/epapages/newsroom_archive/newsreleases/0bee935065eb357a85257145006e34d9.html.
2. *Caraleigh: A Forgotten Village*, 12; "Caraleigh Mills Company," *News and Observer* (Raleigh, NC), August 24, 1899.
3. Neil Morris, "Sports/Entertainment Venue: The Centerpiece of Live, Work, Play Plan Called Downtown South," June 24, 2019. https://www.wralsportsfan.com/sports-entertainment-venue-the-centerpiece-of-live-work-play-plan-called-downtown-south/18471610/; attribution of name "Downtown South," in Zachary Eanes "Developers: Stadium Plan Would Need Public Money," *News and Observer* (Raleigh, NC), June 26, 2019.
4. Michel-Rolph Trouillot, *Silencing the Past: Power and the Production of History*. (Boston: Beacon Press, 1995), xxiii.
5. "This Isn't Leadership," *News and Observer* (Raleigh, NC), January 29, 1969.
6. "How They Work at Caraleigh," *State Chronicle* (Raleigh, NC), October 27, 1891.
7. "Caraleigh Mills," *Evening Visitor* (Raleigh, NC), October 29, 1891.
8. *Ibid.*
9. Crosswell, Jack, "Annexation Is Approved at Caraleigh," *News and Observer* (Raleigh, NC), January 1, 1958.
10. "The Caraleigh Mills," *State Chronicle* (Raleigh, NC), March 12, 1891.
11. *News and Observer* (Raleigh, NC), January 1, 1892.
12. "The Deed for the Land," *State Chronicle* (Raleigh, NC), April 7, 1891.
13. "How They Work at Caraleigh," *State Chronicle* (Raleigh, NC), October 27, 1891.
14. EPA Announces the Availability of the Administrative Record for Caraleigh; Mike Legeros, *Raleigh Fire Department 1880–1899*, Unpublished manuscript July 19, 2009. https://legeros.com/ralwake/raleigh/history/writing/1880-1899.pdf.
15. K. Todd Johnson and Elizabeth Reid Murray, *Wake: Capital County of North Carolina, Vol. II, Reconstruction to 1920* (Raleigh: Wake County Commissioners: 2008), 489; "Raleigh Veteran of Medicine Recalls Old Associates and Practice," *News and Observer* (Raleigh, NC), June 12, 1938.

16. "Caraleigh: A Forgotten Mill Village," ca. 1974, typescript, Caraleigh Mills Survey File, North Carolina State Historic Preservation Office, Raleigh, North Carolina, 12.
17. Quoted here are the words of Hazel V. Carby, in her forward to Trouillot, *Silencing the Past*, xii.
18. Hazel V. Carby quoted in forward to Trouillot, *Silencing the Past*, xii.
19. Trouillot, *Silencing the Past*, 5.
20. Trouillot, *Silencing the Past*, xxii.
21. Kemp P. Battle, *A Centennial Address: Delivered by Invitation of the Committee on the Centennial Celebration of the Foundation of the City October 18, 1892 and an Account of the Centennial Celebration* (Raleigh: Edwards and Broughton, Printers and Binders, 1893), 97.
22. "Register," *State Chronicle* (Raleigh, NC), October 23, 1890.
23. C. Vann Woodward, *Origins of the New South: 1877–1913* (Baton Rouge: Louisiana State University Press, 1951), 51.
24. William J. Cooper and Thomas E. Terrill. *The American South: A History, Volume II*, 3rd edition (Boston: McGraw Hill, 2002), 426, 445.
25. "The Progressive Plutocracy Not Only Survived but Thrived Throughout the Decade of the 1950s. the Major Characteristics of the Party System Remained in Place," Karl E. Campbell quoted in Larry E. Tise and Jeffrey J. Crow, eds., *New Voyages to Carolina: Reinterpreting North Carolina History* (Chapel Hill: University of North Carolina Press, 2017), 255.
26. Karl E. Campbell quoted in Larry E. Tise and Jeffrey J. Crow, eds., *New Voyages to Carolina: Reinterpreting North Carolina History* (Chapel Hill: University of North Carolina Press, 2017), 246.
27. Larry E. Tise and Jeffrey J. Crow, eds., *New Voyages to Carolina: Reinterpreting North Carolina History* (Chapel Hill: University of North Carolina Press, 2017), 247.
28. Dwight B. Billings, Jr., *Planters and the Making of a "New South" Class, Politics, and Development in North Carolina, 1865–1900*. (Chapel Hill: University of North Carolina Press, 1979).
29. Billings, *Planters and the Making of a "New South,"* 130–131.
30. Billings, *Planters and the Making of a "New South,"* 131.
31. "Stockholders of Caraleigh Mills Meet," *Morning Post* (Raleigh, NC), January 18, 1898.
32. "Pension Veterans," *Wilmington Messenger* (Wilmington, NC), June 27, 1891.
33. "Ten Thousand Spindles," *News and Observer* (Raleigh, NC), March 25, 1891.
34. "A Great Enterprise," *State Chronicle* (Raleigh, NC), February 5, 1891.
35. Larry E. Tise and Jeffrey J. Crow, eds., *New Voyages to Carolina: Reinterpreting North Carolina History* (Chapel Hill: University of North Carolina Press, 2017), 3, 386.
36. Larry E. Tise and Jeffrey J. Crow, eds., *New Voyages to Carolina: Reinterpreting North Carolina History* (Chapel Hill: University of North Carolina Press, 2017), 3.
37. *Ibid*.
38. Gunnar Myrdal, *An American Dilemma: The Negro Problem and Modern Democracy* (New York: Harper & Row, 1944), 285–286.
39. *Ibid*.
40. *Ibid*.
41. Trouillot, *Silencing the Past*, 106.
42. Trouillot, *Silencing the Past*, 72–73.
43. Peter Coclanis, "Textiles Spun a New NC, but What Will Replace It?," *News and Observer* (Raleigh, NC), February 22, 2017.

Chapter 1

1. Broadus Mitchell, *The Rise of the Cotton Mills in the South* (Baltimore: Johns Hopkins Press, 1921), 102.
2. Sarah McCulloh Lemmon. "Raleigh—An Example of the 'New South'?" *North Carolina Historical Review* 43, no. 3 (1966): 261–85.
3. "Annual Meeting Mill Captains Is Now on Here," *Charlotte News* (NC), June 23, 1915; *Wilmington Morning Star* (NC), July 22, 1916.
4. Holland Thompson, *From the Cotton Field to the Cotton Mill: A Study of the Industrial Transition in North Carolina* (New York: Norwood Press, 1906), 9.
5. Woodward, *Origins of the New South*, 131.
6. "Home Manufactured Guanos," *News and Observer* (Raleigh, NC) April 4, 1895.
7. *Ibid*.
8. Lemmon, "Raleigh—An Example of the "New South?" 261–85.
9. Brent D. Glass, *The Textile Industry in North Carolina: A History* (Raleigh: Division of Archives and History North Carolina Department of Cultural Resources, 1992), 34.
10. Mitchell, *The Rise of the Cotton Mills in the South*, 68.
11. Thompson, *From the Cotton Field to the Cotton Mill*, 74–76.
12. Mitchell, *The Rise of the Cotton Mills in the South*, 69.
13. Thompson, *From the Cotton Field to the Cotton Mill*, 65–68; David S. Cecelski and Timothy B. Tyson, eds., *Democracy Betrayed: The Wilmington Race Riot of 1898 and Its Legacy* (Chapel Hill: University of North Carolina Press, 2000), 131.
14. "Spirits Turpentine," *Wilmington Morning Star* (Wilmington, NC), August 23, 1899.
15. "An Act to Incorporate the Carraleigh Mills Company," Laws and resolutions of the State of North Carolina, passed by the General Assembly at its session [1891], North Carolina Digital State Documents Collection, State Library of North Carolina, Raleigh, North

Notes—Chapter 1

Carolina. https://digital.ncdcr.gov/digital/collection/p249901coll22/id/434957.

16. Glass, *The Textile Industry in North Carolina*, 38; Randolph Langenbach, "Better Than Steel? (Part 2): Tall Wooden Factories and the Invention of 'Slow-burning.'" This paper continues the historical analysis of tall wooden buildings started in the author's ICSA2010 Keynote paper, "Better Than Steel? the Use of Timber for Large and Tall Buildings from Ancient Times Until the Present," (Langenbach, 2010); "Heavy Timber Construction," Conservationtech Consulting Oakland, California, USA.

17. William A. Link, *The Paradox of Southern Progressivism, 1880–1930* (Chapel Hill: University of North Carolina Press, 1997), 169.

18. Ronald Bujold, Reconnecting Mill Communities: An Architectural Intervention in Fitchburg, Massachusetts, September 2014, Ronald R. Bujold, II B.S., Northeastern University March, University of Massachusetts—Amherst Directed by: Professor Kathleen Lugosch, 8–9. https://scholarworks.umass.edu/cgi/viewcontent.cgi?article=1142&context=masters_theses_2.

19. Bujold, *Reconnecting Mill Communities*, 8–9.

20. *Ibid*.

21. "The Very Severe Loss," *State Chronicle* (Raleigh, NC), August 19, 1892.

22. "The Caraleigh Barbecue," *Morning Post* (Raleigh, NC), August 13, 1899; "The Very Severe Loss," *State Chronicle* (Raleigh, NC), August 19, 1892.

23. "The Caraleigh Barbecue," *Morning Post* (Raleigh, NC), August 13, 1899; "The Very Severe Loss," *State Chronicle* (Raleigh, NC), August 19, 1892.

24. "The Capital City's Tribute to the State's Milling Interest," *News and Observer* (Raleigh, NC) November 28, 1895; Johnson and Murray, *Wake: Capital County of North Carolina, Vol. II*, 203.

25. *Charlotte Observer* (NC), July 14, 1891; see also "A Great Enterprise," *State Chronicle* (Raleigh, NC), February 5, 1891.

26. Read About the Cotton Mill Campaign in Glass, *The Textile Industry in North Carolina*, 30–31; *Wilmington Messenger* (NC), October 20, 1891.

27. "Ten Thousand Spindles," *News and Observer* (Raleigh, NC), March 25, 1891.

28. "How They Work at Caraleigh," *State Chronicle* (Raleigh, NC), October 27, 1891.

29. "Two Big Enterprises," *News and Observer* (Raleigh, NC), January 31, 1891; *Charlotte Observer* (NC), August 12, 1892.

30. "An Act to Incorporate the Carraleigh Mills Company."

31. "Ten Thousand Spindles," *News and Observer* (Raleigh, NC), March 25, 1891.

32. *Evening Visitor* (Raleigh, NC), April 30, 1891.

33. "The Caraleigh Mills," *State Chronicle* (Raleigh, NC), August 25, 1891.

34. *State Chronicle* (Raleigh, NC), July 19, 1892.

35. Daniel L. Watkins, *Caraleigh: Raleigh's Cotton Mill Village* MLS 697 Final Project April 9, 2000. Thesis/Dissertation. North Carolina State University, 8. https://catalog.lib.ncsu.edu/catalog/NCSU1390012.

36. "Spectacular Fire Razes Old Phosphate Structures," *News and Observer* (Raleigh, NC), September 1, 1934; "An Act to Incorporate the Carraleigh Phosphate and Fertilizer Works." Laws and resolutions of the State of North Carolina, passed by the General Assembly at its session [1891], North Carolina Digital State Documents Collection, State Library of North Carolina, Raleigh, North Carolina. https://digital.ncdcr.gov/digital/collection/p249901coll22/id/434955.

37. "How They Work at Caraleigh," *State Chronicle* (Raleigh, NC), October 27, 1891.

38. Johnson and Murray, *Wake: Capital County of North Carolina, Vol. II*, 202; "Two Important Raleigh Enterprises," *Morning Post* (Raleigh, NC), September 21, 1898.

39. "J.R. Chamberlain Passes Suddenly," *News and Observer* (Raleigh, NC), April 27, 1926.

40. "Spectacular Fire Razes Old Phosphate Structures," *News and Observer* (Raleigh, NC), September 1, 1934.

41. Elizabeth Reid Murray, *Wake: Capital County of North Carolina Volume I: Prehistory to Centennial* (Raleigh: Capital County Publishing Company, 1983), 518.

42. Watkins, *Caraleigh: Raleigh's Cotton Mill Village*, 12–13.

43. *Ibid*.

44. *Ibid*., 14.

45. Wilbur Joseph Cash, *The Mind of the South* (New York: Vintage Books Random House, 1941), 143. Johnson and Murray, *Wake: Capital County of North Carolina, Vol. II*, 123.

46. Johnson and Murray, *Wake: Capital County of North Carolina, Vol. II*, 123.

47. Cooper and Terrill, *The American South: A History*, vol. II., 474–475.

48. *Ibid*.

49. *Ibid*., 477.

50. "Our Cotton Interests," *Press-Visitor* (Raleigh, NC), October 19, 1896.

51. *Charlotte Observer* (NC), July 14, 1891.

52. "Ten Thousand Spindles," *News and Observer* (Raleigh, NC), March 25, 1891.

53. "Good Sidewalks," *News and Observer* (Raleigh, NC), November 15, 1893.

54. Glass, *The Textile Industry in North Carolina*, 42.

55. "Such a White Collar Town as Raleigh" found in "Good News," *News and Observer* (Raleigh, NC), March 29, 1938.

56. Watkins, *Caraleigh: Raleigh's Cotton Mill Village* 32.

57. *Ibid*., 23.

58. *Ibid.*, 30. Which quotes Raleigh's *New State Chronicle*, January 26, 1888, as quoted from Sarah McCulloh Lemmon, "Raleigh—An Example of the 'New South'?", 265.

59. Watkins, *Caraleigh: Raleigh's Cotton Mill Village*, 31.

60. *News and Observer* (Raleigh, NC), March 23, 1891; *Wilmington Messenger* (NC), September 19, 1891; Caraleigh Mills, Register of Historic Places Registration Form (National Register Bulletin 16A, https://files.nc.gov/ncdcr/nr/WA3891.pdf; *News and Observer* (Raleigh, NC), March 25, 1891; "Caraleigh Case Settled," *State Chronicle* (Raleigh, NC), September 23, 1891; Watkins, *Caraleigh: Raleigh's Cotton Mill Village*, 35; "Pension Veterans," *Wilmington Messenger* (NC), June 27, 1891.

61. "Caraleigh Mills Company," *News and Observer* (Raleigh, NC), August 24, 1899.

62. *News and Observer* (Raleigh, NC), August 24, 1899.

63. "Caraleigh Mills Company," *Southern Textile Bulletin* (Charlotte, NC), June 21, 1923, V. 25, *Southern Textile Bulletin*, 152–153. https://archive.org/details/southerntextileb1923unse/page/n5/mode/2up.

64. "Caraleigh Mills," RHDC Raleigh Historic Development Commission, section 8, p. 5.

65. Watkins, *Caraleigh: Raleigh's Cotton Mill Village*, 33.

66. "Notice to Stockholders Caraleigh Mills Company," *Morning Post* (Raleigh, NC), February 23, 1898.

67. "10,000 Spindles," *News and Observer* (Raleigh, NC), March 25, 1891.

68. "For Sale: One Hundred Thousand Brick for Immediate Delivery, Four Hundred Thousand Brick for Delivery the Second of August, the Caraleigh Mills Co." *Raleigh Times* (NC), August 10, 1900; "The Company Owns Its Brickworks." *Charlotte Observer* (Charlotte, NC), January 31, 1898.

69. *Raleigh Times* (NC), August 5, 1909; "Caraleigh Mills Company," *News and Observer* (Raleigh, NC), August 24, 1899; On March 25, 1891, the *News and Observer* reported that the Caraleigh Cotton Mills "just to the Southeast of Mr. Upchurch's Brickyard on Caraleigh Lands East of the City Which Have Already Been Secured for This Purpose." In an interview with Caraleigh resident Frank Tuttle on August 6, 1974, the assertion that the original bricks were made at "Goodwin's Brickyard" would seem not wholly accurate since Caraleigh's own brick manufactory was producing over a million bricks annually; *Caraleigh: A Forgotten Village*, 2.

70. Cathy L. McHugh, *Mill Family: The Labor System in the Southern Cotton Textile Industry, 1880–1915* (New York: Oxford University Press, 1988), 18.

71. Rosser H. Taylor, "Fertilizers and Farming in the Southeast, 1840–1950," *North Carolina Historical Review*, Vol. 30, No. 4 (October 1953), 483–523; Harold Woodman, *King Cotton and His Retainers: Financing and Marketing the Cotton Crop of the South, 1800–1925* (Columbia: University of South Carolina Press), 340.

72. *Evening Visitor* (Raleigh, NC), June 4, 1895; "Mill to Employ 300 Here," *News and Observer* (Raleigh, NC), March 28, 1938.

73. Johnson and Murray, *Wake: Capital County of North Carolina, Vol. II*, 202; "Two Important Raleigh Enterprises," *Morning Post* (Raleigh, North Carolina), September 21, 1898; the Phosphate and Fertilizer Company's directors were "J.R. Chamberlain, Ashley Horne, A.Q. Holladay, W.G. Upchurch, F.O. Moring, S.R. Horne, E.C. Smith, J.W. Barber, J.B. Kenney," *Evening Visitor* (Raleigh, NC), June 4, 1895; "By Laws of Caraleigh Mills Co.," Raleigh Banking and Trust Company Papers 1831–1928, Agreements, Specifications, Blueprints, Miscellaneous Papers- 1869–1928. P.C. 136.2. folder: Raleigh Banking and Trust Co. Papers—Miscellaneous Paper, 1869–1920. Courtesy of the State Archives of North Carolina.

74. Woodward, *Origins of the New South*, 76.

75. Watkins, *Caraleigh: Raleigh's Cotton Mill Village* 17; Lemmon, "Raleigh—An Example of the 'New South'?" 261–85.

76. Thompson, *From the Cotton Field to the Cotton Mill*, 68.

77. *Ibid*, 8–9.

78. *Ibid*.

79. "The New South" *Atlanta Daily Herald* (GA), March 14, 1874; Darren Grem, "Henry W. Grady (1850–1889)," *New Georgia Encyclopedia*, https://www.georgiaencyclopedia.org/articles/arts-culture/henry-w-grady-1850-1889.

80. Grem, "Henry W. Grady (1850–1889)."

81. John M. Cooper, "Page, Walter Hines," *Dictionary of North Carolina Biography*, William S. Powell, ed., (Chapel Hill: University of North Carolina Press, 1979).

82. *Charlotte Observer* (NC), July 7, 1915; Brenda Marks Eagles, "Daniel Augustus Tompkins," *Dictionary of North Carolina Biography*, William S. Powell, ed., (Chapel Hill: University of North Carolina Press, 1979).

83. *Charlotte Observer* (NC), July 7, 1915.

84. *News and Observer* (Raleigh, NC) November 9, 1880.

85. Woodward, *Origins of the New South*, 112.

86. Cooper and Terrill, *The American South: A History*, vol. II., 428–429; also see, Edwin DuBois Shurter, ed., *The Complete Orations and Speeches of Henry W. Grady*, South-West Publishing Company, 1910.

87. Cooper and Terrill, *The American South: A History*, vol. II., 428–429.

88. Paul M. Gaston, *The New South Creed: A Study in Southern Mythmaking* (Montgomery: NewSouth Books, 1970, 2002), 28; Mitchell, *The Rise of the Cotton Mills in the South*, 68–69.

Notes—Chapter 2

89. Mitchell, *The Rise of the Cotton Mills in the South*, 68–69.

90. Ibid.

91. "The Caraleigh Mills," *News and Observer* (Raleigh, NC), November 28, 1895.

92. "A Local Poet Penned a Poem 'Hurrah for Caraleigh' and This Was Set to Music" and played at the opening ceremony of Caraleigh Mills, as reported in the *News and Observer* (Raleigh, NC), March 28, 1938; the text of the "Caraleigh Anthem" decorates the wall inside the Caraleigh Mills mailroom to provide a deeper sense of history for the building's residents when it opened as a condominium living complex, in 2003.

93. "The Caraleigh Mills," *News and Observer* (Raleigh, NC), November 28, 1895.

94. "Caraleigh Mills Fabrics," *News and Observer* (Raleigh, NC) October 23, 1897.

95. "Two Important Raleigh Enterprises," *Morning Post* (Raleigh, NC), September 21, 1898.

96. "The Caraleigh Cotton Mills," *News and Observer* (Raleigh, NC), July 2, 1899.

97. "Of the Most Elaborately Laid Out Mill Propositions in the Entire Country," *Charlotte News* (NC), September 21, 1917.

98. "Mill to Employ 300 Here," *News and Observer* (Raleigh, NC), March 28, 1938.

99. "Caraleigh Mills Company," *News and Observer* (Raleigh, NC), August 24, 1899.

100. Peter A. Coclanis, "Textiles Spun a New NC, but What Will Replace It?" *News and Observer* (Raleigh, NC), February 22, 2017.

101. "The Caraleigh Mills," *Evening Visitor* (Raleigh, NC), July 24, 1891.

102. Don H. Kennedy, *Ship Names: Origins and Usages During 45 Centuries* (Charlottesville: University Press of Virginia, 1974), 10–13, 127–131.

103. Kennedy, *Ship Names*, 10–13, 127–131.

104. "The Caraleigh Mills," *News and Observer* (Raleigh, NC), November 28, 1895.

105. "Caraleigh Musicale," *News and Observer* (Raleigh, NC), March 23, 1893.

106. Woodward, *Origins of the New South*, 14.

107. James L. Hunt, "Creating North Carolina Populism, 1900–1960, Part I: The Progressive Era Project, 1900–1930," *North Carolina Historical Review*, Volume XCVII, Number 2, April 2020, 168–199.

108. Ibid.

109. Ibid.

110. Ibid.

111. Ibid.

112. J.G. de Roulhac Hamilton, Robert Digges Wimberly Connor, William Byrd, *History of North Carolina*, in 6 volumes (Chicago: Lewis Publishing Company, 1919). https://catalog.hathitrust.org/Record/006785597; The following Caraleigh founders have biographies in the *History of North Carolina*: F.O. Moring (vol. IV, 293–294), A.A. Thompson (vol. IV, 99) Ashley Horne (vol. III, 341–342), A.Q. Holladay (vol. III, 371), A.S. Merrimon (vol. III, 180–181), Josephus Daniels (vol. III, 264, 282, 335, 342, vol. V 293), R.H. Battle (vol. V, 17) , J.S. Carr (vol. III, 314, 341, 374, vol. VI, 5), J.R. Chamberlain (vol. V, 56), C.J. Hunter (vol. IV, 391), R.B. Raney (vol. IV, 169), E.C. Smith (vol. IV, 98).

113. "Robert E. Lee the Subject," *Raleigh Times* (NC), January 19, 1912; "Lee's Birthday in the Schools," *News and Observer* (Raleigh, NC), January 20, 1912.

114. Charles Reagan Wilson, "The Religion of the Lost Cause: Ritual and Organization of the Southern Civil Religion, 1865–1920." *The Journal of Southern History* 46, no. 2 (1980): 219–38. Accessed February 6, 2021.

115. "Robert E. Lee the Subject," *Raleigh Times* (NC), January 19, 1912; "Lee's Birthday in the Schools," *News and Observer* (Raleigh, NC), January 20, 1912.

116. "Lee's Birthday in the Schools," *News and Observer* (Raleigh, NC), January 20, 1912.

117. H.G. Jones, "Connor, Robert Diggs Wimberly," *Dictionary of North Carolina Biography*, William S. Powell, ed., (Chapel Hill: University of North Carolina Press, 1979).

118. James L. Hunt, "Creating North Carolina Populism, 1900–1960, Part I: The Progressive Era Project, 1900–1930," *North Carolina Historical Review*, Volume XCVII, Number 2, April 2020, 168–199.

119. "Lee's Birthday in the Schools," *News and Observer* (Raleigh, NC), January 20, 1912.

120. Ibid.

121. R.D.W. Connor, *The Story of the Old North State*. (Philadelphia: J.B. Lippincott Company, 1906).

122. Connor, *The Story of the Old North State*, 152.

123. Ibid., 153.

124. Ibid., 156.

125. R.D.W. Connor, ed., *A Manual of North Carolina Issued by the North Carolina Historical Commission for the Use of Members of the General Assembly Session 1913* (Raleigh: E.M. Uzzell & Co. State Printers), 184–185. https://docsouth.unc.edu/nc/manual/manual.html.

126. "R.D.W. Connor Appointed First Archivist of the United States," NC Department of Natural and Cultural Resources. https://www.ncdcr.gov/blog/2015/10/10/wilsons-r-d-w-connor-first-u-s-archivist.

127. "Archivist Dies," *Minneapolis Star* (Minnesota), February 25, 1950.

128. McHugh, *Mill Family*, 7.

129. Harriet L. Herring, *Passing of the Mill Village: Revolution in a Southern Institution* (Westport: Greenwood, 1949), 5.

Chapter 2

1. Fred W. Hobson, ed., Gerald W. Johnson, *South Watching: Selected Essays by Gerald W.*

Johnson, (Chapel Hill: University of North Carolina Press, 1983), 67.

2. Thompson, *From the Cotton Field to the Cotton Mill*, 180.

3. Thompson, *From the Cotton Field to the Cotton Mill*, 165, 166.

4. Harriet L. Herring, *Welfare Work in Mill Villages: The Story of Extra Mill Activities in North Carolina* (Chapel Hill: University of North Carolina Press, 1929), 2.

5. George B. Tindall, *The Emergence of the New South, 1913–1945* (Baton Rouge: Louisiana State University, 1967), 327.

6. Tindall, *Emergence of the New South*, 327.

7. Wake County Register of Deeds, Caraleigh Cemetery January 1924, record number BM1924–00072; Robert Christensen, "Caraleigh: Flourishing Mill, Threadbare Area," *News and Observer* (Raleigh, NC), April 11, 1974.

8. Glass, *The Textile Industry in North Carolina*, 24, 25.

9. Glass, *The Textile Industry in North Carolina*, 25.

10. "By Laws of Caraleigh Mills Co.," Raleigh Banking and Trust Company Papers 1831–1928, Agreements, Specifications, Blueprints, Miscellaneous Papers—1869–1928. P.C. 136.2. folder: Raleigh Banking and Trust Co. Papers—Miscellaneous Paper, 1869–1920. Courtesy of the State Archives of North Carolina.

11. "A.S. Merrimon Was a Noted Member of the Buncombe Bar," *Asheville Citizen-Times* (NC), July 1, 1950; "Augustus Summerfield Merrimon: NC 7th Supreme Court Chief Justice," https://www.carolana.com/NC/Courts/asmerrimon.html.

12. "A Great Enterprise," *State Chronicle* (Raleigh, NC), February 5, 1891; "Two Big Enterprises," *News and Observer* (Raleigh, NC), January 31, 1891; "Chief Justice Merrimon," *Asheville Daily Citizen* (NC), November 14, 1892.

13. "Two Big Enterprises," *News and Observer* (Raleigh, NC), January 31, 1891; "A Great Enterprise," *State Chronicle* (Raleigh, NC), February 5, 1891; "The Caraleigh Mills," *Evening Visitor* (Raleigh, NC), July 24, 1891.

14. A.S. Merrimon, quoted in "A.S. Merrimon Was a Noted Member of the Buncombe Bar," *Asheville Citizen-Times* (NC), July 1, 1950.

15. "A.S. Merrimon Was a Noted Member of the Buncombe Bar," *Asheville Citizen-Times* (NC), July 1, 1950; Jonathan Martin, "Augustus S. Merrimon (1830–1892)," North Carolina History Project, https://northcarolinahistory.org/encyclopedia/augustus-s-merrimon-1830-1892/

16. "Senator and Jurist A.S. Merrimon," *North Carolina Department of Natural and Cultural Resources*, https://www.ncdcr.gov/blog/2013/11/14/senator-and-jurist-a-s-merrimon.

17. "Chief Justice Merrimon," Asheville Citizen-Times (NC), November 14, 1892.

18. "A.S. Merrimon Was a Noted Member of the Buncombe Bar," *Asheville Citizen-Times* (NC), July 1, 1950.

19. "Death of Chief Justice Merrimon," *Wilmington Messenger* (NC), November 15, 1892; "The Kirk-Holden War," North Carolina Department of Natural and Cultural Resources, NCpedia.org,https://www.ncpedia.org/anchor/kirk-holden-war.

20. "Revival of the Ku Klux-Mob Spirit at Milton and Yanceyville, and Caswell County," *Tri-Weekly Era* (Raleigh, NC), July 2, 1872.

21. *Tri-Weekly Era* (Raleigh, NC), July 2, 1872.

22. "Death of Chief Justice Merrimon," *Wilmington Messenger* (NC), November 15, 1892.

23. *Ibid*.

24. *Ibid*.

25. *Ibid*.

26. "A.S. Merrimon Was Noted Member of the Buncombe Bar," *Asheville Citizen-Times* (NC), July 1, 1950.

27. "Death of Judge Merrimon," *Lenoir Topic* (NC), November 23, 1892.

28. *Ibid*.

29. *Ibid*.

30. *Ibid*.

31. "Wm. B. Merrimon," *Greensboro Telegram* (NC), December 1, 1910; *Everything* (Greensboro, NC), February 14, 1914; "Latest Klondike Pilgrim," *Charlotte Democrat* (NC), September 2, 1897; "Had a Great Trip," *Everything* (Greensboro, NC), October 23, 1915.

32. "Two Big Enterprises," *News and Observer* (Raleigh, NC), January 31, 1891.

33. *North Carolinian* (Raleigh), October 17, 1895; *State Chronicle* (Raleigh, NC), February 5, 1891; *News and Observer* (Raleigh, NC), March 25, 1891; *News and Observer* (Raleigh, NC), November 28, 1895; "The Caraleigh Mills," *Evening Visitor* (Raleigh, NC), July 24, 1891; "W.G. Church Dead," *North Carolinian* (Raleigh, NC), October 17, 1895.

34. *State Chronicle* (Raleigh, NC), February 5, 1891.

35. "W.G. Upchurch Dead," *North Carolinian* (Raleigh, NC), October 17, 1895.

36. "Concerning Raleigh People," *Weekly Raleigh Register* (NC), October 21, 1885.

37. "W.G. Upchurch Dead," *North Carolinian* (Raleigh, NC), October 17, 1895.

38. "New Factory Facts," *News and Observer* (Raleigh, NC), November 28, 1895; "A Great Enterprise," *State Chronicle* (Raleigh, NC), February 5, 1891; "Two Big Enterprises," *News and Observer* (Raleigh, NC), January 31, 1891; *News and Observer* (Raleigh, North Carolina), November 28, 1895.

39. "Capt. J.J. Thomas Has Passed Away," *Farmer and Mechanic* (Raleigh, NC), January 10, 1911.

40. "Banks of Raleigh Elect Officers," *News and Observer* (Raleigh, NC), January 11, 1911.

41. *Ibid*.

42. Edward McCrady and Samuel A. Ashe, *Cyclopedia of Eminent and Representative Men of the Carolinas of the Nineteenth Century Volume II* (Madison: Brant & Fuller, 1892), 506.

43. McCrady and Ashe, *Cyclopedia of Eminent and Representative Men*, 506–508.

44. "Capt. J.J. Thomas Has Passed Away," *Farmer and Mechanic* (Raleigh, NC), January 10, 1911; "First Shot Fired," *Goldsboro Daily Argus* (NC), August 15, 1907.

45. "Capt. J.J. Thomas Has Passed Away," *Farmer and Mechanic* (Raleigh, NC), January 10, 1911.

46. "Death of Colonel Horne," *Wilmington Morning Star* (NC), October 24, 1913; William R. Pittman, "Horne, Ashley," 1988, *Dictionary of North Carolina Biography*, William S. Powell, ed., (Chapel Hill: University of North Carolina Press, 1988).

47. "Clayton and Its Commerce," *News and Observer* (Raleigh, NC), December 27, 1898; "A Good Selection," *Farmer and Mechanic* (Raleigh, NC), October 27, 1903; "A Story of Success and Constant Growth," *Morning Post* (Raleigh, NC), January 10, 1904.

48. "Clayton and Its Commerce," *News and Observer* (Raleigh, NC), December 27, 1898.

49. "Hon. Ashley Horne," *Asheboro Courier* (NC), April 9, 1908.

50. "Horne and Harmony," *Robesonian* (Lumberton, NC), May 28, 1908.

51. "Ashley Horne," *News and Observer* (Raleigh, North Carolina), August 24, 1899; "Horne the People's Candidate for Governor," *Progressive Farmer* (Raleigh, NC) April 1, 1908; "Col. Ashley Horne Has Passed Away," *Fayetteville Weekly Observer* (NC), October 29, 1913.

52. "Unveil Monument," *Kinston Free Press* (NC), June 13, 1914; "Col. Ashley Horne Has Passed Away," *Fayetteville Weekly Observer* (NC), October 29, 1913; "North Carolina General Assembly," *Mountain Scout* (Taylorsville, NC), February 26, 1913.

53. "Hon. Ashley Horne," *Asheboro Courier* (NC), April 9, 1908.

54. "Ashley Horne," *News and Observer* (Raleigh, NC), August 24, 1899.

55. Ibid.

56. "William Walton Kitchin, Democratic Nominee," *Concord Daily Tribune* (NC), June 29, 1908.

57. "Col. Ashley Horne Is Laid to Rest," *News and Observer* (Raleigh, NC), October 24, 1913.

58. *Asheville Weekly Citizen* (NC), October 25, 1898; "Caraleigh Mills Stock for Sale," *Press-Visitor* (Raleigh, NC), April 11, 1898.

59. "The Caraleigh Mills," *News and Observer* (Raleigh, NC), November 28, 1895; Billings, *Planters and the Making of a "New South,"* 82–84.

60. McCrady and Ashe, *Cyclopedia of Eminent and Representative Men*, 55–56.

61. Billings, *Planters and the Making of a "New South,"* 82–84.

62. "Speech of Hon. R.H. Battle," *Morning Post* (Raleigh, NC), August 23, 1900.

63. Memory F. Mitchell, "Battle, Richard Henry," *Dictionary of North Carolina Biography*, William S. Powell, ed., (Chapel Hill: University of North Carolina Press, 1979).

64. "The North Carolina Monumental Association," *State Chronicle* (Raleigh, NC), July 16, 1892.

65. "Speech of Hon. R.H. Battle," *Morning Post* (Raleigh, NC), August 23, 1900.

66. Ibid.

67. Memory F. Mitchell, "Battle, Richard Henry," *Dictionary of North Carolina Biography*.

68. "Richard H. Battle Passes at Age of 77," *Raleigh Daily* (NC), May 20, 1912.

69. "The Most Valuable Bull in the World," *News and Observer* (Raleigh, NC), April 5, 1896; "An Act to Incorporate the Carraleigh Mills Company."

70. Louise L. Queen, "Carr, Julian Shakespeare," *Dictionary of North Carolina Biography*, William S. Powell, ed., (Chapel Hill: University of North Carolina Press, 1979).

71. "A Night School," *Press-Visitor* (Raleigh, NC), May 18, 1897; "Will Launch City-wide Appeal to Save John Pullen's Church," *News and Observer* (Raleigh, NC), March 15, 1931.

72. Elizabeth Davis Reid Murray, "Pullen, John Turner," 1994, *Dictionary of North Carolina Biography*, William S. Powell, ed., (Chapel Hill: University of North Carolina Press, 1979).

73. "Great Grief Over Death Mr. Pullen," *News and Observer* (Raleigh, NC), May 3, 1913.

74. *News and Observer* (Raleigh, NC), September 21, 1895.

75. *Caraleigh Baptist Church: One Hundredth Year Anniversary, 1904–2004*, Talmadge Infinger, Pastor. Church publication.

76. Josephus Daniels, *Editor in Politics* (Chapel Hill: University of North Carolina Press, 1941), 340–342; "Governor Glenn in Wake," *News and Observer* (Raleigh, NC), May 22, 1908; *News and Observer* (Raleigh, NC), May 23, 1908; "Prohibition Speaking," *News and Observer* (Raleigh, NC), April 14, 1908.

77. "For Inauguration," *Raleigh Times* (NC), December 19, 1900.

78. "Col. Ashley Horne Is Laid to Rest," *News and Observer* (Raleigh, NC), October 24, 1913.

79. "John Turner Pullen," Find a Grave Memorial ID 24136393, citing Oakwood Cemetery, Raleigh, Wake County, North Carolina, USA; Maintained by Don Stowell (contributor 46794548).

80. John H. Haley, *Charles N. Hunter and Race Relations in North Carolina* (Chapel Hill: University of North Carolina Press, 1987), 26.

81. "Needham Bryant Broughton," *News and Observer* (Raleigh, NC), May 27, 1914.

82. "Memoir in Honor of Mr. N.B. Broughton," *Twin-City Daily Sentinel* (Winston-Salem, NC), September 17, 1914; "Story of Progress: Caraleigh

Baptist Church to Celebrate Golden Anniversary of First Services," *Raleigh Times* (NC), May 22, 1954; "Formal Opening of the Anti-Saloon Campaign," *Morning Post* (Raleigh, NC), September 9, 1903.

83. Moses Neal Amis, *Historical Raleigh: With Sketches of Wake County (from 1771) and Its Important Towns; Descriptive, Biographical, Educational, Industrial, Religious* (Raleigh: Commercial Printing Company, 1913), 181.

84. Murray, *Wake: Capital County of North Carolina* volume I, 569–570.

85. Charles A. Newell, Jr., "Broughton, Needham Bryant," 1979, *Dictionary of North Carolina Biography*, William S. Powell, ed., (Chapel Hill: University of North Carolina Press, 1979).

86. Jennie M. Barbee, *Historical Sketches of the Raleigh Public Schools, 1876–1941–1942* (Raleigh: Barbee Pupils' Association 1943), 67.

87. "Raleigh Historic Property Designation Application and Report, Needham B. Broughton High School," Raleigh Historic Properties Commission, Inc., March 13, 1990.

88. Charles A. Newell, Jr., "Broughton, Needham Bryant," *Dictionary of North Carolina Biography*.

89. "Story of Progress: Caraleigh Baptist Church to Celebrate Golden Anniversary of First Services," *Raleigh Times* (NC), May 22, 1954; "Baptist City Missions of Raleigh," *Biblical Recorder* (Raleigh, NC), April 19, 1899.

90. "Needham Bryant Broughton," *News and Observer* (Raleigh, NC), May 27, 1914; *Caraleigh Baptist Church: One Hundredth Year Anniversary*; "Story of Progress: Caraleigh Baptist Church to Celebrate Golden Anniversary of First Services," *Raleigh Times* (NC), May 22, 1954."

91. "Moral Depravity in Raleigh Portrayed," *Morning Post* (Raleigh, NC), October 18, 1904.

92. "Moral Depravity in Raleigh Portrayed," *Morning Post* (Raleigh, NC), October 18, 1904.

93. Ibid.
94. Ibid.
95. Ibid.
96. Ibid.
97. Ibid.

98. Harriet L. Herring, *Welfare Work in Mill Villages*, 99.

99. "The Temperance Work," *Farmer and Mechanic* (Raleigh, NC), December 19, 1901; "At Caraleigh," *News and Observer* (Raleigh, NC) May 23, 1908.

100. "The Temperance Work," *Farmer and Mechanic* (Raleigh, NC), December 19, 1901.

101. *Caraleigh Baptist Church: One Hundredth Year Anniversary.*

102. Ibid.
103. Ibid.
104. Ibid.
105. Ibid.
106. Ibid.

107. "He Will Not Do It," *Fisherman and Farmer* (Elizabeth City, NC), August 23, 1900.

108. Locke Craig, then state representative and future governor, quoted here in Steven A. Hill, C.M. Eppes, "1858–1942: Uncle Tom or Radical Diplomat?" *North Carolina Historical Review*, April 2019, Volume XCVI, Number 2, p. 157; LeRae Sikes Umfleet, *1898 Wilmington Race Riot Report*, May 31, 2006, Office of Archives and History, North Carolina Department of Cultural Resources.

109. Jerry Gershenhorn and Anna Jones, "The Long Black Freedom Struggle in Northampton County, North Carolina, 1930s to 1970s," *North Carolina Historical Review*, Volume XCVII, Number 1 (January 2020), 6.

110. Hamilton, Joseph Gregoire de Roulhac. *Reconstruction in North Carolina* (New York: Columbia University, 1914), 332, 662–3.

111. "James H. Young, African American Leader in 1890s," North Carolina Department of Natural and Cultural Resources. https://www.ncdcr.gov.

112. Haley, *Charles N. Hunter and Race Relations*, 92; Jeffrey J. Crow "'Fusion, Confusion, and Negroism': Schisms among Negro Republicans in the North Carolina Election of 1896." *North Carolina Historical Review* 53, no. 4 (1976): 364–84.

113. "The Broughton-Young Campaign," *Gazette* (Raleigh, NC), January 9, 1897.

114. "Pure Elections," *Smithfield Herald* (NC), September 16, 1898.

115. "Fear a Fair Trial," *News and Observer* (Raleigh, NC), January 30, 1897.

116. Johnson and Murray, *Wake: Capital County of North Carolina, Vol. II*, 42, 43n; Jeffrey J. Crow, "Fusion, Confusion, and Negroism: Schisms among Negro Republicans in the North Carolina Election of 1896." *The North Carolina Historical Review* 53, no. 4 (1976): 364–84. Accessed June 12, 2021.

117. Eric Anderson, "Race and Politics in North Carolina: 1872–1901," (Baton Rouge: Louisiana State University Press: 1901), 247–8; "James H. Young, African American Leader in 1890s," NC Department of Natural and Cultural Resources; Haley, *Charles N. Hunter and Race Relations*, 92.

118. "Pure Elections," *Smithfield Herald* (NC), September 16, 1898.

119. "The Broughton-Young Campaign," *Gazette* (Raleigh, NC), January 9, 1897.

120. "Pure Elections," *Smithfield Herald* (Smithfield, NC), September 16, 1898.

121. "Mr. Broughton Nominated for State Senator," *News and Observer* (NC), June 10, 1900.

122. Helen G. Edmonds, *The Negro and Fusion Politics in North Carolina: Chapel Hill: University of North Carolina Press, 1951)*, 100.

123. "No Workingman Need Apply," *Raleigh Signal* (NC) May 3, 1888; "Our Next Congressman," *Weekly State Chronicle* (Raleigh, NC), June 1, 1888.

124. "Wake Co. Democrats," *State Chronicle* (Raleigh, NC), May 15, 1892; "Mr. Broughton

Nominated for State Senator," *Farmer and Mechanic* (Raleigh, NC), June 12, 1900.

125. "Democratic Doctrine," *State Chronicle* (Raleigh, NC), November 2, 1892.

126. Charles A. Newell, Jr., "Broughton, Needham Bryant," *Dictionary of North Carolina Biography*, William S. Powell, ed., (Chapel Hill: University of North Carolina Press, 1979); Steven A. Hill, "C.M. Eppes, 1858–1942: Uncle Tom or Radical Diplomat?" *North Carolina Historical Review*, April 2019, Volume XCVI, Number 2, page 157.

127. "Mr. Broughton Nominated for State Senator," *News and Observer* (Raleigh, NC), June 10, 1900.

128. "Afternoon Session of the Convention," *State Chronicle* (Raleigh, NC), September 17, 1892; "Important Meeting," *News and Observer* (Raleigh, NC), October 27, 1892; "Democratic Doctrine," *State Chronicle* (Raleigh, NC), November 2, 1892; *News and Observer* (Raleigh, NC), July 21, 1892; *Smithfield Herald* (NC), September 16, 1898; "Mr. Broughton Nominated for State Senator," *News and Observer* (Raleigh, NC), June 10, 1900.

129. "Mr. Broughton Nominated for State Senator," *News and Observer* (Raleigh, NC), June 10, 1900.

130. "Mr. Broughton Nominated for State Senator," *News and Observer* (Raleigh, NC), June 10, 1900.

131. Charles A. Newell, Jr., "Broughton, Needham Bryant," *Dictionary of North Carolina Biography*.

132. Christopher Crittenden, William S. Powell, Robert H. Woody, et al., eds., *100 Years 100 Men: Raleigh: Edwards and Broughton Company)*, 431–432.

133. Charles A. Newell, Jr., "Broughton, Needham Bryant," *Dictionary of North Carolina Biography*.

134. Johnson and Murray, *Wake: Capital County of North Carolina, Vol. II*, 189.

135. Haley, *Charles N. Hunter and Race Relations*, 149.

136. Haley, *Charles N. Hunter and Race Relations*, 139.

137. Crittenden, Powell, eds., *100 Years 100 Men: 1871–1971*, 433.

138. "Memorial to N.B. Broughton," *News and Observer* (Raleigh, NC), June 24, 1914; "Needham Broughton," *North Carolina Christian Advocate* (Greensboro, NC), June 4, 1914.

139. "Last Rites for N.B. Broughton," *News and Observer* (Raleigh, NC) May 28, 1914.

140. "J.R. Chamberlain Passes Suddenly," *News and Observer* (Raleigh, NC), April 27, 1926. "Money Went Freely," *News and Observer* (Raleigh, NC), March 16, 1895; "The a & M College," *Caucasian* (Clinton, NC), June 17, 1897; *News and Observer* (Raleigh, NC), August 10, 1892.

141. *State Chronicle* (Raleigh, NC), January 13, 1892; *Wilmington Messenger* (Wilmington, NC), January 11, 1894; *News and Observer* (Raleigh, NC), November 21, 1895; *Charlotte Observer* (NC), July 28, 1895; *Morning Post* (Raleigh, NC), January 10, 1904; "Obituaries," *Women's Wear*, April 28, 1926; "Camp Polk to Die Dead as Door Nail," *Wilmington Morning Star* (NC), November 28, 1918; "J.R. Chamberlain Passes Suddenly," *News and Observer* (Raleigh, NC), April 27, 1926; *News and Observer* (Raleigh, NC), May 7, 1926.

142. "J.R. Chamberlain Is Dead at Raleigh Home," *Charlotte Observer* (NC), April 27, 1926. University Archives Photograph Collection. Oversize photographs (UA023.030), Special Collections Research Center at NC State University Libraries; Adolph Oettinger Goodwin, *Who's Who in Raleigh: A Collection of Personal Cartoons and Biographical Sketches of the Staunch Trees That Make the Oak City*, "J.R. Chamberlain," (Raleigh: Commercial Printing Co., 1916).

143. "Money Went Freely," *News and Observer* (Raleigh, NC), March 16, 1895; "The a & M College," *Caucasian* (Clinton, NC), June 17, 1897; *News and Observer* (Raleigh, NC), August 10, 1892; "J.R. Chamberlain Passes Suddenly," *News and Observer* (Raleigh, NC), April 27, 1926; "Orders Mistrial in Wynne Suit," *News and Observer* (Raleigh, NC), May 30, 1924; "A New Copper Mine," *News and Observer* (Raleigh, NC), August 31, 1899.

144. "Adjusting the Tariff," *Wilmington Morning Star* (NC), August 18, 1911; *Newbernian* (New Bern, NC), November 18, 1876.

145. "Potash Tariff Would Deal a Hard Blow to the Tar Heel Farmer," *Greensboro Daily News* "The Populist Handbook Answered," (NC), August 13, 1921.

146. *Charlotte Observer* (NC) March 16, 1895; "A & M College," *Commonwealth* (Scotland Neck, NC), June 17, 1897; *News and Observer* (Raleigh, NC), January 14, 1897.

147. Alice Elizabeth Reagan, *North Carolina State University: A Narrative History* (Ann Arbor: Edwards Brothers, Inc., 1987), 22.

148. "J.R. Chamberlain Passes Suddenly," *News and Observer* (Raleigh, NC), April 27, 1926.

149. Goodwin, *Who's Who in Raleigh*.

150. Goodwin, *Who's Who in Raleigh*.

151. "Funeral Held of J.R. Chamberlain" *News and Observer* (Raleigh, NC), April 26, 1929.

152. "An Act to Incorporate the Carraleigh Mills Company."

153. "Thomas H. Briggs Dies at His Home," *News and Observer* (Raleigh, NC), May 8, 1928; https://www.findagrave.com/memorial/73814759/thomas-henry-briggs; William S. Powell, "Briggs, Thomas Henry," 1979, *Dictionary of North Carolina Biography*, William S. Powell, ed., (Chapel Hill: University of North Carolina Press, 1979).

154. "Thomas H. Briggs Dies at His Home," *News and Observer* (Raleigh, NC), May 8, 1928.

155. "Thomas H. Briggs Dies at His Home," *News and Observer* (Raleigh, NC), May 8, 1928.
156. "Sale of $50,000 in Bonds," *Morning Post* (Raleigh, NC), March 25, 1898.
157. "First Baptists to Recognize Briggs," *News and Observer* (Raleigh, NC), September 21, 1927.
158. "W.G. Briggs Is Appointed," *Raleigh Times* (NC), August 16, 1906.
159. "Thomas H. Briggs Is Laid to Rest," *News and Observer* (Raleigh, NC), May 9, 1928.
160. "Carey J. Hunter to Be Buried Today," *News and Observer* (Raleigh, NC), January 25, 1923.
161. "Two Important Raleigh Enterprises," *Morning Post* (Raleigh, NC), September 21, 1898.
162. *News and Observer* (Raleigh, NC), September 21, 1911.
163. *News and Observer* (Raleigh, NC), September 21, 1911.
164. "News of the Capitol," *Asheville Citizen-Times* (Asheville, NC), April 23, 1908; Goodwin, *Who's Who in Raleigh*.
165. "Present Hunter Portrait to 'Y,'" *News and Observer* (Raleigh, NC), January 7, 1924.
166. "Citizens United for Y.M.C.A. for Raleigh," *News and Observer* (Raleigh, North Carolina), March 24, 1911.
167. "Citizens United for Y.M.C.A. for Raleigh," *News and Observer* (Raleigh, North Carolina), March 24, 1911.
168. "Carey J. Hunter to Be Buried Today," *News and Observer* (Raleigh, NC), January 25, 1923.
169. "The Caraleigh Directors," *News and Observer* (Raleigh, NC), January 14, 1897; *Chatham Record* (Pittsboro, NC), October 19, 1899.
170. Irma Ragan Holland, "Page, Allison Francis (Frank)," 1994, *Dictionary of North Carolina Biography*, William S. Powell, ed., (Chapel Hill: University of North Carolina Press, 1979).
171. *Asheville Citizen-Times* (NC), October 18, 1899; Irma Ragan Holland, "Page, Allison Francis (Frank)," 1994, *Dictionary of North Carolina Biography*.
172. "Death of Mr. A.F. Pope," *Raleigh Christian Advocate* (NC), October 18, 1899; Irma Ragan Holland, "Page, Allison Francis (Frank)" *Dictionary of North Carolina Biography*, William S. Powell, ed., (Chapel Hill: University of North Carolina Press, 1979).
173. Catherine W. Bishir, "Page, Allison F. (1824–1899)," *North Carolina Architects and Builders (2016)* https://ncarchitects.lib.ncsu.edu/people/P000459.
174. "Death of Mr. A.F. Page," *Statesville Record and Landmark* (NC), October 20, 1899.
175. "Builders of Raleigh," *News and Observer* (Raleigh, NC), May 11, 1942.
176. "Methodist Orphanage," *Asheville Citizen-Times* (NC), October 23, 1899.
177. "Death of Mr. A.F. Page," *Statesville Record and Landmark* (NC), October 20, 1899.
178. "Will of Late A.F. Page," *Morning Post* (Raleigh, NC), October 22, 1899.
179. *Norfolk Virginian* (VA), January 11, 1894.
180. "Around the World," *News and Observer* (Raleigh, NC), January 3, 1893.
181. Legeros, *Raleigh Fire Department 1880–1899*.
182. "Chamber of Commerce," *Morning Post* (Raleigh, NC), September 21, 1898.
183. B.W.C. Roberts, "Raney, Richard Beverly," 1994, *Dictionary of North Carolina Biography*, William S. Powell, ed., (Chapel Hill: University of North Carolina Press, 1979).
184. "R.B. Raney, Big Hearted Citizen Dead," *Raleigh Times* (NC), December 8, 1909.
185. B.W.C. Roberts, "Raney, Richard Beverly," 1994, *Dictionary of North Carolina Biography*.
186. "The Olivia Rainey Library," *Farmer and Mechanic* (Raleigh, NC), February 5, 1901.
187. *Ibid.*
188. B.W.C. Roberts, "Raney, Richard Beverly," 1994, *Dictionary of North Carolina Biography*.
189. "For Inauguration," *News and Observer* (Raleigh, NC), December 22, 1900.
190. "R.B. Raney President," *Press-Visitor* (Raleigh, NC) September 22, 1897.
191. "The Olivia Raney Library," *News and Observer* (Raleigh, NC), August 24, 1902; "The Olivia Raney Library," *Farmer and Mechanic* (Raleigh, NC), February 5, 1901; B.W.C. Roberts, "Raney, Richard Beverly," 1994, *Dictionary of North Carolina Biography*.
192. "Raney Library Formally Opened," *Morning Post* (Raleigh, NC), January 25, 1901.
193. "Olivia Rainey Library," *Farmer and Mechanic* (Raleigh, NC), February 5, 1901.
194. "R.B. Raney, Big Hearted Citizen Dead," *Raleigh Times* (NC), December 8, 1909.
195. "Richard Beverly Raney," *News and Observer* (Raleigh, NC), January 16, 1910.
196. "The Caraleigh Mills," *News and Observer* (Raleigh, NC), November 28, 1895; "Death Ends Long Business Career," *News and Observer* (Raleigh, NC), August 8, 1922.
197. "V.C. Royster, Head of Big Candy Business, Will Be Buried Today in Raleigh," *Durham Morning Herald* (NC), August 9, 1922.
198. M. Ruth Little, "Additional Supporting Information for Raleigh Historic Landmark Designation Application of Arkansas Delaware and Vermont Connecticut Royster Confectioners Building 207 Fayetteville Street Raleigh, North Carolina, 27601," Longleaf Historic Resources, Raleigh, July 22, 2008. https://rhdc.org/sites/default/files/Royster%20Landmark%20Report%20text.pdf.
199. "V.C. Royster Is Buried in Oakwood," *News and Observer* (Raleigh, NC) August 10, 1922.
200. "Will of W.A. Linehan Is Filed for Probate," *News and Observer* (Raleigh, NC), July 24, 1931; "By Laws of Caraleigh Mills Co.," Raleigh Banking and Trust Company Papers 1831–1928,

Notes—Chapter 2

Agreements, Specifications, Blueprints, Miscellaneous Papers- 1869–1928. P.C. 136.2. folder: Raleigh Banking and Trust Co. Papers—Miscellaneous Paper, 1869–1920. Courtesy of the State Archives of North Carolina; Wake County Register of Deeds, "Caraleigh Mill Company and Caraleigh Phosphate and Fertilizer Mill, November 4, 1891," record number 000118–00441Wake County Register of Deeds, "Caraleigh Mill Company and Caraleigh Phosphate and Fertilizer Mill, November 4, 1891," record number 000118–00441.

201. *News and Observer* (Raleigh, NC), January 31, 1891; *News and Observer* (Raleigh, NC), January 20, 1914.

202. "S.A. Linehan Buried in Oakwood Cemetery," *News and Observer* (Raleigh, NC), July 20, 1931; the date of birth was June 23, 1897, and place of birth was Raleigh, and he was buried in Oakwood Cemetery, "W.A. Linehan Is Taken by Death," *News and Observer* (Raleigh, NC), July 18, 1931; "Cross & Linehan to Hold Opening," *News and Observer* (Raleigh, NC), September 9, 1927.

203. "Five Firms Top 50 Year Record," *News and Observer* (Raleigh, NC), 1942.

204. "William Augustus Linehan," Find A Grave, Oakwood Cemetery, Raleigh, NC, PLOT A 193, Memorial ID 115169054. https://www.findagrave.com/memorial/115169054/william-augustus-linehan.

205. "The Passing of a Landmark," *News and Observer* (Raleigh, NC), March 5, 1919.

206. *Goldsboro Daily Argus* (NC), March 4, 1919; "Dr. D.E. Everett Passes Away Here," *News and Observer* (Raleigh, NC), March 5, 1919.

207. *Hickory Daily Record* (NC), March 5, 1919; "Dr. D.E. Everett Passes Away Here," *News and Observer* (Raleigh, NC), March 5, 1919.

208. "Worth Bagley Monument," https://docsouth.unc.edu/commland/monument/100; "Unveiling Ceremonies in Capitol Square," *News and Observer* (Raleigh, NC), May 19, 1907.

209. "Commemorative Landscapes, Worth Bagley Monument," https://docsouth.unc.edu/commland/monument/100.

210. "Dr. D.E. Everett Passes Away Here," *News and Observer* (Raleigh, NC), March 5, 1919.

211. "The Caraleigh Fertilizer Works," *News and Observer* (Raleigh, NC), January 11, 1894; "Caraleigh Phosphate and Fertilizer Company," *Evening Visitor* (Raleigh, NC), June 4, 1895; *Raleigh Times* (NC), August 5, 1909.

212. Maurice S. Toler, "Holladay, Alexander Quarles," *Dictionary of North Carolina Biography*, William S. Powell, ed., (Chapel Hill: University of North Carolina Press, 1988).

213. "Life and Services of Dr. A.Q. Holladay," *Farmer and Mechanic* (Raleigh, NC), October 8, 1912.

214. "Life and Services of Dr. A.Q. Holladay," *Farmer and Mechanic* (Raleigh, NC), October 8, 1912.

215. The A & M College," *Caucasian* (Clinton, NC), June 17, 1897.

216. Maurice S. Toler, "Holladay, Alexander Quarles," 1988, *Dictionary of North Carolina Biography*.

217. "Commencement Exercises," *Progressive Farmer* (Winston-Salem, NC), June 20, 1893.

218. "Dr. A.Q. Holladay Dead," *News and Observer* (Raleigh, North Carolina), March 16, 1909.

219. *Norfolk Virginian* (Norfolk, VA), January 11, 1894.

220. Edwards, *Cyclopedia of Eminent and Representative Men, 364–365*.

221. M.R.B. Peacock, "Root, Charles Boudinot," *Dictionary of North Carolina Biography*, William S. Powell, ed., (Chapel Hill: University of North Carolina Press, 1994).

222. McCrady and Ashe, *Cyclopedia of Eminent and Representative Men, 364–365*.

223. McCrady and Ashe, *Cyclopedia of Eminent and Representative Men, 364–365*; "Supreme Court," *Daily Standard* (Raleigh, NC), December 22, 1868.

224. "Negroes for Hire," *Daily Confederate* (Raleigh, NC), December 28, 1864.

225. "Southern Rights Meeting in Wake," *Semi-Weekly State Journal* (Raleigh, NC), April 6, 1861.

226. Murray, *Wake: Capital County of North Carolina* volume 1, 472; "Mr. Charles B. Root Dead," *Morning Post* (Raleigh, NC), May 8, 1903.

227. "The American Union Commission," *Wilmington Herald* (NC), November 29, 1865.

228. "City Elections," *Weekly Standard* (Raleigh, NC), January 30, 1867.

229. *Weekly Raleigh Register* (NC), October 22, 1862; McCrady and Ashe, *Cyclopedia of Eminent and Representative Men, 364–365*; *News and Observer* (Raleigh, NC), September 21, 1902; "North Carolina Mutual Life Insurance Company," *Raleigh Register* (NC), February 21, 1863.

230. "Mr. Charles B. Root Dead," *Morning Post* (Raleigh, NC), May 8, 1903.

231. *News and Observer* (Raleigh, NC), October 16, 1900.

232. "Chambers Smith Dies Here at 83," *News and Observer* (Raleigh, NC), April 4, 1940; "Edward Chambers Smith," https://www.ancestry.com/genealogy/records/edward-chambers-smith-24-1yc9lr; "15th Knight Commander," https://www.kappaalphaorder.org/knight-commanders/edward-chambers-smith/

233. "15th Knight Commander," https://www.kappaalphaorder.org/knight-commanders/edward-chambers-smith/

234. E.C. Smith Province," *News and Observer* (Raleigh, NC), December 7, 1912.

235. "The State Convention," *Wilmington Messenger* (NC), May 20, 1892.

236. "Elias Carr for Governor," *Lenoir Topic* (NC), May 25, 1892.

237. *Ibid.*
238. "A Prominent Negro Bishop's Opinion," *Wilmington Messenger* (NC), February 13, 1890.
239. "Elias Carr for *Governor,*" *Lenoir Topic* (NC), May 25, 1892.
240. "The New State Central Committee," *Fayetteville Weekly Observer* (NC), May 17, 1900.
241. *Morning Post* (Raleigh, NC), March 9, 1900.
242. "Horne for Governor," *News and Observer* (Raleigh, NC), June 20, 1908.
243. "F.O. Moring Dies," *News and Observer* (Raleigh, North Carolina), January 12, 1920; See also, "F.O. Moring Dies After Long Illness," *News and Observer* (Raleigh, NC), January 20, 1920; *History of North Carolina, Volume IV* (Lewis Publishing Company: Chicago, 1919), 293–294.
244. "A Great Enterprise," *State Chronicle* (Raleigh, NC), February 5, 1891; "F.O. Moring Dies After Long Illness," *News and Observer* (Raleigh, NC), January 12, 1920.
245. "F.O. Moring Dies After Long Illness," *News and Observer* (Raleigh, NC), January 12, 1920; *History of North Carolina, Volume IV Biography* (Chicago: Lewis Publishing Company), 293–294.
246. *Charlotte News* (NC), October 6, 1904; Watkins, *Caraleigh: Raleigh's Cotton Mill Village,* 29.
247. "F.O. Moring Dies After Long Illness," *News and Observer* (Raleigh, NC), January 12, 1920; "The New Alderman," *News and Observer* (Raleigh, NC), May 3, 1882; "Board of Alderman," *News and Observer,* December 4, 1886.
248. Billings mistakenly referred to Moring as "Moving" and Moringsville was mistakenly written as "Movingsburg," in Billings, *Planters and the Making of a "New South,"* 206; William D. Snider, "Watauga Club," *Encyclopedia of North Carolina,* William S. Powell, ed., (Chapel Hill: University of North Carolina Press, 2006).
249. Billings, *Planters and the Making of a "New South,"* 206–210.
250. *Ibid.*
251. *Ibid.,* 210.
252. [Support for Democratic Party] "Wake Democrats Meet," *Morning Post* (Raleigh, NC), May 22, 1898.
253. [Support for school taxes], *News and Observer* (Raleigh, NC), April 12, 1908; [support for education, religion, Biblical law] "Blag [sic] Raising at Caraleigh," *News and Observer* (Raleigh, NC), May 11, 1904.
254. Richard L. Watson, "Josephus Daniels," *Dictionary of North Carolina Biography,* William S. Powell, ed., (Chapel Hill: University of North Carolina Press, 1986).
255. Richard L. Watson, "Josephus Daniels," *Dictionary of North Carolina Biography,* 1986.
256. "All Raleigh Is Mourning," *Farmer and Mechanic* (Raleigh, NC) May 17, 1898.
257. Josephus Daniels, *The First Fallen Hero, a Biographical Sketch of Worth Bagley, Ensign, U.S.N.* (Norfolk: S.W. Bowman, 1898), 56.
258. Josephus Daniels, *The First Fallen Hero,* 59.
259. *Ibid.,* 58–59.
260. Richard L. Watson, "Josephus Daniels," *Dictionary of North Carolina Biography,* 1986.
261. "Past, Present, and Future," *State Chronicle* (Raleigh, NC), April 22, 1891; *News and Observer* (Raleigh, NC), November 15, 1899; "A.A. Thompson Has Accepted," *North Carolinian* (Raleigh, NC), July 30, 1903; "Well Known Raleigh Man Died Friday Night," *Asheville Citizen-Times* (NC), June 13, 1920.
262. "Past, Present, Future," *State Chronicle* (Raleigh, NC), April 22, 1891; *History of North Carolina,* Vol. IV (Chicago: Lewis Publishing Company, 1919), 99–100.
263. "Past, Present, Future," *State Chronicle* (Raleigh, NC), April 22, 1891.
264. Cooper and Terrill, *The American South: A History,* vol. II., 426; "Try to Prevent Wood Extortion," *News and Observer* (Raleigh, NC), January 22, 1918.
265. "A.A. Thompson Has Accepted," *North Carolinian* (Raleigh, NC), July 30, 1903.
266. "Well Known Raleigh Man Died Friday Night," *Asheville Citizen-Times* (NC), June 13, 1920; "Past, Present, and Future" *State Chronicle* (Raleigh, NC), April 22, 1891.
267. Amis, *Historical Raleigh: With Sketches of Wake County,* 209–210.
268. *Wilmington Morning Star* (NC), May 18, 1887.
269. "Caraleigh Increases Its Capacity," *Morning Post* (Raleigh, NC), July 2, 1899.
270. *News and Observer* (Raleigh, NC), November 15, 1899; "A.A. Thompson Has Accepted," *North Carolinian* (Raleigh, NC), July 30, 1903.
271. "A.A. Thompson Has Accepted," *North Carolinian* (Raleigh, NC), July 30, 1903; Salary Information from https://panam1901.org/visiting/salaries.htm ; *Farmer and Mechanic* (Raleigh, NC), March 8, 1910.
272. *History of North Carolina, Vol. IV (Chicago:* Lewis Publishing Company, 1919), 99–100.
273. "For Businessmen," *Henderson Gold Leaf* (Henderson, NC), May 18, 1893.
274. "Sale of the Tribune," *North Carolinian* (Raleigh, NC) June 17, 1897; *Raleigh Daily Tribune* (NC), February 28, 1897.
275. Johnson and Murray, *Wake: Capital County of North Carolina, Vol. II,* 237.
276. "Well Known Raleigh Man Died Friday Night," *Asheville Citizen-Times* (NC), June 13, 1920.
277. "Annual Meeting Mill Captains Is Now on Here," *Charlotte News* (NC), June 23, 1915.
278. "Hurrah!" *News and Observer* (Raleigh, North Carolina), August 28, 1888.
279. *Ibid.*
280. James Vickers, *Raleigh City of Oaks: An*

Illustrated History (Sun Valley: American Historical Press, 1997), 85.
281. "Hurrah!" *News and Observer* (Raleigh, NC), August 28, 1888.
282. Ibid.
283. Ibid.
284. Ibid.
285. Ibid.
286. Ibid.
287. Ibid.
288. Ibid.
289. Ibid.
290. "Businessmen at Raleigh," *Twin-City Daily Sentinel* (Winston-Salem, NC), August 11, 1892; "For Businessmen," *Henderson Gold Leaf* (NC), May 18, 1893.
291. "The New Aldermen," *News and Observer* (Raleigh, NC), May 6, 1891.
292. "For Businessmen," *Henderson Gold Leaf* (NC), May 18, 1893.
293. "Speaking Tonight," *Morning Post* (Raleigh, NC), September 8, 1903; *Semi-Weekly Messenger* (Wilmington, NC), March 24, 1908; "The Good Mayor of Raleigh," *Weekly State Chronicle* (Raleigh, North Carolina), April 26, 1889; "Temperance Men for Drewry," *Raleigh Times* (NC), July 3, 1906; "The Devil's Own Drink," *Commonwealth* (Scotland Neck, NC) February 10, 1898.
294. "Governor Glenn in Wake," *News and Observer* (Raleigh, NC), May 22, 1908; *News and Observer* (Raleigh, NC), May 23, 1908; "Prohibition Speaking," *News and Observer* (Raleigh, NC), April 14, 1908.
295. "Only One Woman for Saloons in City," *North Carolinian* (Raleigh, NC), October 1, 1903.
296. "At Caraleigh," *News and Observer* (Raleigh, NC) May 23, 1908.
297. "Governor Glenn in Wake," *News and Observer* (Raleigh, NC), May 22, 1908; *News and Observer* (Raleigh, NC), May 23, 1908; "Prohibition Speaking," *News and Observer* (Raleigh, NC), April 14, 1908.
298. "Don't Belong to Caraleigh," *Raleigh Times* (NC), September 15, 1909.
299. *News and Observer* (Raleigh, NC), November 27, 1903.
300. Grantor Caraleigh Mills Co, Grantee Henry K. Stanton, Deed April 28, 1893, Book-Page 000125–00638, Register of Deeds Tammy L. Brunner, Wake County, Raleigh, North Carolina.
301. "Governor Glenn in Wake," *News and Observer* (Raleigh, NC), May 22, 1908; *News and Observer* (Raleigh, NC), May 23, 1908; "Prohibition Speaking," *News and Observer* (Raleigh, NC), April 14, 1908.
302. "This Is the Last Day to Register," *News and Observer* (Raleigh, NC), May 16, 1908.
303. "Raleigh Goes Dry but Wake Is Wet," *North Carolinian* (Raleigh, NC), May 28, 1908.
304. "Annual Meeting Mill Captains Is Now on Here," *Charlotte News* (NC), June 23, 1915; Amis, *Historical Raleigh: With Sketches of Wake County*, 209–210.
305. Steven A. Hill, "C. M. Eppes, 1858–1942: Uncle Tom or Racial Diplomat?" *North Carolina Historical Review* Volume XCVI, Number 2 (April 2019)149–181.
306. "Wake Democrats Meet," *Morning Post* (Raleigh, NC), May 22, 1898.
307. Ibid.
308. Ibid.
309. "County Convention," *Morning Post* (Raleigh, NC), April 8, 1900; "The Wake Vote Is Now Counted," *Farmer and Mechanic* (Raleigh, NC), June 14, 1904.
310. "County Convention," *Morning Post* (Raleigh, NC) April 8, 1900.
311. *History of North Carolina*, Vol. IV (Chicago: Lewis Publishing Company, 1919), 99–100.
312. "Wake Democrats Meet," *Morning Post* (Raleigh, NC), May 22, 1898; "County Convention," *Morning Post* (Raleigh, NC), April 8, 1900.
313. "Legalized Primaries a Necessary Corollary to the Constitutional Amendment," *North Carolinian* (Raleigh, NC), February 9, 1899.
314. "Former Mayor Thompson," *News and Observer* (Raleigh, NC), June 13, 1920.
315. "Dedication Exercises for Thompson School" *News and Observer* (Raleigh, NC), December 16, 1923; "That Foul Force Bill," *State Chronicle* (Raleigh, NC), July 23, 1890; "Committees for Year Appointed," *Greensboro Daily News* (NC), June 4, 1907; "A Brief History of the A.A. Thompson School: Home of the Wake Young Men's Leadership Academy," https://www.wymlapta.com/historical-archives; Oakwood Cemetery, Raleigh, Wake County, North Carolina, plot identification: BEECHWOOD H 2.

Chapter 3

1. *Robesonian* (Lumberton, NC), April 22, 1909.
2. "Caraleigh Mills Has a Strike," *News and Observer* (Raleigh, NC), March 21, 1907.
3. Myrdal, *An American Dilemma: The Negro Problem and Modern Democracy*, 288.
4. Hobson, ed., *South Watching*, 64–71.
5. Myrdal, *An American Dilemma: The Negro Problem and Modern Democracy*, 285–286.
6. Hobson, ed., *South Watching*, 67.
7. Ibid.
8. Ibid, 69.
9. Gaston, *The New South Creed*, 20, 223.
10. Thompson, *From the Cotton Field to the Cotton Mill*, 277–278.
11. John W. Blassingame, *The Slave Community: Plantation Life in the Antebellum South* (New York: Oxford University Press, 1979), 13, 245.
12. W. Conard Gass, "Battle, Kemp Plummer," *Dictionary of North Carolina Biography*, William

S. Powell, ed., (Chapel Hill: University of North Carolina Press, 1979).

13. Battle, *A Centennial Address*, 130–131.

14. Battle, *A Centennial Address: Delivered by Invitation*, 130–131.

15. A List of men who were on the Board of Aldermen who "authorized the Proposed Steps" for the 100-year celebration of Raleigh included Julius Lewis. Additional citizens were selected to comprise "The Board of Managers of the Raleigh Centennial" that included A.Q. Holladay, Josephus Daniels, A.A. Thompson, R.H. Battle, Dr. R.H. Lewis, Dr. James McKee, Julius Lewis, N.B. Broughton, A.F. Page, Judge A.S. Merrimon, J.J. Thomas, William G. Upchurch. There were twenty-two "Field Marshalls" for the day of celebration, these included Alf. A. Thompson, N.B. Broughton. Assistant Marshalls included Carey J. Hunter, N.W. West, W.H. Pace, Ed. Chambers Smith, Julius Lewis, Thomas H. Briggs, found in Battle, *A Centennial Address: Delivered by Invitation*, 106–108, 122, 131.

16. Jeffrey Leiter, Michael D. Schulman, and Rhonda Zingraff, editors. Hanging by a Thread: Social Change in *Southern Textiles* (Ithaca: ILR Press: 1991), 6.

17. Leiter, Schulman, Zingraff, eds., *Hanging by a Thread: Social Change in Southern Textiles*, 6–7, as quoted from Jay R. Mandle, *The Roots of Black Poverty: The Southern Plantation Economy After the Civil War* (Durham: Duke University Press, 1978).

18. Leiter, Schulman, Zingraff, eds., *Hanging by a Thread: Social Change in Southern Textiles*, 7.

19. Cara A. Finnegan, "Review of Lewis Hine as Social Critic," *Rhetoric & Public Affairs* 13, no. 4 (2010): 741–745. doi:10.1353/rap.2010.0207.

20. McHugh, *The Mill Family*, 8.

21. Harry Boyte. 1972. "The Textile Industry: Keel of a Southern Industrialization." Radical America 6 (2): 4–49 quoted in *Southern Textiles: Contested Puzzles*, 6.

22. W.G. Upchurch Dead," *North Carolinian* (Raleigh, NC), October 17, 1895.

23. "J.R. Chamberlain Passes Suddenly," *News and Observer* (Raleigh, NC), April 27, 1926; *News and Observer* (Raleigh, NC), May 7, 1926; "Funeral Held of J.R. Chamberlain," *News and Observer* (Raleigh, NC), April 29, 1926.

24. C. Vann Woodward, *The Strange Career of Jim Crow* (New York: Oxford University Press, 2002), 95.

25. K. Todd Johnson and Elizabeth Reid Murray, *Wake: Capital County of North Carolina, Vol. II, Reconstruction to 1920* (Raleigh: Wake County Commissioners: 2008), 202; "A Year of Unprecedented Growth: The Textile Industries," *News and Observer* (Raleigh, North Carolina), September 15, 1909.

26. "Trouble at the Caraleigh Mills," *Raleigh Times* (NC), March 21, 1907.

27. Jacquelyn Dowd Hall, James Leloudis, Robert Korstad, Mary Murphy, Lu Ann Jones, Christopher B. Daly, editors. *Like a Family: The Making of a Southern Cotton Mill World*. (Chapel Hill: University of North Carolina Press, 1987), 66.

28. *Charlotte Observer* (NC), April 26, 1907.

29. "Gasses Kill Three Negroes," *Concord Daily Tribune* (NC), June 19, 1908; "Four Negroes Succumb to Sulfuric Acid," *Caucasian* (Clinton, NC), June 25, 1908.

30. *Chatham Record* (Pittsboro, NC), April 22, 1914.

31. *News and Observer* (Raleigh, NC), March 4, 1917.

32. "Caraleigh Mills Has a Strike," *News and Observer* (Raleigh, NC), March 21, 1907.

33. Thompson, *From the Cotton Field to the Cotton Mill*, 248–249.

34. *Ibid L*, 277.

35. Cash, *The Mind of the South*, 317–318.

36. *Ibid*, 91, 317–318.

37. *Ibid*, 91.

38. Thompson, *From the Cotton Field to the Cotton Mill*, 276.

39. *Ibid*.

40. "Break Back Bone of Pit Strike," *Times Dispatch* (Richmond, Virginia), March 23, 1907.

41. *Ibid*.

42. *Semi-Weekly Messenger* (Wilmington, NC), September 13, 1907.

43. "Caraleigh Mills Has a Strike," *News and Observer* (Raleigh, NC), March 21, 1907.

44. "Sent to Court," *News and Observer* (Raleigh, NC), March 22, 1907.

45. "Trouble at Caraleigh Mills," *Raleigh Times* (NC), March 21, 1907.

46. *Ibid*.

47. "Break Backbone of Pit Strike," *Times Dispatch* (Richmond, VA), March 23, 1907.

48. Trouillot, *Silencing the Past*, 146.

49. *Ibid*, 26.

50. "Caraleigh Mills Company," *News and Observer* (Raleigh, NC) August 24, 1899.

51. Trouillot, *Silencing the Past*, 26.

52. *Ibid*, 55.

53. *Ibid*.

54. "Caraleigh Has a Strike," *News and Observer* (Raleigh, NC), March 21, 1907.

55. Trouillot, *Silencing the Past*, 72–73.

56. "Break Backbone of Pit Strike," *Times Dispatch* (Richmond, VA), March 23, 1907.

Chapter 4

1. "Pure Water Question Is Probably Settled," *Morning Post* (Raleigh, NC), March 11, 1899; "Caraleigh Phosphate and Fertilizer Works," *News and Observer* (Raleigh, NC), August 10, 1892.

2. "Hurrah!" *News and Observer* (Raleigh, NC), August 28, 1888.

3. *Ibid*.

4. "City of Oaks," *News and Observer* (Raleigh, NC) March 22, 1890.

5. *Ibid.*

6. "Past, Present and Future," *State Chronicle* (Raleigh, NC), April 22, 1891.

7. *Ibid.*

8. "The Greater Raleigh a Warm Proposition," *North Carolinian* (Raleigh, NC), July 4, 1907.

9. "Caraleigh Increases Its Capacity," *Morning Post* (Raleigh, NC), July 2, 1899.

10. "Blag [sic] Raising at Caraleigh," *News and Observer* (Raleigh, NC), May 11, 1904.

11. "Domestic Classes at Caraleigh Mills," *Charlotte News* (NC), February 21, 1917.

12. "Of the Most Elaborately Laid Out Mill Propositions in the Entire Country," *Charlotte News Textile Industrial Edition* (NC), February 21, 1917.

13. "Caraleigh Mills Company," *Southern Textile Journal*, December 25, 1919, Vol. XVIII, No. 17, Charlotte: Clarke Publishing Company, 146.

14. "Caraleigh Mills Company," *Southern Textile Journal*, Vol. 24, no. 17, June 21, 1923, Charlotte: Clarke Publishing Company, 152–153.

15. Amis, *Historical Raleigh from Its Foundation in 1792*, 161–162.

16. Mitchell, *The Rise of the Cotton Mills in the South*, 154–155.

17. McHugh, *Mill Family*, 41.

18. *Charlotte Observer* (NC), August 19, 1892.

19. "Libel Presentations," *Wilmington Messenger* (NC), July 12, 1895; *Weekly Star* (Wilmington, NC), July 5, 1895; "Raleigh Veteran of Medicine Recalls Old Associates and Practice," *News and Observer* (Raleigh, NC), June 12, 1938.

20. "Plans to Hide Mechanicals Ran Into a Historical Hurdle," *Triangle Business Journal*, Feb 24, 2003. https://www.bizjournals.com/triangle/stories/2003/02/24/focus3.html

21. "Infant Mortality on Big Decrease," *News and Observer* (Raleigh, NC), November 3, 1919.

22. "Water Becomes Prime Concern in Capital City," *News and Observer* (Raleigh, NC), September 13, 1953; Sherman, Fraser, "Raleigh Public Record, a Review of Raleigh's Superfund Sites," February 24, 2012, https://theraleighcommons.org/raleighpublicrecord/news/2012/02/24/a-review-of-raleighs-superfund-sites/.

23. *State Chronicle* (Raleigh, NC), March 16, 1892; "Pure Water Question Is Probably Settled," *Morning Post* (Raleigh, NC), March 11, 1899.

24. *News and Observer* (Raleigh, NC), July 3, 1894.

25. "The Caraleigh Mills," *State Chronicle* (Raleigh, NC), October 21, 1891.

26. "Water Works Case," *News and Observer* (Raleigh, NC), July 12, 1895; Maury York, "Laughinghouse, Charles O'Hagan," *Dictionary of North Carolina Biography*, William S. Powell, ed., (Chapel Hill: University of North Carolina Press, 1991).

27. "Plans to Hide Mechanicals Ran Into a Historical Hurdle" *Triangle Business Journal*, Feb 24, 2003. https://www.bizjournals.com/triangle/stories/2003/02/24/focus3.html

28. David H. Howells, "Historical Account of Public Water Supplies in North Carolina." Report No. 244, 1989. *Water Resources Research Institute of the University of North Carolina*. North Carolina State University, Raleigh, North Carolina.

29. David H. Howells, "Historical Account of Public Water Supplies in North Carolina."

30. Woodward, *Origins of the New South*, 133–134.

31. Johnson and Murray, *Wake: Capital County of North Carolina, Vol. II*, 476. "Water Works Case" *News and Observer* (Raleigh, NC), July 12, 1895.

32. "Water Works Case" *News and Observer* (Raleigh, NC), July 12, 1895.

33. Howells, "Historical Account of Public Water Supplies in North Carolina."

34. *Ibid.*

35. *Ibid.*

36. *Ibid.*

37. *Ibid.*

38. *Ibid.*

39. *Ibid.*

40. *Ibid.*

41. "The Water Works Matter," *News and Observer* (Raleigh, NC), August 24, 1886.

42. Johnson and Murray, *Wake: Capital County of North Carolina, Vol. II*, 477.

43. "The Water Works Matter," *News and Observer* (Raleigh, NC), August 24, 1886.

44. *Ibid.*

45. *Ibid*; Harry McKown, "Dorothea Dix Hospital," https://www.ncpedia.org/dorothea-dix-hospital.

46. "The Water Works Matter," *News and Observer* (Raleigh, NC), August 24, 1886.

47. *Ibid.*

48. *Ibid*; the author's correspondence with the Environmental Protection Agency, "During the 1800s, Gang Drinking Water Wells Were Available for the Public's Consumption." June 29, 2020.

49. "The Water Works Matter," *News and Observer* (Raleigh, NC), August 24, 1886.

50. "Board of Aldermen," *News and Observer* (Raleigh, NC), September 9, 1886.

51. *Ibid.*

52. *Ibid.*

53. Howells, "Historical Account of Public Water Supplies in North Carolina."

54. *Ibid.*

55. *Ibid.*

56. *Ibid.*

57. "The Water Works Matter," *News and Observer* (Raleigh, NC), August 24, 1886.

58. "The City's Water Supply," *News and Observer* (Raleigh, NC), August 29, 1886.

59. *Ibid.*

60. "Our City Water," *News and Observer* (Raleigh, NC) January 31, 1893.
61. "Walnut Creek Water," *News and Observer* (Raleigh, NC), January 31, 1893.
62. *Semi-Weekly Messenger* (Wilmington, NC), August 25, 1892; *State Chronicle*, January 31, 1893; Legeros, *Raleigh Fire Department 1880–1899*.
63. *State Chronicle* (Raleigh, NC), November 3, 1892.
64. *Ibid.*
65. "Notes About the Fire at Caraleigh," *State Chronicle* (Raleigh, NC), August 20, 1892.
66. There has been disagreement over how much sulfuric acid was spilled at the Caraleigh Phosphate fire: *Semi-Weekly Messenger* (Wilmington, NC), August 25, 1892, reported that "240 Tons of Lead Were in the Acid Chambers"; The *State Chronicle* newspaper reported on January 31, 1893, that "over 400 Tons of Sulfuric Acid Was Let Loose..." and 4000 tons were reported in Legeros, *Raleigh Fire Department 1880–1899.*
67. "The Very Severe Loss," *State Chronicle* (Raleigh, NC), August 19, 1892; *Wilmington Messenger* (NC), February 28, 1893; *State Chronicle* (Raleigh, NC), October 21, 1891.
68. "Walnut Creek Water," *News and Observer* (Raleigh, NC) January 31, 1893.
69. *Ibid*; "Our Drinking Water," *Evening Visitor* (Raleigh, NC), February 1, 1893.
70. "Setback for Temperance," *Morning Post* (Raleigh, NC), February 22, 1899.
71. *Ibid.*
72. "At Caraleigh," *News and Observer* (Raleigh, NC), May 23, 1908; "Governor Glenn in Wake," *News and Observer* (Raleigh, NC), May 22, 1908; *News and Observer* (Raleigh, NC), May 23, 1908; "Prohibition Speaking," *News and Observer* (Raleigh, NC), April 14, 1908. "Don't Belong to Caraleigh," *Raleigh Times* (NC), April 15, 1909.
73. "Report on Water," *Raleigh Times* (NC), March 11, 1899.
74. Legeros, *Raleigh Fire Department 1880–1899*; Steps to Protect the City Water," *News and Observer* (Raleigh, NC), March 12, 1899.
75. "Report on Water," *Raleigh Times* (NC), March 11, 1899; Legeros, *Raleigh Fire Department 1880–1899*.
76. "Pure Water Question Is Probably Settled," *Morning Post* (Raleigh, NC), March 11, 1899.
77. Fraser Sherman, "Raleigh Public Record, a Review of Raleigh's Superfund Sites," February 24, 2012, https://theraleighcommons.org/raleighpublicrecord/news/2012/02/24/a-review-of-raleighs-superfund-sites/.
78. "EPA Announces the Availability of the Administrative Record for Caraleigh."
79. Fraser Sherman, "Raleigh Public Record, a Review of Raleigh's Superfund Sites."
80. *Ibid.*
81. EPA Announces the Availability of the Administrative Record for Caraleigh.
82. *Ibid.*
83. "Raleigh Happenings," *Weekly Star* (Wilmington, NC), July 5, 1895; "Water Works Case," *News and Observer* (Raleigh, NC) July 12, 1895.
84. "Caraleigh News," *Evening Visitor* (Raleigh, NC), July 5, 1894; "At Caraleigh," *Evening Visitor* (Raleigh, NC), July 3, 1894; John T. Pullen in 1895 was "still Conducting Services at the Caraleigh Mills Chapel and Is Meeting with Much Encouragement." *News and Observer* (Raleigh, NC), September 21, 1895.
85. "Caraleigh News," *Evening Visitor* (Raleigh, NC), July 5, 1894.
86. "Water Works Case," *News and Observer* (Raleigh, NC), July 12, 1895; Maury York, "Laughinghouse, Charles O'Hagan," *Dictionary of North Carolina Biography*.
87. "Caraleigh News," *Evening Visitor* (Raleigh, NC), July 5, 1894.
88. "Plans to Hide Mechanicals Ran Into a Historical Hurdle," *Triangle Business Journal*, February 24, 2003. https://www.bizjournals.com/triangle/stories/2003/02/24/focus3.html.
89. "Plans to Hide Mechanicals Ran Into a Historical Hurdle" *Triangle Business Journal*, Feb 24, 2003. https://www.bizjournals.com/triangle/stories/2003/02/24/focus3.html.
90. "Caraleigh News," *Evening Visitor* (Raleigh, NC), July 5, 1894; "The 28 Brick Cottages for Operatives Are Also to Be Constructed Immediately," *State Chronicle* (Raleigh, NC), May 10, 1892.
91. *Evening Visitor* (Raleigh, NC), May 26, 1894.
92. "Caraleigh News," *Evening Visitor* (Raleigh, NC), July 5, 1894; "...Dr. McGee of the Penitentiary..." quoted in "Sensational Rumors," *Wilmington Messenger* (NC), July 8, 1894.
93. "At Caraleigh: There Is Yet Much Suffering and Sickness," *Evening Visitor* (Raleigh, NC), July 3, 1894; *Patron and Gleaner* (Lasker, NC), November 28, 1895.
94. "A Just Complaint," *Evening Visitor* (Raleigh, NC), April 12, 1894.
95. *Ibid.*
96. "Caraleigh News," *Evening Visitor* (Raleigh, NC), July 5, 1894.
97. *Ibid.*
98. *Evening Visitor* (Raleigh, NC), July 5, 1894.
99. *News and Observer* (Raleigh, NC), July 3, 1894.
100. "A Concert for Caraleigh," *Evening Visitor* (Raleigh, NC), July 10, 1894.
101. "A Reformer's Bad Day," *Charlotte Observer* (NC), July 25, 1894; "Notes from Caraleigh," *Evening Visitor* (Raleigh, NC), July 9, 1894.
102. "A Reformer's Bad Day," *Charlotte Observer* (NC), July 25, 1894.
103. *Charlotte Observer* (NC), July 25, 1894; "Notes from Caraleigh," *Evening Visitor* (Raleigh, NC), July 9, 1894.
104. "Notes from Caraleigh," *Evening Visitor* (Raleigh, NC), July 9, 1894.

Notes—Chapter 4

105. *Ibid.*
106. Michael P. McCarthy, "Typhoid and the Politics of Public Health in Nineteenth-Century Philadelphia" (American Philosophical Society, Independence Square, Philadelphia, 1987), 4.
107. Howells, "Historical Account of Public Water Supplies in North Carolina."
108. *Ibid.*
109. *Ibid.*
110. *Ibid.*
111. Michael P. McCarthy, "Typhoid and the Politics of Public Health," 10–11.
112. *Courier-Journal* (Louisville, KY), January 27, 1901.
113. Michael P. McCarthy, "Typhoid and the Politics of Public Health," 1.
114. *Ibid*; "Fear Is Felt for Inventor," *Dayton Daily News* (OH), May 18, 1912.
115. William Cain, *North Carolina Board of Health: Sanitary Engineering*, 3rd edition, 1885 (Raleigh: P.M. Hale, State Printer and Binder: 1885), 9.
116. *Ibid.*
117. "Water Works Case," *News and Observer* (Raleigh, NC), July 12, 1895.
118. *Ibid.*
119. "Caraleigh News," *Evening Visitor* (Raleigh, NC), July 5, 1894.
120. "At Caraleigh," *Evening Visitor* (Raleigh, NC), July 3, 1894.
121. *News and Observer* (Raleigh, NC), July 3, 1894; *Wilmington Messenger* (NC), July 20, 1895; "Water Works Case," *News and Observer* (Raleigh, NC), July 12, 1895.
122. "Water Works Case," *News and Observer* (Raleigh, NC), July 12, 1895; *News and Observer* (Raleigh, North Carolina), July 3, 1894; *Evening Visitor* (Raleigh, NC), May 26, 1894.
123. "Past, Present and Future," *State Chronicle* (Raleigh, NC), April 22, 1891.
124. *Weekly Star* (Wilmington, NC) July 5, 1895.
125. "Water Works Case," *News and Observer* (Raleigh, NC), July 12, 1895.
126. *Ibid*; *Wilmington Morning Star* (NC), July 3, 1895; *Patron and Gleaner* (Lasker, NC), November 28, 1895.
127. "To Cure Typhoid," *Boston Post* (MA), June 21, 1896.
128. "How Typhoid Spreads," *Messenger* (Marion, NC), September 9, 1898.
129. *Sixth Biennial Report of the North Carolina Board of Health 1895–1896* (Winston: M.I. & J.C. Stewart, Public Printers and Binders: 1897), 179.
130. *Sixth Biennial Report of the North Carolina Board of Health 1895–1896*, 178.
131. Francis E. Cox, "History of the Discovery of the Malaria Parasites and Their Vectors." *Parasites & Vectors* vol. 3,1:5. February 1, 2010, doi:10.1186/1756–3305–3–5.
132. "Damage Suit Decision Today," *News and Observer* (Raleigh, NC), October 26, 1899.
133. *Ibid.*
134. "Water Works Case," *News and Observer* (Raleigh, NC), July 12, 1895.
135. *Ibid.*
136. *Ibid.*
137. *Ibid.*
138. *Ibid.*
139. *Ibid.*
140. *Ibid.*
141. *Ibid.*
142. *Ibid.*; Maury York, "Laughinghouse, Charles O'Hagan," 1991, *Dictionary of North Carolina Biography*.
143. "Water Works Case," *News and Observer* (Raleigh, NC), July 12, 1895; Maury York, "Laughinghouse, Charles O'Hagan," 1991, *Dictionary of North Carolina Biography*.
144. "Water Works Case," *News and Observer* (Raleigh, NC), July 12, 1895.
145. *News and Observer* (Raleigh, NC), January 11, 1895.
146. *Patron and Gleaner* (Lasker, NC), November 28, 1895; *Warren Record* (Warrenton, NC), July 19, 1895.
147. "Walnut Creek Must Be Canalled," *News and Observer* (Raleigh, NC), July 18, 1895.
148. "Damage Suit Decision Today," *News and Observer* (Raleigh, NC), October 26, 1899.
149. *Ibid.*
150. "A Damage Suit Against the City," *North Carolinian* (Raleigh, NC), October 26, 1899.
151. *Ibid.*
152. *Ibid.*
153. *Ibid.*
154. *Ibid.*
155. *Ibid.*
156. *Ibid.*
157. *Ibid.*
158. *Ibid.*
159. *Ibid.*
160. *Ibid.*
161. "Damage Suit Decision Today," *News and Observer* (Raleigh, NC), October 26, 1899.
162. *Ibid.*
163. *Ibid.*
164. *Ibid.*
165. *Ibid.*
166. *Ibid.*
167. *Ibid.*
168. "A Damage Suit Against the City," *North Carolinian* (Raleigh, NC), October 26, 1899.
169. "Past, Present and Future," *State Chronicle* (Raleigh, NC), October 26, 1899.
170. *Ibid.*
171. *Ibid.*
172. *Ibid.*
173. "Damage Suit Decision Today," *News and Observer* (Raleigh, NC), October 26, 1899.
174. "The City Wins Its Damage Suit," *Farmer and Mechanic* (Raleigh, NC), October 31, 1899.
175. *Ibid.*
176. Glass, *The Textile Industry in North Carolina*, 25.

177. *Ibid.*
178. *Ibid.*
179. "Caraleigh News," *Evening Visitor* (Raleigh, NC), July 5, 1894.
180. "Water Works Case," *News and Observer* (Raleigh, NC), July 12, 1895.
181. *Ibid.*
182. "The Capital City's Tribute to the State's Milling Interests," *News and Observer* (Raleigh, NC), November 28, 1895.
183. Gaston, *The New South Creed*, 203–204.
184. Nicholas Worth [pseud., Walter Hines Page], *The Southerner* (New York, 1909), 17, as quoted in Gaston, *The New South Creed*, 203–204.
185. Wynes, Charles E., "Lewis H. Blair (1834–1916)" *The Dictionary of Virginia Biography* https://www.encyclopediavirginia.org/Blair_Lewis_Harvie_1834-1916.
186. Gaston, *The New South Creed*, 203–204.
187. *Ibid.*, 60.
188. *Ibid.*, 205.
189. *Ibid.*, 203–204.
190. *Ibid.*
191. *State Chronicle* (Raleigh, NC), July 8, 1892.
192. "The City's Water Supply," *News and Observer* (Raleigh, NC), August 29, 1886; Another report of "danger to Raleigh's water supply" was "The Nuisance," *Raleigh Times* (NC), July 11, 1898.
193. "The City's Water Supply," *News and Observer* (Raleigh, NC), August 29, 1886.
194. *Ibid.*
195. *Ibid.*
196. *Ibid.*
197. *Ibid.*
198. Chamber of Commerce and Industry and the Merchants Association, *Raleigh Illustrated: Commercial, Financial, Educational, Manufacturing, Illustrated* (Raleigh: Edwards and Broughton, 1910).
199. *Ibid.*
200. "Caraleigh Mills Company," *News and Observer* (Raleigh, NC) August 24, 1899; "Water Works Plant To Change Ownership," *North Carolinian* (Raleigh, NC), November 28, 1901.
201. *Raleigh Illustrated: Commercial, Financial, Educational, Manufacturing, Illustrated.*
202. "Wake Water Company Buys Raleigh Waterworks," *Morning Post* (Raleigh, NC), November 27, 1901.
203. *New Berne Weekly Journal* (NC), November 29, 1901.
204. "Walnut Creek Must Be Canalled," *News and Observer* (Raleigh, NC), July 18, 1895.
205. *Ibid.*
206. *Ibid.*
207. "Scored" is used correctly in this instance, meaning to strongly criticize; Wilmington Messenger (NC), July 20, 1895.
208. *Bulletin of the North Carolina Board of Health* [1894–1895: v.9], 48. https://digital.ncdcr.gov/digital/collection/p249901coll22/id/257358/rec/1.
209. "30 cases" reported *Evening Visitor* (Raleigh, NC), July 5, 1894.
210. "Six cases" reported in *Evening Visitor* (Raleigh, NC) July 9, 1894; "30 cases" reported *Evening Visitor* (Raleigh, NC), July 5, 1894; "There are more cases than are reported..." also in the *Evening Visitor* (Raleigh, NC), July 5, 1894; *News and Observer* (Raleigh, NC), July 3, 1894.
211. *Bulletin of the North Carolina Board of Health* [1894–1895 : v.9], August 1894 edition. https://digital.ncdcr.gov/digital/collection/p249901coll22/id/257358/rec/.
212. *Analyses of Drinking Water*, Public documents of the State of North Carolina [1895], Publisher: Josephus Daniels, North Carolina Office of the Governor State Document, 135–137, Health Sciences Library. University of North Carolina at Chapel Hill Public documents of North Carolina, OCLC Number-Original, 0001053167NYG; https://digital.ncdcr.gov/digital/collection/p249901coll22/id/119829/rec/41.
213. "Bacillus Coli Communis: The Cause of an Infection Clinically Identical With Typhoid Fever: Agglutination Reactions. 1 Against Bacillus Typhosus. Against Bacillus Paratyphosus (Types A And B). Against Bacillus Coli (Strain A)." Bibliography. Coleman, Warren; Hastings, T.W. *The American Journal of the Medical Sciences* (1827–1924); Philadelphia Vol. 137, Iss. 2 (Feb 1909): 199.
214. *Analyses of Drinking Water*, Public documents of the State of North Carolina [1895].
215. *Sixth Biennial Report of the North Carolina Board of Health 1895–1896*, 96–97, 143.
216. *Ibid.*, 96–97.
217. *Ibid.*
218. *Sixth Biennial Report of the North Carolina Board of Health 1895–1896*, 179.
219. *Ibid.*, 145–147.
220. *Ibid.*
221. *North Carolina Board of Health Bulletin*, August 1894, Vol. IX, No. 5. Pg. 57–58.
222. *Patron and Gleaner* (Lasker, NC), November 28, 1895.
223. New Jersey Department of Health, September 2016, Hazardous Substance Fact Sheet," https://nj.gov/health/eoh/rtkweb/documents/fs/0931.pdf; "A Damage Suit Against the City," *North Carolinian* (Raleigh, NC), October 26, 1899.
224. *Biennial Report of the North Carolina Board of Health 1895–1896*, 59–60.
225. *Ibid.*
226. *Ibid.*
227. *Ibid.*
228. Woodward, *Origins of the New South*, 225.
229. "City of Oaks," *State Chronicle* (Raleigh, NC), March 22, 1890.
230. "The progressive plutocracy not only survived but thrived throughout the decade of the 1950s. The major characteristics of the party

system remained in place," Karl E. Campbell quoted in Larry E. Tise and Jeffrey J. Crow, eds., *New Voyages to Carolina: Reinterpreting North Carolina History* (Chapel Hill: University of North Carolina Press, 2017), 255.

231. "The Caraleigh Mills," *News and Observer* (Raleigh, NC), November 28, 1895.

232. "Wealth From Industry," *Morning Post* (Raleigh, NC), December 2, 1897.

233. *Ibid.*

234. "Blag [sic] Raising at Caraleigh," *News and Observer* (Raleigh, NC), May 11, 1904.

235. *Ibid.*

236. Washington Herald (District of Columbia), October 21, 1912.

237. *Ibid.*

238. "Of the Most Elaborately Laid Out Mill Propositions in the Entire Country," *Charlotte News Textile Industrial Edition* (NC), February 21, 1917.

239. "Miss Carolina Champion, an employee at the Caraleigh mills, died this morning at her home in the southern part of the city, of fever. Her brother is very sick." *Evening Visitor* (Raleigh, NC), May 26, 1894.

240. *Southern Textile Bulletin* Vol. 25 (June 21, 1923), 152–153. https://archive.org/details/southerntextileb1923unse/page/n5/mode/2up.

241. Herring, *Welfare Work in Mill Villages*, 160, 274.

242. *Ibid*; also see Harriet L. Herring Papers #4017, Folder 263, Series 3, Research Materials, 1928–1950, Southern Historical Collection, University of North Carolina at Chapel Hill. https://dc.lib.unc.edu/cdm/singleitem/collection/04017/id/15123.

243. Herring, *Welfare Work in Mill Villages*, 160, 274.

244. *Ibid.*
245. *Ibid.*
246. *Ibid.*
247. *Ibid.*

248. "Caraleigh Mills," *News and Observer* (Raleigh, NC), August 24, 1899.

249. Tindall, Emergence of the New South, 588–589.

250. Samuel Huntington Hobbs, Jr., *North Carolina: Economic and Social* (Chapel Hill: University of North Carolina, 1930), 82.

251. *Ibid.*

252. *Caraleigh: A Forgotten Mill Village*, ca. 1974.

253. Daniel L. Watkins, *Caraleigh: Raleigh's Cotton Mill Village* MLS 697 Final Project, April 9, 2000. Thesis/Dissertation. North Carolina State University, 8. https://catalog.lib.ncsu.edu/catalog/NCSU1390012.

254. "Caraleigh-Survey Area XVI."

255. Nancy Van Dolsen, *National Register of Historic Places Registration Form.*

256. *Caraleigh: A Forgotten Mill Village*, ca. 1974.

257. *Ibid.*

258. Watkins, *Caraleigh: Raleigh's Cotton Mill Village*, 4–6.

259. "Statement Relative to $100,000 of First Mortgage Bonds Issued by the Caraleigh Mills Company of Raleigh, N.C.," North Carolina Collection, Cp 677.1 C25, Wilson Library, University of North Carolina at Chapel Hill, pp. 6–7, quoted in Watkins, *Caraleigh: Raleigh's Cotton Mill Village*, 32–33.

260. Watkins, *Caraleigh: Raleigh's Cotton Mill Village*, 7–8.

261. *Ibid.*
262. *Ibid.*
263. *Ibid.*

264. Herring, *Welfare Work in Mill Villages*, 169–172.

265. Watkins, *Caraleigh: Raleigh's Cotton Mill Village*, 65.

266. "The 'State of the Art': A Comparative Analysis of Newspaper Digitization to Date," April 10, 2015. https://www.crl.edu/sites/default/files/d6/attachments/events/ICON_Report-State_of_Digitization_final.pdf.

267. "Caraleigh-Survey Area XVI," 2.

268. *Ibid.*

269. Trouillot, *Silencing the Past*, 147.

270. "The Caraleigh Mills," *News and Observer* (Raleigh, NC), November 28, 1895.

271. "Raleigh Veteran of Medicine Recalls Old Associates and Practice," *News and Observer* (Raleigh, NC), June 12, 1938.

272. "Dr. James R. Rogers Dies; Oldest Raleigh Physician," *News and Observer* (Raleigh, NC) July 6, 1940.

273. "Raleigh Veteran of Medicine Recalls Old Associates and Practice," *News and Observer* (Raleigh, NC), June 12, 1938.

274. *Ibid.*
275. *Ibid.*
276. *Ibid.*
277. *Ibid.*
278. *Ibid.*

279. Johnson and Murray, *Wake: Capital County of North Carolina, Vol. II*, 489.

280. *Ibid.*
281. *Ibid.*, 202.

282. "The Danger to the City Water," *News and Observer* (Raleigh, NC) March 11, 1899.

283. "Microbe of Sloth," *Brooklyn Daily Eagle* (NY), December 5, 1902.

284. "Operatives in Southern Mills," *News and Observer* (Raleigh, NC), December 11, 1902.

285. *Ibid.*

286. Woodward, *Origins of the New South*, 425–426; "Laziness Is Offspring of Germ," *Buffalo Courier* (NY), December 14, 1902.

287. Carmena B. Zimmerman, "Dirt Eaters," *Dictionary of North Carolina Biography*, William S. Powell, ed., (Chapel Hill: University of North Carolina Press, 2006).

288. *Ibid.*

289. Margaret Humphreys, "How Four Once Common Diseases Were Eliminated From the

American South," *HEALTH AFFAIRS*, Volume 28, No.6. https://www.healthaffairs.org/doi/full/10.1377/hlthaff.28.6.1734.

290. Col. F.A. Olds, "Gossip of Current Topics," *Charlotte Observer* (NC), November 14, 1909.

291. C. Vann Woodward, *Origins of the New South 1877-1913*. (Baton Rouge: Louisiana State University Press, 1951), 425-426.

292. Col. F.A. Olds, "Gossip of Current Topics," *Charlotte Observer* (NC), November 14, 1909; *Salisbury Evening Post* (NC), September 30, 1915.

293. "Laziness Is Offspring of Germ," *Buffalo Courier* (NY), December 14, 1902.

294. Woodward, *Origins of the New South*, 426-427.

295. Margaret Humphreys, "How Four Once Common Diseases Were Eliminated from the American South," *HEALTH AFFAIRS*, Volume 28, No.6. https://www.healthaffairs.org/doi/full/10.1377/hlthaff.28.6.1734.

296. *Wilmington Morning Star* (NC), March 22, 1914.

297. Margaret Humphreys, "How Four Once Common Diseases Were Eliminated From the American South," *HEALTH AFFAIRS*, Volume 28, No. 6. https://www.healthaffairs.org/doi/full/10.1377/hlthaff.28.6.1734.

Chapter 5

1. Tindall, *Emergence of the New South*, 325.
2. *Ibid.*, 326.
3. Herring, *Welfare Work*, 107.
4. "The Caraleigh Mill," *Charlotte News* (NC), January 17, 1915.
5. Herring, *Welfare Work*, 9-10.
6. Watkins, *Caraleigh: Raleigh's Cotton Mill Village*, 61.
7. "Caraleigh Moves for Village Improvement," *News and Observer* (Raleigh, NC), February 20, 1915.
8. *Ibid.*
9. Hobson, ed., *South Watching*, 64, 65, 71.
10. *Ibid.*, 70.
11. *Ibid.*, 70.
12. Hobson, ed., *South Watching*, 70.
13. Leiter, Schulman, Zingraff, eds., *Hanging by a Thread: Social Change in Southern Textiles*, 7-8.
14. *Ibid.*, 9.
15. *News and Observer* (Raleigh, NC), August 13, 1899.
16. "Caraleigh Moves for Village Improvement," *News and Observer* (Raleigh, NC), February 20, 1915.
17. *Ibid.*
18. Herring, *Welfare Work in Mill Villages*, 206-208.
19. "Mill Betterment at Caraleigh," *Charlotte News* (NC), March 14, 1915.
20. *Ibid.*
21. "They Win Prizes on Pretty Home," *News and Observer* (Raleigh, NC) August 14, 1916.
22. *Ibid.*
23. *Ibid.*; I.T. Littleton, "Hill, Daniel Harvey, Jr.," *Dictionary of North Carolina Biography*, William S. Powell, ed., (Chapel Hill: University of North Carolina Press, 1988).
24. "They Win Prizes on Pretty Home," *News and Observer* (Raleigh, NC), August 14, 1916.
25. *Ibid.*
26. Link, *The Paradox of Southern Progressivism*, 177.
27. "Mill Betterment at Caraleigh," *Charlotte News* (NC), March 14, 1915.
28. Dorothy Mitchell, "Mill Village Betterment at Caraleigh," *Charlotte News* (NC), March 14, 1915.
29. *Ibid.*
30. Lena Rivers Smyth, "Welfare Work in Cotton Mills of North Carolina—Progress Operatives Have Made," *June 15, 1916, Industrial Development and Manufacturers' Record*. c.1 v.69 1916 (Baltimore: Conway Publications, 1916), 48, 50. https://babel.hathitrust.org/cgi/pt?id=chi.096443385&view=1up&seq=1095&q1=Caraleigh.
31. Herring, *Welfare Work in Mill Villages*, 135.
32. "Mill Betterment at Caraleigh," *Charlotte News* (NC), March 14, 1915.
33. Herring, *Welfare Work in Mill Villages*, 137.
34. "City News," *State Chronicle* (Raleigh, NC), April 7, 1892. "Baseball To-Day," *News and Observer* (Raleigh, NC), July 25, 1896.
35. "Caraleigh Defeats Pilot by Exciting Score of Six to Five," *News and Observer* (Raleigh, NC), June 21, 1910.
36. *Ibid.*
37. "City Baseball League," *News and Observer* (Raleigh, NC), January 30, 1915.
38. Herring, *Welfare Work in Mill Villages*, 137.
39. "Mill Betterment at Caraleigh," *Charlotte News* (NC), March 14, 1915.
40. *Ibid.*
41. Herring, *Welfare Work in Mill Villages*, 141.
42. Basil Frank Farlow interview by Daniel Watkins, March 6, 2000, Watkins, *Caraleigh: Raleigh's Cotton Mill Village*, 62; Dorothy Mitchell, "Mill Village Betterment at Caraleigh" *Charlotte News* (NC), March 14, 1915; Watkins, *Caraleigh: Raleigh's Cotton Mill Village* 62-63; "Local Tax Rally," *News and Observer* (Raleigh, NC), April 12, 1908.
43. *News and Observer* (Raleigh, NC), September 24, 1908. "Big Free Barbecue Today," *North Carolinian* (Raleigh, NC), September 24, 1908; "Local Tax Rally," *News and Observer* (Raleigh, NC), April 12, 1908; *Raleigh Times* (Raleigh, NC), July 20, 1909; "A Big Rally

Monday Night," *Caucasian* (Clinton, NC), October 29, 1908; "Many Fine Lots Go At Auction," *Daily Journal* (New Bern, NC), January 23,1913; *Greensboro Daily News* (NC), August 16, 1908; "Pilot Mills Defeated," *Raleigh Times* (Raleigh, NC), August 2, 1910.

44. "Making Good Music," *News and Observer* (Raleigh, NC), February 5, 1907; "In and About the City," *News and Observer* (Raleigh, NC), December 22, 1907; "Caraleigh Mills Band Resplendent in New Uniforms," *News and Observer* (Raleigh, NC) February 5, 1907.

45. "Great Meeting at Caraleigh," *Raleigh Times* (NC), October 30, 1906.

46. "City Celebrates Signal Victory," *News and Observer* (Raleigh, NC), December 28, 1907.

47. "A Rousing Welcome Given the Fighters in the Capital Monday," *Greensboro Daily News* (NC), March 25, 1919.

48. Link, *The Paradox of Southern Progressivism*, 169.

49. "Caraleigh Mills Company," *Southern Textile Bulletin* (Charlotte, NC), December 25, 1919, Vol. 18, No. 17. https://archive.org/details/southerntextileb1919unse/page/142/mode/2up?q=Caraleigh.

50. *Southern Textile Bulletin*, "Caraleigh Mills Company," December 25, 1919.

51. *Ibid.*

52. *Ibid.*

53. *Ibid.*

54. "Destruction of Flies During Baby Week," *Western Sentinel* (Winston-Salem, NC), May 30, 1919.

55. *Ibid.*

56. Herring, *Welfare Work in Mill Villages*, 160.

57. Harriet L. Herring Papers #4017, Folder 263, Series 3, Research Materials, 1928–1950, Southern Historical Collection, University of North Carolina at Chapel Hill. https://dc.lib.unc.edu/cdm/singleitem/collection/04017/id/15123.

58. Watkins, *Caraleigh: Raleigh's Cotton Mill Village*, 107.

59. Herring, *Welfare Work in Mill Villages*, 9–10.

60. *Ibid.*, 152–160.

61. "The Caraleigh Mill" *Charlotte News* (NC), January 17, 1915; Watkins, *Caraleigh: Raleigh's Cotton Mill Village*, 58–59.

62. Watkins, *Caraleigh: Raleigh's Cotton Mill Village*, 60.

63. *Ibid.*

64. Herring, *Welfare Work in Mill Villages*, 106–107.

65. Watkins, *Caraleigh: Raleigh's Cotton Mill Village*, 55.

66. Harriet L. Herring Papers #4017, Folder 263, Southern Historical Collection, University of North Carolina at Chapel Hill. https://dc.lib.unc.edu/cdm/singleitem/collection/04017/id/15123.

67. "Caraleigh Women Stage Fine Fair," *Greensboro Daily News* (NC), October 2, 1921.

68. *Ibid.*

69. Watkins, *Caraleigh: Raleigh's Cotton Mill Village*, 104; Hall, Leloudis, et al., *Like a Family*, xvii.

70. *Ibid.*

71. Watkins, *Caraleigh: Raleigh's Cotton Mill Village*, 104–105.

72. *Ibid.*, 104.

73. Herring, *Welfare Work in Mill Villages*, 88.

74. Gerald W. Johnson, *South Watching: Selected Essays by Gerald W. Johnson*, Fred W. Hobson, ed. (Chapel Hill: University of North Carolina Press, 1983), 68.

75. *News and Observer* (Raleigh, NC), November 13, 1892; *Union Herald* (Raleigh, NC), April 27, 1922; *Charlotte Observer* (NC), April 23, 1893.

76. "Church to Observer 25th Anniversary Here Today," *News and Observer* (Raleigh, NC), June 23, 1929; Ora Junius Baker, "History of the Caraleigh Baptist Church 1892–1979; *Caraleigh Baptist Church: One Hundredth Year Anniversary*; Watkins, *Caraleigh: Raleigh's Cotton Mill Village*, 53; *Wilmington Messenger* (NC), May 31, 1894.

77. "Church to Observer 25th Anniversary Here Today," *News and Observer* (Raleigh, NC), June 23, 1929; Ora Junius Baker, "History of the Caraleigh Baptist Church 1892–1979; "Caraleigh Baptist Church: One Hundredth Year Anniversary; Watkins, *Caraleigh: Raleigh's Cotton Mill Village*, 53; *Wilmington Messenger* (NC), May 31, 1894.

78. "Caraleigh Baptist Church: One Hundredth Year Anniversary."

79. *Ibid.*

80. Watkins, "*Caraleigh: Raleigh's Cotton Mill Village*," 53–4.

81. *Ibid.*

82. "Caraleigh Baptist Church: One Hundredth Year Anniversary."

83. *Ibid.*

84. Watkins, *Caraleigh: Raleigh's Cotton Mill Village*, 54.

85. Leiter, Schulman, Zingraff, *Hanging by a Thread: Social Change in Southern Textiles*, 115; Watkins, *Caraleigh: Raleigh's Cotton Mill Village*, 54.

86. "Caraleigh Baptist Church: One Hundredth Year Anniversary."

87. *Ibid.*

88. *Ibid.*

89. *Ibid.*

90. *Ibid.*

91. *Ibid.*

92. *Ibid.*

93. *Ibid.*

94. Watkins, *Caraleigh: Raleigh's Cotton Mill Village*, 55.

95. "Raleigh Juniors Spreading Out," *News and Observer* (Raleigh, NC) July 4, 1903; "Blag [sic] Raising at Caraleigh," *News and Observer*

(Raleigh, NC), May 11, 1904; Watkins, *Caraleigh: Raleigh's Cotton Mill Village*, 55.
96. Crittenden, Powell, eds., *100 Years 100 Men: 1871–1971*, 433.
97. Albert C. Stevens, *The Cyclopaedia of Fraternities: A Compilation of Existing Authentic Information and the Results of Original Investigation as to the Origin, Derivation, Founders, Development, Aims, Emblems, Character and Personnel of More Than Six Hundred Secret Societies in the United States* (E.B. Treat and Company: New York, 1907), 302–303.
98. "The State Council," *Wilmington Morning Star* (NC), February 19, 1902; *Semi-Weekly Messenger* (Wilmington, NC), March 14, 1905.
99. Herring, *Welfare Work in Mill Villages*, 147–148.
100. Stevens, *the Cyclopaedia of Fraternities*, 302–303.
101. *Ibid.*
102. *Ibid.*
103. "Blag [sic] Raising at Caraleigh," *News and Observer* (Raleigh, NC), May 11, 1904.
104. *Ibid.*
105. *Ibid*; "Past, Present and Future," *State Chronicle* (Raleigh, NC), April 22, 1891.
106. "Blag [sic] Raising at Caraleigh," *News and Observer* (Raleigh, NC), May 11, 1904; "Past, Present and Future," *State Chronicle* (Raleigh, NC), April 22, 1891.
107. *Ibid.*
108. "Blag [sic] Raising at Caraleigh," *News and Observer* (Raleigh, NC), May 11, 1904.
109. Herring, *Welfare Work in Mill Villages* 147–8; Watkins, *Caraleigh: Raleigh's Cotton Mill Village*, 55.
110. Watkins, *Caraleigh: Raleigh's Cotton Mill Village*, 55- 57 interview of Doris Dean Joyner, March 4, 1999.
111. Watkins, *Caraleigh: Raleigh's Cotton Mill Village*, 55–57.
112. Watkins, *Caraleigh: Raleigh's Cotton Mill Village* 55, quoting Herring, *Welfare Work*, 147.
113. Watkins, *Caraleigh: Raleigh's Cotton Mill Village*, 55, quoting Harriet L. Herring, *Welfare Work*.
114. "Attendance Large," *North Carolinian* (Raleigh, NC), September 26, 1907.
115. Lena Rivers Smyth, "Welfare Work in Cotton Mills of North Carolina—Progress Operatives Have Made," *June 15, 1916 Industrial Development and Manufacturers' Record* vol. 69 (Baltimore: Conway Publications, 1916), 48.
116. Link, *The Paradox of Southern Progressivism*, 134.
117. "A Night School," *Press-Visitor* (Raleigh, NC), May 18, 1897.
118. *Morning Post* (Raleigh, NC), 14 Nov 1899; *Morning Post* (Raleigh, NC), December 6, 1899.
119. Both Barbee's *Historical Sketches of the Raleigh Schools* and Watkins, *Caraleigh: Raleigh's Cotton Mill Village*, states that the school named for Eliza Pool was done so in 1924; however, in William S. Powell's *Dictionary of North Carolina Biography*, it states 1926 as the date, William S. Powell, "Pool, Eliza Anne," *Dictionary of North Carolina Biography*, William S. Powell, ed., (Chapel Hill: University of North Carolina Press, 1994).
120. William S. Powell, "Pool, Eliza Anne," *Dictionary of North Carolina Biography*, William S. Powell, ed., (Chapel Hill: University of North Carolina Press, 1994).
121. https://raleighnc.gov/places/eliza-pool-park; Watkins, *Caraleigh: Raleigh's Cotton Mill Village*, 53.
122. Watkins, *Caraleigh: Raleigh's Cotton Mill Village*, 53.
123. *Ibid.*, 52.
124. "Local Tax Rally," *News and Observer* (Raleigh, NC), April 12, 1908.
125. "Raleigh Redeemed by Patriotic Votes," *News and Observer* (Raleigh, NC), March 17, 1909.
126. Watkins, *Caraleigh: Raleigh's Cotton Mill Village*, 52, interview of Doris Jean Joyner, March 4, 1999.
127. Watkins, *Caraleigh: Raleigh's Cotton Mill Village*, 52, interview of Doris Jean Joyner, March 4, 1999.
128. "Of the Most Elaborately Laid Out Mill Propositions in the Entire Country," *Charlotte News Textile Industrial Edition* (NC), February 21, 1917.
129. *News and Observer* (Raleigh, NC), April 3, 1922.
130. Watkins, *Caraleigh: Raleigh's Cotton Mill Village*, 52, interview of Doris Jean Joyner, March 4, 1999.
131. Watkins, *Caraleigh: Raleigh's Cotton Mill Village*, 57.
132. In November 1924, the Hugh Morson High School was not yet opened and was "being erected on the corner of Hargett and Person streets...found in "Srygley Will Ask for Full Limit Possible Bond Issue," *News and Observer* (Raleigh, NC), November 26, 1924; for a situation report on Raleigh schools in 1924, also see "Committee Will Discuss-Election," *News and Observer* (Raleigh, NC), November 27, 1924.
133. Watkins, *Caraleigh: Raleigh's Cotton Mill Village*, 86.
134. "The Caraleigh Cotton Mills," *News and Observer* (Raleigh, NC) July 2, 1899.
135. Thompson, *From the Cotton Field to the Cotton Mill*, 3.
136. *Ibid.*, 221.
137. *Ibid.*
138. *Ibid.*
139. "Child Labor in Mills," *Charlotte News* (NC), November 29, 1899.
140. Watkins, *Caraleigh: Raleigh's Cotton Mill Village*, 15.
141. Schulman, Leiter et al., eds., *Southern Textiles: Contested Puzzles Continuing Paradoxes*, 74–75.

142. Schulman, Leiter et al., eds., *Southern Textiles: Contested Puzzles Continuing Paradoxes*, 73.
143. "Child Labor in Mills," *News and Observer* (Raleigh, NC), *Roanoke-Chowan Times* (NC), December 20, 1900; *Weekly Star* (Wilmington, NC), June 23, 1899.
144. Cash, *The Mind of the South*, 203.
145. "Child Workers In North Carolina Cotton Mills," photographs by Lewis W. Hine for the National Child Labor Committee, *The Survey: Common Welfare*, February 27, 1915, Volume XXXIII, No, 22. Author's collection.
146. Link, *The Paradox of Southern Progressivism, 1880–1930*, 182.
147. Alexander McKelway, "The Awakening of the South Against Child Labor," in "Proceedings of the Third Annual Meeting of the National Child Labor Committee," Annals of the American Academy of Political and Social Science 29 (1907), 12, quoted in "Conservation of the Child Is Our First Duty": Clubwomen, Organized Labor, and the Politics of Child Labor Legislation in Florida, Sarah Burns, "Conservation of the Child is Our First Duty": Clubwomen...fsu.digital.flvc.org.
148. Thompson, *From the Cotton Field to the Cotton Mill*, 222, 225.
149. "Child Welfare in the State of North Carolina," 10–11.
150. Watkins, *Caraleigh: Raleigh's Cotton Mill Village*, 54.
151. Ibid.
152. *Raleigh Times* (NC), December 24, 1909.
153. "Caraleigh Boy Held for Theft from Mill," *News and Observer* (Raleigh, NC), August 20, 1919.
154. Walter B. Cooper, "Child Labor in Mills," *Charlotte News* (NC), November 29, 1899.
155. Ibid.
156. Ibid.
157. In reference to this "pernicious form of slavery. It mentions especially ...the Caraleigh Mills at Raleigh." "Child Labor in the Mills," *Progressive Farmer* (Winston-Salem, NC), July 9, 1901; "Mill Village Betterment at Caraleigh," *Charlotte News* (NC), March 14, 1915; "Carolina Cotton Mills Leads in Welfare Work," *Charlotte Observer* (NC), June 17, 1916; *News and Observer* (Raleigh, NC), January 3, 1920.
158. Link, *The Paradox of Southern Progressivism*, 175.
159. "Child Labor in the South," *Graphic* (Nashville, NC), July 4, 1901.
160. Watkins, *Caraleigh: Raleigh's Cotton Mill Village*, 21–22.
161. Emily S. Harrison, "Miss Ashby on Child Labor Legislation," Emily Stewart Harrison papers, 1829–1979, Collection #556, series 3, Box 13, Folder 12, Stuart A. Rose Library, Emory University Archives; Link, *The Paradox of Southern Progressivism*, 60, 169.
162. Harrison, "Miss Ashby on Child Labor Legislation."
163. Watkins, *Caraleigh: Raleigh's Cotton Mill Village*, 54.
164. Lena Rivers Smyth, "Welfare Work in Cotton Mills of North Carolina—Progress Operatives Have Made," *June 15, 1916 Industrial Development and Manufacturers' Record.* c.1 vol. 69, (Baltimore: Conway Publications, 1916), 48. https://babel.hathitrust.org/cgi/pt?id=chi.096443385&view=1up&seq=1095&q1=Caraleigh.
165. *Child Welfare in North Carolina: An Inquiry by the National Child Labor Committee for the North Carolina Conference for Social Service, Under the Direction of W.H. Swift (1918)* (New York: National Child Labor Committee, 1918), 10–11.
166. Tindall, *Emergence of the New South*, 324.
167. "Child Workers in North Carolina Cotton Mills," photographs by Lewis W. Hine for the National Child Labor Committee, *The Survey: Common Welfare*, February 27, 1915, Volume XXXIII, No, 22. Author's collection.
168. "Child Workers In North Carolina Cotton Mills," photographs by Lewis W. Hine for the National Child Labor Committee, *The Survey: Common Welfare*, February 27, 1915, Volume XXXIII, No, 22. Author's collection.
169. Russell Freedman, *Kids at Work: Lewis Hine and the Crusade Against Child Labor* (Clarion Books: New York, 1998).
170. Finnegan, Cara A. "Review of Lewis Hine as Social Critic," *Rhetoric & Public Affairs* 13, no. 4 (2010): 741–745. doi:10.1353/rap.2010.0207.
171. "Child Workers in North Carolina Cotton Mills," photographs by Lewis W. Hine for the National Child Labor Committee, *The Survey: Common Welfare*, February 27, 1915, Volume XXXIII, No, 22. Author's collection.
172. "Child Labor in Mills," *News and Observer* (Raleigh, NC); *Roanoke-Chowan Times* (NC), December 20, 1900; *Weekly Star* (Wilmington, NC), June 23, 1899.

Chapter 6

1. Cooper and Terrill, *The American South: A History*, vol. 2., 583–584.
2. Ibid.
3. *Durham Morning Herald* (NC), March 29, 1918.
4. "McDonald's Specials," *Wilmington Morning Star* (NC), April 11, 1915; *News and Observer* (Raleigh, NC), October 11, 1917.
5. *Industrial Development and Manufacturers' Record.*, c.1 vol. 69 (Baltimore: Conway Publications, 1916), 59, February 17, 1916.
6. A.O. Sulzberger, Jr., "Cemetery cleanup pressed," *Raleigh Times* (NC) December 2, 1974.
7. "Sixteen More Men Will Leave on April 2," *News and Observer* (Raleigh, NC), March 18, 1918.
8. "Help Caraleigh Pay for Liberty Bond,"

News and Observer (Raleigh, NC), May 27, 1918.
  9. "Nearly $75,000 Secured Monday," *News and Observer* (Raleigh, NC), October 8, 1918.
  10. United States President. Proclamation by the President to the people. [Buffalo, Printed by the Rochester & Pittsburgh Railway Co., 1917]. https://www.loc.gov/item/29022842/, p. 4.
  11. "Accomplishments in Canning," *Charlotte News* (NC), January 5, 1918.
  12. "Cotton Mills Employ Home Demonstrator," *News and Observer* (Raleigh, NC), June 29, 1917.
  13. *Ibid*.
  14. "Accomplishments in Canning," *Charlotte News* (NC), January 5, 1918.
  15. "Cotton Mills Ask For Home Agents," *News and Observer* (Raleigh, NC), June 3, 1918.
  16. *Ibid*.
  17. Hall, Leloudis, et al., *Like a Family*, xv.
  18. *News and Observer* (Raleigh, NC), August 22, 1918.
  19. *Ibid*.
  20. Glass, *The Textile Industry in North Carolina*, 56.
  21. "Under the Dome," *News and Observer* (Raleigh, NC), October 7, 1939.
  22. A.O. Sulzberger, Jr., "Cemetery Cleanup Pressed," *Raleigh Times* (NC) December 2, 1974.
  23. Watkins, *Caraleigh: Raleigh's Cotton Mill Village*, 104–105.
  24. "Caraleigh Mills in Receivership," *News and Observer* (Raleigh, NC), August 7, 1931.
  25. William S. Joyner, "Infectious Diseases," *Dictionary of North Carolina Biography*, William S. Powell, ed., (Chapel Hill: University of North Carolina Press, 2006).
  26. "Flu Waning," *Kinston Free Press* (NC), March 6, 1920.
  27. Watkins, *Caraleigh: Raleigh's Cotton Mill Village*, 59–60.
  28. Jacquelyn Dowd Hall, James Leloudis, Robert Korstad, Mary Murphy, Lu Ann Jones, Christopher B. Daly, eds. *Like a Family: The Making of a Southern Cotton Mill World*. (Chapel Hill: University of North Carolina Press, 1987), 235.
  29. "Caraleigh Folks Have Moving Day," *News and Observer* (Raleigh, NC), June 29, 1920; Hall, Leloudis, et al., *Like a Family*, 190.
  30. Larry E. Tise and Jeffrey J. Crow, eds., *New Voyages to Carolina: Reinterpreting North Carolina History* (Chapel Hill: University of North Carolina Press, 2017), 381.
  31. "Strike of Weavers," *News and Observer* (Raleigh, NC), January 6, 1914; "Weavers Walk Out" *Concord Times* (NC), January 8, 1914.
  32. "Textile Workers Decline Raise," *News and Observer* (Raleigh, NC), December 25, 1919.
  33. "Caraleigh Mill Employees Strike," *News and Observer* (Raleigh, NC), May 13, 1920.
  34. "No Recognition at Other Mills," *News and Observer* (Raleigh, NC), December 31, 1919.
  35. "Caraleigh Mill Employees Strike," *News and Observer* (Raleigh, NC), May 13, 1920.
  36. *Ibid*.
  37. "Caraleigh Folks Have Moving Day," *News and Observer* (Raleigh, NC), June 29, 1920.
  38. *Ibid*; "Proceedings to Eject Workers," *Cleveland Star* (Shelby, NC), June 8, 1920.
  39. "*Detective Is Held for Forcible Entry,*" *News and Observer* (Raleigh, NC), June 21, 1920.
  40. "Mill Operatives Strike," *Asheville Citizen-Times* (NC), May 18, 1920.
  41. "Caraleigh Folks Have Moving Day," *News and Observer* (Raleigh, NC), June 30, 1920.
  42. *Ibid*.
  43. *Ibid*.
  44. *Ibid*.
  45. *Salisbury Evening Post* (NC), June 25, 1920.
  46. *Ibid*
  47. "Caraleigh Folks Have Moving Day," *News and Observer* (Raleigh, NC), June 30, 1920.
  48. Hall, Leloudis et al., *Like a Family*, 183.

Chapter 7

  1. Cooper and Terrill, *The American South: A History*, vol. 2, 640.
  2. Price V. Fishback, Michael R. Haines, and Shawn Kantor, "Births, Deaths, And New Deal Relief During the Great Depression," T*he Review of Economics and Statistics*, Vol. LXXXIX, no. 1. February 2007.
  3. Price V. Fishback, Michael R. Haines, and Shawn Kantor, "Births, Deaths, And New Deal Relief During the Great Depression," T*he Review of Economics and Statistics*, Vol. LXXXIX, no. 1. February 2007.
  4. "Caraleigh Mills in Receivership," *News and Observer* (Raleigh, NC), August 7, 1931.
  5. Price V. Fishback, Michael R. Haines, and Shawn Kantor, "Births, Deaths, And New Deal Relief During the Great Depression," T*he Review of Economics and Statistics*, Vol. LXXXIX, no. 1. February 2007.
  6. "Free Dentistry Is Worth $2,500," *News and Observer* (Raleigh, NC), May 28, 1922.
  7. *Ibid*.
  8. *Ibid*.
  9. *Ibid*.
  10. *Caraleigh: A Forgotten Mill Village*, ca. 1974; "Machinery Going into Caraleigh Cotton Mill," *News and Observer* (Raleigh, NC), September 14, 1938.
  11. Jimmy C. Wilder, *From Then Until Now: A Caraleigh Story*, unpublished manuscript, October 3, 1999.
  12. Wilder, *From Then Until Now: A Caraleigh Story*.
  13. Thompson, *From the Cotton Field to the Cotton Mill*, 276.
  14. *Ibid*.
  15. "Caraleigh People in Need" *News and Observer* (Raleigh, NC), August 3, 1930.

16. "Offer Help for Caraleigh Poor," *News and Observer* (Raleigh, NC), August 7, 1930.
17. Watkins, *Caraleigh: Raleigh's Cotton Mill Village*, 68–69.
18. Ibid., 69.
19. *News and Observer* (Raleigh, NC), November 30, 1937; *News and Observer* (Raleigh, NC), December 1, 1937.
20. Watkins, *Caraleigh: Raleigh's Cotton Mill Village* 69–70.
21. Ibid., 81–82.
22. Ibid., 67–68.
23. Ibid., 82–84.
24. Ibid., 83.
25. Ibid., 82.
26. Ibid., 83.
27. Ibid., 81.
28. Ibid., 81–82.
29. Ibid.
30. National Register of Historic Places Registration Form, Raleigh Water Works and E.B. Bain Water Treatment Plant, October 21, 1999. https://files.nc.gov/ncdcr/nr/WA4179.pdf.
31. Watkins, *Caraleigh: Raleigh's Cotton Mill Village*, 81–82.
32. "New Water System Looks to Future Development of Raleigh," *News And.*
Observer (Raleigh, NC), June 18, 1940.
33. "Ordinance No.: (1999) 564, An Ordinance Designating the E.B. Bain Water Treatment Plant, 1810 Fayetteville Road, in the Planning Jurisdiction of Raleigh, North Carolina, a Historic Landmark," December 2, 1997. https://rhdc.org/sites/default/files/EB%20Bain%20LD%20Ordinance.pdff.
34. "National Park Service, Raleigh: A Capital City, A National Register of Historic Places Itinerary, Raleigh Water Works and E.B. Bain Water Treatment Plant," https://www.nps.gov/nr/travel/raleigh/ebb.htm.
35. Watkins, *Caraleigh: Raleigh's Cotton Mill Village*, 82.
36. "Views and Observations," *News and Observer* (Raleigh, NC), January 15, 1936.
37. "Raleigh-Durham Airport Secures CAA Allocation," *News and Observer* (Raleigh, NC), August 2, 1941.
38. Ibid.
39. *News and Observer* (Raleigh, North Carolina). February 3, 1931.
40. "C.E. Walker Master of Wm. G. Hill Lodge," *News and Observer* (Raleigh, NC), June 23, 1931.
41. "Junior Woman's Club Meets," *News and Observer* (Raleigh, NC), January 8, 1931.
42. Ibid.
43. "To Give Seeds in Mill Community," *News and Observer* (Raleigh, NC), March 31, 1931.
44. "Reports Much Welfare Work," *News and Observer* (Raleigh, NC), June 5, 1931.
45. Ibid.
46. "Raleigh Civitan Club Donates to Children," *News and Observer* (Raleigh, NC), February 11, 1931.
47. *News and Observer* (Raleigh, NC), February 8, 1931.
48. "Gives Box Party," *News and Observer* (Raleigh, NC), December 23, 1931.
49. "Junior League Plays," *News and Observer* (Raleigh, NC), May 2, 1932.
50. A Wise Provision," *News and Observer* (Raleigh, NC), August 13, 1934.
51. "The People's Forum: A Wise Provision," *News and Observer* (Raleigh, NC), August 13, 1934, for more information about Dr. Kirbye read "Kirbye Accepts Government Job," *News and Observer* (Raleigh, NC), July 24, 1935.
52. "Plan Community Play at Caraleigh Village," *News and Observer* (Raleigh, NC), July 23, 1935.
53. "Negro Park Project for City Not Clear," *News and Observer* (Raleigh, NC), November 6, 1935.
54. "Citizens Go Sightseeing to Nine City Playgrounds," *News and Observer* (Raleigh, NC), June 16, 1937.
55. Ibid.
56. Ibid.
57. Ibid
58. Ibid.
59. Ibid.
60. "Women of Caraleigh Request Playground," *News and Observer* (Raleigh, NC), November 17, 1937.
61. "Mayor Iseley Answers Playgrounds Petition," *News and Observer* (Raleigh, NC), November 18, 1937.
62. "Caraleigh People in Need," *News and Observer* (Raleigh, NC), August 6, 1930.
63. Ibid.
64. "Citizens of Caraleigh Claim Misrepresentation," *News and Observer* (Raleigh, NC), November 17, 1937.
65. "Offer Help for Caraleigh Poor," *News and Observer* (Raleigh, NC), August 7, 1930; *Caraleigh: A Forgotten Village*, 5.
66. *News and Observer* (Raleigh, NC), August 6, 1930.
67. "Offer Help for Caraleigh Poor," *News and Observer* (Raleigh, NC), August 7, 1930.
68. Ibid.
69. Thompson, *From the Cotton Field to the Cotton Mill*, 167.
70. Ibid.
71. Ibid., 168.
72. Ibid., 167.
73. "Amanda of the Mill," *Concord Daily Tribune* (NC), April 18, 1905; Marie Van Vorst, "Amanda of the Mill," (New York: Dodd, Meade, and Company, 1905).
74. "Amanda of the Mill," *Los Angeles Evening Express* (CA), July 8, 1905.
75. "Hill Folk," *New York Times*, April 22, 1905.
76. "Amanda of the Mill," *Sun* (New York, NY), April 22, 1905.

77. *Concord Daily Tribune* (NC), February 2, 1907.
78. "Community Chest Pennies Make Healthy Youngsters Here," *News and Observer* (Raleigh, NC), November 10, 1937.
79. *Ibid.*
80. "Citizens of Caraleigh Claim Misrepresentation," News and Observer (Raleigh, NC), November 17, 1937.
81. *Ibid.*
82. *Ibid.*
83. *Ibid.*
84. *Ibid.*
85. *Ibid.*
86. *Ibid.*
87. *Caraleigh: A Forgotten Mill Village*, ca. 1974, 4.
88. Watkins, *Caraleigh: Raleigh's Cotton Mill Village*, 30.
89. *Ibid.*
90. Watkins, *Caraleigh: Raleigh's Cotton Mill Village*, 65.
91. *Ibid.*
92. Watkins, *Caraleigh: Raleigh's Cotton Mill Village*, 76.
93. *Ibid.*
94. Watkins, *Caraleigh: Raleigh's Cotton Mill Village*, 77.
95. *Ibid.*
96. Watkins, *Caraleigh: Raleigh's Cotton Mill Village*, 78.
97. *Ibid.*
98. "J. Percy Card," *News and Observer* (Raleigh, NC), June 27, 2000.
99. *Ibid.*; *News and Observer* (Raleigh, NC), August 23, 1992.
100. "Annual Fees for Course Reduced," *News and Observer* (Raleigh, NC), July 3, 1931.
101. "Says Cripples Fortunate in Having Aid Continued," *News and Observer* (Raleigh, NC), June 4, 1933.
102. "Circus Packs 'em in Here for Good, Thrilling Show," *News and Observer* (Raleigh, NC), October 29, 1940; "To Be Seen At Circus Tomorrow," *News and Observer* (Raleigh, NC), October 25, 1937; *News and Observer* (Raleigh, NC), April 6, 1939; *News and Observer* (Raleigh, NC), September 18, 1941.
103. "Ringling Circus Offers Lavish Entertainment," *News and Observer* (Raleigh, NC), October 22, 1933.
104. *News and Observer* (Raleigh, NC), August 12, 1934; *News and Observer* (Raleigh, NC), September 13, 1936.
105. *News and Observer* (Raleigh, NC), April 8, 1940.
106. "Jack Dempsey Heads Long List of Stars with Show Coming Here Monday," *News and Observer* (Raleigh, NC) September 19, 1941.
107. Watkins, *Caraleigh: Raleigh's Cotton Mill Village*, 86.
108. *Ibid.*, 87.
109. *Ibid.*, 85.
110. "Old Clothes Making Poor Children Happy," *News and Observer* (Raleigh, NC), February 4, 1936.
111. "Children Lack Warm Clothing," *News and Observer* (Raleigh, NC), February 2, 1936.
112. "Old Clothes Making Poor Children Happy," *News and Observer* (Raleigh, NC), February 4, 1936.
113. Watkins, *Caraleigh: Raleigh's Cotton Mill Village*, 70.
114. *Ibid.*
115. *Ibid.*, 88.
116. *Ibid.*
117. "Unemployed Caraleigh Resident Kills Self," *News and Observer* (Raleigh, NC) April 5, 1932.
118. *News and Observer* (Raleigh, NC), November 27, 1903.
119. *News and Observer* (Raleigh, NC), March 10, 1937.
120. Bryan LeClaire, "Beer in North Carolina," *Dictionary of North Carolina Biography*, William S. Powell, ed., (Chapel Hill: University of North Carolina Press, 2010).
121. "State's Liquor History Enters Another Chapter," *News and Observer* (Raleigh, NC) July 3, 1935.
122. *Ibid.*
123. "Deplores Reception Given to Beer," *News and Observer* (Raleigh, NC), May 2, 1933.
124. *Ibid.*
125. K. Todd Johnson, "Prohibition," *Dictionary of North Carolina Biography*, William S. Powell, ed., (Chapel Hill: University of North Carolina Press).
126. "Arrested with Booze," *News and Observer* (Raleigh, NC), July 2, 1933.
127. "Liquor Den Broken Up," *News and Observer*, March 21, 1934.
128. *News and Observer* (Raleigh, NC), August 24, 1934.
129. "Divorce Action Started by Wife of Dave H. Pope," *News and Observer* (Raleigh, NC), May 16, 1934.
130. Watkins, *Caraleigh: Raleigh's Cotton Mill Village*, 95.
131. *Ibid.*, 99.
132. Watkins, *Caraleigh: Raleigh's Cotton Mill Village*, 99.
133. "Servicemen Honored at Caraleigh Church," *News and Observer* (Raleigh, NC), December 13, 1943.
134. Watkins, *Caraleigh: Raleigh's Cotton Mill Village*, 96; "Servicemen Honored at Caraleigh Church," *News and Observer* (Raleigh, NC), December 13, 1943.
135. Watkins, *Caraleigh: Raleigh's Cotton Mill Village*, 96.
136. "Killed in Action," *News and Observer* (Raleigh, NC), November 14, 1943.
137. "Dies of Wounds," *News and Observer* (Raleigh, NC), May 31, 1945.
138. "Eastern North Carolina Soldiers Who

Gave Their Lives Listed," *News and Observer* (Raleigh, NC), June 27, 1946. https://www.newspapers.com/image/651424996. Downloaded on Jan 31, 2021.

139. Watkins, *Caraleigh: Raleigh's Cotton Mill Village*, 94.
140. *Ibid.*, 98.
141. *News and Observer* (Raleigh, NC), April 16, 1943.
142. *Ibid.*
143. Watkins, *Caraleigh: Raleigh's Cotton Mill Village*, 97.
144. "Places Closed on Court Order," *News and Observer* (Raleigh, NC), September 16, 1942.
145. *Ibid.*
146. Watkins, *Caraleigh: Raleigh's Cotton Mill Village*, 97.
147. "Appeal Is Dropped in Air Raid Charge," *News and Observer* (Raleigh, NC), July 18, 1942.
148. *News and Observer* (Raleigh, NC), April 16, 1943.
149. "Marine Is Wounded at Caraleigh," *News and Observer* (Raleigh, NC), August 9, 1943.
150. "Economic Consequences of War on the U.S. Economy," Institute for Economics and Peace, 2011. https://www.economicsandpeace.org/wp-content/uploads/2015/06/The-Economic-Consequences-of-War-on-U.S.-Economy_0.pdf.
151. *Ibid.*
152. Watkins, *Caraleigh: Raleigh's Cotton Mill Village*, 93.
153. "Changes In Street Names Voted by Commissioners," *News and Observer* (Raleigh, NC), November 10, 1944.
154. "Caraleigh's Houses Will Be Renumbered," *News and Observer* (Raleigh, NC), May 2, 1945.
155. *Ibid.*

Chapter 8

1. "Under the Dome," *News and Observer* (Raleigh, NC), October 7, 1939.
2. *Ibid.*
3. Rita Angelica Scotti, *Sudden Sea: The Great Hurricane of 1938.* Little, Brown, Back Bay Books, 2003.
4. *Ibid.*
5. "Machinery Going Into Caraleigh Mill," *News and Observer* (Raleigh, NC), September 14, 1938; "Fifteen New Full Fashion Mills in State In March," *Daily Times-News* (Burlington, NC), April 27, 1938; "Charter Is Granted Caraleigh Enterprise," April 23, 1938, clippings file, North Carolina State Archives, Raleigh, North Carolina; "Caraleigh: A Forgotten Village," 5.
6. *Morning Call* (Paterson, NJ), April 6, 1938; "Charter is Granted Caraleigh Enterprise," *News and Observer* (Raleigh, NC) April 23, 1938; "Caraleigh Mills Will Open Soon in Raleigh," *Charlotte Observer* (NC), March 28, 1938; "Fifteen New Full Fashion Mills in State In March," *Daily Times-News* (Burlington, NC), April 27, 1938; "Machinery Going Into Caraleigh Mill," *News and Observer* (Raleigh, NC), September 14, 1938.
7. Crito, "Off and On the Record," *Morning Call* (Paterson, NJ), April 6, 1938.
8. *Morning Call* (Paterson, NJ), April 6, 1938; "Under the Dome," *News and Observer* (Raleigh, NC), October 7, 1939.
9. "Fifteen New Full Fashion Mills in State in March," *Daily Times-News* (Burlington, NC), April 27, 1938.
10. "Will Renovate Plant," *Charlotte Observer* (Charlotte, NC), November 4, 1941; "Start Monday," *High Point Enterprise* (NC), November 3, 1941.
11. Jane Hall, "Premier Worsted Mill at Caraleigh," *News and Observer* (Raleigh, NC), September 3, 1944; *Charlotte Observer* (NC), November 7, 1943; *Charlotte Observer* (NC), February 4, 1945.
12. Jane Hall, "Premier Worsted at Caraleigh," *News and Observer* (Raleigh, NC), September 3, 1944.
13. Caraleigh Mills, Register of Historic Places Registration Form (National Register Bulletin 16A, https://files.nc.gov/ncdcr/nr/WA3891.pdf.
14. "Textile Union Wins," *Charlotte Observer* (NC), September 1, 1949.
15. "Circuit Jurists Uphold NLRB," *Charlotte Observer* (NC), June 20, 1950.
16. *Ibid.*
17. "Raleigh Chosen," *Rocky Mount Telegram* (NC), July 19, 1951.
18. *Ibid*; "Caraleigh: A Forgotten Village," 5–6; "Joseph Ely, Former Mass. Leader, Dies," *Daily Times-News* (Burlington, NC), June 13, 1956.
19. "American Woolen's Raleigh Plant Expects to Open In March," *News and Observer* (Raleigh, NC), January 10, 1952.
20. Jimmy Wilder was listed as a watchman at the Fred Whitaker Company, and he authored a two-page typed history that was included in small collection of papers obtained from longtime Caraleigh condominium residents Mike and Susan Hanley, Jimmy C. Wilder, *From Then Until Now a Caraleigh Story,* October 8, 1999; "Plant to Open," *Statesville Daily Record* (NC), January 10, 1952; "Plant to Open," *Statesville Daily Record* (NC), January 10, 1952.
21. "Plans Laid for Merger of 3 Mills," *Charlotte Observer* (NC), August 5,1954; "American Woolen-Textron Legal Battle Comes to an End," *Charlotte Observer* (NC), July 28, 1954.
22. "American Woolen-Textron Legal Battle Comes to an End," *Charlotte Observer* (NC), July 28, 1954.
23. Caraleigh Mills, Register of Historic

Places Registration Form (National Register Bulletin 16A, https://files.nc.gov/ncdcr/nr/WA3891.pdf, page 8 of 12; Jimmy C. Wilder, "From Then Until Now: A Caraleigh Story" October 8, 1999; *Daily Times-News* (Burlington, NC), October 29, 1956.

24. Henry Lesesne, "Textile Merger Fever," *Rocky Mount Telegram* (NC), September 29, 1957.

25. Jimmy C. Wilder, "From Then Until Now: A Caraleigh Story," October 8, 1999; "Caraleigh: A Forgotten Village," 5–6.

26. Letter from Larry J. Vass to employees of Charles Whitaker Company, author of letter, "Notice of Plant Closing and Layoffs To Affected Employees Pursuant to the Worker Adjustment And Retraining Notification Act (WARN), August 4, 1999; Letter to Rayford G. Hamilton, "Personal and Confidential," August 4, 1999.

Chapter 9

1. "Council Approves Zoning Rules for Area Outside City Limits," *News and Observer* (Raleigh, NC), January 24, 1952.

2. Chittaranjan Pathak, "A Spatial Analysis of Urban Population Distribution in Raleigh, North Carolina," *Southeastern Geographer*, Volume 4, 1964, 41–50, University of North Carolina Press. https://doi.org/10.1353/sgo.1964.0002.

3. Pathak, "A Spatial Analysis of Urban Population Distribution in Raleigh."

4. *Ibid.*
5. *Ibid.*
6. *Ibid.*
7. *Ibid*

8. "James Wesley 'Willie' York," *News and Observer* (Raleigh, NC), March 3, 2004.

9. Thomas W. Hanchett, "U.S. Tax Policy and the Shopping-Center Boom of the 1950s and 1960s," *American Historical Review*, Oct.,1996, Vol. 101, No. 4 (October 1996), 1082–1110. http://www.jstor.com/stable/2169635.

10. Kenneth T. Jackson, *Crabgrass Frontier: The Suburbanization of the United States*. (New York: Oxford University Press, 1985), 259; "Cameron Village Stores Hold Formal Opening This Morning," *News and Observer*, November 17, 1949.

11. Jackson, *Crabgrass Frontier*, 259; "Cameron Village Stores Hold Formal Opening This Morning," *News and Observer*, November 17, 1949.

12. "Caraleigh Homes Being Numbered," *News and Observer* (Raleigh, NC), March 17, 1949; "Caraleigh Mail," *News and Observer* (Raleigh, NC), August 10, 1949.

13. Pathak, "A Spatial Analysis of Urban Population Distribution in Raleigh."

14. *Ibid.*
15. *Ibid.*
16. *Ibid.*
17. *Ibid.*

18. "Economic Consequences of War on the U.S. Economy," Institute for Economics and Peace, 2011. https://www.economicsandpeace.org/wp-content/uploads/2015/06/The-Economic-Consequences-of-War-on-U.S.-Economy_0.pdf.

19. Margaret Ruth Little, "Getting the American Dream for Themselves: Postwar Modern Subdivisions for African Americans in Raleigh, North Carolina," *Buildings & Landscapes: Journal of the Vernacular Architecture Forum*, vol. 19, no. 1 (Spring 2012), pp. 73–86.

20. Little, "Getting the American Dream for Themselves."

21. *Ibid.*

22. Jackson, *Crabgrass Frontier*, 232, 246.

23. Little, "Getting the American Dream for Themselves."

24. Andrew Wiese, *Places of Their Own: African American Suburbanization in the Twentieth Century* (Chicago: University of Chicago Press: 2004), 124–125.

25. *Ibid.*, 172.

26. Little, "Getting the American Dream for Themselves."

27. Wiese, *Places of Their Own*, 165.

28. Little, "Getting the American Dream for Themselves."

29. Wiese, *Places of Their Own*,165.

30. "The Development of Modernism in Raleigh, 1945–1965," Prepared for the Raleigh Historic Districts Commission, by Longleaf Historic Resources, Raleigh, North Carolina, August 2006.

31. "Housing Project for Negroes Going Up on Old Garner Road," *News and Observer* (Raleigh, NC), November 8, 1959.

32. "Whites Voice Objections to Negro Housing Project," *News and Observer* (Raleigh, NC), September 11, 1956.

33. Jackson, *Crabgrass Frontier*, 203–204.

34. "Housing Project Plan Threatened," *Carolinian* (Raleigh, NC), September 15, 1956; "Council Takes Up Agenda," *News and Observer* (Raleigh, NC), September 14, 1956.

35. "Council Takes Up Agenda," *News and Observer* (Raleigh, NC), September 14, 1956.

36. "Housing Project Plan Threatened," *Carolinian* (Raleigh, NC), September 15, 1956.

37. "Whites Voice Objections to Negro Housing Project," *News and Observer* (Raleigh, NC), September 11, 1956.

38. "Housing Project Plan Threatened," *Carolinian* (Raleigh, NC), September 15, 1956.

39. *Ibid.*

40. "Paul Jervay's Legacy," *Charlotte Observer* (NC), December 15, 1993; "Housing Project Plan Threatened," *Carolinian* (Raleigh, NC), September 15, 1956.

41. "Housing Project Plan Threatened," *Carolinian* (Raleigh, NC), September 15, 1956.

42. "Plan Cancelled for Negro Housing in White Section," *News and Observer* (Raleigh, NC), October 5, 1956.

43. "Plan Cancelled for Negro Housing in White Section," *News and Observer* (Raleigh, NC), October 5, 1956.

44. "Four Areas Oppose Annexation," *News and Observer* (Raleigh, NC), November 5, 1957; "Annexation Plan Okayed by Council," *News and Observer*, October 8, 1957.

45. "Annexation Plan Meeting Opposition," *News and Observer* (Raleigh, NC), December 10, 1957; "Annexation Plan Changed," *News and Observer* (Raleigh, NC), October 4, 1957.

46. "Annexation Plan Meeting Opposition," *News and Observer* (Raleigh, NC), December 10, 1957.

47. "Caraleigh: A Forgotten Village," 12; "Four Areas Oppose Annexation," *News and Observer* (Raleigh, NC), November 5, 1957; "Annexation Plan Okayed By Council," *News and Observer* (Raleigh, NC), October 8, 1957.

48. "Caraleigh: A Forgotten Village," 11; Jack Croswell, "Annexation is Approved At Caraleigh," *News and Observer* (NC), January 1, 1958; A.C. Snow, "Will They Vote To Enter the City?" *Raleigh Times* (NC), December 12, 1957.

49. Interview of Frank Tuttle on August 6, 1974, located in "Caraleigh, a Forgotten Village."

50. "In Caraleigh, Some Still Wait for Promised Sewer Services," *News and Observer* (Raleigh, NC), June 17, 1960.

51. Interview of Frank Tuttle on August 6, 1974, located in "Caraleigh, a Forgotten Village.

52. "In Caraleigh, Some Still Wait for Promised Sewer Services," *News and Observer* (Raleigh, NC), June 17, 1960.

53. Ibid.

54. *Caraleigh: A Forgotten Mill Village*, ca. 1974, 11.

55. Robert Christensen, "Caraleigh: Flourishing Mill, Threadbare Area," *News and Observer* (Raleigh, NC), April 11, 1974.

56. Ibid.

57. Ibid.

58. Ivan Illich, *Deschooling Society* (London: Marion Boyars, 1970, 2002), 3.

59. Ibid.

60. Ibid.

61. Rob Christensen, "Neighborhood Activism Rises," *News and Observer* (Raleigh, NC), February 3, 1975.

62. Robert Christensen, "Caraleigh: Flourishing Mill, Threadbare Area," *News and Observer* (Raleigh, NC), April 11, 1974.

63. Ibid.

64. A.O. Sulzberger, Jr., "Cemetery Cleanup Pressed," *Raleigh Times* (NC) December 2, 1974.

65. Ibid.

66. Rob Christensen, "Caraleigh: Flourishing Mill, Threadbare Area," *News and Observer* (Raleigh, NC), April 11, 1974.

67. Ibid.

68. Rob Christensen, "Neighborhood Activism Rises," *News and Observer* (Raleigh, NC), February 3, 1975.

69. Richard Pearson, "Former Ala. Gov. George Wallace Dies," *Washington Post* (Washington, D.C.), September 14, 1998.

70. Nicholas Graham, *NC Miscellany*, "May 1972: First Presidential Primary," North Carolina Collection, Wilson Special Collections Library, University of North Carolina Chapel Hill, 2007. https://blogs.lib.unc.edu/ncm/2007/05/01/this_month_may_1972/.

71. "Wake Voters Pick Carter, Reagan," *News and Observer* (Raleigh, NC), March 24, 1976.

72. Rob Christensen, "Caraleigh: Flourishing Mill, Threadbare Area," *News and Observer* (Raleigh, NC), April 11, 1974.

73. Philip Shabecoff, *A Fierce Green Fire: The American Environmental Movement* (Washington: Island Press:2003), 92-94, 121-127.

74. Caraleigh Neighborhood Association, Inc., PROJECT REPORT, undated, unsigned typed one-page letter, author's collection.

75. Faye Senter to William R. Knight, typed letter, December 9, 1976, Caraleigh Neighborhood Association, Inc., Scrapbook page, author's collection.

76. "Home Neighborhood Development Sponsors 25-Year History 1957-1982," Caraleigh Neighborhood Association Papers, author's collection.

77. "HANDS Organization Marks Its 20th Anniversary" *News and Observer* (Raleigh, NC) March 30, 1977.

78. "Philosophy of HANDS," Caraleigh Neighborhood Association, Inc., author's collection.

79. Joyce C. Mills and Martha R. Maynard to the Editor *News and Observer* and *Raleigh Times*, April 8, 1987, Caraleigh Neighborhood Association Papers, author's collection.

80. Joyce C. Mills, "1982-83 Project Report," Caraleigh Neighborhood Association Papers, author's collection.

81. David E. Hayes to Mr. J.D. Blackburn, December 9, 1976, Caraleigh Neighborhood Association Papers, author's collection; "City Council approves street paving projects for 1977," *Raleigh Times* (NC) January 19, 1977.

82. Mildred Flynn to Archie F. Henderson, Jr., January 29, 1976, Caraleigh Neighborhood Association Papers, author's collection.

83. Caraleigh Neighborhood Association, Inc. "Report 1979," Caraleigh Neighborhood Association Papers, author's collection; "Caraleigh rezoning gets 'no.'" *Raleigh Times* (NC), April 9, 1979.

84. Caraleigh Neighborhood Association, Inc., Scrapbook, two-page, typed, undated and unsigned document, Caraleigh Neighborhood Association Papers, author's collection.

85. Dudley Price, "Caraleigh rezoning stirs up hornets' nest," *Raleigh Times* (NC), January 13, 1978.

86. Judy Sarasohn, "Caraleigh rezoning plea gets support," *Raleigh Times* (NC), April 23, 1974; Dudley Price, "Coggins backs half-way

homes," *Raleigh Times* (NC), January 14, 1977; Joyce Mills, "RE: Zoning Case Z-43-76," Typed letter, February 13, 1977, Caraleigh Neighborhood Association, Inc., Scrapbook page, author's collection; Caraleigh Neighborhood Association, Inc. "Report 1978," Caraleigh Neighborhood Association Papers, author's collection.

87. Caraleigh Neighborhood Association, Inc., Scrapbook page that includes a photograph of Mayor Cannon at the CNA meeting and a pamphlet entitled "Inaugural Ceremony Mayor and City Council of Raleigh 13 December 1977, author's collection; "'I'm mama to all Raleigh,' new mayor says," *Philadelphia Inquirer* (PA), April 28, 1978; "Death Notices, Dr. Isabella Walton Cannon," *News and Observer* (Raleigh, NC), February 15, 2002.

88. Joyce C. Mills, "Caraleigh Neighborhood Assn., Inc. April 29, 1988, Caraleigh Neighborhood Association Papers, author's collection.

89. "Hands Dinner May 27, 1976, YMCA," Caraleigh Neighborhood Association Papers, author's collection; Miriam P. Block to Faye Senter, May 28, 1976, Caraleigh Neighborhood Association Papers, author's collection.

90. Rob Christensen, "Downsizing, the 'Fad Now,' Is Trend Across the U.S.," *News and Observer* (Raleigh, NC) June 26, 1975.

91. Rob Christensen, "Downsizing, the 'Fad Now,' Is Trend Across the U.S.," *News and Observer* (Raleigh, NC) June 26, 1975; Dudley Price, "Caraleigh wins on rezoning," *Raleigh Times* (NC) January 18, 1978.

92. Undated newspaper clipping, Caraleigh Neighborhood Association Scrapbook, 1975-1976; "South Belt Line Rezoning Sought," *News and Observer* (NC), January 16, 1976.

93. Undated newspaper clipping, Caraleigh Neighborhood Association Scrapbook, 1975-1976; "South Belt Line Rezoning Sought," *News and Observer* (NC), January 16, 1976.

94. "Christmas Comes Early," *Raleigh Times* (NC), May 14, 1984.

95. Julie Powers Rives, "Dawson/McDowell extension said good for city, but calamity for area," *Raleigh Times* (NC), November 10, 1986.

96. "Christmas Comes Early," *Raleigh Times* (NC), May 14, 1984.

97. Judy Sarasohn, "Road extensions in Caraleigh hit," *Raleigh Times* (NC), July 16, 1975; "Street Route Change Asked," *News and Observer* (Raleigh, NC), January 16, 1976; A.O. Sulzberger, Jr., "Street plans worrying residents," *Raleigh Times* (NC), January 16, 1976.

98. David Zucchino, "Residents Rail Against Interchange on Beltline," *News and Observer* (Raleigh, NC), March 10, 1976; Tom Ayres, "Fears of interchange unanswered," *Raleigh Times* (NC), March 10, 1976.

99. "Study: Keep Two Roads," *News and Observer* (Raleigh, NC), August 13, 1977.

100. Julie Powers Rives, "Dawson/McDowell extension said good for city, but calamity for area," *Raleigh Times* (NC), November 10, 1986.

101. Sylvia Adcock, "Closed: Street project dead-ends grocer," *Raleigh Times* (NC), March 27, 1982.

102. Sylvia Adcock, "Closed: Street project dead-ends grocer," *Raleigh Times* (NC), March 27, 1982.

103. Joyce Mills, "1981-1982 Project Report Caraleigh Neighborhood Association, INC.," author's collection.

104. Joyce C. Mills, "1982-83 Project Report," Caraleigh Neighborhood Association Papers, author's collection.

105. Julie Powers Rives, "Dawson/McDowell extension said good for city, but calamity for area," *Raleigh Times* (NC), November 10, 1986.

106. Julie Powers Rives, "Dawson/McDowell extension said good for city, but calamity for area," *Raleigh Times* (NC), November 10, 1986.

107. Julie Powers Rives, "Dawson/McDowell extension said good for city, but calamity for area," *Raleigh Times* (NC), November 10, 1986.

108. Joyce Mills to Bob Mosher, October 14, 1987, Caraleigh Neighborhood Association Papers, author's collection; Gerald P. Traub to Joyce C. Mills, November 14, 1987, Caraleigh Neighborhood Association Papers, author's collection; Joyce C. Mills to Thomas W. Bradshaw, Jr., February 23, 1988, Caraleigh Neighborhood Association Papers, author's collection.

109. "Downtown I-40 link opens for traffic," *News and Observer* (Raleigh, NC), July 17, 1987.

110. Rob Christensen, "Raleigh's Voters Fashion New Type of City Council," *News and Observer* (Raleigh, NC), November 8, 1973; Rob Christensen, "Councilwoman Block Gaining Political Power," *News and Observer* (Raleigh, NC), July 5, 1974.

111. Rob Christensen, "Raleigh's Voters Fashion New Type of City Council," *News and Observer* (Raleigh, NC), November 8, 1973.

112. Josh Shaffer, "Ex-Councilor Dies," *News and Observer* (Raleigh, NC), February 27, 2005; Rob Christensen, "Councilwoman Block Gaining Political Power," *News and Observer* (Raleigh, NC), July 5, 1974.

113. Josh Shaffer, "Ex-Councilor Dies," *News and Observer* (Raleigh, NC), February 27, 2005; "Memorial Pondered for Miriam Block," *News and Observer* (Raleigh, NC), January 11, 2006.

114. Josh Shaffer, "Ex-Councilor Dies," *News and Observer* (Raleigh, NC), February 27, 2005.

115. Rob Christensen, "Neighborhood Activism Rises," *News and Observer* (Raleigh, NC), February 3, 1975.

116. "Mrs. Block, DeAngelis Discuss Election Issues," *News and Observer* (Raleigh, NC), October 31, 1975; "Memorial Pondered for Miriam Block," *News and Observer* (Raleigh, NC), January 11, 2006.

117. Josh Shaffer, "Ex-Councilor Dies," *News and Observer* (Raleigh, NC), February 27, 2005;

"Memorial Pondered for Miriam Block," *News and Observer* (Raleigh, NC), January 11, 2006.

118. Rob Christensen, "Miriam Block Seeks Post," *News and Observer* (Raleigh, NC), August 8, 1973.

119. Nadine Cohodas, "Council Naming Backed Grudgingly," *News and Observer* (Raleigh, NC), April 4, 1973; "Politics' building Block," *News and Observer* (Raleigh, NC) September 10, 1990; Miriam J. Preston Block, *News and Observer* (Raleigh, NC), February 27, 2005.

120. Rob Christensen, "Councilwoman Block Gaining Political Power," *News and Observer* (Raleigh, NC), July 5, 1974; Josh Shaffer, "Ex-Councilor Dies," *News and Observer* (Raleigh, NC) February 25, 2005.

121. Rob Christensen, "Development, Beltline District D issues," *News and Observer* (Raleigh, NC), October 4, 1973.

122. Rob Christensen, "Councilwoman Block Gaining Political Power," *News and Observer* (Raleigh, NC), July 5, 1974.

123. Nadine Cohodas, "Council Naming Backed Grudgingly," *News and Observer* (Raleigh, NC), April 4, 1973.

124. Rob Christensen, "Miriam Block Seeks Post," *News and Observer* (Raleigh, NC), August 8, 1973.

125. *Ibid.*

126. *Ibid.*

127. Rob Christensen, "Development, Beltline District D issues," *News and Observer* (Raleigh, NC), October 4, 1973.

128. Miriam J. Preston Block, *News and Observer* (Raleigh, NC), February 27, 2005.

129. Rob Christensen, "Development, Beltline District D issues," *News and Observer* (Raleigh, NC), October 4, 1973.

130. Rob Christensen, "Councilwoman Block Gaining Political Power," *News and Observer* (Raleigh, NC), July 5, 1974.

131. Josh Shaffer, "Ex-Councilor Dies," *News and Observer* (Raleigh, NC), February 27, 2005.

132. Rob Christensen, "Councilwoman Block Gaining Political Power," *News and Observer* (Raleigh, NC), July 5, 1974.

133. *Ibid.*

134. Jeff Gordinier, "Politics' Building Block," *News and Observer* (Raleigh, NC), September 10, 1990.

135. Rob Christensen, "Development, Beltline District D issues," *News and Observer* (Raleigh, NC), October 4, 1973.

136. Rob Christensen, "Councilwoman Block Gaining Political Power," *News and Observer* (Raleigh, NC), July 5, 1974.

137. Josh Shaffer, "Ex-Councilor Dies," *News and Observer* (Raleigh, NC), February 27, 2005.

138. Rob Christensen, "Councilwoman Block Gaining Political Power," *News and Observer* (Raleigh, NC), July 5, 1974.

139. *Ibid.*

140. "Mrs. Block, DeAngelis Campaigns Hard-Fought," *News and Observer* (Raleigh, NC), October 31, 1975.

141. *Ibid.*

142. *Ibid.*

143. *Ibid.*

144. *Ibid.*

145. *Ibid.*

146. Rob Christensen, "Business Coalition to Seek Change in Voting," *News and Observer* (Raleigh, NC), November 6, 1975.

147. Rob Christensen, "Caraleigh: Flourishing Mill, Threadbare Area," *News and Observer* (Raleigh, NC), April 11, 1974.

148. Rob Christensen, "Development, Beltline District D issues," *News and Observer* (Raleigh, NC), October 4, 1973.

149. *Ibid.*

150. Phosphorus is an element, and phosphate is a compound that contains phosphorus.

151. Miriam J. Preston Block, *News and Observer* (Raleigh, NC), February 27, 2005.

152. Rob Christensen, "Neighborhood Activism Rises," *News and Observer* (Raleigh, NC), February 3, 1975.

153. *Ibid.*

154. "Council Acts on Public Drinking," *News and Observer* (Raleigh, NC), November 20, 1974.

155. Rob Christensen, "Neighborhood Activism Rises," *News and Observer* (Raleigh, NC) February 3, 1975; One mile of streets paved in Caraleigh by the State Highway Department in 1953, "Caraleigh Village Gets Paved Streets," *News and Observer* (Raleigh, NC), October 3, 1953.

156. Rob Christensen, "Neighborhood Activism Rises," *News and Observer* (Raleigh, NC) February 3, 1975.

157. *Ibid.*

158. Chip Pearsall, "Council hears Caraleigh rezoning bid, sign proposal," *News and Observer* (Raleigh, NC) April 6, 1979; Rob Christensen, "Neighborhood Activism Rises," *News and Observer* (Raleigh, NC), February 3, 1975.

159. Rob Christensen, "Neighborhood Activism Rises," *News and Observer* (Raleigh, NC), February 3, 1975.

160. "Charles Craven," *News and Observer* (Raleigh, NC), April 5, 1979.

161. "Re-Routing Action Held Up," *News and Observer* (Raleigh, NC), April 6, 1949.

162. U.S. Department of Transportation, Federal Highway Administration and North Carolina Department of Transportation, "Administrative Action Final Environmental Impact Statement" regarding "Southward Extension of Dawson and McDowell Streets and Related Improvements to Wilmington and South Saunders Streets from Cabarrus Street to the U.S.-70–401 interchange in Raleigh, Wake County, North Carolina." State Project No. 9. 8052060, U-83. Federal Aid Project U-56–1. October 2, 1978, b-42 /17. https://hdl.handle.net/2027/ien.35556031007511.

163. *Ibid.*

164. *Ibid.*

165. Cole C. Campbell, "Proposed Street Routes Debated," *News and Observer* (Raleigh, NC), April 15, 1977.

166. Miriam P. Block, Councillor for the Caraleigh Community Neighborhood Association, April 15, 1977, page 134–136 of the *U.S. Department of Transportation, Federal Highway Administration and North Carolina Department of Transportation* "Administrative Action Final Environmental Impact Statement," https://hdl.handle.net/2027/ien.35556031007511.

167. U.S. Department of Transportation, Federal Highway Administration and North Carolina Department of Transportation "Administrative Action Final Environmental Impact Statement" https://hdl.handle.net/2027/ien.35556031007511.

168. *Ibid.*

169. Caraleigh-Survey, page 2.

170. U.S. Department of Transportation, Federal Highway Administration and North Carolina Department of Transportation "Administrative Action Final Environmental Impact Statement" https://hdl.handle.net/2027/ien.35556031007511.

171. *Ibid.*; Wayne L. Horton to Letter to William A. Garrett, Jr., 139–140.

172. U.S. Department of Transportation, Federal Highway Administration and North Carolina Department of Transportation "Administrative Action Final Environmental Impact Statement" https://hdl.handle.net/2027/ien.35556031007511.

173. William S. Powell, "Ramsgate Road," NCpedia, 2006. https://www.ncpedia.org/ramsgate-road.

174. "Uglification—Ramsgate Road," *News and Observer* (Raleigh, NC) October 3, 1945.

175. Depending on the particular time in history a map was made, Lake Wheeler Road has been known as "Ramsgate Road," "Rhamkatte Road," "Tryon Road," "Asylum Road," and the "Holly Springs Road," see "Uglification—Ramsgate Road," *News and Observer* (Raleigh, NC) October 3, 1945.

176. "Annais in North Carolina," *Dispatch* (Lexington, NC), September 24, 1891.

177. "A Combination Not Wanted," *State Journal* (Raleigh, NC), April 21, 1916; Murray, *Wake: Capital County of North Carolina* volume 1, 494–496.

178. "Old Grave Found by Ditch Diggers," News and Observer (Raleigh, NC) February 9, 1960.

179. "Civil War Relics are Salvaged in Dig," *Rocky Mount Telegram* (NC), July 19, 1988.

Chapter 10

1. Sylvia Adcock, "Closed: Street project dead-ends grocer," *Raleigh Times* (NC), March 27, 1982.

2. Joyce Mills, *Caraleigh Neighborhood Association, Inc. 1985-86 Report*, Caraleigh Neighborhood Association, Inc. Caraleigh Neighborhood Association Papers, author's collection.

3. "Caraleigh loves its landlord," *News and Observer* (Raleigh, NC) December 20, 2010.

4. Dennis E. Gale, *The Misunderstood History of Gentrification: People, Planning, Preservation, and Urban Renewal, 1915–2020* (Philadelphia: Temple University Press, 2021), 16.

5. *Ibid.*, 5.

6. *Ibid.*, 4.

7. *Ibid.*, 5.

8. *Ibid.*, 11–13.

9. *Ibid.*, 11.

10. *Ibid.*, 12.

11. *Ibid.*, 13.

12. James (Jim) Gerardi and Betty Gerardi in conversation with the author, July 26, 2021.

13. Samantha Thompson Smith, "Furniture World Gets Rearranged," *News and Observer* (Raleigh, NC), October 14, 2000.

14. "Southside Payments Hike," *News and Observer* (Raleigh, NC), November 17, 1971; Samantha Thompson Smith, "Furniture World Gets Rearranged," *News and Observer* (Raleigh, NC), October 14, 2000.

15. James (Jim) Gerardi and Betty Gerardi in conversation with the author, July 26, 2021.

16. *Ibid.*

17. *Ibid.*

18. *Ibid.*

19. "Capital housing squeeze hurts," *News and Observer* (Raleigh, NC), May 10, 1986.

20. *Ibid.*

21. "Caraleigh loves its landlord," *News and Observer* (Raleigh, NC) December 20, 2010.

22. *Ibid.*

23. *Ibid.*

24. William J. Dumont in conversation with the author, July 22, 2021.

25. Joanna Kakissis, "City Weighs Shift in Housing Code," *News and Observer* (Raleigh, NC), July 20, 1999; Sarah Lindenfeld, "Group Rejects Relaxing Rule on Housing," News and Observer (Raleigh, NC) October 12, 1999.

26. Joanna Kakissis, "City Weighs Shift in Housing Code," *News and Observer* (Raleigh, NC), July 20, 1999.

27. Sarah Lindenfeld, "Group Rejects Relaxing Rule on Housing," *News and Observer* (Raleigh, NC), October 13, 1999.

28. Joanna Kakissis, "Raleigh to Rework Prefab-Home Plans," (News and Observer), October 20, 1999.

29. Richard Stradling, "Council Test-Drives Manufactured Home in Raleigh," *News and Observer* (Raleigh, NC), June 11, 2000.

30. Sarah Lindenfeld, "Homeless Shelter Advances in Raleigh," *News and Observer* (Raleigh, NC), November 17, 1999.

31. None of the original 1890s mill homes

built in Caraleigh remain. Here is a sampling of new homes in Caraleigh listed by decade: 1628 Thompson Street built in 1901; 409 Maywood built in 1910; 101 Maywood Avenue built in 1922; 35 Summit Avenue built in 1932; 19 Summit Avenue built in 1940; 138 Summit Avenue built in 1959; 121 Gilbert Avenue built in 1968; 139 Gilbert Avenue built in 1972; 27 Summit Avenue built in 1984; 1508 Green Street built in 1999; 420 Maywood Avenue built in 2003; 609 Maywood Avenue built in 2017, Wake County Geographic Information (GIS) Services, https://maps.raleighnc.gov/imaps/.

32. The Caraleigh Furniture store was described to be in a building that had once been "an old schoolhouse" in Samantha Thompson Smith, "Caraleigh Furniture Closing," *News and Observer* (Raleigh, NC), September 23, 2000.

33. Samantha Thompson Smith, "Caraleigh Furniture Closing," *News and Observer* (Raleigh, NC), September 23, 2000.

34. Samantha Thompson Smith, "Furniture World Gets Rearranged," *News and Observer* (Raleigh, NC), October 14, 2000.

35. Samantha Thompson Smith, "Furniture World Gets Rearranged," *News and Observer* (Raleigh, NC), October 14, 2000.

36. USDI/NPS NRHP Registration Form, Caraleigh Mills, Wake County, North Carolina, NPS Form 10–900 (Rev. 10–90) United States Department of the Interior, National Park Service, 2000. https://files.nc.gov/ncdcr/nr/WA3891.pdf.

37. *Ibid.*

38. Steve Cannon, "A New Bid to Convert Raleigh's Last Mill," *News and Observer* (Raleigh, NC), November 20, 2001.

39. *Ibid.*

40. *Ibid.*

41. "Mill Reincarnation," *News and Observer* (Raleigh, NC), November 23, 2001.

42. *Ibid.*

43. *Ibid.*

44. Steve Cannon, "A New Bid to Convert Raleigh's Last Mill," *News and Observer* (Raleigh, NC) November 20, 2001; "Mill Reincarnation," *News and Observer* (Raleigh, NC), November 23, 2001.

45. "Mill Reincarnation," *News and Observer* (Raleigh, NC), November 23, 2001.

46. *Ibid.*

47. Steve Cannon, "A New Bid to Convert Raleigh's Last Mill," *News and Observer* (Raleigh, NC) November 20, 2001; "Mill Reincarnation," *News and Observer* (Raleigh, NC), November 23, 2001.

48. "Mill Reincarnation," *News and Observer* (Raleigh, NC), November 23, 2001.

49. *Ibid.*

50. Steve Cannon, "A new bid to convert Raleigh's last mill," *News and Observer* (Raleigh, NC) November 20, 2001; author in discussion with Jack Finley, March 7, 2021.

51. USDI/NPS NRHP Registration Form, Caraleigh Mills, Wake County, North Carolina, NPS Form 10-900 (Rev. 10-90) United States Department of the Interior, National Park Service, 2000. https://files.nc.gov/ncdcr/nr/WA3891.pdf.

52. Steven Cannon, "A Historic Tax Incentive," *News and Observer* (Raleigh, NC) August 19, 2002.

53. *Ibid.*
54. *Ibid.*
55. *Ibid.*
56. *Ibid.*

57. USDI/NPS NRHP Registration Form, Caraleigh Mills, Wake County, North Carolina, NPS Form 10–900 (Rev. 10–90) United States Department of the Interior, National Park Service, 2000. https://files.nc.gov/ncdcr/nr/WA3891.pdf.

58. USDI/NPS NRHP Registration Form, Caraleigh Mills.

59. *Ibid.*
60. *Ibid.*

61. "Plans to Hide Mechanicals Ran Into a Historical Hurdle" *Triangle Business Journal*, February 24, 2003. https://www.bizjournals.com/triangle/stories/2003/02/24/focus3.html.

62. Jeffrey Johnson, senior principal engineer for Bass, Nixon & Kennedy Inc. quoted in "Plans to Hide Mechanicals Ran Into a Historical Hurdle," *Triangle Business Journal*, February 24, 2003.

63. *Ibid.*

64. Raleigh Cotton Mills, Wake County Historic Preservation Commission Landmark Designation Application, 1996. https://rhdc.org/sites/default/files/Raleigh%20Cotton%20Mills%20Landmark%20Report.pdf.

65. North Carolina Listings in the National Register of Historic Places as of 6/16/2020, *North Carolina State Historic Preservation Office* http://www.hpo.ncdcr.gov; Caraleigh Mills; Raleigh Historic Development Commission. https://rhdc.org/caraleigh-mills; Ordinance No. (2002) 337, "An Ordinance Designating Caraleigh Mill 421 Maywood Avenue in the Planning District of Raleigh, North Carolina, A Historic Landmark." Wake County Register of Deeds, December 18, 2002.

66. "Plans to Hide Mechanicals Ran Into a Historical Hurdle," *Triangle Business Journal*, February 24, 2003. https://www.bizjournals.com/triangle/stories/2003/02/24/focus3.html.

67. *Ibid.*
68. *Ibid.*
69. *Ibid.*
70. *Ibid.*
71. *Ibid.*
72. *Ibid.*
73. *Ibid.*
74. *Ibid.*

75. USDI/NPS NRHP Registration Form, Caraleigh Mills.

76. "Plans to Hide Mechanicals Ran Into a Historical Hurdle," *Triangle Business Journal*, February 24, 2003.

77. *Ibid.*

78. *Ibid.*

79. Nilsen, Kim, *Triangle Business Journal*, Vol. 18 Iss. 28 (Mar 14, 2003): 3; "More condos set near Caraleigh," Kim Nilsen, *Triangle Business Journal,* Vol. 18, Iss. 46 (Jul 18, 2003): 3; "Plans to Hide Mechanicals Ran Into a Historical Hurdle," *Triangle Business Journal*, February 24, 2003. https://www.bizjournals.com/triangle/stories/2003/02/24/focus3.html; Historic Landmark application page 4; On November 14, 2003, the first of 84 residential condominium units was sold to Eleanor T. Jones, Wake County Department of Tax Administration, Real Estate Data, 1535 Caraleigh Mills Court, Raleigh, NC 27603–6452.

80. "Plans to Hide Mechanicals Ran Into a Historical Hurdle," *Triangle Business Journal*, February 24, 2003.

81. "Appearance Matters," *News and Observer* (Raleigh, NC), October 19, 2004.

82. Iris June Vinegar, "Historic Mills Find New Glory," *News and Observer* (Raleigh, NC) June 25, 2005.

83. *Ibid.*

84. Andrew Kenney, "South Raleigh Becomes Downtown's Final Frontier," *News and Observer* (Raleigh, NC), April 13, 2015.

85. *Ibid.*

86. *Ibid.*

87. Cindy George, "South Raleigh Strikes Alliance," *News and Observer* (Raleigh, NC) November 20, 2004.

88. *Ibid.*

89. Andrew Kenney, "South Raleigh Becomes Downtown's Final Frontier," *News and Observer* (Raleigh, NC), April 13, 2015.

90. Richard Stradling, "Storm's Chaos Brief But Potent," *News and Observer* (Raleigh, NC), April 17, 2011.

91. Andrew Kenney, "South Raleigh Becomes Downtown's Final Frontier," *News and Observer* (Raleigh, NC), April 13, 2015.

92. *Ibid.*

93. Chris Cioffi, "Two Downtown Raleigh Neighborhoods Get New Housing," *News and Observer* (Raleigh, NC), April 22, 2017; Andrew Kenney, "South Raleigh Becomes Downtown's Final Frontier," *News and Observer* (Raleigh, NC), April 13, 2015.

94. Raleigh City Council, Southern Gateway Corridor Study Final Report, February 7, 2017.

95. *Ibid.*

96. *Ibid.*

97. *Ibid.*

98. *Ibid.*

99. *Ibid.*

100. *Ibid.*

101. *Ibid.*

102. *Ibid.*

103. *Ibid.*

104. Neil Morris, "Sports/Entertainment Venue The Centerpiece Of Live, Work, Play Plan Called Downtown South," June 24, 2019. https://www.wralsportsfan.com/sports-entertainment-venue-the-centerpiece-of-live-work-play-plan-called-downtown-south/18471610/.

105. Zachary Eanes "Developers: Stadium plan would need public money, *News and Observer* (Raleigh, NC), June 26, 2019.

106. Neil Morris, "Sports/Entertainment Venue the Centerpiece of Live, Work, Play Plan Called Downtown South."

107. *Ibid.*; The attribution of name "Downtown South," in Zachary Eanes "Developers: Stadium Plan Would Need Public Money," *News and Observer* (Raleigh, NC), June 26, 2019.

108. Neil Morris, "Sports/Entertainment Venue the Centerpiece of Live, Work, Play Plan Called Downtown South."

109. *Ibid.*

110. *Ibid.*

111. Zachary Eanes, "Developers: Stadium Plan Would Need Public Money," *News and Observer* (Raleigh, NC), June 26, 2019.

112. Neil Morris, "Sports/Entertainment Venue the Centerpiece of Live, Work, Play Plan Called Downtown South."

113. *Ibid.*

114. *Ibid.*

115. *Ibid.*

116. *Ibid.*

117. *Ibid.*

118. *Ibid.*

119. Zachary Eanes, "Developers: Stadium Plan Would Need Public Money," *News and Observer* (Raleigh, NC), June 26, 2019.

120. Neil Morris, "Sports/Entertainment Venue the Centerpiece of Live, Work, Play Plan Called Downtown South."

121. Gale, *The Misunderstood History of Gentrification*, 5.

122. Jen Gomez, "Latinos Face Health Obstacles," *News and Observer* (Raleigh, NC), July 24, 1999; Cindy George, "South Raleigh Makes Alliance," News and Observer (Raleigh, NC), November 20, 2004; "Caraleigh Loves Its Landlord," *News and Observer* (Raleigh, NC), December 20, 2010.

123. Larry E. Tise and Jeffrey J. Crow, eds., *New Voyages to Carolina: Reinterpreting North Carolina History* (Chapel Hill: University of North Carolina Press, 2017), 379.

124. James L. Hunt, "Creating North Carolina Populism, 1900–1960, Part I: The Progressive Era Project, 1900–1930," *North Carolina Historical Review*, Vol. XCVII, No. 2, April 2020, 168–199; Thompson, *From Cotton Field to Cotton Mill*, 165.

125. "The Caraleigh Mills," *Evening Visitor* (Raleigh, NC), July 24, 1891; Larry E. Tise and Jeffrey J. Crow, eds., *New Voyages to Carolina: Reinterpreting North Carolina History* (Chapel Hill: University of North Carolina Press, 2017), 379.

126. Larry E. Tise and Jeffrey J. Crow, eds., *New Voyages to Carolina: Reinterpreting North Carolina History* (Chapel Hill: University of North Carolina Press, 2017), 5, 379.

127. Larry E. Tise and Jeffrey J. Crow, eds., *New Voyages to Carolina: Reinterpreting North Carolina History* (Chapel Hill: University of North Carolina Press, 2017), 3.

128. "Caraleigh Loves Its Landlord," *News and Observer* (Raleigh, NC) December 20, 2010.

129. Larry E. Tise and Jeffrey J. Crow, eds., *New Voyages to Carolina: Reinterpreting North Carolina History* (Chapel Hill: University of North Carolina Press, 2017), 382.

130. Nilsen, Kim. *Triangle Business Journal*, Vol. 18, Iss. 28 (March 14, 2003): 3; "More Condos Set Near Caraleigh," Kim Nilsen, *Triangle Business Journal*, Vol. 18, Iss. 46 (July 18, 2003): 3; "Plans To Hide Mechanicals Ran Into A Historical Hurdle" *Triangle Business Journal*, February 24, 2003; Historic Landmark application page 4; On November 14, 2003, the first of eighty-four residential condominium units was sold to Eleanor T. Jones, Wake County Department of Tax Administration, Real Estate Data, 1535 Caraleigh Mills Court, Raleigh, NC 27603–6452.

131. Raleigh City Council, Southern Gateway Corridor Study Final Report, February 7, 2017.

132. *Ibid.*

133. *Ibid.*

134. *Ibid.*

Bibliography

Books

Amato, Joseph A. *Rethinking Home: A Case for Writing Local History.* Berkley: University of California Press, 2002.

Amis, Moses Neal. *Historical Raleigh from Its Foundation in 1792. Descriptive, Biographical, Educational, Industrial, Religious.* Raleigh: Edwards & Broughton, printers, 1902.

Amis, Moses Neal. *Historical Raleigh: With Sketches of Wake County (from 1771) and Its Important Towns: Descriptive, Biographical, Educational, Industrial, Religious.* Raleigh: Commercial Printing Company, 1913.

Anderson, Eric. *Race and Politics in North Carolina: 1872–1901.* Baton Rouge: Louisiana State University Press, 1901.

Ashe, Samuel A., Stephen B. Weeks, Charles L. Van Noppen, eds. *Biographical History of North Carolina from Colonial Times to the Present.* Greensboro, NC: Charles L. Van Noppen, 1907.

Baker, Ora Junius. *History of the Caraleigh Baptist Church 1892–1979.*

Barbee, J.M. *Historical Sketches of the Raleigh Schools 1876–1941–1942.* Raleigh: Barbee Pupils' Association, 1943.

Blassingame, John W. *The Slave Community: Plantation Life in the Antebellum South.* New York: Oxford University Press, 1979.

Battle, Kemp B. *A Centennial Address: Delivered by Invitation of the Committee on the Centennial Celebration of the Foundation of the City October 18, 1892 and an Account of the Centennial Celebration.* Raleigh: Edwards and Broughton, 1893.

Billings, Dwight B., Jr. *Planters and the Making of a "New South" Class, Politics, and Development in North Carolina, 1865–1900.* Chapel Hill: University of North Carolina Press, 1979.

Caraleigh Baptist Church: One Hundredth Year Anniversary, 1904–2004, Talmadge Infinger, Pastor.

Cash, Wilbur Joseph. *The Mind of the South.* New York: Vintage Books, 1941.

Chamber of Commerce and Industry and the Merchants Association. *Raleigh Illustrated: Commercial, Financial, Educational, Manufacturing, Illustrated,* Raleigh: Edwards and Broughton, 1910.

Connor, Robert Digges Wimberly, ed. *A Manual of North Carolina Issued by the North Carolina Historical Commission for the Use of Members of the General Assembly Session 1913* Raleigh: E.M. Uzzell, 1913.

Connor, Robert Digges Wimberly. *The Story of the Old North State.* Philadelphia: J.B. Lippincott Company, 1906.

Cooper, William J., and Thomas E. Terrill. *The American South a History, vol. II, 3rd Edition.* Boston: McGraw-Hill, 2002.

Cox, William E. *Southern Sidelights.* Raleigh: Broughton and Edwards, 1942.

Daniels, Josephus. *The First Fallen Hero, a Biographical Sketch of Worth Bagley, Ensign, U.S.N.* Norfolk: S.W. Bowman, 1898.

Daniels, Josephus. *Josephus Daniels, Editor in Politics.* Chapel Hill: University of North Carolina Press, 1941.

Edmonds, Helen G. *The Negro and Fusion Politics in North Carolina: 1894–1901.* Chapel Hill: University of North Carolina Press, 1951.

Freedman, Russell. *Kids at Work: Lewis Hine and the Crusade Against Child Labor.* New York: Clarion Books, 1998.

Gale, Dennis E. *The Misunderstood History of Gentrification: People, Planning, Preservation, and Urban Renewal, 1915–2020.* Philadelphia: Temple University Press, 2021.

Gaston, Paul M. *The New South Creed: A Study in Southern Mythmaking.* Montgomery: New South Books, 1970, 2002.

Glass, Brent D. *The Textile Industry in North Carolina: A History.* Raleigh: North Carolina Department of Cultural Resources, 1992.

Goodwin, Adolph Oettinger. *Who's Who in Raleigh: A Collection of Personal Cartoons and Biographical Sketches of the Staunch "Trees" That Make the "Oak City."* Raleigh: Commercial Printing Co., 1916. https://hdl.handle.net/2027/loc.ark:/13960/t30294d4p.

Hamilton, Joseph Gregoire de Roulhac. *Reconstruction in North Carolina.* New York:

Columbia University, 1914. https://archive.org/details/reconstructioni00hami.

Hall, Jacquelyn Dowd, James Leloudis, Robert Korstad, Mary Murphy, Lu Ann Jones, Christopher B. Daly, eds. *Like a Family: The Making of a Southern Cotton Mill World.* Chapel Hill: University of North Carolina Press, 1987.

Haley, John H. *Charles N. Hunter and Race Relations in North Carolina.* Chapel Hill: University of North Carolina Press, 1987.

Hamilton, J.G. de Roulhac, Robert Digges Wimberly Connor, William Byrd. *History of North Carolina*, 6 volumes. Chicago: Lewis Publishing Company, 1919.

Herring, Harriet L. *Welfare Work in Mill Villages: The Story of Extra Mill Activities in North Carolina.* Chapel Hill: University of North Carolina Press, 1929.

Herring, Harriet L. *Passing of the Mill Village: Revolution in a Southern Institution.* Westport, CT: Greenwood, 1949.

History of North Carolina, vol. IV Biography. Chicago: Lewis Publishing Company, 1919.

Hobbs, Samuel Huntington, Jr. *North Carolina: Economic and Social.* Chapel Hill: University of North Carolina Press, 1930.

Hobson, Fred W., ed. *South Watching: Selected Essays by Gerald W. Johnson.* Chapel Hill: University of North Carolina Press, 1983.

Illich, Ivan. *Deschooling Society.* London: Marion Boyars, 1970, 2002.

Jackson, Kenneth T. *Crabgrass Frontier: The Suburbanization of the United States.* New York: Oxford University Press, 1985.

Johnson, K. Todd, and Elizabeth Reid Murray. *Wake: Capital County of North Carolina, vol. II, Reconstruction to 1920.* Raleigh: Wake County Commissioners, 2008.

Kennedy, Don H. *Ship Names: Origins and Usages During 45 Centuries.* Charlottesville: University Press of Virginia, 1974.

Link, William A. *The Paradox of Southern Progressivism, 1880–1930.* Chapel Hill: University of North Carolina Press, 1997.

Mandell, Jay R. *The Roots of Black Poverty: The Southern Plantation Economy After the Civil War.* Durham: Duke University Press, 1978.

Martin, Jonathan. *Augustus S. Merrimon (1830–1892).* North Carolina History Project, https://northcarolinahistory.org/encyclopedia/augustus-s-merrimon-1830-1892.

McCrady, Edward, and Samuel A. Ashe. *Cyclopedia of Eminent and Representative Men of the Carolinas of the Nineteenth Century vol. II.* Madison: Brant & Fuller, 1892.

McCarthy, Michael P. *Typhoid and the Politics of Public Health in Nineteenth-Century Philadelphia.* Philadelphia: American Philosophical Society, 1987.

McHugh, Cathy L. *Mill Family: The Labor System in the Southern Cotton Textile Industry, 1880–1915.* New York: Oxford University Press, 1988.

Mitchell, Broadus. *The Rise of the Cotton Mills in the South.* Baltimore: Johns Hopkins Press, 1921.

Murray, Elizabeth Reid. *Wake: Capital County of North Carolina vol. I: Prehistory to Centennial.* Raleigh: Capital County Publishing Company, 1983.

Powell, William S., ed. *Dictionary of North Carolina Biography*, 6 volumes. Chapel Hill: University of North Carolina Press, 1994. https://www.ncpedia.org.

Raleigh Illustrated, published by the Chamber of Commerce and Industry and the Merchants Association, 1910.

Reagan, Alice Elizabeth. *North Carolina State University: A Narrative History.* Ann Arbor: Edwards Brothers, 1987.

Schulman, Michael D., Jeffrey Leiter, and Rhonda Zingraff, eds. *Southern Textiles: Contested Puzzles Continuing Paradoxes, Hanging by a Thread: Social Change in Southern Textiles.* Ithaca: ILR, 1991.

Scotti, Rita Angelica. *Sudden Sea: The Great Hurricane of 1938.* Back Bay Books, 2003.

Shabecoff, Philip. *A Fierce Green Fire: The American Environmental Movement.* Washington: Island Press, 2003.

Stampp, Kenneth. *The Peculiar Institution: Slavery in the Ante-Bellum South.* New York: Alfred A. Knopf, 1956.

Thompson, Holland. *From the Cotton Field to the Cotton Mill, a Study of the Industrial Transition in North Carolina.* New York: Macmillan, 1906.

Tindall, George B. *The Emergence of the New South, 1913–1945.* Baton Rouge: Louisiana State University, 1967.

Tise, Larry E., and Jeffrey J. Crow, eds. *New Voyages to Carolina: Reinterpreting North Carolina History.* Chapel Hill: University of North Carolina Press, 2017.

Trouillot, Michel-Rolph. *Silencing the Past: Power and the Production of History.* Boston: Beacon Press, 1995.

Vickers, James. *Raleigh, City of Oaks: An Illustrated History.* Sun Valley: American Historical Press, 1997.

Vorst, Marie Van. *Amanda of the Mill.* New York: Dodd, Meade, and Company, 1905.

Washington, Booker T. *Up from Slavery: An Autobiography.* Garden City: Doubleday, 1900.

Woodman, Harold D. *King Cotton and His Retainers: Financing and Marketing the Cotton Crop of the South, 1800–1925.* Columbia: University of South Carolina Press.

Woodward, C. Vann. *Origins of the New South: 1877–1913.* Baton Rouge: Louisiana State University Press, 1951.

Woodward, C. Vann. *The Strange Career of Jim Crow.* New York: Oxford University Press, 1955.

Journal Articles

Bartley, Numan V. "In Search of the New South: Southern Politics After Reconstruction." *Reviews in American History*, vol. 10, no. 4 (1982): 150–163.

Bishir, Catherine W. "Page, Allison F. (1824–1899)." *North Carolina Architects and Builders*, NC State University Libraries Copyright & Digital Scholarship Center (2016). https://ncarchitects.lib.ncsu.edu/people/P000459.

"Bulletin of the North Carolina Board of Health" [1894–1895]. *State Archives of North Carolina and the State Library of North Carolina*. https://digital.ncdcr.gov/digital/collection/p249901coll22/id/257358/rec/1.

Chittaranjan Pathak. "A Spatial Analysis of Urban Population Distribution in Raleigh, North Carolina." *Southeastern Geographer*, vol. 4 (1964): 41–50.

Coleman, Warren, and T.W. Hastings. "Bacillus Coli Communis: The Cause of an Infection Clinically Identical with Typhoid Fever: Agglutination Reactions Against Bacillus Typhosus. Against Bacillus Paratyphosus (Types A and B). Against Bacillus Coli (Strain A). Bibliography." *American Journal of the Medical Sciences*, vol. 137, iss. 2 (February 1909): 199.

"Commemorative Landscapes, Worth Bagley Monument." *Documenting the American South*. University of North Carolina at Chapel Hill. https://docsouth.unc.edu/commland/monument/100.

Cox, F.E. "History of the Discovery of the Malaria Parasites and Their Vectors." *Parasites Vectors* vol. 3, no. 5 (2010). https://doi.org/10.1186/1756-3305-3-5.

Crow, Jeffrey J. "'Fusion, Confusion, and Negroism': Schisms Among Negro Republicans in the North Carolina Election of 1896." *The North Carolina Historical Review* vol. 53, no. 4 (1976): 364–84.

Ellis, Leonara Beck. "A Study of Southern Cotton-Mill Communities. Child Labor, the Operatives in General." *American Journal of Sociology*, vol. 8, no. 5 (March 1903): 623–630.

Fibre and Fabric: A Record of American Textile Industries in the Cotton and Woolen Trade, vol. 58 (November 22, 1913).

Finnegan, Cara A. "Review of Lewis Hine as Social Critic." *Rhetoric & Public Affairs* vol. 13, no. 4 (2010): 741–745.

Gershenhorn, Jerry, and Anna Jones. "The Long Black Freedom Struggle in Northampton County, North Carolina, 1930s to 1970s." *North Carolina Historical Review*, vol. XCVII, no. 1 (January 2020): 1–31.

Hancett, Thomas W. "U.S. Tax Policy and the Shopping-Center Boom of the 1950s and 1960s." *American Historical Review*, vol. 101, no. 4 (October 1996):1082–1110.

Hill, Steven A. "C.M. Eppes, 1858–1942: Uncle Tom or Radical Diplomat?" *North Carolina Historical Review*, vol. XCVI, no. 2 (April 2019): 149–181.

Hine, Lewis. "Child Workers in North Carolina Cotton Mills." *National Child Labor Committee, the Survey: Common Welfare*, vol. 33, no. 22 (February 27, 1915).

Howells, David H. "Historical Account of Public Water Supplies in North Carolina." *Water Resources Research Institute of the University of North Carolina*. North Carolina State University Report no. 244 (1989).

Humphreys, Margaret. "How Four Once Common Diseases Were Eliminated from the American South." *Health Affairs*, vol. 28, no. 6.

Industrial Development and Manufacturers' Record, vol. 69 (Baltimore: Conway Publications, 1916).

Lemmon, Sarah McCulloh. "Raleigh—An Example of the 'New South'?" *North Carolina Historical Review* vol. 43, no. 3 (1966): 261–85.

Little, M. Ruth. "Additional Supporting Information for Raleigh Historic Landmark Designation Application of Arkansas Delaware and Vermont Connecticut Royster Confectioners Building 207 Fayetteville Street Raleigh, North Carolina, 27601." *Longleaf Historic Resources*, Raleigh (July 22, 2008).

Maly, Ico, and Piia Varis. "The 21st-century Hipster: On Micro-populations in Times of Superdiversity." *European Journal of Cultural Studies* (August 18, 2015). https://doi.org/10.1177/1367549415597920.

Mattson, Richard. "The Evolution of Raleigh's African-American Neighborhoods in the 19th and 20th Centuries." *City of Raleigh and the North Carolina Division of Archives and History* (November 1988).

Newsome, A.R. "The A.S. Merrimon Journal, 1853–1854." *North Carolina Historical Review* vol. 8, no. 3 (July 1931): 300–330.

Southern Textile Bulletin (Charlotte, NC), vol. 18, no. 17 (December 25, 1919).

Southern Textile Bulletin (Charlotte, NC), vol. 25 (June 21, 1923).

Taylor, Rosser H. "Fertilizers and Farming in the Southeast, 1840–1950." *North Carolina Historical Review*, vol. 30, no. 4 (October 1953): 483–523.

NCpedia Articles

Cooper, John M. "Page, Walter Hines." *Dictionary of North Carolina Biography*, William S. Powell, ed. Chapel Hill: University of North Carolina Press, 1994. https://www.ncpedia.org.

Eagles, Brenda Marks. "Daniel Augustus Tompkins." *Dictionary of North Carolina Biography*, William S. Powell, ed. Chapel Hill: University of North Carolina Press, 1996. https://www.ncpedia.org.

Gass, W. Conrad. "Battle, Kemp Plummer." *Dictionary of North Carolina Biography*, William S. Powell, ed. Chapel Hill: University of North Carolina Press, 1979. https://www.ncpedia.org.

Holland, Irma Ragan. "Page, Allison Francis (Frank)." *Dictionary of North Carolina Biography*, William S. Powell, ed. Chapel Hill: University of North Carolina Press, 1994. https://www.ncpedia.org.

Johnson, K. Todd. "Prohibition." *Dictionary of North Carolina Biography*, William S. Powell, ed. Chapel Hill: University of North Carolina Press, 1994. https://www.ncpedia.org.

Jones, H.G. "Connor, Robert Diggs Wimberly." *Dictionary of North Carolina Biography*, William S. Powell, ed. Chapel Hill: University of North Carolina Press, 1979. https://www.ncpedia.org.

Joyner, William S. "Infectious Diseases." *Dictionary of North Carolina Biography*, William S. Powell, ed. Chapel Hill: University of North Carolina Press, 2006. https://www.ncpedia.org.

LeClaire, Bryan. "Beer in North Carolina." *Dictionary of North Carolina Biography*, William S. Powell, ed. Chapel Hill: University of North Carolina Press, 2010. https://www.ncpedia.org.

Littleton, I.T. "Hill, Daniel Harvey, Jr." *Dictionary of North Carolina Biography*, William S. Powell, ed. Chapel Hill: University of North Carolina Press, 1988. https://www.ncpedia.org.

McKown, Harry. "Dorothea Dix Hospital." *This Month in North Carolina History* series, North Carolina Collection, 2006. https://www.ncpedia.org/dorothea-dix-hospital.

Mitchell, Memory F. "Battle, Richard Henry." *Dictionary of North Carolina Biography*, William S. Powell, ed. Chapel Hill: University of North Carolina Press, 1979. https://www.ncpedia.org.

Murray, Elizabeth Davis Reid. "Pullen, John Turner." *Dictionary of North Carolina Biography*, William S. Powell, ed. Chapel Hill: University of North Carolina Press, 1994. https://www.ncpedia.org.

Newell, Charles A., Jr. "Broughton, Needham Bryant." *Dictionary of North Carolina Biography*, William S. Powell, ed. Chapel Hill: University of North Carolina Press, 1979. https://www.ncpedia.org.

Peacock, M.R.B. "Root, Charles Boudinot." *Dictionary of North Carolina Biography*, William S. Powell, ed. Chapel Hill: University of North Carolina Press, 1994. https://www.ncpedia.org.

Pittman, William R. "Horne, Ashley." *Dictionary of North Carolina Biography*, William S. Powell, ed. Chapel Hill: University of North Carolina Press, 1988. https://www.ncpedia.org.

Powell, William S. "Briggs, Thomas Henry." *Dictionary of North Carolina Biography*, William S. Powell, ed. Chapel Hill: University of North Carolina Press, 1979. https://www.ncpedia.org.

Powell, William S. "Pool, Eliza Anne." *Dictionary of North Carolina Biography*, William S. Powell, ed. Chapel Hill: University of North Carolina Press, 1994. https://www.ncpedia.org.

Queen, Louise L. "Carr, Julian Shakespeare." *Dictionary of North Carolina Biography*, William S. Powell, ed. Chapel Hill: University of North Carolina Press, 1979. https://www.ncpedia.org.

Roberts, B.W.C. "Raney, Richard Beverly." *Dictionary of North Carolina Biography*, William S. Powell, ed. Chapel Hill: University of North Carolina Press, 1994. https://www.ncpedia.org.

Snider, William D. "Watauga Club." *Dictionary of North Carolina Biography*, William S. Powell, ed. Chapel Hill: University of North Carolina Press, 2006. https://www.ncpedia.org.

Toler, Maurice S. "Holladay, Alexander Quarles." *Dictionary of North Carolina Biography*, William S. Powell, ed. Chapel Hill: University of North Carolina Press, 1988. https://www.ncpedia.org.

Watson, Richard L. "Josephus Daniels." *Dictionary of North Carolina Biography*, William S. Powell, ed. Chapel Hill: University of North Carolina Press, 1986. https://www.ncpedia.org.

York, Maury. "Laughinghouse, Charles O'Hagan." *Dictionary of North Carolina Biography*, William S. Powell, ed. Chapel Hill: University of North Carolina Press, 1991. https://www.ncpedia.org.

Zimmerman, Carmena B. "Dirt Eaters." *Dictionary of North Carolina Biography*, William S. Powell, ed. Chapel Hill: University of North Carolina Press, 2006. https://www.ncpedia.org.

Newspapers

Asheboro Courier (NC)
Asheville Citizen-Times (NC)
Asheville Daily Citizen (NC)
Asheville Weekly Citizen (NC)
Atlanta Constitution (GA)
Atlanta Daily Herald (GA)
Baltimore Sun (MD)
Biblical Recorder (Raleigh, NC)
Brooklyn Daily Eagle (NY)
Buffalo Courier (NY)
Caucasian (Clinton, NC)
Charlotte Democrat (NC)
Charlotte News (NC)
Charlotte News Textile Industrial Edition (NC)
Charlotte Observer (Charlotte, NC)
Chatham Record (Pittsboro, NC)
Cleveland Star (Shelby, NC)
Commonwealth (Scotland Neck, NC)

Concord Daily Tribune (NC)
Concord Times (NC)
Courier-Journal (Louisville, KY)
Daily Confederate (Raleigh, NC)
Daily Journal (New Bern, NC)
Daily Times-News (Burlington, NC)
Dayton Daily News (Dayton, OH)
Dispatch (Lexington, NC)
Durham Morning Herald (NC)
Durham Sun (NC)
Evening Visitor (Raleigh, NC)
Everything (Greensboro, NC)
Farmer and Mechanic (Raleigh, NC)
Fayetteville Weekly Observer (NC)
Fisherman and Farmer (Elizabeth City, NC)
Gazette (Raleigh, NC)
Goldsboro Daily Argus (NC)
Graphic (Nashville, NC)
Greensboro Daily News (NC)
Greensboro Patriot (NC)
Greensboro Telegram (NC)
Henderson Gold Leaf (Henderson, NC)
Hickory Daily Record (NC)
Kinston Free Press (NC)
Lenoir Topic (NC)
Los Angeles Evening Express (CA)
Morning Call (Paterson, NJ)
Morning Post (Raleigh, NC)
Mountain Scout (Taylorsville, NC)
Mountain Scout (Taylorsville, NC)
New Berne Weekly Journal (NC),
New York Times
Newbernian (New Bern, NC)
News and Observer (Raleigh, NC)
North Carolina Christian Advocate (Greensboro, NC)
North Carolinian (Raleigh, NC)
Orange County Observer (Hillsborough, NC)
Patron and Gleaner (Lasker, NC)
Philadelphia Inquirer (PA)
Press-Visitor (Raleigh, NC)
Raleigh Christian Advocate (NC)
Raleigh Daily (NC)
Raleigh Daily Tribune (NC)
Raleigh Enterprise (NC)
Raleigh Signal (NC)
Raleigh Times (NC)
Review (High Point, NC)
Roanoke Beacon (NC)
Roanoke-Chowan Times (NC),
Robesonian (Lumberton, NC)
Robesonian (Lumberton, NC)
Rocky Mount Telegram (NC)
Salisbury Evening Post (NC)
Semi-Weekly Messenger (Wilmington, NC)
Smithfield Herald (NC)
State Chronicle (Raleigh, NC)
Statesville Daily Record (NC)
Statesville Record and Landmark (NC)
Sun (New York, NY)
Times Dispatch (Richmond, VA)
Tri-Weekly Era, Raleigh (NC)
Triangle Business Journal (Raleigh, NC)
Twin-City Daily Sentinel (Winston-Salem, NC)
Union Herald (Raleigh, NC)
Warren Record (Warrenton, NC)
Washington Post (Washington, D.C.)
Weekly Raleigh Register (NC)
Weekly Star (Wilmington, NC)
Western Sentinel (Winston-Salem, NC)
Wilmington Messenger (NC)
Wilmington Morning Star (NC)
Women's Wear

Unpublished Manuscripts

"Caraleigh: A Forgotten Mill Village." Unnamed author, typescript, Caraleigh Mills Survey File, North Carolina State Historic Preservation Office (Raleigh: ca. 1974).

Legeros, Mike. "Raleigh Fire Department 1880–1899." Unpublished manuscript (July 19, 2009). https://legeros.com/ralwake/raleigh/history/writing/1880-1899.pdf.

Watkins, Daniel L. "Caraleigh: Raleigh's Cotton Mill Village." MLS 697 Final Project, Thesis/Dissertation. (North Carolina State University: April 9, 2000). https://catalog.lib.ncsu.edu/catalog/NCSU1390012.

Wilder, Jimmy C. "From Then Until Now a Caraleigh Story." October 8, 1999.

Government Documents

"Administrative Action Final Environmental Impact Statement" regarding "Southward Extension of Dawson and McDowell Streets and Related Improvements to Wilmington and South Saunders Streets from Cabarrus Street to the U.S.-70–401 Interchange in Raleigh, Wake County, North Carolina." U.S. Department of Transportation, Federal Highway Administration and North Carolina Department of Transportation. State Project No. 9. 8052060, U-83. Federal Aid Project U-56-1. October 2, 1978, B-42 /17. Https://hdl.handle.net/2027/ien.35556031007511.

"Analyses of Drinking Water." North Carolina Office of the Governor State Document, 135–137, Health Sciences Library. University of North Carolina at Chapel Hill Public documents of North Carolina, OCLC Number-Original, 0001053167NYG; https://digital.ncdcr.gov/digital/collection/p249901coll22/id/119829/rec/41.

Cain, William. "North Carolina Board of Health: Sanitary Engineering," third edition. Raleigh: P.M. Hale, State Printer and Binder, 1885.

Caraleigh Mills, Register of Historic Places Registration Form (National Register Bulletin 16A, https://files.nc.gov/ncdcr/nr/WA3891.pdf.

"Caraleigh Mills." RHDC Raleigh Historic Development Commission. Ordinance No. 337,

Wake County Register of Deeds, December 18, 2002. https://rhdc.org/caraleigh-mills.Child Welfare in North Carolina: An Inquiry by the National Child Labor Committee for the North Carolina Conference for Social Service (New York: National Child Labor Committee, 1918).

"'Conservation of the Child Is Our First Duty': Clubwomen, Organized Labor, and the Politics of Child Labor Legislation in Florida" in Sarah Burns, "Conservation of the Child Is Our First Duty."

"EPA Announces the Availability of the Administrative Record for Caraleigh Phosphate and Fertilizer Works Removal Site in Raleigh, N.C." April 3, 2006. https://archive.epa.gov/epapages/newsroom_archive/newsreleases/0bee935065eb357a85257145006e34d9.html.

"Hazardous Substance Fact Sheet." New Jersey Department of Health, September 2016. https://nj.gov/health/eoh/rtkweb/documents/fs/0931.pdf.

McKelway, Alexander. "The Awakening of the South Against Child Labor" in "Proceedings of the Third Annual Meeting of the National Child Labor Committee." Annals of the American Academy of Political and Social Science 29 (1907).

"Proclamation by the President to the People." United States President. Buffalo, Rochester & Pittsburgh Railway Co, 1917. https://www.loc.gov/item/29022842/.

"Raleigh Cotton Mills, Wake County Historic Preservation Commission Landmark Designation Application," 1996. https://rhdc.org/sites/default/files/Raleigh%20Cotton%20Mills%20Landmark%20Report.pdf

"Raleigh Historic Property Designation Application and Report, Needham B. Broughton High School." (Raleigh Historic Properties Commission: March 13, 1990).

Sixth Biennial Report of the North Carolina Board of Health 1895–1896 (Winston: M.I. & J.C. Stewart, 1897).

United States Department of the Interior, National Park Service, 2000. https://files.nc.gov/ncdcr/nr/WA3891.pdf.

USDI/NPS NRHP Registration Form, Caraleigh Mills, Wake County, North Carolina, NPS Form 10-900 (Rev. 10-90).

Van Dolsen, Nancy, *National Register of Historic Places Registration Form,* Typescript, Caraleigh Mills Survey File, North Carolina State Historic Preservation Office (Raleigh: 2000).

Wake County Register of Deeds.

Digital Resources

Dictionary of Virginia Biography. https://www.encyclopediavirginia.org.

Find a Grave. https://www.findagrave.com.

Interfaith Creation Care of the Triangle (ICCT). https://interfaithcreationcare.org/.

"James H. Young, African American Leader in 1890s." *NC Department of Natural and Cultural Resources.* https://www.ncdcr.gov/blog/2013/10/26/james-h-young-african-american-leader-in-1890s.

Kappa Alpha Order. https://www.kappaalphaorder.org/.

NCpedia. www.ncpedia.org/.

New Georgia Encyclopedia. https://www.georgiaencyclopedia.org/.

North Carolina History Project. https://northcarolinahistory.org/about/.

Wake County Geographic Information (GIS) Services. https://www.wakegov.com/departments-government/geographic-information-services-gis.

Wake Young Men's Leadership Academy. https://www.wymlapta.com/.

Interviews, Archival, and Other Resources

Author in conversation with James Gerardi and Betty Gerardi, July 2021.

Author in conversation with Matthew Archibald, University Arborist, Tree Supervisor. North Carolina State University.

Author in conversation with William J. Dumont, July 22, 2021.

Caraleigh Neighborhood Association Papers, author's collection.

"Caraleigh-Survey Area XVI." unnamed author, 1991, Typescript, Caraleigh Mills Survey File, North Carolina State Historic Preservation Office, Raleigh, North Carolina.

"Harriet L. Herring Papers #4017, Folder 263, Series 3." Research Materials, 1928–1950. Southern Historical Collection, University of North Carolina at Chapel Hill, North Carolina. https://dc.lib.unc.edu/cdm/singleitem/collection/04017/id/15123.

Harrison, Emily S. "Miss Ashby on Child Labor Legislation." Emily Stewart Harrison papers, 1829–1979, Collection #556, series 3, Box 13, Folder 12 Stuart A. Rose Library, Emory University Archives.

State Archives of North Carolina.

"Statement Relative to $100,000 Of First Mortgage Bonds Issued by the Caraleigh Mills Company Of Raleigh, N.C." North Carolina Collection, Cp 677.1 C25, Wilson Library, University of North Carolina at Chapel Hill.

University Archives Photograph Collection. Oversize photographs (UA023.030), Special Collections Research Center at North Carolina State University Libraries.

Index

African Americans (Negroes) 4, 5, 7, 9, 10–12, 23, 29–30, 34, 37–38, 44–46, 50, 54, 56, 63, 65–71, 93, 97, 100, 113, 126, 142–145, 153, 157
Agricultural and Mechanical College in Greensboro 48
air raid drills 135
Alabama 112, 149
alcohol (includes prohibition, temperance, saloons, beer, whiskey, liquor) 37, 41, 42, 44, 45, 46, 56, 62, 58, 78, 103, 106, 107, 127, 133, 134, 135, 136, 162, 164, 174, 176
Alcoholic Beverage Control bill 133
alderman/aldermen City of Raleigh 39, 54, 56, 75–76, 78
Amanda of the Mill 128–129
Amato, Joseph 3
Amendment of 1900 37, 44, 45, 63
An American Dilemma: The Negro Problem and Modern Democracy 12
American Federation of Labor 112
American Union Commission 54
American Woolen 5, 138–139
Anderson, J.T. 137
Andrews, Graham 123
Annexation of Caraleigh 5, 8, 109, 143, 145–146, 148, 157, 181
Anti-Saloon League 42
Appomattox Court House 36
Arendell, F.B. 61
arsenic 79
Ashby, Irene 112–113
Ashe, Samuel A. 12, 31, 34
Ashely Horne Democratic Club 37
Asheville, NC 123, 126
Asheville-Citizen Times 34

Atlanta Daily Herald 25
Aycock, Charles B. 31, 42, 49, 51, 56, 58

Bagley, Worth 52, 57, 59
Bailey, J.W. 30
Band, Caraleigh 99, 102, 103, 105, 126
Baptist Church 42; Baptist State Convention 49; Caraleigh Baptist Church 4, 12, 18, 41–44, 62, 92, 105–107, 109, 125, 130, 133–134, 158, 180
Barajas, Dionacio 165
baseball, Caraleigh teams 101–102, 126
Bass, Nixon & Kennedy Inc. (BNK) 172
Battle, Richard H. 19, 38–40, 42, 52, 54
Beauty and the Beast 125
Becker, Dan 169
Bellevue Terrace 145
Beltline, Raleigh Interstate 144, 152, 167, 174
Bennett, Marshall W. 159
Betts, Sylvester 43–44
Beveridge, Albert J. 129
Biblical Recorder Publishing Company 49
Billings, Dwight B., Jr. 11
Biltmore Hills 144
Blair, Lewis H. 87
Bledsoe's Grove 82
Block, Miriam P. 5, 150–151, 153–158, 181
Block, William J. 154
Blount, John Gray 51
Booker, W.H. 101
Boston Manufacturing Company 18
Boylan Heights 126
Boylan Heights Preservation and Restoration Society 156
Brazil 20
Briggs, Thomas H. 48–49, 61
Briggs, W.D. 105, 119, 121

Brooklyn Daily Eagle 97
Broughton, John M. 106
Broughton, Needham B. 12, 42–46, 55, 61–63, 106, 116; school named 43
Brunner, Tammy L. 75, 117
Bull Durham trademark 40
Bulletin of the North Carolina Board of Health 88–89
Bunker Hill Cemetery *see* cemeteries
Bureau of Animal Industry of the Agricultural Department 97
Bureau of Infant Hygiene of the State Board of Health 104
Burgwyn, William H.S. 57
Burnham, Rex 144
Busbee, F.H. 80

Cain, William 75
Cameron Village 142
Campbell, Karl E. 11
Canning clubs 116
Cannon, Isabella W. 150
Capitol Square 37, 39, 40, 57, 59
Capudine Chemical Company 47, 49
Caraleigh Neighborhood Association (CNA) 149
Card, J. Percy 131
Card, Tommy 131
Cardinal Hills subdivision 154
Carolina Pines 131, 144, 149, 156
Carolina Pines Golf Course 131
Carolina Power and Light Company 132, 136
The Carolinian 60, 144, 145
Carr, Elias 79, 86
Carr, Julian S. 37, 40, 41, 45
Carson, Rachel 149
Carter, Jimmy 149
Cary, Samuel F. 50

Index

Cary, NC 50
Cash, Wilbur J. 20, 66, 69, 111
Cemetery, Bunker Hill 4, 10, 32, 115–117, 148
Cemetery, Oakwood 10, 35, 40, 42, 46, 48–54, 57, 59, 60, 64
Centennial Campus 167
Centennial School 30, 110
Chamberlain, Joseph R. 46–48, 50, 52, 68, 70
Charlotte, NC 141
Charlotte Daily Observer 25
Charlotte Evening News 25
Chatham County 58, 69
Chatham Record 69
Cheviot Hills Golf Course 131
child labor 1, 4, 7, 13, 29, 99, 101, 110–114, 129, 130, 153
childcare (birth) 104
circuses 4, 131
CitySpace Homes 176, 182
Civil War 2, 6, 7, 10, 12, 13, 15, 20, 25, 28, 31–37, 39, 40, 48, 51, 52, 54, 56, 67, 75, 91, 98, 108, 159, 180
Civilian Conservation Corps (CCC) 123
Civitan Club, Raleigh 125
Cleveland, Grover 57
Cleveland-Carr Club 45
Coclanis, Peter A. 13
Cole Brother's Combined Circus 131
Coley Forest Ridge Road 145
Commercial and Farmers Bank 36, 50–51, 60
Commercial and Industrial Association of North Commercial National Bank 48
Community Chest 124, 129
Concord Daily Tribune 129
Confederate (Confederacy) 7, 10, 15, 20–21, 25, 28, 30–31, 33–34, 36–41, 51–54, 56–57, 59, 61, 66, 70, 87, 91, 159
The Congressional Globe 42
Connor, R.D.W. 12, 29–31
Constitutional Convention of 1875 39
Cook, Robert M. 115
Cooper, Roy 38
Copperville Mining Company 47
Coss, Jack 145
Cowper, Pulaski 51
Craven, Charles 157
Cross & Linehan Clothiers Company 52

Dabney, Charles W. 76
Daily Confederate newspaper 54

Daniels, Josephus 11–12, 25, 36, 42, 44–45, 50–51, 56–58, 62–63, 71–72, 91–93, 97, 107–109, 116
Davidson College 40
Davis, Jefferson 30
Dawson/McDowell Street 152
Dayton, Ohio 88
DeAngelis, Amedo 155–156
Democratic Party 11, 28–29, 34, 37, 39, 41–42, 44–46, 48, 54–57, 60, 62–63, 149, 155, 157
Dempsey, Jack 131
Denson, Kate Whiting 51
Department of Conservation and Development 137
Department of Labor 116
Deveraux Meadow 126
Dirt Eaters 97
Dix Hill (Hospital) (Park) 23, 76; 87, 142, 147, 177–178
Doffer boys 101, 112
Downtown South 1, 2, 5, 7, 178–181
Drury's Bluff, Battle of 36
Duke University (Trinity) 40
Dumont, William 3, 5, 164, 165, 181
Dupuy, Bernard 54
Dye, J.J. 70

Eatmon's Pond 80
eavesdropping committee 44
Eberth, Karl Joseph 82
Eckerd's Store 133
Edenton Street United Methodist Church 35
Edmonds, Helen G. 45
education: Caraleigh School 4, 29, 30, 31, 34, 54, 62, 108, 109, 110, 121, 125, 129, 132, 135; Eliza Pool School 123, 125, 132, 135; Hugh Morson High School 132
Edwards, Cornelius B. 42, 46
Edwards and Broughton 42
Egypt 20
Eighteenth Amendment 133
electricity 8, 73, 24, 40, 51, 119, 162; *see also* Raleigh Electric Company
Ellis, Mrs. Richard A. 112
Elon College 40
The Emergence of the New South, 1913–1945 32, 113
Enloe, W.G. 145
Environmental Protection Agency (EPA) 78, 149
Erwin, W.A. 112
Evans, Claud 70
Evening Visitor 19, 27, 79–80, 86

Everett, David E. 52
Executive Committee of the Fourth Congressional district 45

Fairview Acres 144, 156
Farmer and Mechanic newspaper 51
Farmers Market, State 1, 174
Farmers' Cotton Oil Company of Wilson, NC 47
Farmers' Guano Company of Norfolk, VA 47
Farrow, Frank 102
Fayetteville Street 52, 84, 110
Fayetteville Street Baptist Church 42
Federal Housing Administration (FHA) 144
fertilizer *see* phosphate
Filter Theory 161–162
Finley, Jack 168
Fire of 1892, phosphate 77
First Presbyterian Church 106
floriculture 100
Flynn, Mildred 153, 175–176
Ford, Gerald 147
Fred Olds School 126
Fred Whitaker Company 5, 139, 140, 147–148, 153, 166
From the Cotton Field to the Cotton Mill 25, 32
Fuller Heights 144, 148, 156
furniture store, Caraleigh 166
Fusion Movement 28, 44–45, 47–48

Gale, Dennis E. 161
Gatling, Bart N. 85
Gay, R.D. 134
gentrification 5, 161, 162, 164, 180, 181
Georgia 112
Gerardi, Betty 3, 5, 163, 164, 181
Gerardi, James 3, 5, 163, 164, 181
Gettysburg, Battle of 36
Gilbert Street 106
Glass, Brent D. 22, 32, 86
Glass, Ruth 161
Glenwood South 169
Glover, Rommey 105
Goldsboro, NC 52
golf 153
Goodale, Amy 176
Grady, Henry W. 25
Great Depression 7, 95, 107, 116, 121–125, 127, 129–137, 143, 147, 148, 162, 166, 180, 181
Great Sanitary Awakening 75
Green Street 106, 110

Index

Greencastle, Pennsylvania 36
Greensboro, NC 40, 48, 51, 126, 141
Greensboro Daily News 105
Greenville, NC 2, 49, 84
Greenville [South Carolina] News 25
Greenway 79, 94; Capital Area Greenway system 177; Greenway Commission 155; Triangle Greenway System 178
Greenway, W. Clyde 149
Grimes, Bryan 51

Hachmeister, Mariah 175
Haley, John M. 46
Hamilton, Joseph Gregoire de Roulhac 29, 12
Harper, F.M. 30, 109
Harrison, William 54
Haywood County 33
The Herald 42
Herring, Harriet L. 31–32, 92, 95, 99–100, 104–105
Hertford Village 144–145
Highway 15 A 122, 135, 158
Hill, D.H. 101
Hill, Luke 69
Hine, Lewis 1, 67
Hinton, Henry 2
Historical Account of PUBLIC WATER SUPPLIES in North Carolina 76
Hobbs, Samuel H., Jr. 93
Hoekstra, R. 127–128
Hoke, Robert F. 36
Holden, William W. 34
Holding, Willis P. 145
Holladay, Alexander Q. 52–54
Holland, Dave 85
Holleman Road 84
Horne, Ashley 11, 19, 36–38, 42, 50, 55
Home and Neighborhood Development Sponsors (HANDS) 149–150
hookworm 97–98
Horton, Pauline 135
Horton, Wayne A. 147–149, 152, 157–158; Horton's Store 136, 157
Howell, David H. 76
Howells, David H. 76
Hoyt, Homer 161–162
Hunt, James L. 30
Hunter, Carey J. 18, 49–50
Hunter, Charles N. 42, 46

Illich, Ivan 147
India 20
Indiana 129
International Building Code (IBC) 172

Interstate 40 (I-40) 1, 94, 152, 167, 177–178
Iseley, George A. 126

Jarvis, Thomas J. 34, 55
Jefferson, Thomas 55
Jervay, Paul R. 145, 113–114
Johnny J. Jones Exposition 131
Johnson, Gerald W. 99
Johnson, Jeffrey 172
Johnson, K. Todd 96
Johnson, Richard 176
Jones, Eleanor 168
Jones, Sarah 96
Joyner, Barney 166
Joyner, Doris 108, 110, 117
Joyner, James 133
Joyner, James Y. 108–109
Joyner, Thomas 135
Joyner Realty 166
Junior League, Raleigh 125
Junior Order of United American Mechanics 4, 46, 105, 107, 108, 109, 110, 125, 128, 136
Junior Woman's Club of Raleigh 125

Kane, John 7, 178–180
Kappa Alpha Order 55
Kentwood Subdivision 154
King, Vaughn 5–6, 166–169, 171–172, 174, 181, 183
Kirby, G.L. 83
Kirbye, J. Edward 125–126
Kirk-Holden War 34
Kirkpatrick, T.L. 60
Kiwanis Club, Raleigh 131
KKK (Ku Klux Klan) 30–31, 34, 38, 68

Lacy, B.R. 108
Lake Johnson 154–156
Lake Wheeler Road 77, 158–160, 177
Lee, Robert E. 29–30, 36
Leiter, Jeffrey 67
Lewis, Julius 88
Lewis, Richard H. 61, 76, 79, 96
Liberty Bond 115
Lightner, Clarence E. 153
Lincoln, Abraham 33
Linehan, William A. 52
Little Rock, Arkansas 40
Lost Cause 57
Lowell, Francis Cabot 18

Madonna Subdivision 143
Mahler, Fred W. 85
malaria 4, 9, 74, 77, 79–86, 89–90, 95, 97

Malik, Steve 178–180
Mandle, Jay R. 67
Manly Street Church 126
Mansion Park Hotel 50
Manufacturers Record 113
Marine Hospital Service 89
Marines, United States 136
Mary Talbert House 126
Massachusetts 54
Matthews, Douglass 156
Maye, Foster 134
Maywood Avenue 1, 5, 9, 16, 23, 65, 74, 79, 107, 108, 117, 136, 140, 147, 152, 157–159, 161, 164–165, 168, 174–176, 182
Maywood Dairy Farm 23
McCarthy, Michael 81
McHugh, Cathy L. 73
McKee, James 75, 78–80, 83–84, 86, 89, 108
McKinley's Tariff 47, 55
Meeker, Charles 172, 174–175
Melrose Knitting Company 49
Melrose Knitting Company 49
Memorial Day (Confederate) 91, 108
Memphis, TN 52
Meredith College 43, 49, 106
Merrimon, Augustus S. 11, 33–35
Messer, Hannah 104, 117
Method community 156
Methodist Church 35, 40, 50
Metropolitan Life Insurance Company 104
Meyer, Harold 126
Miasmas 81, 83
Miller, Conrad 155
Model T Ford 109
monuments: Confederate Monument, State Capitol, Raleigh 39; George Washington Statue 58; North Carolina Women of the Confederacy 37–38; North Carolina Monumental Association 39; Worth Bagley Monument 52, 59; Zebulon Vance Statue 39
Moore, Paul 155
Moore County 50
Morgan, J.B. 134
Morgan Street 110
Moring, Frank O. 18, 52, 55–56, 76, 83, 97, 112
Morning Post 18, 27, 31, 39, 72, 78, 91
Morrisville, NC 56
Moses, E.P. 108
Murray, Elizabeth R. 96

Index

Mutual Publishing Company 49
Myrdal, Gunnar 12, 65

National Bank of Raleigh 35, 39
National Child Labor Committee (NCLC) National Nutrition Program 135
National Park Service 172
National Priorities List 78
National Register of Historic Places 5, 68, 72, 93, 168–169
National Youth Administration (NWA) 123
Nazareth community 156
Neuse River Cotton Mills 39, 60, 124
New Bern Weekly Journal 88
New Deal, PWA 123, TVA
New England Hurricane 137
New South 11, 15–16, 22, 25–26, 32, 48, 50, 52, 54–55, 57, 67, 87, 98, 110, 112, 113
New York City 42
New York Times 129
News and Observer 45, 48, 57, 61–63, 72, 74, 82, 84–86, 88, 91–93, 96, 100, 102–103, 107, 112, 115–116, 118–119, 124–130, 132, 144, 147, 157, 159, 161, 164–165, 167–168, 174
Nixon, Richard 149
Norfolk-Southern Railroad 23, 131
North Carolina Agricultural Experiment Station 47
North Carolina Agricultural Extension Service 116
North Carolina Agricultural Society 40, 49
North Carolina Alcoholic Beverage Control Commission 133
North Carolina Board of Health 74, 75, 81, 88–90, 98, 101, 104
North Carolina Cotton Growers Association 60
North Carolina Dentists' Association 52
North Carolina Department of Transportation 152
North Carolina Fisheries Commission 55
North Carolina Good Roads Association 60
North Carolina Historical Commission 31
North Carolina Historical Review 28, 31
North Carolina Home Insurance Agency 39, 51

North Carolina House of Commons 33
North Carolina Office of Archives and History 31
North Carolina Railroad 23
North Carolina Rehab Code (NCRC) 172
North Carolina State Historic Preservation Office 67, 93, 172, 174
North Carolina State University/North Carolina Agricultural and Mechanic College 39–40, 43, 53–55, 66, 75–76, 87, 93, 126, 155–156, 167, 175
North Carolinian 62

Oakwood Cemetery *see* cemeteries
Oberlin School for Negroes 126
Observer Printing House 25
Occupational Safety and Health Administration (OSHA) 149
Office of Price Administration (OPA) 135
O'Hagan, O.J. 84
Olds, F.A. 30
Olivia Raney Library 39, 51
Orphanage and Preachers' Home 50
Orrel, Corporal 135
Overman, Lee 129
Owens, J.E. 119
Oxford Orphan Asylum 43

Page, Alison F. 50–51, 56
Page, Walter H. 25, 87, 98
Parker-Hunter Realty Company 49
Parkland 144
Passing of the Mill Village: Revolution in a Southern Institution 31
Pathak, Chittaranjan 142
Peace College 55
Pearce, Lillie 136
Penn Mutual Life Insurance Company 51
Perry, Thomas 155
Philadelphia 52, 107, 109, 139
Philadelphia College for Dentistry and Surgery 52
Philadelphia Sesquicentennial Celebration 109
Phillips, W.B. 76, 87, 88
Phipps, Joyce 110
Phipps, William 131
Phosphate and Fertilizer Plant, Caraleigh 4, 6, 9, 15, 18, 19, 20, 23, 24, 33, 35–37, 46–47,
51, 53, 56, 63, 65–70, 72–79, 93, 96, 115–116, 118, 157
Pickle Eaters 97
Pilot Mills 18, 21, 86, 91, 102, 109–110, 116, 118–119, 125, 130, 168
Planters and the Making of a New South 11
Pool, Eliza 5, 109, 123, 125, 132, 135
Pope, David H. 134
Populist Party 28–29, 44, 47, 63
potash 47
Premier Worsted 5, 137–138
prostitution 43, 128, 162
Public Works Administration (PWA) 123
Pullen, John T. 11–12, 18, 36, 41–44, 62, 79, 106, 109, 116

Railroad Freight Commission 60
Raleigh Associated Charities 39
Raleigh Banking and Trust Company 35, 47, 52
Raleigh Cemetery Association 40, 52
Raleigh Chamber of Commerce 42, 51, 61, 88, 153
Raleigh City Commissioners 126, 136
Raleigh City Council 5, 35, 124, 141, 144, 145, 150–151, 153–157, 166, 181
Raleigh Cotton Mills 21, 51, 60, 91, 102
Raleigh Council Parent-Teacher Associations 125
Raleigh Dental Society 52
Raleigh Electric Company 60
Raleigh Gas Company 54
Raleigh Gazette 45
Raleigh Golf Association 131
Raleigh High School 30
Raleigh Register 41
Raleigh Rifles 54
Raleigh School Committee 48
Raleigh Standard 35
Raleigh Telephone Company 47
Raleigh Times newspaper 48
Raleigh Water Company 78, 123
Raleigh's Sesqui-Centennial celebration 50
Randolph County 41
Raney, Richard B. 51–52
Rankin, W.S. 98
Reagan, Ronald 147
Reconstruction 75, 96, 180

Index

Redeemers 10–11, 24–25, 60
Redmond, Billie 178, 180
Regulators 159
Republican (Party) 12, 28–29, 34, 44, 47–49, 55, 60, 62–63, 102, 149
Revolutionary War 159
Rex Hospital 39, 52, 156
Rhamkatte Road 77, 83, 87, 117, 159
Rhyne, Jennings 104
Richards, E.N. 144–145
Ringling Brothers and Barnum and Bailey's Circus 131
Robinwood subdivision 156
Rochester Heights 144
Rockefeller Sanitary Commission for the Eradication of Hookworm 98
Rogers, James R. 96
Roman Catholic Church 106
Roosevelt, Franklin D. 31, 58, 121–122
Roosevelt, Theodore 48
Root, Charles B. 54, 61
Rotary Club, Raleigh 125, 131
Royster, Vermont Connecticut 39, 52
Rural Post Office, Caraleigh 5, 136, 152
Russell, Daniel L. 48

Saint Augustine's School 40
Saint Mary's School 40
Salisbury Street 110
Salvation Army 108, 127, 128
Sanford, Terry 149
Sanitary Engineering 81
Santa Claus 112
Sauls, Christopher E. 171, 182
Schulman, Michael D. 67
Sears, Roebuck and Company 149
Sechler, Joseph 172
Senter, Faye 104
Senter, Robert 131
serum test 90
Sexton, J.A. 83, 85
Sherman, William T. 52, 53, 159
Silencing the Past 10, 71
Slater System 17–18
slavery 10, 12, 20, 25, 30, 39, 50, 54, 56, 65, 66, 67, 70, 97, 100, 113, 129; hiring out system 54
Smith, Charles L. 30
Smith, Edward C. 35, 54–55, 63
Smith, Lena Rivers 99
Smith, Nannie Mae Hussey 112
Smith, W.A. 42

South Carolina 25, 55, 112, 129, 141
South Hill's Twin Cinema 156
South Saunders Street 5, 94, 109, 122, 144, 148, 149, 152, 153, 158, 159, 164, 166–167, 175, 177, 178, 181
South Street 110
Southern Colored Goods Association 56
Southern Gateway Corridor Study 5, 177–178, 181
Southern Textile Bulletin 102, 103
Spacedye 5, 139, 140
Spanish American War 52
Spanish flu 116
stadium 179
Standard Gas and Electric Company 51
State Board of Improvements 55
State Chronicle 8, 18, 25, 72, 77, 85
State School for the Deaf, Dumb and Blind 43, 55
Stiles, Charles W. 97
Streets in Caraleigh 157
strike, Caraleigh workers 4, 69, 70–71, 118–120
Suggs, Viola 139
sulfuric acid 78
Summit Avenue (Street) 133, 153, 157
The Sun newspaper 129

Tabernacle Baptist Church 43
The Textile Industry in North Carolina: A History 32
Thomas, James J. 4, 11, 18, 34, 35, 36, 39, 50
Thompson, Alfred A. 4, 11, 15, 18, 30, 36, 42, 44, 50, 56, 58, 60–64, 72, 82, 85, 88, 91–92, 95, 106, 108, 116, 118, 126, 148, 153–154, 157; Thompson School 126
Thompson, Holland 15–16, 25, 32, 69–70, 111–112, 128–129
Tindall, George B. 32, 113
Todd's Café 136
Tom Mix Circus 131
Tompkins, Daniel A. 22, 25
Transylvania County 33
trees 101
Trophy Brewery 2, 174–176
Trouillot, Michel-Rolph 10, 71
Tucker, R.S. 61
Tucker's Meadow 80
Twenty-First Amendment 133
typhoid 4, 53, 74, 75, 77, 79, 80–82, 84–86, 89–91, 96–97, 127

Union Army 28
Union Central Life Insurance Company 49
Union Whig 33
United Daughters of the Confederacy 30, 36
United States Department of the Interior 57
United Textile Workers of America 118
University of North Carolina–Chapel Hill 13, 38, 93, 226
Upchurch, W.G. 4, 18, 24, 27, 35, 36, 48, 50, 61, 68, 125

Valand, Mark 172
Vance, Zebulon B. 33–34, 39–40, 58
Veterans' Administration (VA) 144
Virginia 47, 49, 53, 55, 112, 140
Volk, Richard 155
Vorst, Marie Van 129

Wadesboro, NC 38
Wake: Capital County of North Carolina, Vol. II, Reconstruction to 1920 10, 46, 96
Wake County Beautification Committee 150
Wake County Board of Commissioners 80, 134
Wake County Cattle Club 48
Wake County Register of Deeds 19, 117
Wake County Savings Bank 48
Wake County's Southern Rights Association 54
Wake Forest College 4, 40, 43, 48–49
Wallace, George C. 149, 180
Walnut Creek 2, 4, 6, 9, 23, 72, 74–80, 82–85, 87–91, 93–95, 107–108, 128, 131, 136, 147, 148
Walnut Creek Sporting Club 74
Waltham System 17–18
War Savings Stamps 115
Washington, D.C. 35, 42, 55–58, 89, 92
Washington, NC 56
Washington High School 126
Watauga Club 56
Water Treatment Plant (Ernest B. Bain) 5, 123-124
Water Works, Raleigh 123
Watkins, Daniel 3, 67, 93, 95, 105, 117, 122, 123
Watkins, Rex 3

Watkins, Tyree 134, 136
Watkins, Wesley 117, 123
Weekly Star 82
Welfare Work in Mill Villages 32, 92, 99
West, N.W. 88
West End Hotel in Winston 51
West Raleigh Civic Association 154–156
Wheeler, Fred B. 144–145
Whitaker, George 135; Whitaker's Place 135
White Supremacy 10–12, 25, 29–30, 55, 57, 62–63, 66, 68, 71, 148–149

Wiese, Andrew 143
Wiley School 30
Wilkins, Ruth 104
Williams, James 69
Williams, Mary L.H. 36
Williams, Sam 115
Williamson, B.P. 36
Wilmington, NC 52
Wilmington Messenger 88, 34
Wilmington Race Riot 44, 63
Wilmington Street 152
Wilson, Woodrow 50, 57, 115
Winston-Salem, NC 51, 141
Winters, John W. 143
Woodward, C. Vann 25, 28, 75

Works Progress Administration (WPA) 123
World War I 38, 70, 92, 99, 103–104, 115, 116, 118, 119, 180
World War II 121, 123–125, 127, 129, 131, 133–137, 139, 142–143, 152, 162
Wright, Orville 81
Wright, Wilbur 81

Yarborough House 51
York, James W. 142
Young, Jams H. 44, 45
Young Men's Christian Association (YMCA) 48, 50, 126

www.ingramcontent.com/pod-product-compliance
Lightning Source LLC
Chambersburg PA
CBHW060341010526
44117CB00017B/2915